GREATER NEW YORK

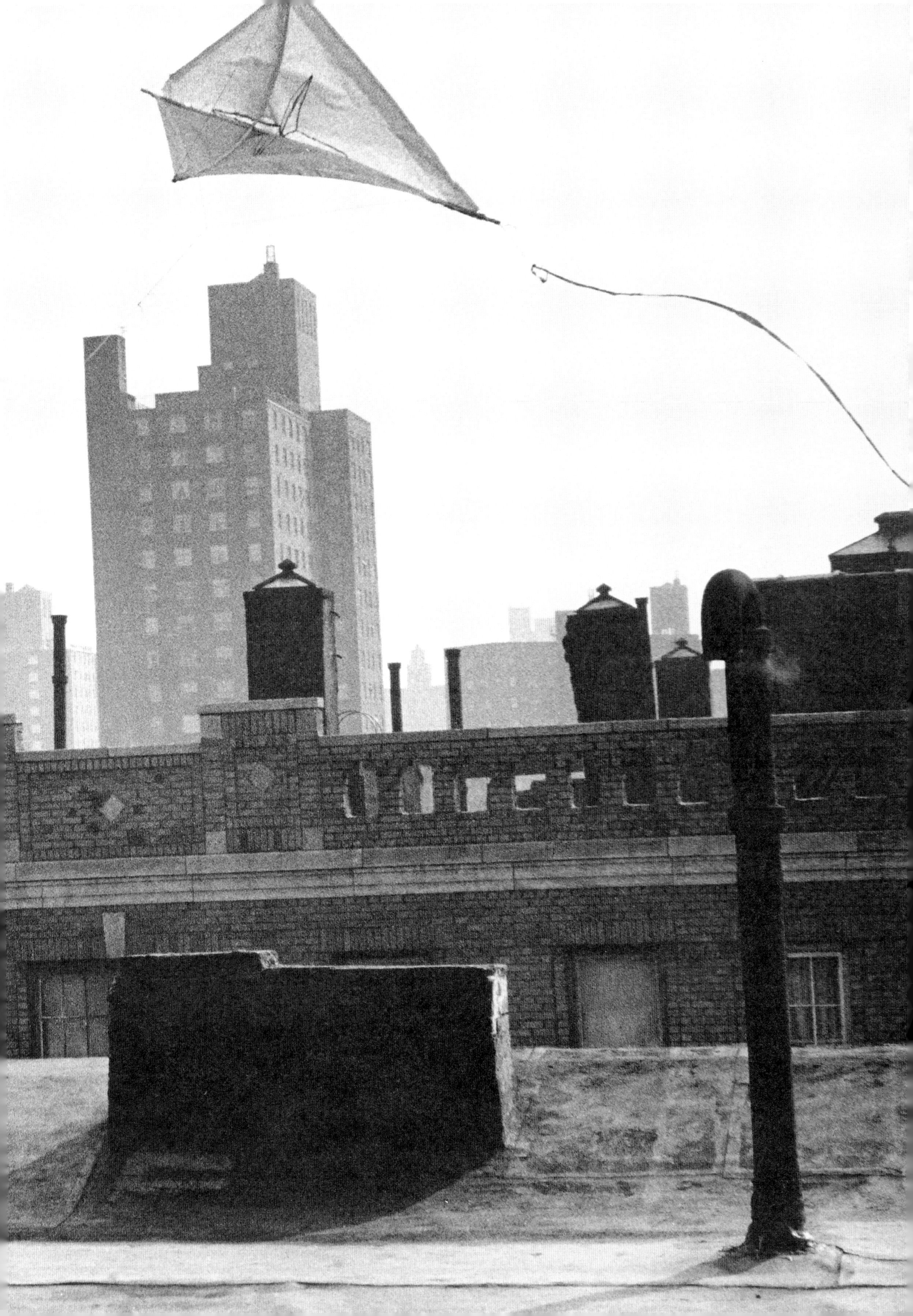

Table of Contents

Table of Contents

Table of Contents

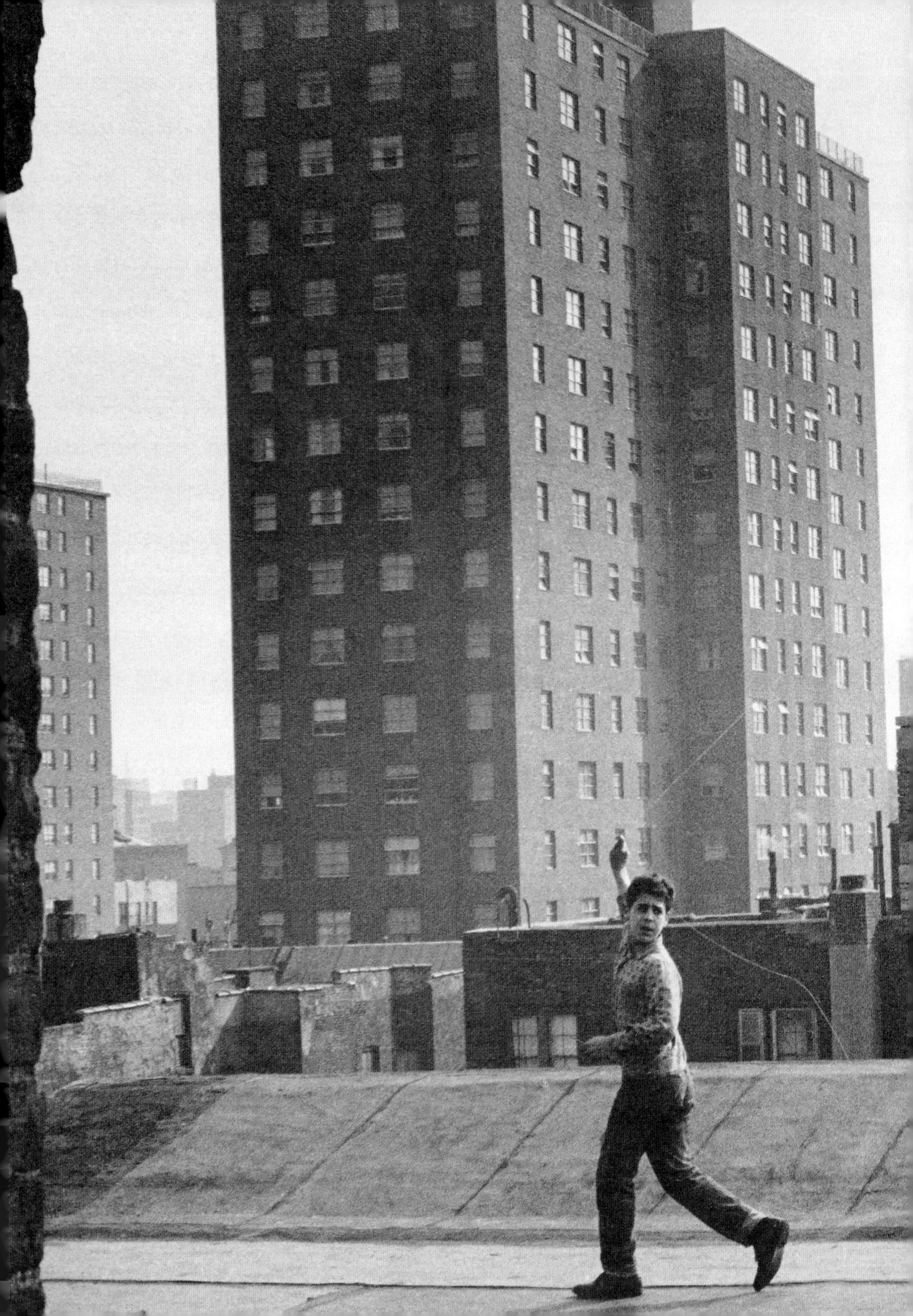

Foreword

Greater New York 2021, the fifth iteration of the exhibition since its conception in 2000, brings together the work of forty-seven artists and collectives to offer a fresh look at practices that shape, and have been shaped by, New York. Recurring every five years, the exhibition offers a moment to take stock of the social, political, and cultural contexts that impact thinking and making—from an era before 9/11, or Twitter, or Trumpism, to our current moment amid a global pandemic, the advent of cryptocurrency, and increasing environmental crisis. Equally important, it allows us to reflect on the ways that artists crystallize the tangled, often difficult histories and lives that propel this city.

The first edition of *Greater New York* in 2000 featured works by 168 artists, all of which had been made within the previous five years, under the mandate "New Art In New York Now." Every moment demands its own kind of exhibition, and subsequent iterations of *Greater New York* have shifted impetus accordingly. This year's is no exception. Organized by a curatorial team led by Ruba Katrib, Curator at MoMA PS1, and writer and independent curator Serubiri Moses, with Inés Katzenstein, Curator of Latin American Art and Director of the Patricia Phelps de Cisneros Research Institute for the Study of Art from Latin America at the Museum of Modern Art, and myself, this *Greater New York* puts pressure on each of the terms in the original formulation: What counts as new? Where can New York be said to begin and end? How, exactly, do we encapsulate the now? *Greater* than what?

Delayed by a year due to the global pandemic, developed in large part over Zoom, and opening in the aftermath of a year marked by the city's complete shutdown and eventual reawakening amid protests in support of Black Lives Matter, this iteration of *Greater New York* serves in part as an homage to all the artists that breathe life into this city, even in difficult moments. Its realization has challenged so many of our assumptions around proximity, contact, and distance.

The show brings together a relatively small group of practitioners in comparison to former iterations, enabling us to focus more resources on supporting the production of work at a time when many artists are facing financial precarity. Within the cohort, there is a surprising temporal and geographical range, with artists born from 1901 (Paulina Peavy) to 1991 (Sean-Kierre Lyons), and those whose lives span multiple cities and continents but who nonetheless conceive of New York as a nexus. This particular selection of artists also champions intergenerational and diasporic affinities, celebrating camaraderies among peers and reminding us how artists across generations and backgrounds collectively make New York.

I deeply appreciate my fellow curators for their incredible commitment to learning from and with artists, and for thinking through crucial questions of history, geography, and belonging in a moment of profound uncertainty. I learned so much from each of you. The realization of this show is testament to the tenacity and patience of many. It is also the manifestation of collaboration between the PS1 teams, from finance, operations, and security to communications, visitor engagement, and development. Respect goes to Ruba Katrib, Jody Graf, and Michael Henry for stewarding the exhibition to completion amid many transformations within the institution.

I am also beyond grateful to the entire PS1 Board of Directors, led by the inimitable Sarah Arison, who never swerved in their support and their confidence that we could pull off this project in spite of the extraordinary conditions of the last eighteen months. Similarly, we have felt the solidarity of our municipal partners: Gonzalo Casals and the New York City Department of Cultural Affairs; Donovan Richards, Queens Borough President; Jimmy Van Bramer, Council Member; and the New York City Council. Thank you. I also thank Glenn D. Lowry, the David Rockefeller Director of the Museum of Modern Art, for his continuous support, from the very first *Greater New York* twenty-one years ago to now.

A number of key individuals, groups, and foundations were instrumental in bringing this ambitious show and publication into the world. Alongside the rest of the curatorial team, I extend many thanks to Ben Rodriguez-Cubeñas and the Charles E. Culpeper Arts and Culture Program of the Rockefeller Brothers Fund for your early and lead support; the pioneering founding members of the Greater New Yorkers donor group at MoMA PS1; Gerald Marolf, Ruth Heenan, and Sam del Pilar from On; the Contemporary Arts Council of the Museum of Modern Art; the International Council of the Museum of Modern Art; MoMA's Wallis Annenberg Director's Fund for Innovation in Contemporary Art; Janet Neschis and Barbara Campisi from the Jacques and Natasha Gelman Foundation; Lise Stolt-Nielsen; the Junior Associates of the Museum of Modern Art; the Black Arts Council of the Museum of Modern Art; the Ava Olivia Knoll Fund; and the Tom Slaughter Emerging Artists Endowment Fund; as well as Bark Frameworks and the Billion Oyster Project.

Finally, on behalf of the curators and the entire team at MoMA PS1, a heartfelt thank you to all the artists in the show. May this be the beginning of many conversations and collaborations to come.

Kate Fowle
Director, MoMA PS1

Acknowledgments

An exhibition of this magnitude is always an immense effort, requiring the dedicated labor and care of many. *Greater New York* was no exception, and was made all the more challenging because it occurred in the midst of a global pandemic. This exhibition would not have been possible without the support of many intersecting networks of collaborators and colleagues. We extend our gratitude to the following individuals, whose insight and assistance was invaluable in facilitating loans and bringing the show and publication to fruition: Miguel Abreu, Caio Meirelles Aguiar, Ramsey Alderson, Luke Alvine, Katherine Armstrong, Daniele Balice, Yto Barrada, Cassandra Belliston, Derek Bishton, Andrew Blackley, Charlotte Boesch, Kim Bouras, Jennifer Brennan, Hal Bromm, Susanna Callegari, Lucas Casso, Marie Catalano, Marina Chao, Zhiwei Chen, Tony Chrenka, Mark Christman, Rob Colvin, Jenni Crain, Patrick Creedon, Dean Daderko, Claudia Delaplace, Elyse Derosia, Amparo Discoli, Andrew Edlin, Mike Egan, Becky Elmquist, Martha Fleming-Ives, Iliya Fridman, Alissa Friedman, Gabrielle Giattino, Thelma Golden, Sam Gordon, Maxwell Graham, Taymour Grahne, Renita Graves and the Graves family, Jeanne Greenberg Rohatyn, Carol Greene, Jennifer Grimyser, Janice Guy, Kaara Henriquez, Alexander Hertling, Hannah Hoffman, Janae Huber, Andrew Kreps, Sabrina Lefkowitz, Josh Lenten, Weston Lowe, Miguel Luciano, Caitlin Mahony, Pete Malinowski, Jaqueline Martins, Sarah Miller, Sherine Morsi, Nabil Moufarrej and the Moufarrege family, Liz Mulholland, Renée Mussai, Wendy Olsoff, Shannon O'Neill, Gary Owen, Gabriele Papa, Siddharth Patel, Penny Pilkington, Scott Portnoy, Alexander Provan, Kari Rittenbach, Jacob Robichaux, Esther Ruiz, Britta Ruona, Tim Saltarelli, Jay Sanders, Rachel Shabica, Sandra Schulman, Ross Simonini, David B. Smith, Robert Snowden, Richard Sorensen, Hedi Sorger, Isabella St. Ivany, Mina Stone, Katie Svensson, Jasmin Tsou, Eric Veit, Nicole Wallace, Taylor Walsh, Zachary Wampler, Marie Warsh, Max Warsh, Kira Wilson, Troy Wong, Chavisa Woods, and Aurélie Bernard Wortsman.

Huge thanks are due to the following individuals, galleries, and institutions, who so generously lent artworks to the exhibition: Andrew Edlin Gallery; Andrew Kreps Gallery; Annet Gelink Gallery; Aarne and Tina Anton; Balice Hertling; Bodega; Bureau; Cosmocosa; Collection Cross and Couteau; Lonti Ebers; Collection Mr. Michael Ettner; Fridman Gallery; Fundacion Medianoche0; Galerie Jaqueline Martins; Gordon Robichaux; the Estate of Milford Graves; Greene Naftali; Hal Bromm Gallery; Hale Schulman Archives; Hannah Hoffman Gallery; The Helios Trust; Bob Holman; JTT; Kravis Collection; Larrie; the Estate of Rosemary Mayer; Maxwell Graham / Essex Street; Miguel Abreu Gallery; National Museum of the American Indian, Smithsonian Institution; Office Baroque; Collection Alec Oxenford; The Estate of Paulina Peavy; Collection Francesco Pellizzi; the Peter Hujar Archive; Collection Mr. Ferdinand Porak; PPOW Gallery; Ramiken; Salon 94; Collection Joshua P. Smith; the Studio Museum in Harlem; Sweetwater; Taymour Grahne Projects; Carol Ann Thompson; the Walther Collection; and Washington State Arts Collection.

The devoted efforts and attention of the incredible staff at MoMA PS1 made this exhibition possible; we thank them for collaborating with us and the artists to manifest the exhibition and the artists' visions. Special thanks are due to Jody Graf, Assistant Curator, for her work on the exhibition, as well as Taja Cheek, Associate Curator, and Elena Ketelsen González, Assistant Curator, for their invaluable assistance on the many programs that accompany this exhibition. We are grateful to Andrea Sánchez, Administrative Assistant in the Curatorial Department, Jack Radley, Special Projects Coordinator and Executive Assistant, Director's Office, and Stephanie Del Carpio, former Special Projects Coordinator and Executive Assistant, Director's Office, for keeping us organized and on track, as well as Muheb Esmat and May Makki, former Research Associates, and Lily Engelmaier, former Curatorial Intern, for their incisive research. The Exhibitions team, led by former Director of Programs Michael Henry, managed the installation with finesse. We extend particular gratitude to Richard Wilson, Exhibition and Production Designer; Joya Erickson, Registrar; Angela Hallinan, Project Manager, Exhibitions; Anna Grofik, Exhibition Assistant; and the entire team of art handlers, who brought such care and skill to an ambitious installation. Taja Cheek; Chris Masullo, Project Manager, Performance and Events; and Alex Sloane, former Assistant Curator, were crucial in bringing Freya Powell's performance to the exhibition. Molly Kurzius, Director of External Affairs; Amber Sasse, Assistant Director of Institutional Giving; Hannah Howe, Director of Individual Giving; Alison Cuzzolino, former Director of Finance; and the entire press and communications team were instrumental in bringing this exhibition to the broader world. An exhibition at this scale is truly a building-wide effort, and we thank our Administration department, led by Jose A. Ortiz, Deputy Director, and Operations team, led by Samuel N. Denitz, as well as the

Visitor Engagement associates and security guards that have been so crucial in engaging and assisting visitors to the show.

Vance Wellenstein, former Head of Design, and Julia Schäfer brought a keen eye and attention to detail to the design of this catalogue. Additionally, we would like to acknowledge Jody Graf for stewarding the process of making this book; Dana Kopel for her thoughtful copyediting; Nora Rodriguez, Digital Strategy and Content Manager, for supervising the roundtable conversations; and each of the participants and authors who contributed to the conversations and texts we are honored to highlight in this book.

We also thank the communities of colleagues, family, and friends who think alongside us, and whose conversations and support were invaluable: Patrick Charpenel, Lauren Cornell, Beto De Volder, Verónica Flom, Danielle Jackson, Ana Janevski, Lawrence Kumpf, Rodrigo Moura, Leila N.M. Mpanga, Abubaker Mulindwa, Gabi Ngcobo, Oluremi C. Onabanjo, Renaud Proch, Alan Segal, Leon Villagran, and Emma Wolukau-Wanambwa.

Finally, and most importantly, we are profoundly grateful to the forty-seven artists and collectives included in this exhibition, and to the family members and estates who have been key supporters in cases of the artist's absence. The vision—and visionary artworks—of this group of artists and thinkers provided both the framework and inspiration for this show. Their daring, generous, and collaborative spirit guided us throughout.

Kate Fowle, Ruba Katrib, Inés Katzenstein, and Serubiri Moses

Introduction

But while contact may be, by comparison, "random" (but doesn't one move to—or from—a particular neighborhood as part of a desire to be among, or to avoid—certain types of people, whether that neighborhood be Greenwich Village, Bensonhurst, or Beverly Hills?), and while networking may be, by comparison, "planned" (yet how many times do we return from the professional conference unable, a month later, to remember having met anyone of particular interest or, next Monday morning in the office, not having retained any useful idea?), it is clear that contact is contoured, if not organized, by earlier decisions, desires, commercial interests, zoning laws and immigration patterns. The differences seem to be rather matters of scale (the looser streets of the neighborhood versus the more condensed hotel or conference center spaces) and the granularity that allows others to dilute the social density with a range of contrasting needs and desires, as well as differences in social skills and, yes, institutional access.
—Samuel R. Delany, *Times Square Red, Times Square Blue*, 1999

In October of 2021 at MoMA PS1, we opened *Greater New York*, an exhibition that has taken place every five years since 2000 with a mandate to survey New York artists. Our plans were underway, yet still in formation, when the COVID-19 pandemic hit New York: we switched to online Zoom studio visits and postponed the exhibition by a year as we dealt with a slew of new obstacles—as well as opportunities. Samuel R. Delany's book *Times Square Red, Times Square Blue*, a personal history of New York City, became a key touchpoint as the city went under lockdown. Written in the late 1990s, as the city—and Times Square in particular—was undergoing a pronounced process of gentrification, the effects of which continue today, Delany considered the social effects of these changes to the built environment. Building on Jane Jacobs's notion of contact as integral to vibrant interclass relationships in an urban landscape, Delany posits that the city can facilitate a broad range of close and fleeting interactions, creative connections, and charged encounters that are shaped by social space but also defy the top-down directives of politicians, urban planners, and commercial interests. These interactions, when allowed to flourish, have the potential to cut through barriers of class and race. During the pandemic, as people became increasingly isolated and discouraged from even the most banal "contact," the facets of the city that foster interaction among strangers were suddenly emptied; in its absence, the idea of contact became even more pronounced as a defining aspect of urban life.

With this present crisis of contact in mind, we found it important to consider the diverse, interconnected, and expansive artist communities that make up New York now and over the last decades. We began looking more closely at relationships between artists that transcend or defy established hierarchies, and at recent histories that have been excluded from the art historical canon, thinking through the ways in which the city and its institutions can better support the many who call this place home. The result, an exhibition that brings together the work of forty-seven artists and collectives in an intergenerational and international conversation, acknowledges New York City as Native land and a meeting place for Indigenous artists from different parts of the world, and provides a glimpse into the many artists and art worlds that comprise New York.

The exhibition and this publication seek to honor long-standing relationships and connections between artists, as well as to forge new contact between artists who met for the first time on the occasion of the exhibition or through the conversations we arranged for this book. Some of these preexisting relationships stem from friendships and mentorships between artists like E'wao Kagoshima and Nicolas Moufarrege, or Yuji Agematsu and Milford Graves. Artists such as G. Peter Jemison, Hiram Maristany, and Marilyn Nance have been mentors to many artists and keepers of stories for decades. Their works document the city and their communities, offering historical insight into radical movements and artists who have contributed to struggles for justice. The legacies of artists pushing for social change, whether they are ultimately successful or not, also inspire younger artists. The collectives BlackMass Publishing and Shanzhai Lyric, placed in conversation with Maristany for this publication, use experimental and improvisational means to produce materials that reveal under-recognized stories about the city and its inhabitants, past and present. Artistic influence cascades through generations; sometimes younger artists are the first to appreciate elders who were ahead of their time. Bettina Grossman, for instance, has been championed and cared for by the younger Yto Barrada, who connected with Grossman toward the end of her life and reflects on her legacy for this publication. Grossman sadly passed away a few weeks after the exhibition opened, at the age of ninety-four.

Relationships among artists, and the communities they form, will always exceed the generational and geographic limits of traditional art-historical framings. Many younger artists we spoke to were keen to uncover histories, particularly those that have been overlooked or even shunned, as a way to understand the present—but also to shape the future. As Shanzhai Lyric aptly states in these pages, "The past isn't past." Following these cues, this publication extends the exhibition and its methodologies, centering artists' voices intermixed across decades and generations. A series of newly produced roundtable conversations between artists, some of whom already knew each other and others whom hadn't yet met, chart the main through lines of the exhibition: the documentary impulse and the archive; surrealism, trauma, and the posthuman; Native New York; and abstraction, mourning, and time. Grounded in the perspectives of their participants, these discussions offer insight into the shared considerations and conditions many artists face today. Other artists are represented in this publication by oral histories—personal narratives focusing on key aspects of their works—either in their own words or those of people close to them. We have also reprinted texts by artists, ranging from criticism to film scripts and poetry. Many artists in the exhibition are themselves writers of various kinds: Diane Burns, Ahmed Morsi, and Paulina Peavy are prolific poets; Rotimi Fani-Kayode, Steffani Jemison, and Nicolas Moufarrege use essays and criticism to contextualize the conceptual underpinnings of their work; and artists such as Raque Ford, Marie Karlberg, Matthew Langan-Peck, Rosemary Mayer, and Shanzhai Lyric employ notes and scripts as crucial parts of their practices. Their perspectives on the city, as well as their thoughts on the artistic process, provide essential documents that illuminate the interdisciplinary, multifaceted, and immediate manner of writing through which artists continue to work.

In thinking about how artists represent themselves and the world around them, we became interested in the concept of the *longue durée*. If they are able, artists work for decades, some until the end of their lives. Meanwhile, the idea of newness is constantly evolving, and the "emerging artist" is not the only signifier of the contemporary. The present is fundamentally nonlinear and heterogeneous; there are pockets of the present in the past—which we want to offer back today, through this exhibition. Robin Graubard's installation, for example, features photographs taken from 1979 through the summer of 2021, right before the opening of *Greater New York*, in no linear chronological order. Paulina Peavy made some of her paintings over decades, with a single work dating from the 1930s, the 1960s, and the 1980s. Shelley Niro's photographs of fossils embedded in the shores of Lake Erie, titled *Resting Place of our Ancestors* (2019), point to our longer origins and unknowable futures. Works by Alan Michelson and Athena LaTocha also speak to deeper histories of land and Indigenous geographies, as well as the impact of ecological and cultural shifts. A tension between ruin, decay, and regeneration pervades the exhibition. Steffani Jemison "tumbles" materials like rocks, shards of glass, and pennies in her sculptures, a process that accelerates the effects of time by wearing down and buffing their surfaces. In Dolores Furtado's sculpture, architectural remains made of paper pulp are installed in front of the ever-growing New York City skyline, glimpsed through the museum's windows.

Numerous artists articulate the sense of the city as an aural as well as visual place. In her diaristic drawings, Rosemary Mayer notates the disruptive noises of construction near her longtime Tribeca home, alongside the coughs and sneezes of passersby.

Other artists, such as Freya Powell and Regina Vater, use the human voice and its reverberation in the city, while Raha Raissnia and Andy Robert approach sound as a visual experience. In one gallery, the car horns and traffic sounds in Matthew Langan-Peck's *Red Light Trouble* (2021)—an audio piece dramatizing the inner monologue of a New York City building super stuck at a never-ending red light—merge and periodically clash with Diane Burns's reading of her poem "Alphabet City Serenade" on the streets of the Lower East Side, recorded thirty-four years earlier. Yuji Agematsu catalogues his intimately scaled sculptural practice, visualizing the unique treasures-*cum*-detritus he gathered daily from the streets of Brooklyn during 2020, yet he also explains in his contribution to this book that his practice is tied to the experience of *listening*. His works serve as both maps and scores of urban life. Similarly, both Milford Graves and Carolyn Lazard visualize not only sound, but listening, as corporeal and embodied. Lazard's *Red* (2021) touches on the bodily effects of abstraction—tethering a space typically read as disconnected from the body to its visceral rhythms and reactions.

Other artists document and distort the space of the city—its streets, architectures, and the bodies that move through it. Through very different means and working decades apart, Kristi Cavataro and Bettina Grossman turn to glass to speak to the sometimes-warped experience of urban space. Curtis Cuffie, who lived unhoused for many years, made work that existed in and for the city streets. Luis Frangella's large-scale paintings from the 1980s emerged from a practice of adorning the walls of abandoned sites in Lower Manhattan. Diane Burns, working around the same time, turned to the street as both stage and subject for her poems. Many artists are drawn to making new sense out of the refuse and excess material culture of the city, as Regina Vater captures in her film *LuxoLixo* (1973/1974) documenting New York's markets and trash piles, and Kayode Ojo explores in gleaming sculptures made of low-cost and knockoff luxury goods.

A number of artists in the exhibition take on issues of representation by locating the personal within historic materials and references. In her video work, filmed during the height of the COVID-19 lockdown, Marie Karlberg restages Doris Lessing's 1985 novel *The Good Terrorist*, transforming an empty luxury apartment in a New York City skyscraper into a squat of disgruntled radicals. Stanley Wolukau-Wanambwa mines archives and produces his own photographs to create a choreography of images and objects that probe the racialized and sexualized residues of photographic representation, while Avijit Halder manipulates his deceased mother's saris in a series of intimate portraits through a queer lens. Many of the artists, including Hadi Fallahpisheh, Doreen Garner, Julio Galán, Raque Ford, Lachell Workman, and Rotimi Fani-Kayode, explore desire, longing, mourning, and representation, often in relation to systems of oppression or violence. Using more abstracted means, artists Bill Hayden,

Kayode Ojo, Servane Mary, and Diane Severin Nguyen investigate notions of attraction and repulsion, withholding or circumventing forms of direct representation and legibility.

Surrealism is a central thread running through the exhibition, complicating the many ways artists use the documentary to represent, map, and archive. While one approach is grounded in a sense of reality and the other is based in fiction, the two modes work together to share truths that may appear unfamiliar, fantastic, or farfetched to some. In works by Nadia Ayari, Las Nietas de Nonó, Sean-Kierre Lyons, Emilie Louise Gossiaux, and Tammy Nguyen, animals, plants, and fantastical beings intermingle with—and at times overpower—the human realm. These artists construct images and worlds in which relationships between humans and nonhuman organisms are transformed. Gossiaux's drawings and sculpture merge her body with that of her guide dog, London; the interdependence between the artist and her companion animal entangles distinctions between necessity and love. In their sculptures, drawings, and painting, Sean-Kierre Lyons looks to the realm of the botanical, creating an army of flowers through which to contend with societal trappings of race and gender. As an approach to feelings of belonging and estrangement, surrealism is key in thinking through notions of contact: How do artists process their lived experience beyond conventional narratives? How can the hyper subjective document and foster resilience during challenging times? How do artists' visions of place and being offer new perspectives? As Surrealist artist and poet Ahmed Morsi's daughter says of her father, who has called New York City home since 1974, "Ahmed knows the city, but the city doesn't know him." Like Morsi, other artists in the exhibition—among them Julio Galán, Shanzhai Lyric, Hadi Fallahpisheh, Nicolas Moufarrege, Avijit Halder, E'wao Kagoshima, and Yuji Agematsu—deploy surrealist approaches to consider experiences of diaspora.

Looking critically at existing art histories of the city, we chose to push against the ways that various institutions of art—museums, galleries, publications, etc.—have segregated artists from one another. Notably, many of the artists in the exhibition have started their own institutions or spaces, or worked at culturally specific institutions in New York. Collectives Shanzhai Lyric and BlackMass Publishing mimic, critique, and intervene in cultural institutions while, importantly, not solidifying into institutions themselves. Hiram Maristany was a founder of El Museo del Barrio and worked as director there for many years, and G. Peter Jemison served as a curator at the American Indian Community House. With fellow artists Mike Bidlo and David Wojnarowicz, Luis Frangella helped establish the abandoned Pier 34 as an unofficial site for experimental artmaking. Rosemary Mayer was a founding member of A.I.R. Gallery, a cooperative that supports women artists, and Diane Burns cofounded the Nuyorican Poets Cafe, a downtown hub for a diverse group of artists and poets. Many younger artists in the exhibition similarly run collective spaces and experimental initiatives. These examples attest to the fact that artists not only make their work, but contribute to the layered communities that bring life to the city. These artists attend to that which has been disregarded by the mainstream and the forces of capital, helping shape new pathways for future generations.

This publication provides an entry point into the work of the forty-seven artists brought together in *Greater New York*, while also offering a snapshot of key concerns for artists more broadly. To do this, we relied on artists' own words, their own ways of framing their practices and experiences, rather than commissioning essays on their work or the themes of the exhibition. With new dialogues between artists placed alongside historical conversations, included as reprints or previously unpublished material, this publication will, we hope, function as a sourcebook for the future—one grounded in the incredible output and complex thinking of so many artists of our time.

Ruba Katrib with Kate Fowle, Inés Katzenstein, and Serubiri Moses

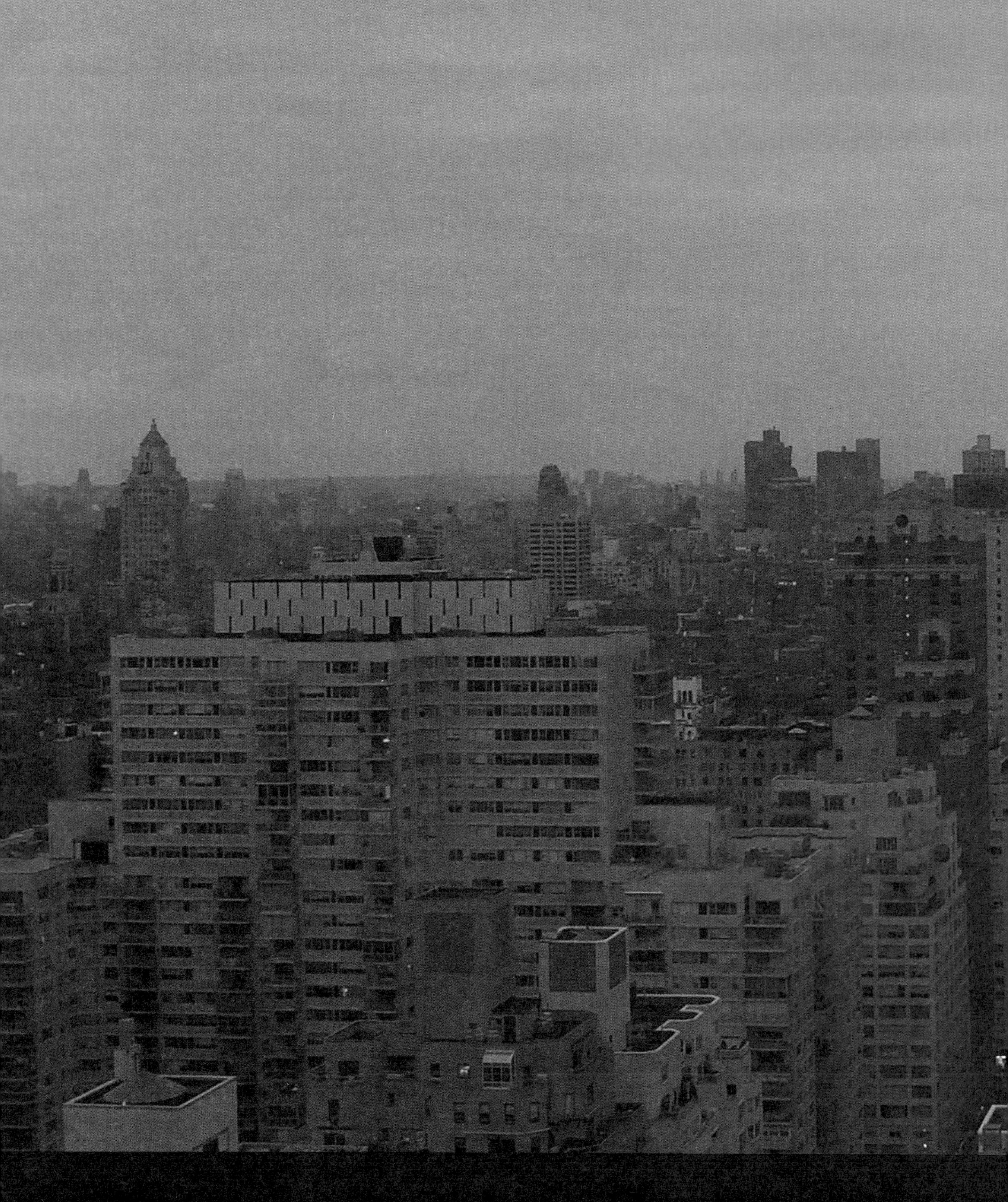

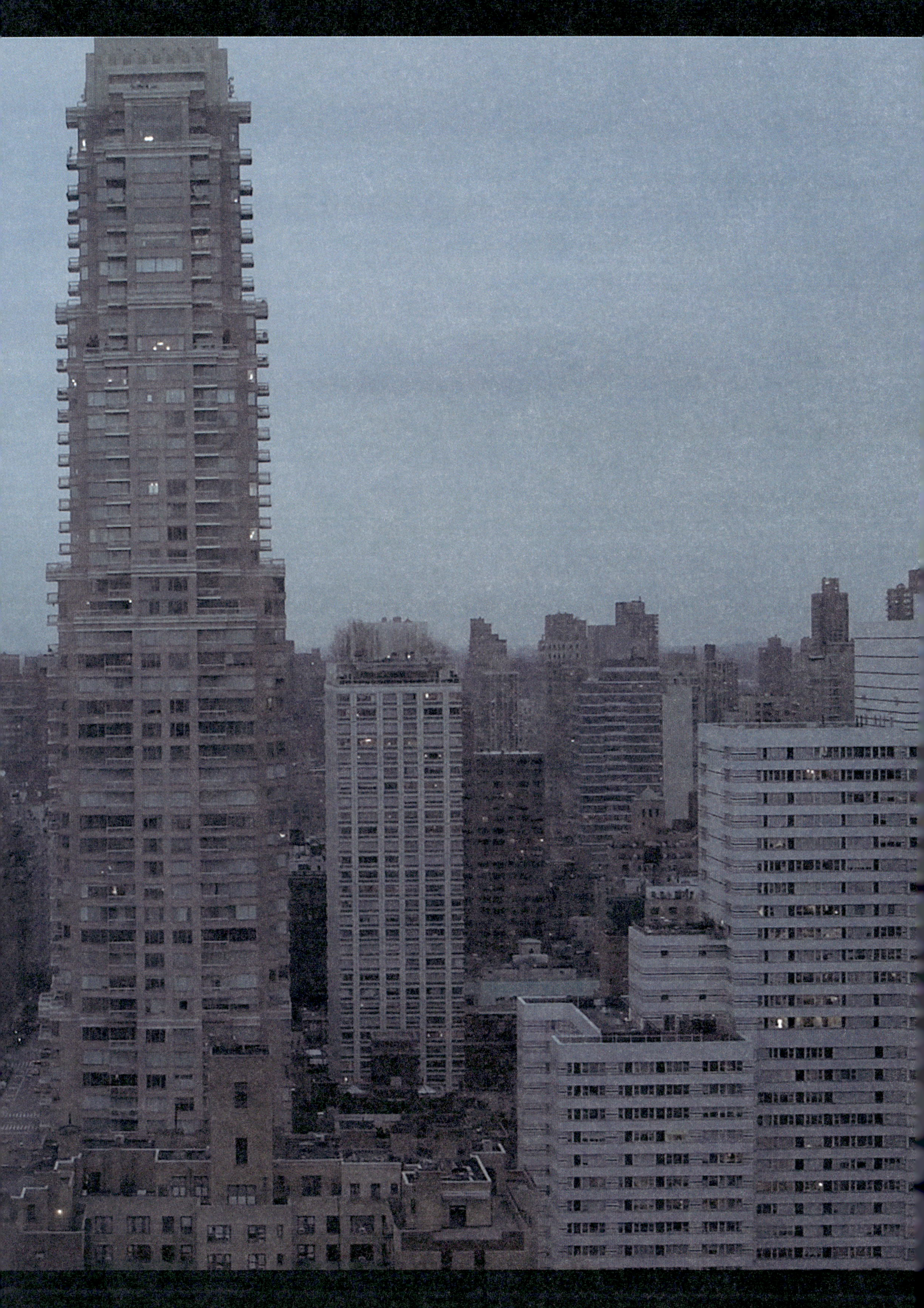

THE DOCUMENTARY IMPULSE AND THE ARCHIVE:

A conversation between BlackMass Publishing, Hiram Maristany, and Shanzhai Lyric

Kwamé Sorrell
(BlackMass Publishing):
Can you explain the origin and significance of the name Shanzhai Lyric?

Shanzhai Lyric:
Shanzhai is the Mandarin word for "counterfeit," but it translates literally to "mountain hamlet." It allegedly refers to a Song dynasty legend of robbers taking goods from the empire to redistribute among those at the margins, where they were protected by a mountain hamlet. It offers a different mode of thinking about trade and redistribution of resources, and also ownership and authorship. We've been very inspired by this terminology as a way of thinking about a more liberatory notion of counterfeit.

The research first started looking specifically at *shanzhai* garments, mostly made in China but distributed and beloved around the world, that were blanketed in this very beautiful, experimental, often supra-sensical English text. Shanzhai Lyric was a way for us to reconceive of this phenomenon of experimental languages that we saw traveling across bodies around the world. We think of them as bootleg poems, which comment on and often critique the circumstances of their own production.

KS:
I grew up in Flushing, Queens, and it was funny because as a kid, we would see an old grandpa on the bus or something, and he would have a hat that said, "World's best daughter"—something that just didn't seem to make sense at all.

SL:
Yeah! We're really excited about celebrating that kind of irreverent relationship to language and branding. We've been collecting shirts for six years, since we went on a research trip to China and spent a month commuting to this multilevel wholesale clothing market there. At that time, we had no funds, so we were just taking photo documentation of the T-shirt poems. Slowly, over time, however, we've been able to amass a large collection that has been in circulation around the globe—in libraries, archives, personal closets, private institutions, community centers. Since we've been at PS1, we've been meaning to take a trip to Flushing to gather some more items for the archive. Let's turn the question that you asked us back to you, in terms of the origins and resonance of your name. What does BlackMass Publishing mean for you? What's the origin of the name?

Yusuf Hassan
(BlackMass Publishing):
BlackMass Publishing started in 2018 in response to the lack of representation of Black publishers contributing to contemporary printed matter. The name originated from a play by Amiri Baraka called *A Black Mass* (1966). At the time, I was working on a book compiled of documents, which I had friends contribute to. It started off with three friends, Kwamé being one of them, along with Devin B. Johnson and Jacob Mason-Macklin. We all did different things, and we started to see how our work would feed off of each others'. I titled the book *Project BlackMass*, and that's how the first body of work was created. This document never went into print. It just floated around for a little while. Later that year, in the fall of 2018, I started BlackMass Publishing as a way to extend my contribution to other Black artists and the diaspora at large. I wanted to create a mass of Black artists working together in different mediums on the presentation of printed matter and archives.

KS:
Yusuf and I work very closely together in producing a lot of these publications. What we focus on is how to continue to build the

Mass through print medium specifically. Yusuf always says he wants to figure out how to put music in print: How do you take a song and translate it to music through print medium, without having lyrics or a score or sound? We try to put a lot of movement and rhythm into the practice as well. We're heavily influenced by music.

Hiram Maristany:

What you're saying about a lack of representation in terms of Black issues in printed matter is very important. I think that applies to many other things as well. It applies to many other groups that are poor and are treated in a similar way. I'm a photographer. I was born and raised in East Harlem. My parents immigrated to New York from Puerto Rico. I have been engaged with the civil rights movement from a very young age. I'm very privileged to say that I actually went to the March on Washington. I was by myself. Many of my contemporaries didn't believe that the March on Washington was important, and I disagreed. It's not about pitting one group against another. I'm from the generation of the '60s and '70s. There were enormous things going on, enormous battles. Battles with institutions like MoMA over the lack of representation of people of color, women, and gay people. Lack of representation of a whole list of things.

I've been documenting my community for many decades, and the photographs I am exhibiting in *Greater New York* show aspects of my community that are positive and document the Young Lords, a political movement that was active in East Harlem. The Young Lords is a Puerto Rican group that is fashioned after the Black Panther Party for Self-Defense. I emphasize the word *self-defense*. They formed because they felt they had to defend their communities. They didn't come from a perspective of political analysis; they came from a practical reality. They had to defend their community because they felt they were under attack and under siege. What I'm showing are key elements and moments of those events. I am a documentarian, and I'm trying to tell the narrative. Because, unfortunately, the media always distorts our story and somehow puts us in a position where we're fighting the wrong enemies; they're very sophisticated in dividing and conquering, pitting poor people against poor people. I was also one of the key players in the Puerto Rican arts movement, and helped develop El Museo del Barrio. I was one of the earliest members of the Young Lords, and I became the official photographer of the organization.

SL:

Thank you for sharing this personal history embedded in a collective history. Recently, in the fall of 2020, we invented a fictional office entity called Canal Street Research Association. We began inhabiting this empty storefront on Canal Street, near where we grew up, which was largely boarded up and vacant due to many factors: high rent, blight, landlords' fear of so-called looting following the uprisings in the summer. We stepped into this empty retail space to just be there all day, look out the window, and talk to whoever came in about the unofficial markets and industries—semi-illicit and illicit—of Canal Street, which have created so much important New York history.

One of the things that struck us while we were on Canal Street was a history of the block as perpetually processing waste and overflow. Canal Street was originally an actual canal that was built in order to channel excess sewage and industrial runoff from Collect Pond in Chinatown into the Hudson and East rivers. This created a very fetid waterway that they then tried to beautify by placing trees along its edge. They eventually had to fill it back in, and it became the chaotic, polluted, noisy, crowded thoroughfare that it is today. While we were down there in our storefront, we were aware of the fact that as artists, we were the trees of the situation: we were placed there in order to participate in an upscaling project that landlords there have been undertaking for the past ten years or so. We were placed there to "artwash," essentially, the neighborhood—until our presentation was found to be at odds with the landlord's agenda. Since then, we have not had an office. For *Greater New York*, we will have a storage unit where all of the archival objects that we had been collecting over time—the Shanzhai Lyric archive, which is about two hundred or so T-shirts, and the materials from our former storefront—will be with us in the space. We'll be accessing these objects throughout the six months [of the show], creating a kind of relay between Long Island City and Canal Street.

One guiding metaphor for us in this work has been tracing the waterways of New York and finding that which has been buried and covered up—these hidden flows, channels, and currencies that literally run from Canal Street in Lower Manhattan to Long Island City. We've become very inspired by the classic New York coffee cup, which is a kind of visualization of the research methodology that we will be attempting to embody while at PS1: the meander. This research methodology defies linearity and finds discoveries in the most inefficient and winding way between points. That's been our guiding philosophy as of late.

KS:

It's quite beautiful that you will grow this project over time. Having a research-based practice, you always want to add something else, right? I think it's beautiful that you all will be creating this conversation between Canal Street, the museum, and your practice in between.

HM:

One of the realities of Canal Street for me was the great art supply store, Pearl Paint. I used to hang out at Pearl Paint when I was still a starving artist—and I mean a real starving artist. We used to go down there, and the owner knew that we were "liberating" things, to put it mildly. What I witnessed was a form of subtle gentrification that was incredible. It's important to document it, to show it—because a lot of communities are gentrified and they don't realize that it takes a very long time. When they finally realize, it's way too late and they're already displaced. So I'm very intrigued by what you guys are doing.

SL:

We're big Pearl Paint fans! Many folks who have come to share memories with us have talked about how important Pearl Paint was. But none, before you, have expressed this important phrase of "liberating" the goods you need.

HM:

I met some really famous artists. They used to say, "I remember when I used to liberate, too, and everybody knew that I was a starving artist." I came back to pay homage to this place that understood that artists could not afford half the prices. The irony of this is that it's no longer there because the property was worth more than the business.

I believe that whenever we have great artists that unify different communities, that is an embellishment that is profound. One of the artists that did this is Gil Scott-Heron. He has a poem that I suggest you check out. It's a poem for José Campos Torres, a Latin American brother who was brutally beaten. The second artist I would mention is Sekou Sundiata, a dear friend of mine. He was born and raised in Central Harlem, but he lived most of his life in East Harlem. He was inspired by a lot of great poets, such as Pedro Pietri—an artist that also transcends his community. As artists, there's an unstated reality that we have to look at injustice, wherever it is, and respond to it. That doesn't mean that we have to take on other people's issues, but we cannot be silent.

YH:
One of the biggest inspirations for BlackMass Publishing is Larry Paul Neal. He was very good friends with Amiri Baraka/LeRoi Jones. While I was researching at the Schomburg Center for Research in Black Culture, I found a document called *The Rise of Black Consciousness* that inspired BlackMass to expand. Neal died before this document was actually published. This set the fire under me to push my practice forward and continue the narrative of what Neal was doing, and to think about how to expand and distribute our work. We started to distribute information through paper pamphlets, which are approachable and easy to disseminate. Right before the pandemic started, we were heading over to France for a show, and then everything came to a halt. We were trying to think about how to continue this conversation around what we would do during this time, and one of the best contributions to BlackMass Publishing was this mailing program that Kwamé developed.

KS:
The mailing program essentially was a way for us to expand our conversation during the pandemic. Being that we couldn't travel, being that it was a weird time for everyone, we wanted to open up our practice to people we were in conversation with but couldn't directly speak with or see. People would send us poems, letters, photos, mixtapes. The whole purpose was to archive. We would open it up to the public to then contribute to the archive that we're building. We don't have a bigger picture in mind for this archive as of yet, but we are continuously building.

I have a question for you, Hiram, about your archiving practice. Were you aware that you were building an archive for a future purpose, or were you simply shooting and documenting because you felt the need to? What was your ultimate goal?

HM:
I was not aware that I was archiving. One of the things that I had to deal with as a young man was that all the images depicting Puerto Ricans were negative. We were either committing a crime or a crime was being perpetrated against us. We were always in handcuffs. Our sisters were depicted as teenage mothers—without any morals or ethics. I was very distressed and angry about it. I wanted to try and do something about it. Being naive, I felt that I could address all those negative issues. I just went out and I said, "Let me try and document what's good about us." Yes, I grew up extremely poor, but there were values that were incredibly beautiful. But I had no reference for learning how to become a documentarian. A lot of it was trial and error. When I started out, I didn't even understand the word "narrative." I did understand that there were people who were Puerto Ricans who were creating history. And I also understood that I had to try and document it because if I didn't, it would be gone, and gone forever. Through my example, I influenced quite a few other artists; I had a photography workshop where I trained quite a few other artists. But to go back to the core of your question, most of it was not planned.

The reality is that for artists of color, we do not have a system that will nurture or support us financially. Then, when I started to document East Harlem, I was always borrowing money to buy film. There are people who see me in the street and they always remind me: "Hiram, you need $2?" It is a joke, but it was kindness. I never had enough. Always needed something in order to do what I wanted to do. The lone wolf part of it was that we had no institutions that believed in us and supported us. I had to raise my own funds. I had to sell prints in order to sustain myself. I had to do things that, frankly, other artists don't have to do. And then, when we were finally accepted into certain institutions, they behaved as if they were doing us a favor.

SL:
It becomes evident through this conversation how much important knowledge travels through conversation and unofficial spaces—places and modes that often don't have a formal method of documentation. Who gets to determine officialness and the formality of something? The legibility of something? By restaging—or, as we sometimes say, bootlegging—histories, you actually create the possibility of envisioning a different future. You show that time isn't this linear path of so-called progress or development, but is in fact circular and cyclical, repeating and glitching in exciting ways.

HM:
We were a little crazy back then. We took a lot of risks. I want to speak about El Museo del Barrio. The idea started in the dead of winter, in someone's basement. It was cold as hell. We said, "Hey, we're going to build a museum." We asked the collective question, "Who knows anything about a museum?" And every one of us said, "I don't know what the hell you're talking about. We do not know anything." As artists, we had gone to all the museums, and they told us the following: "Your work is not good enough. Your work is not valid. Your work does not represent art. Your work is not . . ." And they gave every excuse in the world not to engage us. So our response was, "Well, then we will build our own." We set out to build this museum. We made tremendous mistakes. We did things backwards. But we learned a profound lesson, that the strength of the institution lies in its people.

SL:
Something that's important for us is that we view all the different entities we operate as, as fictional. Canal Street Research Association is what we call a fictional office entity. It arose spontaneously in the midst of a certain context, and we don't know how long it will last. Part of the impulse to be shape-shifting has to do with wanting to view the accumulation of research as a collective process, to bring it back to the *shanzhai* idea. *Shanzhai*, according to the philosopher Byung-Chul Han, continues the lineage of East Asian landscape painting, which has a lot of emptiness in it. That emptiness inspires inscription. In fact, these landscape paintings accumulate value through collective inscription by subsequent owners/authors over time. We're inspired to create a space for these kinds of collective inscriptions in our various entities.

We're also excited by the word "counternarrative," because we've been thinking more deeply into the etymology of counterfeit, and thinking of etymology itself as a kind of digging back into the past. "Counterfeit" goes back to the Latin, counter-*facere*, which is anti-making or against making—an unmaking. We've been excited to think about archiving as a kind of unmaking of the official history. This gets at some of our skepticism, let's say, of institutions, and a desire to trouble the boundary between fake and real. Who generally decides what is fake and what is real? What is important and what is unimportant? What is to be protected and what is to be banned?

HM:
To speak to some of these questions: In our tenth year, El Museo del Barrio was somewhat legitimate, and we had to deal with the American Alliance of Museums. They came in to evaluate us. And they

started saying, "Well, first of all, you don't have a collection. Second of all, you do not have major artists in your institution. So how do you call yourselves a museum? You do not have patrons." They are using their modality to set the standards for us. Use your own modality. Set whatever standard you want and need. All they wanted to do was to control it. As artists, you're going to find that there is always a battle between liberation and control. You're going to have to figure out what side you're going to be on. We did not get accreditation from the American Alliance of Museums, and we lost quite a bit of funding. The National Endowment for the Arts, the National Endowment for the Humanities, all these people just bailed out. Fifteen years later, they all came back because we did not disappear. We did not run for shelter.

KS:
What you're speaking of, Hiram, has a lot to do with why Yusuf initially started this practice—wanting to be in control of the narrative. We pay homage to your generation as well. You all laid this groundwork; we're just following suit.

HM:
Well, I tell a lot of young artists, "You don't follow my path." You take what I started and you make it better. You don't have to do it the way I do it, but you have to do it better. You will know when you're kicking butt because you will be creating a whole bunch of enemies. It will not be a peaceful existence.

YH:
Preserving the past is a foundation and significant research hub for BlackMass Publishing. We think about how we're preserving what we're creating right now—not just through archiving it, but how we're distributing information. One of the most significant things for us is distributing information instantly. Archives aren't just being distributed in the standard way, where you need to have access to a physical space. Now, the archive lives in a digital format as well, which we are using. I have a love-hate relationship with the internet. But the internet, to tell you the truth, has helped me build a very significant number of relationships.

One of the most prominent aspects of our installation in *Greater New York* is that it will continuously change throughout the duration of the show. Information will be added, things will be represented in different ways and through different mediums. Printed matter is the base, but it's not the only source of information—we're using music, poetry. Even right now, what we're doing via Zoom—I mean, this conversation is happening in real time. At some point it will be transcribed onto paper and will be read as a text. Information doesn't start with us. It doesn't end with us. We're here to pass the torch that was passed to us over to whoever is willing to run with it and distribute information.

SL:
We've heard this echoed in the way that you all have talked about your practices, but we wanted to add that, for us, the past isn't past. Even the opposition of past and future sets up a way of relating to time that doesn't feel quite right to us. Knowledge and stories often do not enter into an official archive or history, and so they seem to disappear to some. What we're devoted to is surfacing the ways in which they have *not* disappeared and how they can be brought back to life, like a resurrection process: research as resurrection.

Canal Street holds history in its name: the canal itself continues to run underneath the street. It's not gone, even though it's covered up. That feels really important to us in terms of thinking about the flow of time and channels of information. Even when they are hidden, and trees, let's say, are planted to cover up the stench of history and oppression, these flows of stories are in fact still there. What we're hearing from you all, and what we hope we can continue to figure out how to do, is that the job of the archivist is to reveal that the stream is still flowing. It's still there. The history never went away.

SURREALISM, TRAUMA, AND THE POSTHUMAN:

A conversation between Nadia Ayari, Doreen Garner, Sean-Kierre Lyons, Tammy Nguyen, and Diane Severin Nguyen

Nadia Ayari:
When we got the questions prior to this conversation, one in particular opened things up for me as far as how I look at the origin of things currently happening in my work: "In what ways does surrealism open up a realm beyond the human—and does it remain a resonant strategy today or not?" I make what I refer to as conceptual narrative painting, where elements of a plant become primary protagonists that set up a central event. The works in the exhibition span two years, during which I synthesized previous forms into a pink flower.

My interest has always been in painting, and becoming a painter was always political. At a certain point, I stopped painting the figure or referring explicitly to anything that had to do with the human figure, in a moment where I was trying to paint a very particular political landscape. I was making paintings of acts of war: a drone strike or a car bomb. I remember feeling really, really exhausted and looking at the painting and thinking: What if I painted a small section of this? What if I only painted the corner where the tree is enveloped in smoke? This was the aha moment that I had while thinking about this question. I realized that whatever I imagined happening in the tree—the leaves, the fruit, the branches—became witness to the act of violence, rather than me or the viewer. That sense of uncanniness in my work, which I could never really figure out the origins of, was that heightened space of post-violence.

Doreen Garner:
For me, surrealism has come into my work more as a traumatic experience. A lot of my work focuses on ways that the medical industry has exploited Black bodies throughout history. I've been focusing on J. Marion Sims, a white gynecologist who would torture enslaved Black women. In his clinic, he purchased sixteen cots so he could maximize the number of patients that he could operate on and torture. The piece that I'm making for the exhibition is essentially a torture device, but in the form of a sex sling.

I created a piece a few years ago at Pioneer Works, which consisted of a series of objects that were hanging and that looked like meat, but I had cast Black women's bodies to create the silicone. That piece ended up going to the Art Basel fair in Switzerland, and I had a unique experience with viewers and how they were interacting with the work. The piece sold, fortunately, but I felt a lot of remorse about what it means to create work like that and then have it be sold to someone that doesn't look like you or the people represented in the work. There's also always this negotiation of the price, because the buyer wants to get the best deal. It made me really uncomfortable, the idea of negotiating prices of things that represent Black bodies. So from that point on, I decided that I need to locate my ideas in objects that aren't totally representative of the Black body. Blackness could instead be seen somewhere in the object, whether in color or texture. I started to use wood grain, plants, and other types of creatures to stand in for the body.

Diane Severin Nguyen:
There's a really important relationship between trauma and surrealism. I think trauma is about not having a state of purity to return to—about a destabilization of categories on a kind of basic level. Sometimes trauma can be about a moment that's reoccurring, but to present one's trauma isn't necessarily an inherently healing or liberatory process. Trauma is something that you might reexperience over and over again, but you can't reunify with your original state of being once the event has occurred. Maybe I mean that it's about irreversibility. I think a lot about how surrealism operates now and how it

might aesthetically look different than when the term came into popularity one hundred years ago. Maybe we need to desanctify certain categories. They might visually look different—we have to be inventive with the forms that we use to represent this space of trauma.

Sean-Kierre Lyons:
I really loved what Doreen said about the buying of work. That hits hard because most of my work is blackface and there is already a market where a bunch of non-Black people buy blackface work. I think that's why I stopped making figures and started putting Blackness in other things and making them more anthropomorphic. I honestly didn't even know I was doing that until I learned more about the word anthropomorphism. It's used to define the other vis-à-vis whatever "normal" is. I'm a fan of cartoons and things that are childlike or whimsical. I never really thought that I was anthropomorphizing when I was drawing cartoons and making my own characters. When I learned the term a couple of years ago, it blew my mind because I was just like, wow, we watch cartoons and there's like a sassy Black character, and she's probably a poodle or some shit.

Before this, the way that I would make work was a little more violent. I made a hair whip out of my old locks, and I think a lot of people thought that it was about me hating white people, or weaponizing myself. It wasn't; it was like I was the weapon and I was harming myself. Now I have this world that I've built out of flower people, who are like these forgotten entities in a lot of ways. Whimsy and humor are two points that I like to reach more than anything. In the show, there is a large sculptural version of the figure I've been drawing for the past year. An accompanying drawing and a painting recount this figure's life. I feel like the figure has made these paintings and drawings, not me—it's what the figure is going through. It's a part of me, but it's also so *not* a part of me at this point that I think about a character and I'll be like, "Oh yeah, she would do that." It's really coming from visualizing life, but putting it in this context where bad shit happens in this world, which is actually on the brink of destruction. However, these entities still figure out a way to cohabitate. I guess it helps me accept what is actually happening and offers me a weird way of dealing with it, through a portal. So, for me, it's more about escapism. About visualizing a better future within this world that can give me hope. I think that's how I come into surrealism—because I feel like our world is very bleak, and I don't normally want to live in our world.

Tammy Nguyen:
I'd like to connect a few points that I heard that I have a lot of affinity with. Diane, you said something about surrealism and liberation, and Nadia, this idea of zooming into one part of the painting. Doreen and SK, you made me think about surrealism and the use of proxies—how things can speak about internal tensions via a proxy.

When I was in grad school, I had just finished living in Vietnam for a long period of time. I came back to the US with a bit of confusion about contradictions that I was witnessing around ideas of family and success. I kept trying to find a vehicle to discuss those tensions and those contradictions in art. One day, on a whim, with the advice of a professor, I went over to Yale's ornithology lab and volunteered as a taxidermist. I learned how to skin birds. I started to paint from that experience, and through the process of observation, I ended up making what you might call stylistically surrealist paintings. People called them surrealist paintings because they couldn't track the origin point, which was actually highly observational. I feel that my work is very deeply rooted in research and the juxtaposition of things, not inventing them per se.

This conversation about surrealism is really provocative to me because it suggests how things can suddenly turn into an escape when we don't share the same history. In thinking about trauma, some of the works that I create are an extension of traumatic history, such as the histories of the Vietnam War or the histories of different trade wars and conflicts in the South China Sea. My two paintings in the exhibition explore the Allegory of the Cave as it is superimposed on different narratives and histories about regions in Southeast Asia, particularly the Phong Nha-Ké Bàng karst in Vietnam and Forest City in Malaysia. But when you put them in this artistic space, the trauma can transform itself into escapism, which is challenging to think about because then you then fold in ideas of entertainment, seduction, and leisure—and sometimes those things are in opposition to the original intentions.

I wanted to share my excitement but also my sadness about this idea of escapism, because I feel like part of the reason why it's so seductive is that surrealism and fabulation allow, in some ways, the viewer to run away with their own experience of the artwork. One of the things that has inspired me about surrealism was that it seemed like the artists had authority to break all the rules. In this context, I guess breaking the rules may mean introducing histories that nobody's ever heard about and introducing people that nobody's ever really cared about. I'm a big fan of surrealism as a process of collapsing histories and symbols and cultural heritages that seem disparate into an entity that audiences have to contend with.

NA:
The sadness that you were describing, Tammy, reminds me of a lot of the grief that I have contended with around the limitations of painting. I'm now at this other place where I see the limits to the limits of painting, and what this escapist possibility allows for is perhaps a familiarity that a viewer will have with a situation that might or might not engender some emotional clarity related to contemporary politics.

DSN:
I think what is interesting about the surrealist framework and the history that it came from is that it does question use value. Especially if we're talking broadly about the environment and surrealism, I always think about whether revolution is a rational or an irrational act. Obviously, as artists, we all want to have some kind of political effect with our work, but I think what surrealism offers is that it allows us to question whether we have to have progress on the same terms as the broader political sphere. I think surrealism is very good at doing that in terms of speaking to the repressed: Are we trying to redeem the repressed or let it loose on some level? These are questions that I think about in my work, because I wonder what the point is of defunctionalizing something. How do I defunctionalize this thing and turn it into something that is functional in another way? But the very question of functionality and use value also recourses to a capitalistic way of thinking about value and usefulness.

DG:
I have a hard time locating elements of escapism in my work because a lot of it is research-based and involves me constantly reading traumatic accounts of history and trying to figure out a way to regurgitate that in a visual language that viewers can observe. It's more like I'm hyper-engaged at all times. Besides, my experience as a Black person I believe to be surreal, living in two opposites—greatness and fear—at the same time, constantly. I don't have any moments where I feel like

I'm escaping. I feel like to be a surrealist sculptor or a surrealist artist is to constantly be trying to pioneer new visual languages and figure out ways for people to process the same information in a different way. I'm always thinking about people interpreting things the wrong way or in a way that I'm not intending, so this surrealist experience is pretty torturous, in my opinion, because I use a lot of trauma in my work, which usually finds its way into my daily experience in ways that I wish it didn't.

Trying to find objects to stand in for traumatic events is a means for me to locate empathy in someone that wouldn't normally empathize with a Black figure. Using different materials with high-gloss textures and crystals and silicone—things that we're used to interacting with—allows people to tap into that information without feeling like it's a burden.

S-KL:
What Doreen said about using something that makes someone feel comfortable to explain a truth is, I think, how approaching the raw truth is done now. I think there's a double-edged sword to that, because I want to be able to just tell people to shut the fuck up. But you have to be like, "Please, shut the fuck up." People forget that my characters are constantly carrying weapons. They're so pretty. They're flowers. When you think of a flower, you think that it's yours to take. But you don't really think about how many flowers could kill you just by you touching them. I do think that there is a way to send rawness and light and cuteness at the same time.

DSN:
Continuing on the rawness thing for a second—I think there's a lot of mediation that you end up constructing to cover yourself because you're dealing with a capitalist logic that seeks to have direct access to you. In my work, I think about surrealism as a method of transforming ideas into materials, and mediation and opacity are things that I feel I have to be very conscious of in terms of how they work against the idea of the raw.

DG:
It's tough thinking about rawness and the body, because a lot of my work talks about a history of bodies being cut and torn apart and stitched back together, or possibly dug up and dissected. So when I think about rawness in my work, obviously I can zoom in on parts of the body, like Nadia, which takes a little bit of the context away. Then you're able to just view the detail as a composition itself, but it also takes away from the shock value. How do I get this person to process information? There's a lot of consideration that goes into finishing edges and details. The processing actually allows people to forget how raw it is and accept it as something that has been considered and presented to them. A lot of the stories are really traumatic. Just think about Anarcha, a fifteen-year-old girl who was most likely raped and experienced a lot of malnutrition during her pregnancy and suffered a vesicovaginal fistula. She was operated on more than thirty times over the course of five years. How do you take a story like that and present it to people without them being horrified to the point that they can't learn any more? How do you get them to sit with that but still be interested in hearing more, when a lot of people want to deny the rawness of human experience or the rawness of colonization and what it really looks like to be in power? There's a lot of blood that was shed in the gaining of that power and that privilege. I think as far as today is concerned, a lot of people would rather not hear about the cost and what it took to get to this point.

For a lot of my work, it's not only about getting people to empathize with these histories but also, for my audience members of color, it's important to know about this history because it's happening right now. Instead of turning a blind eye to it, we can see the patterns and the similarities and figure out how to prevent what happened before from happening now.

NA:
I wanted to talk about the question of surrealism and posthumanism. It made me realize that I have a lot to unpack, because now I'm in this other phase of my work which has a science-fiction vibe and that brings up other questions for me. I am really curious to hear what you all felt: Does the surreal allow us to think beyond the human or expand our understanding? My initial thoughts were, well, no, because I'm human. Everything I make is from a very human place. But in thinking about posthumanism, I see possibilities for my work to enter this other arena.

S-KL:
I'm always thinking about posthumanism. I think because I am trans, I never want to think about the body because the body is limiting. I don't think this is just dedicated to trans people; I think everyone knows that the body is limiting. Part of the reason why I make the work I do is because flowers are all trans—they have both genders and they exist freely without any kind of judgment. It's not so much about the judgment, because I can give a fuck about what someone thinks about me; it's more about the idea that they exist naturally this way. So I do think about the posthuman and what that looks like. I think it doesn't even look like a body. I think of the flowers and how they'll be here after we're gone and have been taking in all this data, like emotions, atrocities, beauty.

DSN:
I also play with beauty a lot in my work, and how beauty can be the space where intellect is decentralized and hidden. It can almost be seen as an anti-intellectual space. Somehow that relates, for me, to how we view nature. So much of Western thinking is premised on this ultimate mind/body split, where the body and nature can be spaces of beauty that are nonintellectual and unstructured—a split that I don't really believe in.

DG:
That really resonates with me. As a person who takes mushrooms from time to time, I find there is a big difference in my experience of taking them during the day versus at night. During the day everything is really beautiful and sparkly, but at night I do experience a lot of fear because of the number of dark spaces around. And I feel like when there are dark spaces around, that leaves a void where your brain has to make up the rest of the information. I think that that's where a lot of my creativity has been thriving right now, a place that is not totally conscious or in my body, but a place where Indigenous and diasporic ancestors can influence me and speak to me and lead me. As an artist, I am creating work that is pre- and posthuman. In some ways, I feel the work I make is for the spiritual realm, not necessarily for where we are and what we're experiencing right now. I'm thinking about ancestral vengeance and being a kind of vessel or a catalyst for ideas on their behalf. That's where I'm at right now.

31

A conversation between
Nadia Ayari, Doreen Garner, Sean-Kierre Lyons,
Tammy Nguyen, and Diane Severin Nguyen

NATIVE NEW YORK:

A conversation between G. Peter Jemison, Athena LaTocha, Alan Michelson, and Shelley Niro

G. Peter Jemison:
Nya weh sgenoh gah:gwegoh. I give greetings and thanksgiving to all of you. My name given to me by the Heron clan is *Gah:non:zah:deh:deon*. It alludes to my responsibilities as a Faithkeeper in our traditional way of life. I have been the manager of a place called Ganondagan for many years, which is the site of a seventeenth-century Seneca town. The work that I'm showing in *Greater New York* is about treaties between the United States and the Haudenosaunee. I'm one of the organizers of an annual commemoration of a treaty between ourselves and the United States, called the Canandaigua Treaty, which was originally signed on November 11, 1794. The US has blown off most of its obligations that were included in the treaty, such as land they guaranteed to the Onondaga and Seneca people, which included all of Western New York. I know that might sound a little greedy, that we think we still should have all that land, but that land was a part of our Aboriginal territory. In my work, I draw attention to these treaty violations that have occurred and the ongoing attitude that the US Congress knows what's best for the Ongweoweh (meaning we Native people), which is preposterous, really. They don't even know who we are, let alone know what we need.

I'm also showing some paper bag works. *Party Bag* (1982) features an image of one of my very good friends, Bobby Onco. Bobby Onco was one of those who occupied Wounded Knee. He's the guy that knew how to take apart and assemble an AK-47, but he was also a very good electrician. When I was running the American Indian Community House Gallery on Broadway in SoHo (which I became director of in 1978), I would always say he wired it with a can of Bud in one hand and a pair of pliers in the other; when he hit one switch, all the lights came on.

One of the first things I focused on in my art was the fact that Broadway was originally a trail that the Lenape created and the Seneca used when visiting the island of Manahatta—this long trail that went all the way down the island. I came across a site that was all about the fur trade, and the French, Dutch, and English vying for control of the fur trade. They used to say that you can get anything you want in New York. They thought that a long time ago, too: they could go hunt there, go shell fishing there. It was a place of abundance.

Alan Michelson:
New York City probably preserves less of its history than any city in the Eastern US. I've lived here for a long time and I love it, but I'm always thinking about what's underfoot, what's under the concrete, what the shoreline looked like, what the pond was like. There's something about connecting time with space that has fascinated me as an artist. This inevitably brings me to the colonial overlay of the landscape, and wanting to understand the moves that created the landscape that we have now and our position within it, which is no longer one of stewardship. Rather, we have been demoted to witnessing all these things going on without necessarily having much voice.

I was in New York in the '70s as an undergrad, and a piece I did for the Public Art Fund, *Earth's Eye* (1990), brought me back to New York to stay in 1989. I was interested in a site in Lower Manhattan that was previously a large freshwater pond called Collect Pond, which was ruined by early industry and filled in by the early 1800s—it's literally buried history. Later, it became the site of a notorious prison and execution ground nicknamed "The Tombs." The research I did for that piece led me to the piece that I'm doing now for *Greater New York*, which is based on shell middens. There was a large shell midden on the western shore of Collect Pond that had been left by countless generations of

Lenape people. There were many such in the area, but now they're almost all gone or hard to see. The piece I'm doing commemorates that history. It speaks to the richness of the estuary environment that was New York before it was industrialized, and to the lifeways of Indigenous people who coexisted with other life forms in ways that allowed them to flourish. A midden may just be looked upon as a garbage pile, but sometimes these lacunae, these absences, speak volumes.

When I was first working in this manner, there weren't that many artists doing it. It's good to see that more and more people are interested in this history because it's multiplying the awareness of this history amongst non-Native people. It also causes people to contrast the values of the culture that they're in with that culture that preceded them, which is still here—a culture that lived *with* the land, not over it in some sort of dominating position.

Shelley Niro:
It sounds like we're kind of on the same wavelength, Alan. I started exploring fossils on rock faces in Lake Erie a few years ago, and becoming attached to the small creatures that these fossils once held. Of course, this work has been in process for millions of years, so I can't take credit for it. I started becoming a bit obsessed with taking photographs of these guys, thinking about my own mortality and how something happened to these creatures that obliterated them but left them in a condition where I can now look at them and almost communicate with them.

A lot of my work also revolves around the placement of women in history, and I've really concentrated on putting images of Indigenous women out there. Not stylized or romantic, but something kind of realistic. These depictions come from the need to create economies for women who are often the caretakers of families. As we all know, Native women have been put in a position where they're almost invisible. From images, you can branch out and continue into so many different things, like advocating for economic stability and opportunities for women. And I think those opportunities are starting to manifest.

GPJ:
One of the first pieces of Shelley's that I really liked was of women under a hairdryer (*The Iroquois is a Highly Developed Matriarchal Society*, 1991). It just spoke so much about the rez and home and all the rest. It really touched me. I still think about that image, Shelley.

Athena LaTocha:
It's thought-provoking to listen to everybody's perspectives because there is a lot of continuity, but there are also differences in where we come from and how we approach the work that we do. I wasn't born on a reservation, but growing up in Alaska we spent a lot of time outdoors, going out hunting, fishing. And with those experiences, there were stories. I'm not Alaska Native, but being surrounded by the Alaska Native community, there were a lot of stories about the land and how things are the way they are. For example, the northern lights—where the northern lights come from and the stories of people walking in the sky. During the time before us, before humans as we know them existed, it was a time of giants. These were the stories that I often thought about as a child when we would be outdoors in the winter, seeing the northern lights, being out in the tundra plaines, walking on the marshy, swampy, boggy terrain and thinking about how we move and how our experience of place informs us. I think being immersed in that has greatly informed my practice in ways that I never set out for it to do. Just living, ideas manifest in ways that we may not always be conscious of. So my perspective is a little different in that I'm very interested in following an intuitive response to place: looking at space, colors, formations, and also looking at it through the greater historical lens of geology. For *Greater New York*, I'm making a work based upon my experience of New York, looking at glacial striations around the city, and particularly the bedrock that has glacial striations and grooves etched into it. I'm very interested in ideas of time and place that precede our own human understanding of them.

AM:
Should we talk more about New York as a site of Indigenous artistic production and dissemination? I think Pete is probably a better historian of the earlier days of contemporary Native art in New York. When I came back in 1989, Pete, you'd already left, right?

GPJ:
Yeah, I came back to our area of the country in 1985. I first went to New York in 1967, then I went back in '78 and stuck around till '85, when I came back to Ganondagan.

AM:
In '89, when I arrived, the scene was largely separate from the larger New York art scene. It was centered around a gallery that Pete had founded at the American Indian Community House when it used to be on Broadway, in a big loft. Even though it didn't have the biggest budget in the world, it was pulling contemporary Native artists from all over Turtle Island to show there. It was also an amazing locus of community. That changed a bit when the National Museum of the American Indian (NMAI) opened in 1989. There was a second locus, and one that was better funded and could do things like [publish] catalogues and hold larger events. That was an expansion.

For a while there, I think in the '90s, at least a few of our artists, like Pete and others, emerged and gained visibility within the larger art world. But it was still very few, and the artists for the most part weren't picked up by commercial galleries. Kay WalkingStick and Jaune Quick-to-See Smith are some of the few that I can remember from that era. Artists like Edgar Heap of Birds, James Luna, and Jimmie Durham also gained some traction within the larger art world and were being shown in alternative spaces like Artists Space, Art in General, and Exit Art. This led to being shown in places like the Whitney and even internationally, because in 1992, the quincentennial of Columbus sparked interest in Native art. Suddenly there were invitations that hadn't been there before, and in venues that hadn't necessarily been interested in us before. James Luna was against it; he said, "Call me in '93," knowing that it was going to be a flash in the pan, which it was. But all through the '90s, people steadily worked from their different perspectives. One thing that I think really changed the scene here for the worse was when NMAI stopped holding openings at the customs house, because it was one of these loci of community. Indigenous artists, even from places like Australia and New Zealand, would come to some of these things. And that built a new energy.

In 2016 and 2017, I partnered with the Vera List Center for Art and Politics at the New School on an initiative called Indigenous New York, which convened Indigenous curators, critics, and artists with their non-Indigenous counterparts in New York institutions. And that did seem to open some minds and doors. Ten years ago, if an Indigenous friend from another country came, let's say a Sámi from Norway, and said, "Okay, where are the Indigenous shows?" I would have to say, "Well, there aren't any." Now I can say that there are probably a few at any given moment.

It's been broken open a bit, and I think it's probably never been a better time for visibility and opportunities that are opening up to Indigenous artists here in the US. It's always been different and better in Canada, but I'd say that we're in a good period right now, which really stands out from the earlier days.

AL:
I've always felt like a bit of an outsider. When I came to New York in the mid '90s, I was coming more or less right out of art school in Chicago. A lot of my background was steeped in academics. And right around that time, I was starting to look at what this Native America is. Growing up in Alaska, surrounded by the Alaska Native community, there was never really any kind of self-reflection or understanding of what that meant. It was all about living life and just trying to get by.

I was living at the YWCA in Downtown Brooklyn and I thought, well, what is this American Indian Community House? I started showing up and everyone was very inclusive and supportive and it was almost like a family of sorts. I had never even thought about notions like: What is Native art? What is Indigenous art? What does that mean, and what does that look like? I had no concept, no background or premise with which to enter into it. Coming to New York and being introduced to the American Indian Community House and gallery was for me like walking into a different part of the world that I had never truly experienced before. I haven't been in New York long enough to really understand the scope of the arc of its movement with regard to Indigenous art, but it's always been fascinating to me to hear those questions, because it makes you think: What does that mean? What does it imply? Whose history is it, and why do we have to think about it as separate?

AM:
I'm hoping that younger artists will continue to come to New York to experience it and grow here. But I'm afraid that there's been a decline in people showing up like you did in the '90s, because of the high rents. Artists also used to come via Cooper Union, which had free tuition. There'd be the odd Native artists who came through that route, and who might not be able to come now. I'm hoping that there can be some sort of action to create residencies for Native artists in New York, to bring people back here to experience it and to be part of the scene here.

GPJ:
I guess I have to speak to this history for a minute. I made a conscious decision, in about 1974 or '73, to start showing with Native American artists. Not very long after I made that decision, I was advised not to do that. I was advised by an African American artist who became quite prominent. He was quite successful and he always maintained that he would never want to be shown as a Black artist. It was seen as the kiss of death—you would always be limiting yourself. But I really felt in my own heart that I saw myself as Seneca, because I grew up in a Seneca community. When I met other Native artists, I found I could really relate to them. We had connections and it was something that I wanted to hold on to.

Of course, it didn't make things easier, because racism really and truly affected our ability to get any place. Yet throughout, especially the period between '78 and '85, I had reviews of shows that I curated in the *New York Times* and *New York* magazine and the *Village Voice*. The one museum that took a chance on us was the Queens Museum, in 1984. I did an entire Haudenosaunee show with the support of the curators there. But it's been an uphill battle. Like Alan mentioned, things are beginning to open up for us; museums that didn't previously pay attention to us are interested and it's good. It only took me sixty-three years to get here, and as I see it, I still got a lot of time left.

SN:
I can speak a bit to the American Indian Community House. At the time, the curator was Joanna Bigfeather, and she gave me my first solo show there. I often forget to acknowledge that she played a big part in that. I've had shows at the NMAI as well. Canada is really strong with Canadian Native art, and it's just a matter of producing—just keep producing. I've had work that has never really been outside of my studio and now suddenly people want to show it. I can't predict where it's going to be shown or when, but I just think it's important to keep producing what your heart wants to do. Just keep on keeping on.

AM:
We used to envy the Canadian First Nations artists, because they were better supported than we were down here. The Canada Council for the Arts grants and the provincial art galleries would show them and produce really nice catalogues and things like that that were helpful to careers in ways that just weren't happening down here. NMAI would be the first venue where that could happen. And we should acknowledge our curators here: Lloyd Oxendine, Pete, Joanna Bigfeather, and Kathleen Ash-Milby, who was, I think, the last curator at the Community House before they let go of the gallery. They lost their lease, or whatever it was, on the Broadway space, which was another blow to the scene. There's still not really a gathering place anymore. The Community House has been a sort of fugitive organization for a while. They've moved around from smaller space to smaller space and so forth. It'd be good to see some sort of centralized place where we could meet like we used to in the old times.

GPJ:
The other thing that existed back at that time was something called Museums Collaborative, whose members included the Brooklyn Museum, MoMA, the American Museum of Natural History, and a couple others that I'm forgetting. A graphic department from one of these museums might, for example, design the poster for an exhibit that I was putting on, or they might even do the text panel. That was gratis, and they also provided training. We would go to a graphic designer around Midtown and he would walk us through different things that we as young curators did not know about, and it was really helpful. The guy that was very helpful to me was an Ojibwe named John Garrigan; he worked for MoMA in the graphic arts department at the time. This is going back to about 1980 or so. And then, as Alan pointed out, I became very friendly with Lloyd Oxendine, a real character, who did a lot of good work. He and I worked together on putting together some shows. That was sort of what I had as a foundation. When I took over the Community House gallery in '78, I was just flying by the seat of my pants really. We then moved to SoHo, to a loft space, which we totally renovated on literally a shoestring budget.

AM:
I think the next phase will be the inclusion of Native curators in some of the arts spaces in New York. The Metropolitan Museum of Art recently hired Patricia Marroquin Norby as Associate Curator of Native American Art. Hopefully more will follow, which will Indigenize the scene a little bit more. I think the future looks good right now; there's a lot of activity. I think there were seven Natives in the 2019 Whitney Biennial. That hadn't happened before. There's at least four of us in this one, which probably hasn't happened before in a *Greater New York* show. I always wondered why NMAI, with its resources, never took the steps necessary to become a contemporary art destination in the city. I never understood that as

policy; maybe it had something to do with being a federal cultural entity.

GPJ:

They did attempt to, because of course Kathleen Ash-Milby was a curator there, and they have exhibits and so forth. But I feel as though they were cautious in their approach.

AL:

I'm also wondering if it's something that happens in the art world too, how curators sometimes go after the same artists over and over again. You get a lot of repetition, but there are a lot of artists out there doing different things. I really challenge curators to go out there to look for artists. I wonder if we can find some way to help encourage that, and to think about who is taking the risks, who can afford to take the risks.

ON ABSTRACTION, MOURNING, AND TIME:

A conversation between Carolyn Lazard, Raha Raissnia, Andy Robert, and Lachell Workman

Lachell Workman:
One of the ways I think about abstraction is through how I've experienced audiences, or people who've entered my studio, relating to the ways in which the body shows up in my work. My work explores memorials—specifically memorials that are born out of inner-city communities in which there often aren't larger official, communal monuments or memorials present. I'm thinking about things like the street sign memorial and the cultural iconography of the memorial T-shirt—how people use their bodies as an extension of the memorial and how that relates to what we often see as the emptiness of many inner-city landscapes. These ideas are born out of specific landscapes—such as sites in Bridgeport, Connecticut—that are either empty, underserved, or have just sat for multiple generations without any specific human interaction.

I'm also thinking about a way of deconstructing the memorial T-shirt, freeing up the body from having to be the wearer of the memorial. Abstraction gives greater agency to people who are in mourning by breaking down the formula of text, photography, and garment. I'm interested in abstracting the formula of the monument, and in the particular way that most state-sanctioned monuments are erected. Through this exploration of abstraction, I'm considering ways that people living in particular communities can retake ownership and agency over these landscapes and extend mourning from objects into real space. It's also a way of accessing some sort of freedom from tropes of how one represents the body, specifically the Black body, and addressing the limitations of representing the body within contemporary art more broadly. Abstraction is a way to think through what my dear friend, art historian Genevieve Hyacinthe, describes as the "ineffable Black body"—something that cannot be represented specifically within the context of loss, especially public loss. I found myself having many of these conversations starting around 2014, when people were trying to make a connection between the work and public acts of violence that circulate on the internet.

I'm often thinking about the street-side memorial, where people just leave objects. These moments seem to supersede public and private space, and there seems to be a kind of communal reverence around these moments of loss, in which people are using not only their bodies but everyday objects to mark a particular place and hold space to memorialize someone. Throughout my practice, I've continued to observe and be in conversation with these materials—such as asphalt and T-shirts—and abstracting and deconstructing them highlights for me the ways that abstraction is really active in many quotidian spaces. People are regularly accessing abstraction. It connects to the vernacular languages used in these sites of mourning and to whether something is perceived as coded language—whether one chooses to actually display the image of a person who has passed, or whether there are moments in which we want to conceal those things.

Carolyn Lazard:
I really love what you were saying about abstraction in quotidian spaces. As artists, our relationship to abstraction is framed in this incredibly formalized art history, and yet we engage with abstraction all the time. I think about this a lot, particularly about the ways that Black people communicate with each other and the ways that we've stretched language to the peripheries of intelligibility, like in Black American vernaculars, but also patois and Creole. We sequester abstraction as this specific mode of perception, when in fact it's just a way of thinking and engaging with the world around us. It's mundane in some ways. A lot of my work is made from appropriated materials, media, and objects.

It is mostly about care—care practices and care labor. I also make work about how we relate to different kinds of institutions—museums, hospitals, prisons, and universities. In relation to museums, I think a lot about how people move through museums and who can occupy space in museums, and how art is or is not intelligible to different kinds of people. My work is also about consent and accessibility; I like to think through the radical possibilities of incapacity and debility. Incapacity itself is a really generative and beautiful force in the world and something that is endemic to being alive. For *Greater New York*, I'm presenting a new work from this year called *Red* (2021). It's a two-channel video installation. One of the channels is a "flicker film" made by pressing the pad of my thumb on the camera of my iPhone and lifting it up and down. The second channel is a synced video in a separate room that you see before you walk into the larger installation, and on this second channel is a video that lets viewers know when the film in the larger room is stroboscopic and when it's not, so that people who are sensitive to strobe can navigate the work on their own terms.

Raha Raissnia:

The way I think of abstraction relates to what you were saying in the sense that it allows more content in; it expands the area in which the viewer can interpret or experience the work in very personal, subjective ways. I relate to abstraction in the way I feel an affinity with music. We experience the works rather than understand the works. It's very open to evocation and perception, rather than limited to one specific subject. Also, ironically, I might say that there is no such thing as abstraction, even in painting. You're still experiencing line, color, movement—and these are very real things. With music, there's actual vibrations. So, in a way, there is no such thing as abstraction. But it does inspire the mind to go beyond the apparent reality of facts—to go beyond what we can see and tap into very deep areas within the psyche.

I've been a painter for a very long time, since I was ten or eleven. But I also work with film, and the film work I do is very connected to my painting and drawing. When I moved to New York in 1995, I became involved with Anthology Film Archives, a space for avant-garde cinema. I moved here to go to school, but I couldn't afford school and Anthology became a kind of education for me. For the exhibition, I am presenting a film installation which uses a 16-millimeter film print in black and white that is projected onto two layered panels, making up a kind of a box that creates an optical illusion of three-dimensional imagery. The material for this film came by chance, from a series of 35-millimeter slides that were found in the trash at the media center at Brooklyn College and given to me by a friend. The slides document a fourteenth-century mosque in India in ruins. I rephotographed them in my studio using various analog and digital techniques, and combined them with new imagery. I make film through a very layered process of superimposition. As a result, there's a lot of abstract imagery in it, but there are also recognizable architectural elements.

Andy Robert:

For me, abstraction is a deeply contemplative and interior space where you're wrestling with the lyrical and the concrete. I've also thought about how a painting comes into being, how a subject finds form over time through the process of painting. For me, that's where ideas of abstraction are parallel to or entangled with representation. I ended up in a place that was very dialectical when thinking about abstraction: abstraction is found in detail, in its oscillation, and in how it comes apart—how it all unravels. The process and the subject and the painting are interwoven. For me, there is no real, true way of starting a painting; I try to just get into the painting, but then there are moments of doubt and loss. There are questions of how to treat the subject, and of legibility.

In the painting *Mid Atlantic* (2020), I was circulating around several thinkers and conversations that ruminate on and look to the idea of the horizon. It reflects on Long Beach, California, and the traffic jam at the port there at the moment, but it's also me thinking about my late professor and mentor Allan Sekula's work and his writing on Claude Lévi-Strauss, as well as working through my thoughts on Édouard Glissant. In the painting, there is the question of whether it is day or night, sunrise or sunset—but there are also questions around the horizon as a site of becoming or deep forgetting, a space that is both internal and recurring, different and unpredictable every time, that looks to both here and the heavens. For Sekula, the Atlantic is an elusive site—a site of oblivion, deep forgetting, and extraction of material and labor, whose sea routes birthed global capital. For Glissant, it is a site of mourning and bereavement of a massive, irretrievable loss that is unrepresentable. The loss of a kind of humanity, of solidarity. It's where we became something else, something *para-*. There is no going back, I don't think? And it is the site of an event we hold collectively in memory—the transatlantic slave trade.

In response to the question of abstraction and the vernacular, I do think that painting's very specific history of abstraction isn't going away. From Georgia O'Keeffe to Piet Mondrian, Hans Hofmann to [Paul] Cézanne, and definitely when thinking about the works of Alma Thomas, Norman Lewis, and Beauford Delaney, the city can be distilled, but that back-and-forth between what happens to the subject of the painting, its process, and its representation on canvas is negotiable. With [Wassily] Kandinsky there is composition; in Eugène Leroy's magnificent paintings, an abstract and layered density of light; in Sol LeWitt, you find systems and instructions that share a conceptual and geometric sensibility with François Morellet, whose work has a thought process akin to that of a game or puzzle. There is also the question of function and design that arises out of the concrete, as well as questions of cannibalism, savagery, and Indigeneity within the lineage of avant-garde abstraction. For me, artists like Wilfredo Lam, Lygia Pape, Jean-Paul Riopelle, and Carmen Herrera speak to the global networks that sprung from the emancipatory and revolutionary consciousness of the avant-garde and Surrealists, in the "digesting" and abstraction of Cubism into a kind of anthropomorphic consciousness—of being simultaneously human, plant, earth, and animal.

I've been thinking about the geometric and abstract concerns of memory and nature, too, as found in works by artists like Thomas Nozkowski, Etel Adnan, Howard Hodgkin, Jack Whitten, and Frank Bowling. Equally, I have been looking at a lot of masks—specifically Bolo masks—textiles, reliquary figures, and documentation of ceremonial practices like scarification, tattooing, and body painting, which decorate and abstract the body. I likewise found these ideas in Glissant: *créolité* in painting is deeply complicated because there isn't a single marker of the origin, but as a space of orality it functions as a sign or pictograph of a community. Or call it a sample; there is a transformation in displacement, as in the crossing over. A kind of doublespeak—call it shorthand, code, or slang—it is an utterance meant for a specific ear, and it hits and sounds different depending on the listener. It becomes a voice or marker divorced from text or the written laws and grammar that once defined it; it is now moving and at play, a mark that sounds a call of alarm, insightful and yet piercingly deafening and disorienting. The other question this raises for me is around modernity and how we deal with our past. This conversation around abstraction, mourning, the audience, and legibility and illegibility, for me, is really a question of modernity.

RR:
Do you think that the subject of abstraction has evolved and means something else? Do we use abstraction more now as a language, as a tool for language, than before? Does it have more meaning in contemporary life than before?

CL:
It is hard for me to think of abstraction as something that's historically progressive. I'll give two examples: My work in the show is a flicker film—a hyper-specific genre of filmmaking from the 1960s and '70s that emerges from structural filmmaking, where people really focused on the materials of film production and completely abstracted the idea of the image in cinema. Concurrently, there were landmark representational works being made. If you think about Tony Conrad's work *The Flicker* (1966), the film itself is a psychedelic assault on the eyes. Yet before it starts, there's a trigger warning that basically says, "This is stroboscopic, it causes photosensitive epilepsy. You can have a stroke every time this film is screened, there must be a doctor on hand in the cinema." It seems funny to pair this super abstracted work with a text that is so grounded in the material repercussions of this very abstraction.

For me, abstraction and representation are in constant interplay. To give another example: as structural film got more and more severe in the '70s and '80s—and it was primarily a bunch of white men who were making this work—Black and brown people were gaining access to the tools of production to make movies at the same time. There's avant-garde film, and then there's an actual radical democratization of the media that happens after this formal extremism. What I'm trying to say is that the idea of abstraction as a formal progression feels a little bit simplistic. Things are constantly happening at the same time, responding to each other, and antagonizing each other.

RR:
Do you think abstraction has always existed?

CL:
Yes. My feeling is that it has always existed. Maybe, for example in painting, it has crystallized in periodic breaks, but I'm interested in thinking of it as something that's continuous rather than something that happened and now we are living in the period after it.

LW:
There also seems to be a continued effort toward revision, toward looking critically at this history of abstraction and thinking about the other participants. I'm always interested in writers who interrogate the canon of abstraction and talk about the ways that we have perhaps missed some key moments. To me, it seems the most subversive dialogue arises in this idea of where abstraction becomes more democratic—where it has always been more democratic, both within and outside of the art world. What does it look like for enough people to develop a democratic relationship with abstraction, so they can participate in that writing of that language, that contextualizing, for themselves?

RR:
Yeah, I think it's interesting. I'm familiar with Tony Conrad and the structural filmmakers that Carolyn was mentioning, and I associate my work with them. I'm not sure if I would necessarily call the process, the manipulation and expansion of structural elements, an abstract thing. It's a physical process: a matter of using a certain screen, maybe doing away with the traditional cinematic screen, manipulating the mechanical parts of the projector, or taking it out of its conventional use, let's say, and expanding on its various elements. For me, it's very concrete, it's not abstract in any way.

CL:
I agree with you. I think all of this work comes out of materialism and thinking about a material relationship to the medium, but fundamentally, what it is—and what I think Lachell really picked up on—is this way in which the reduction of cinema to its material means is also something that has to do with light and sound and all of these things that are actually elements of perception. So, for me, what happens in the materialist breakdown of the medium is that we start to understand that cinema can actually exist in a lot of different forms. If it's just light and projection and a surface, then it can become a lot of other things: we can start to see cinema all around us, so that when we think about Lachell's work, which involves projections onto T-shirts, we understand that the T-shirts themselves are screens and the projection a form of cinema.

It is radical to think through one's medium from a materialist perspective, and I'm interested in how that can lead to abstraction. And this has other repercussions—for thinking about embodiment, for example. I'm thinking about what Andy was saying earlier about interiority. I'm interested in interiority and I'm also interested in systems. What I'm less interested in is representing the bodies that seem to experience the interiority and are entangled in the systems, because I think that's already implicit. I love representational work, I feel like it's critically important; it's just that I'm interested in the far edges of what bodies imply. It has to do with stretching the capacity of what we think embodiment means. Embodiment is interior experience and it's also the ways in which we're interpolated by the world around us—it's not just this physicality right here.

AR:
I think of abstraction as contemplation, and about how memory comes with its bends and folds. When I brought up tradition, it wasn't necessarily in regards to tradition in painting. I'm thinking about tradition in the broader sense, too. I don't think we should talk about the past purely with nostalgia—you can't talk about things purely as great, or only focus on that which you want to remember—but we can ponder or mourn what is lost and irretrievable. The site of ruin—this barren, salty floodland that, at any moment, can flood or break—it's like a basin; its levees, which some call eyelids, heavy at times, flow over. Our psyche makes references to these images and sites—almost metaphors—of the mind. And they have an effect on our lives today, on modernity. These are questions of memory, and memory is alive today. You see what I mean? It's our modernity that is in question when wrestling with the past.

39

A conversation between
Carolyn Lazard, Raha Raissnia,
Andy Robert, and Lachell Workman

YUJI AGEMATSU

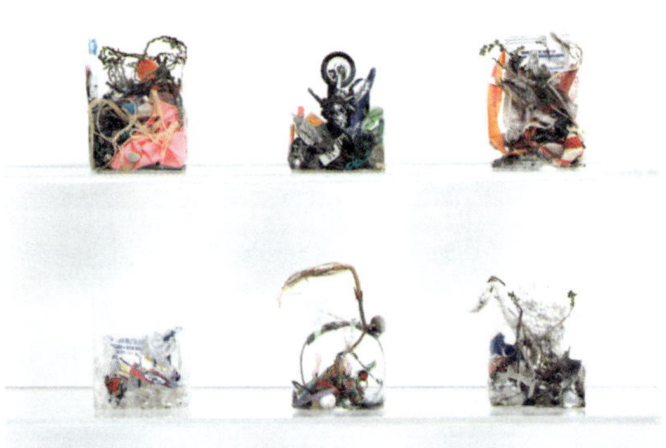

In college, in Japan, my major was management. I really hated going to school. Then I got a saxophone and started to play free jazz. It was the mid-seventies, so many hippie people who came from Europe and the US got together in Japan, especially in Kyoto or the mountains. I had so many friends who came from other countries and hung around together. And then in 1980, I joined Friends World College, an experimental Quaker college in Long Island, which was sort of related to Black Mountain College. Tuition was really inexpensive and I got an I-20 visa. Each student had to decide on a field advisor because of the experimental learning process. I knew of Milford Graves's activities through magazines. I found his telephone number in the phone book and kept calling, calling. For six months I called, and eventually in 1981 I joined his Yara class. For five or six years, I took his class intensively. I had to survive, so I became a little bit busy because of taking jobs, but I still took the class. I quit his class in 1996, fifteen years later.

It was mostly movement. Milford was always asking me, "What do you want to do?" It was very, very hard. I could pretend to dance their way, but they always told me, "You can trace us, and then you have to do your own thing." Milford told me, "You want to play, you want to learn drumming? You have to know your own heartbeat first—that's your heart. You are beating yourself already, so just learn from your heartbeat by touching the skin. What can I teach you? You have to reach in your heartbeat." In class, there was a very fundamental practice of just walking around making circles. I practiced a lot. Walking around is a thing I really love, even when I was a kid. No purpose, just walking. And then I started to walk around the city with no purpose, and then started to touch the ground instead of touching the body. It was a transfer from the class. During the class, we touched each other, but then I started touching the ground. Then I gradually started picking up stuff. For me, movement was first and the object secondary.

Sensation is very important. Seeing and staring are one sensation. That's why contemporary visual art exists. But I wanted to touch the stuff. Touching is very important for human beings. My activity is to touch, to notice, like with chewing gum. Of course we shouldn't touch chewing gum on the street. My really fundamental desire to feel is related to Milford. Materials are very sensitive, and also anonymous. What did the object used to be? Fragments of green glass used to be a Heineken bottle or something like that. I'm really interested in objects becoming totally anonymous from the original product. I'm interested in mutations. Everything changes in time. But there is a human desire to keep an original shape all the time. My own thing is watching how shapes change like time. Maybe that's typical of Oriental aesthetics. It's a longer view of history. It relates to religion, too. In Japan, there are so many gods: Stone has a god. Wood has a god. Even rotten gum, chewing gum. Change is better than new. Like cheese and wine and pickles in Western culture. Dried flowers.

I started picking up objects in 1985. I walk in the street and there are so many strange, interesting objects spread all over the city. Each object gives me a signal, you know? Then I stop and touch it. A car honks, there's street noise—I react to the street noise and the visual object on the street. I'm like an unknown street dancer or something, and I was very nimble because of Milford's class. That's how I invented my own way to practice, instead of with the body. More like a phenomenon of the surface. I started putting the objects on a shelf in my house, as an archive. A friend of mine who was an artist explained all kinds of art history, like Duchamp and the so-called readymade. And then I started to get jobs in art galleries in the '90s, at John Weber Gallery. I didn't think to make art. But I noticed that this kind of activity I was already doing was related to art. Gradually, I learned a lot through the gallery, working with artists. I met the Sol LeWitt crew and I started to work with them. The first time I showed my own art was in 1994 at TZ'Art & Co. on Wooster, next to American Fine Arts. Ziplock bags were the first show.

At first, there was no regulation; I just put the stuff I collected into the box. Then I started to carry a pedometer to count my steps. Gradually, I started notating location and time. I like New York. People leave me alone because I'm not going to steal anything. I'm just touching the ground and picking up the trash. New Yorkers think, "Oh, you must be crazy. Okay." A doorman around Water Street—where it's very beautiful, so many great fragments—said, "Oh, the crazy guy came." I'm not going to explain, "I'm an artist and I have a show at the PS1, please, come to see my artwork." I want to be anonymous.

New York is a rough city. I pick up fragments of glass, stone, and asphalt. So many objects are plastic. I couldn't do it in another city, especially Tokyo. There's nothing. Just the concrete, perfect. I've been collecting glass for a long time. I know the character of materials, and I've collected all kinds of materials already. But ten, fifteen years ago, we didn't have any iPhones, so of course products have changed and then broken down. But the elements are the same: plastic is plastic, glass is glass. Chewing gum color is different also. I don't hang around Times Square that much anymore, but I used to. It's very interesting for me to collect objects there because of the many international sightseers in that area. They bring their own chewing gum. Sometimes totally black chewing gum. Wall Street people chew Dentyne Ice. Each district has a character.

Every day I balance attention and inattention—the conscious and subconscious are always switching around. I walk around just staring at the atmosphere, like, "Oh, the sky is blue. Oh, I feel so good, today's cold, a little bit chilly or hot." I just go, just swimming into the air. Then I hit an object and switch on, staring and watching. This kind of paying attention is more like the documentary impulse. But staring relates to a surrealism too—like sleeping, you know? Surrealism and realism are very interesting themes because they are always related to each other. While picking things up, I'm getting into the spot, the sense of time, the sense of the place. Everything is involved in change, just like a surrealistic experience.

These days, there are really so many regulations. We need freedom in the moment so we can create our own spot. We've been paying taxes so we should be able to enjoy public space. We have the right. The kinds of materials I pick up are already outside property, already anonymous. That's why we call it trash. Trash has freedom already. It doesn't belong to anyone. It's a way of finding what Hakim Bey calls "temporary autonomous zones"—because we have freedom to create a temporary space or utopia. There's always that possibility, before it gets absorbed, where we could be free. We need utopia right now because there is no dream, you know? COVID hits, the rent goes high, grocery prices go high, we can't afford to get into the movie theater that much. But I believe that we can create our own space in our mind very easily. That's the artist's way, I guess—how to survive with this ridiculous studio rent. But okay. I pay.

Tina and Aarne Anton on

CURTIS CUFFIE

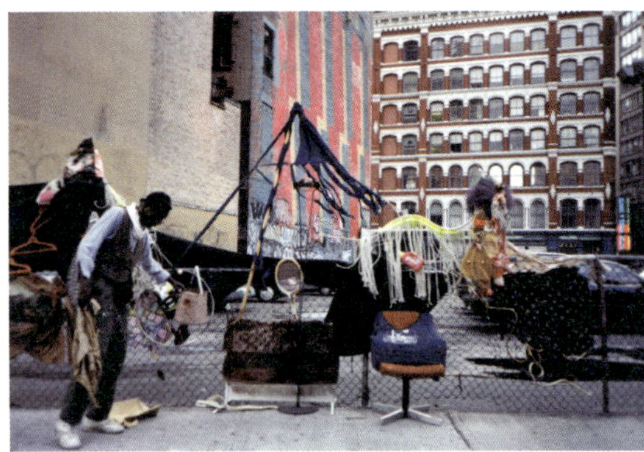

Aarne Anton:
My name is Aarne Anton and I formerly ran American Primitive Gallery in New York, and under that auspice showed Curtis Cuffie.

Tina Anton:
My name is Tina Anton, and I started a program called Art on the Edge, an art program for the homeless, in which I worked both in shelters and on the street. That's when I met Curtis and introduced him to Aarne, and showed his work both in the gallery and at the Outsider Art Fair. It was '94 when we met him, on the street.

AA:
He was usually near Cooper Union and the big parking lot by the *Village Voice* [office].

TA:
We heard of Curtis through some of the artists I was working with who were homeless. There was a bit of camaraderie between the downtown homeless artists. They'd say, "Oh, you should see this person." I'm pretty sure that's how we met and became aware of him. It wasn't like we just stumbled upon him in the street.

AA:
Actually it took a little while—weeks almost, it seemed like—to find him where he was working.

TA:
We just befriended him, hung out, and then I talked to him about the program I was running and asked him if perhaps I could show some of his work. At that time, I was working on the Outsider Art Fair and wanted to bring some of his work to the booth. He was receptive to it.

AA:
He liked us and we liked him. We spent time just hanging out with him, watching him work on the street. He had a canvas cart that was full of materials that he would pull things out of.

TA:
Like a magician.

AA:
It was like watching Jimi Hendrix perform. He had what were almost dance movements, and he would sing, rap poetry, and react and interchange with people walking by on the sidewalks—some of whom he knew, because he was a fixture in that location. Sometimes, just out of the blue, he would grab a Frisbee and throw it out into the street at an angle. It would come back to him, or he'd run out into the street if it was a bad throw.

TA:
Many of his works were taken down or thrown out.

AA:
He talked about falling asleep on the sidewalk and waking up and seeing the last of some construction that he had been doing thrown into the dump truck. He asked, "Where are you taking that?" And they said, "It's going to the museum, that one in Staten Island." The dump. There wasn't a permanence to much of what he did. If he did a whole big thing on a given day, the next day he might rearrange half of it and it would become something else. He became very adept at taking cloth and draping it and wrapping it and knotting it, using it as an art material and animating it. There was always an element of performance art, though at the time I didn't think

of it in those terms. I was always looking at the aesthetics of what he had created. Some of it didn't work for me, and some of it I thought was brilliant. We did a show at the gallery of work we had selected from the sidewalk on a given day or days.

I've been waiting over twenty years for Curtis to be recognized as part of twentieth-century art history. He was part of the art world but he hasn't been recognized, though he was recognized by other artists in the East Village, because all kinds of people interacted with him. I see it as indicative of a time in the 1990s when, let's face it, the art world really didn't give a shit about homeless people. Otherwise he would've been getting recognition while he was alive. He was getting recognition from David Hammons and Robert Frank, and other people that were in the neighborhood, but still a recognition like, "Here's this wacky homeless Black dude making stuff on a fence." It wasn't, by and large, taken seriously as art. It's just indicative of that time. Art has always had a hierarchy and blind spots. In Curtis's obituary, David Hammons describes meeting with European curators and inviting them to come down and meet Curtis to see something different. Curtis was homeless and David wasn't, but they were working in the same neighborhood and sometimes even showing in the same place, for example A Gathering of the Tribes. I love both of them, David Hammons and Curtis, but sometimes there's no fairness or justice in this world. There are so many institutions, so many arts foundations, that are able to support artists or facilitate art making, but Curtis wasn't able to connect with that.

TA:

He touched so many people. For him, art was never about being finished. It was performance and it was ongoing.

AA:

But he did do individual pieces that were freestanding. The fence was like a wall. He had things that he picked up and made bases with. A store would throw out a stand for some display and he'd take the bottom of the X and he'd have a freestanding piece. He did that more when he was on that little triangular island right in front of Cooper Union. He had all these art students, since he was across from Cooper. People sometimes suggested that the students were more influenced by Curtis than by what the teachers were teaching. Watching him was like an art theater.

TA:

There's also a jazz, an improvisation, to all the work. He was saying, "What's missing?" Now it may have been because I was younger and was an artist in the city, so I felt that vibe more then, but I think the city has changed. It doesn't have quite that jazz feeling downtown. His work expressed that by grabbing disparate things. All of his work, to me at least, relates to the city.

Besides the work, he had an incredible heart—you felt it. If he loved you, he loved you. To me, it comes out in the work. He's got this soul and a sweetness to him. That was always uplifting. You could be down and then you'd go see Curtis and it would change your whole mindset.

Tina Anton is an artist who ran American Primitive Gallery alongside her husband, Aarne Anton, for many years. Aarne Anton is a collector and dealer of contemporary art and antique folk art who runs American Primitive Gallery, formerly located in New York City and now based in Pomona, NY.

Guillermo Kuitca on

JULIO GALÁN

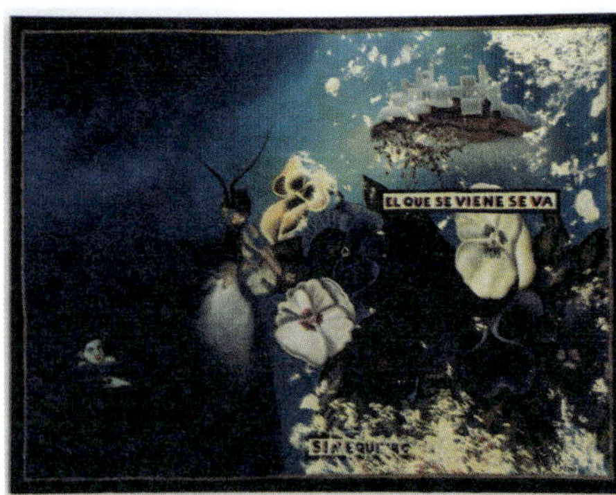

I first came across Julio's work because I heard about this other Latin American artist that was showing here and there. We happened to share not only two galleries that were representing us at that time, Annina Nosei in New York and Barbara Farber in Amsterdam, but we were also part of parallel shows. Nevertheless, it took us both a long time to meet. I think this all happened between '88 and '96, and we only met in '95 or '96. As personalities, we were very different; our work was super different too. There was this moment that I think is very important in Latin American art, when the center of the scene moved from Mexico to Brazil, and simultaneously moved more from an imaginary, almost surrealist fantasy realm to the non-fantastic or concrete. If there is a confrontation, it's the fantastic versus the concrete. Of course, Julio represented a very fantastic world. To me, it was fascinating how he was one of the sole inheritors of Frida Kahlo's world. I don't know if he really thought of himself in those terms. Maybe he did. Maybe he didn't. Self-portrayal, queerness, and freedom of depiction played such central roles in his work. And pain. Atavism was also a central theme in his work, and the way he approached themes of sex and suffering.

Julio moved to New York from Monterrey, Mexico, where he was from, which was a very oppressive milieu. I know he had this epiphany moment when he crossed paths with Andy Warhol. I think he might have seen himself as some kind of Warholian character. Of course, art-wise they couldn't be more different, but I mean in the way that he explored ways to express himself. When I finally met him, I met a character who was completely eccentric and over the top, flamboyant—the way he dressed, the way he talked, the gestures. To me it was like, *wow*. We could hardly communicate in the same language, really. We did eventually communicate through paintings. He set up this meeting where we would both paint a painting for the other one by creating a sort of wall in the middle of the room, so neither of us could see what the other was doing. Equal-size canvases. We both painted something in relation to the fact that we were living a parallel life. He painted two lobsters that were fucking each other. He literally called the piece *Julio and Guillermo*. We didn't have any sexual contact at all, this is just to tell you a little bit about how over-the-top his approach was. It was a beautiful painting.

I'm not sure if his work was transformed by living in New York. At some point, he started creating black gestural marks on top of more elaborated figures. He might paint something quite realistic, and then alter the painting by doing this very fast black painting on top. There was an immediacy to that gesture, which we traditionally connect with the New York school, or a New York speed. It's an interesting thing because on one hand, I met an isolated artist who was in a sort of a limbo, but on the other hand, it could only happen in New York. A city like New York can provide a particular kind of isolation. He lived a New York kind of isolation.

Guillermo Kuitca is an artist based in Buenos Aires.

ROBIN GRAUBARD

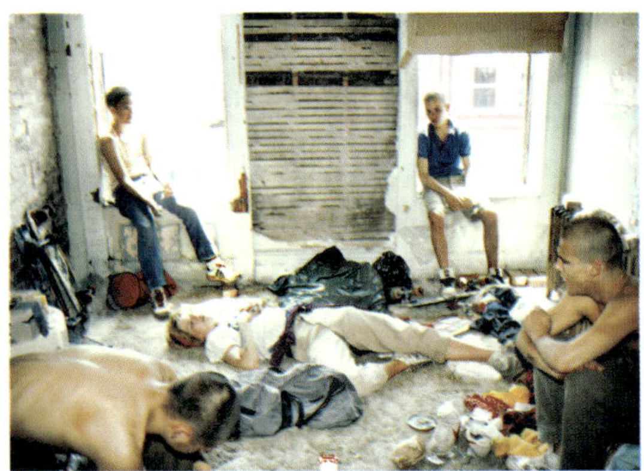

When I was nine years old, I made a drawing for a nationwide art contest about safety belts. I drew the picture sitting in my dining room and ended up winning the contest, so newspapers all over the country published it. It's interesting to me that I made it when I was nine and the theme of it is very similar to what I do now, though not purposefully. I never thought about this drawing until a couple of years ago. It's a girl, bandaged. That set the course for me a bit. But people in my town said, "She has to go to art school, she has to study painting." I had an image of an artist with a beret and everything, and I felt like it was a bit old school, so I eventually ended up doing photography. I thought it was more cutting edge.

I always feel a bit of an outsider—even in grade school and high school, I was always a bit of an outsider wherever I went. My work is about finding common ground, really. I left my home in Westchester County when I was about sixteen, in the 1960s, and lived with other kids my age. I had read the Andy Warhol book when I was a teenager and was influenced by him, so I started going to the city a lot. I never actually met Warhol when I was really young—I met him much later—but I was really interested in what he was doing. I went and lived with people in New York City, downtown, in crash pads. I hitchhiked cross country, read Jack Kerouac's *On the Road* (1957), and all that. I didn't have a camera then, so I just lived my life. Later, I was living with my boyfriend on the Lower East Side. I saved up $100 and went to Europe. I had one of those Brownie cameras, and so I started taking some pictures in Scotland.

When I came back, I went to NYU film school. First, I wanted to be a dance therapist, but after a short while, I was working on lighting for dance productions. I got interested in that because I had been going to the Fillmore and other venues. I was probably a poster child for the hippies. Actually, I was on a poster once. It said, in Spanish, "This is a hippie." There's no such thing as hippies, really; it was just this constructed notion. It was like there were two sides to the '60s: Woodstock was all the suburban kids doing the '60s thing, and I felt like that was the end of the '60s. But there was really a lot of very dark stuff going on as well. I had wanted to make a film about my experiences during the '60s. I never made that film when I was in school, which was in the '70s, but when I got out of school, I started taking some photography classes. I started going back down to the Lower East Side and taking pictures of punks and skinheads who were living a lifestyle that I had lived during the '60s, or similar to it, though punks did not like hippies. That was kind of my way to go back in time to process the '60s. I'm still trying to do that, believe it or not. I feel like I'm still trying to materialize what happened during that time.

A lot of what I do is a kind of reaction to what came before. I didn't set out to photograph the kids on the Lower East Side as a way of photographing myself during that time, but after the fact, I realized that that's partly what I was doing. I'll photograph situations and then conceptualize it after the fact, rather than have a plan. I feel like if I had an absolute plan, I would just be setting up people and situations and it would be more like a studio practice. I've always been more interested in real life. Not that a studio is not real life, but I've always been more interested in reality. I try not to pose anybody. There's definitely something about catching people. A lot of times, my pictures look like crime scenes.

I started out in journalism by photographing the Mafia. I was interested in photographing power. That's basically how my entire journalism career started. I followed John Gotti to a restaurant one time and there was this really burly, tough photographer standing outside the restaurant with me. I said to him, "I think I'm going to go inside," and he said, "Nuh-uh—negative." I went inside and I photographed all these Mafia guys around a dinner table. At one point I was in an elevator with them, and they said, "Where do you live?" I didn't tell them, but they said, "Well, how would you like it if we went to your house and photographed you having dinner?" Someone recently told me that the FBI used that picture to identify a lot of the people that were in that particular group of the Mafia. Before I started working for the big papers, I also did work for the *East Village Eye* and the *New York Rocker*, where Lance Loud and I worked together.

The world feels so different right now, with how many images there are. I have mixed feelings about it. In a way, January 6, 2021, was the most photographed event in all of history, and I'm glad I wasn't there, considering they probably would have gotten a whiff of my politics. At a certain point, I felt like I had to photograph things that were going on in the world in my lifetime. Now I feel like there's plenty of people around doing that. I'm not really sure what direction I'm going to go in from here. It's difficult. It's like a circle. When I was really young and we were protesting against Vietnam, I thought, well, we ended the war, that's going to be the last war ever. And no—I think things have just gotten worse and worse. Things are way more chaotic than they've ever been, with more death, destruction, wars, inequities. I guess part of taking photographs is trying to make sense of it all, trying to put some order into disorder and create your own world out of the world. If it makes sense to you, it might make sense to other people as well. If you're doing art that's just a white painting or something, like Robert Ryman, I guess that's a way of creating some sort of order as well. It's about choices. I tend to pick things that are visible. But there's also an element, or the way I put order into some of the photographs, that is in my head; maybe other people will see, maybe they won't. There's an element of abstraction in the choice of images. It's deceptively concrete.

Yto Barrada on

BETTINA GROSSMAN

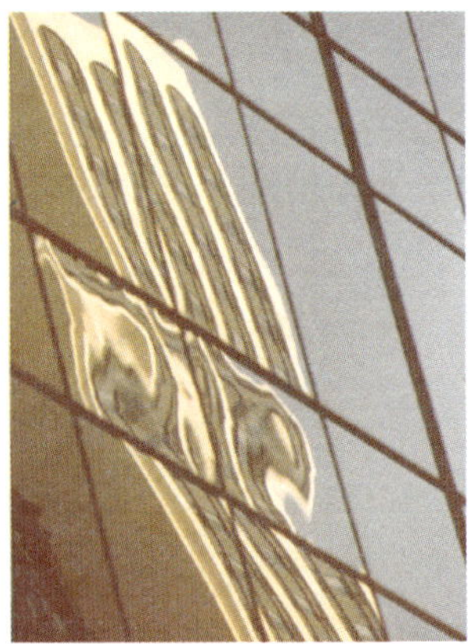

The first time I heard about Bettina was in a film a friend of mine, Corinne van der Borch, made about her in 2010 called *Girl with Black Balloons*. It's a portrait of an eccentric, charming lady who's been living as a recluse in the legendary Chelsea Hotel, trapped in her room and inventing new cosmogonies. I glimpsed bits and pieces of her artwork in the documentary in 2018, and I told the filmmaker, "I want to meet her and see the work." She responded, "Well, it's a bit complicated." Bettina did not show her work, so you would only get a glimpse of it if you visited her. I met Bettina in her apartment at the Chelsea when she was ninety-one. Much of her work was packed and stored in boxes, but some of it was on display. It started from the door, the hallway—there were images collaged everywhere, reinvented elements of work that she made mixed with quotes. There was a strong relation between abstract art and the written word. When you squeezed into the apartment, every shelf was full of sculptures, paintings and photographs on the wall, lots of Super 8 and film.

So the origin story with Bettina—a story which remains full of holes—is that she lost everything in a fire in '66; she lost all her work when she was at a high point in her career. I think it took many years before she could figure out a ritual and a system to move on. Her work has to do with perpetual renewal, a circulation of visual ideas which is never repetitive: the same form you'd see in her photography would reappear transfigured in a collage, then in sculpture, then back to photography as a photogram. Similar forms of renewal through difference appear throughout her writing and text-based artworks.

Bettina lived and travelled in Europe for a number of crucial years where she made some central pieces in her work. Later in her life, she became very close to nature, too, collecting and working with botanical raw materials. After the fire, she moved to the Chelsea Hotel where she lived and worked until the end. She was already painting, drawing, and making sculptures, but her photography practice developed a lot in the years at the hotel, with series shot from her balcony. She said that after she lost everything, she started to reproduce everything that she had made from memory, and that it took her devotion, ritual, and being confined in her room to do it. The last exhibition she had was in the '80s at OK Harris, and after that she didn't show work at all until 2019, when I asked her to join me in a two-woman exhibition at the Lower Manhattan Cultural Council's space on Governors Island. I also included her in my Artist's Choice exhibition at MoMA, *The Raft*, in 2021. Other than that, incredibly, her work had hardly been shown at all.

I'm finding now, as I organize her archives, notes where she says clearly that as a woman in New York in those days there was no way you were going to make it. There were many artists who lived at the Chelsea Hotel, and lots of guys having careers around her in New York. Bettina was certainly aware that the New York art community, the people who celebrated and supported so many artists, had overlooked her. I think that brought her frustration, rage, because she was also conscious of her greatness. It was just so clear to her. She was keeping tabs: she would photocopy works by other artists from art magazines, and put them facing the work that she had done that it resembled, and write her name with the date of her work. For example, showing that François Morellet did a piece, and she had made a similar innovation two or three years before.

She knew she wasn't getting the career she deserved. Sure, she has a strong personality and a great sense of humor, but think how many male artists are a pain in the ass, and with them it's considered a sign of strength.

What she really would have loved is large-scale commissions. She always said of her works, "Those are models, I'm working small because I'm in here. I want them to be huge sculptures in the streets of the city. My work is finite and perfect and super well organized." Finite, meaning that the circle was closed. Then she would start a new thing. There was something of a closing and reopening of circles, and a ritual play that has to do with forms of transcendence, like energy. Something ceremonial. In the mid-1800s, paleographic drawings on walls were discovered, and it was a huge shock for artists that there was art being made 40,000 years ago. There was a strong spiritual force in Bettina's belief that art was a natural function of humans, and all she was doing was serving that force.
It's as if she was carried by something else.

Earlier in her life, she worked as a textile designer. She was self-taught and she celebrated that. That space of non-formal knowledge was a huge part of her freedom. She's not an outsider artist, but she was self-taught. She was very adamant that she had made the decision not to go to school and to work right away instead. She did get commercial gigs and travelled a lot for her work. She says she invented the pinstripe shirt turned into sheets for men. She probably did! Now I have the proof, in all the stores in New York. She claims a few other inventions that I have to look into, but I wouldn't be surprised if they are true, because everything Bettina said has turned out to be true.

There's something systemic about neglect, when it involves women from that generation. A lot of art was destroyed when the Chelsea Hotel was sold. They put Bettina's work in bins and her friends and neighbors had to rescue it. Maybe we need to put together a little group of artists who can be trained to support older artists in the professional space, and also be their mentees creatively.

Bettina was ninety-four when she died in November of 2021. She was happy to see her work starting to be recognized, even if we all knew it was decades too late. She has survived many attempts to destroy her, but I think, to her, the worst threat is oblivion. That's why the work of building her legacy is just starting. I've had sleepless nights in the winter of 2021, worrying about the Hotel management taking back her room before we can get her work safely packed and archived. Curating Bettina, even now, is a handful. And it's all worth it.

Yto Barrada is a multimedia visual artist living and working in Tangier, Morocco, and New York City. She is currently working with the estate of Bettina Grossman to archive and preserve Grossman's work, as well as organizing a forthcoming monograph on the artist to be published in Paris by Atelier EXB / Éditions Xavier Barral.

E'WAO KAGOSHIMA

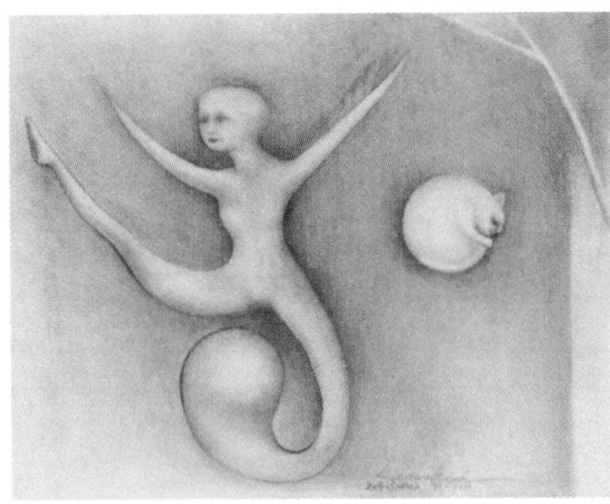

I didn't like school. I wanted to go through the bushes and trees, among animals, swimming in the river. I was not interested in the city. But later, after high school, I liked the city life. I don't think about childhood much. As I get older, I lose interest in my past. I am still getting to what time my dream is. I stick to my dream. I don't compare myself to other people but I always want to be more intelligent than I am. This is why I started reading. I went to the bookstore to get art books and I went to galleries, because I didn't speak English but I wanted to understand art. I wanted to know the New York art scene. I am ambitious. I can do more, you know; I still have a dream and I'm not satisfied. People think that when you are young you are ambitious, but I am old and ambitious. Some people dream of being a doctor but I still dream about being a fine artist.

I have to make money, my own money in life, and I cannot do this with art. But I want to stick with art. I remember when something inside of me changed and I became a hungry guy. I'm primitive now. I need food. This is my situation—every day. Physically, when I was young, it was easy, but getting older might not make it so easy to be an artist. I want to live longer so I can do this. If I see something hopeful, I want to live longer.

Now I am also in *Greater New York*. There are forty-seven artists in the show. This is just like the forty-seven samurai story—the most famous story from Japan. There are forty-seven samurai who live in a castle in Tokyo and want to take revenge on the lord of the castle.

I am a practical guy. I need strategy. Like a company, the most successful artists in the United States have strategy. It's just business, even though most artists believe they are next to God. But if someone pays me $1000, I will make work for them. I am not a rich artist. I come from Japan. I don't want to be wealthy; I want to survive. In 1983, I had a show at the New Museum. I had a few collectors. One of them had a museum and he was the only one who stuck with me. But most rich people are very . . . fickle.

I know Ruba [Katrib] from SculptureCenter. As an artist, you need to be connected. Otherwise, you get no attention. I am at MoMA now, so I get attention. Maybe this is the last chance . . . or no! It's my beginning! But it is also my last chance. Last weekend, I looked at the *New York Times* and there was my name, E'wao Kagoshima, right in the center [slaps his hands against his leg]. But no one has heard of me still. This show will be open for six months, which is very unusual, and it only happens every five years. So the next few years might be something. It's like the forty-seven samurai story. Who will kill the lord?

Look at Picasso: the most powerful creator in history. He was always changing. Having no style is important. But no style is an invisible idea; it's difficult to recognize. So why I am changing? If I do one style that would allow me support myself, I would focus on that style. But I cannot find that. I can't live on what I make. So I change. This show is a programmatic idea of what I am going to do now. In ten years, I may be in the ground somewhere. If I were young, I would not feel hurried, but this my last opportunity to do something. Today, I feel good; tomorrow, I might be in a rush. Last night, I was worried that I cannot talk like a philosopher or an NYU professor for this interview, because my thoughts cannot fully be expressed in English. My English is only as good as, "Give me money!" Today, a man on the street told me, "Give me money!" So I asked him, "Do I look like a rich guy?" He said, "Give me money!" But I only have a few hundred dollars in the bank.

This is why I don't want to talk about art—because my art is for eyes only. My mouth is like an advertiser: "My work is great, you know? One million dollars." You see who buys. That is stupid. My job is only to make good art, not to speak. My work is more serious than what I am saying. Nobody can see their own face except in the mirror. And that is not correct. Left becomes right and right becomes left in the mirror: nobody can see their real face. This is why I ask myself: Who am I? I am stupid or intelligent or a god? My art is always asking this question. Always, when I wake up, I start thinking about this: What do I do? What do I make? Finally, I eat, I go to the bathroom, always thinking about what's inside of me. What is the real thing? Nobody knows that infinity.

This text is excerpted from a conversation between E'wao Kagoshima and Ross Simonini, originally published in the January 2022 issue of *ArtReview*.

AHMED MORSI

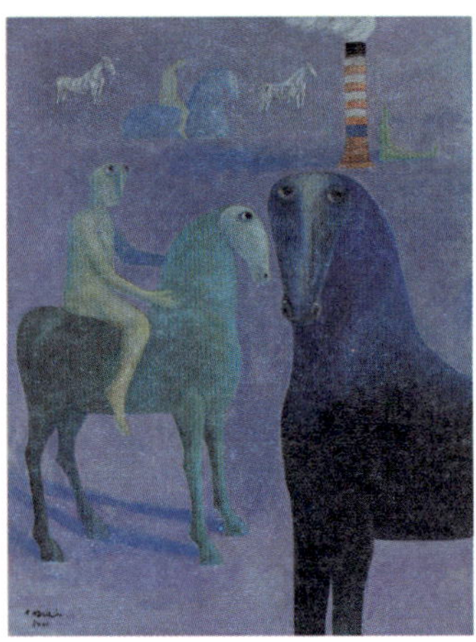

It was in Alexandria, where I grew up, that I first saw the works of Picasso and Matisse. With France ravaged by war, Parisian galleries moved their exhibitions across the Mediterranean to the port city of Alexandria, which at that time was home to a significant number of wealthy people of Italian, Greek, Armenian, Levantine, and Egyptian backgrounds. It's where I bought my first art books as well as poetry. The French school was still the center of influence on the arts. By the time I made my last move, in 1974, that center was undeniably New York.

Though I was well acquainted with the "teachers and friends" from Europe, in New York I discovered the wide expanse of American artists and American writers and poets. It was a tumultuous time, politically, economically, and socially in the US. These aren't unfamiliar elements to me, so I was not shaken by them. But they seemed to fuel the art and literary output. There were more museums and more galleries and more biennials for me to visit than I was accustomed to, with these venues proudly showcasing American art, and I was happy for the introductions into this world that had been so distant and so foreign. The geographic distance separating Europe from the US, the "old" world and the "new," created something distinctly different in the art and literary worlds, something "American"—born of a unique environment with its personal set of circumstances and modes of expression. Of particular interest to me was the discovery of Black American writers, playwrights, and most especially poets. I read them, I studied them, and I wrote about them. There's an intimacy we share—an understanding of sorts. Gradually, but undeniably and most unfortunately, the art scene in New York lost its innocence to the temptations of capitalism, and the old and new worlds came together, catering to Euro-American taste and sensibilities.

I moved homes and geographies many times in my life. At twenty-six, I left Alexandria and moved to Baghdad for two years. At twenty-eight, I returned from Iraq and moved to Cairo. At thirty-three, as a newlywed, my wife and I moved to Kabul for six months—that was the shortest of moves. And at forty-four, I moved with the family to NYC—the last and longest of relocations. With each new address, there was a conscious intent to cut my umbilical cords, the influence of my birth city, Alexandria. Strangely, though I have now lived longer in New York than I have in my birth city or Egypt as a whole, I have not succeeded in freeing myself from her. But though New York is the furthest away from Alexandria geographically, in many ways it is also the closest.

My body physically gravitated toward the less-urban places, those areas that were uncharacteristically New York. I found myself walking cobblestone streets of lower Manhattan, specifically in the area now known as South Street Seaport, but which in the '70s was a space where fishermen sold their catch to the island's various retailers. Here I entered a wormhole that transported me to Alexandria. Manhattan defies space and time in my poetry and in my paintings. I knew these ancient fishermen. I was acquainted with that smell. The sounds were familiar. My New York, the one that allowed this transcendence, of course resides in my memory, which is not based on record and fact. Just like Alexandria, my recollections are later understood as manifestations of my imagination, and by definition that is a place of aloneness—whether in New York or Alexandria. But any existing sense of alienation grows harder, with deeper roots, when fed by other experiences that are related to emigration. Foreign beings have to take up unrecognizable masks to assimilate in a strange expanse that knows no horizon, seems to go as far as the eye can see and perhaps even further. Age also plays a role here. My imagination matured—grew detailed, seemingly rich and boundless.

To me, surrealism is not just an art movement. I know this contradicts one hundred years of art history. But allow me to explain. I was first introduced to this "new" concept as a teenager in Alexandria, a young poet who was mining the bookstores and libraries for reading material. I was already writing poetry in Arabic and was proficient in English. I taught myself French so I could read the poetry of Arthur Rimbaud in its original. Once I gained fluency, I expanded until I read Paul Éluard and Louis Aragon in French, which ultimately led to my translation of selected works by each of these Surrealist writers from French to Arabic. This is important because, until then, the 1960s, this new "idea" was not available to readers or audiences who spoke non-Western languages, Arabic included.

If surrealism now is understood as the "revolutionary" and quite conscious efforts made first by writers and then by visual artists to unlock the doors of the subconscious, I must confess that I had no need for these methods. In fact, my sense of deep alienation since my youth is rooted in my attempts to understand this existence, our existence, from the seat of my imagination, where I comfortably reside among my "beings" and "creatures." In other words, this "new" idea was neither novel nor an idea. I had always lived surreally, even before knowing of the widely used term. So I prefer to describe surrealism as a philosophy, a way of being. Simply being, with little to no effort. "You close your eyes in order to see the unseen"—that's a line from a poem I wrote in a collection called *Dress Rehearsal for a Season in Hell* (2001), which pays homage to Rimbaud's seminal poem "A Season in Hell." Rather than action, inaction—because experiencing the unseen or the subconscious cannot be done by conscious means.

What are we? You and I? We are animals. I make no distinctions. My animals and creatures are all experiencing, too, without the constructs of time and space and without labels. They are all sentient, seeing through my eyes and feeling through my heart, and I through them. My relationship with animals started with dogs, when I rescued a German Shepherd abandoned by the British Army at the end of WWII. I was fifteen, and there was never a doubt that this being was deserving of something better. In my late thirties, I was forced to take my dog to be put down. A few rogue children pelted him with rocks over the garden walls "for fun" and he was left blind and paralyzed from an injury to the head. We shared a car ride to death, no . . . to murder. Who was the human and who was the "animal," the being of lesser consciousness? It is clear the universally accepted definitions are a product of a human need to have dominion over all. Thankfully I don't subscribe to such ambitions of the fittest. I prefer to give my voice to the creatures that speak to me in silence and share my void.

1 min

SURE YOU CAN ASK ME A PERSONAL QUESTION DIANE BURNS 1983

How do you do?
No, I'm not Chinese.
No, not Spanish.
No, I'm American Indi- uh, Native American.
No, Not from India.
No, we're not extinct.
No, not Navajo.
No, Not Sioux.
Yes, Indin.
Oh, so you've had an Indian friend?
    That close.
Oh, so you've had an Indian lover?
    That tight.
Oh, so you've had an Indian servant?
    That much.
Oh, so that's where you got those high cheekbones.
Your great grand-mother, eh?
Hair down to there?
Let me guess - Cherokee?
Oh, an Indian Princess.
No, I didn't make it rain tonight.
No, I don't know where you can get Navajo rugs real cheap.
No, I don't know where you can get peyote.
No, I didn't make this - I bought it at Bloomingdale's
Yes, some of us drink too much.
Some of us can't drink enuf.
This ain't no stoic look
This is my face.

378 Pacific
Bklyn 11217

718-

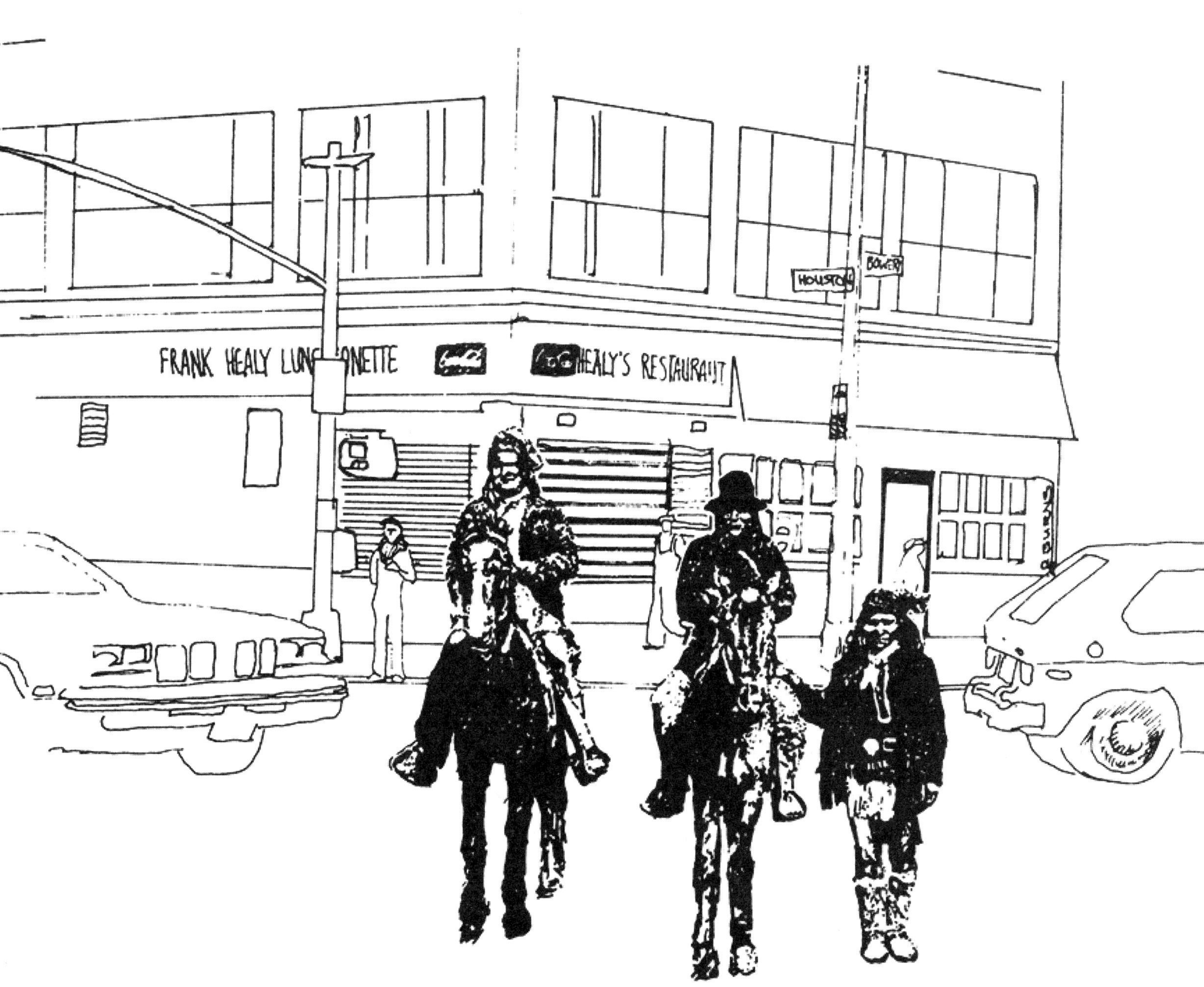

Diane Burns, “Sure You Can Ask Me A Personal Question,” 1983

DIANE BURNS INTERVIEWED BY JUSTINA MEJIAS

Justina Mejias:

My name is Justina Mejias. And today is November 20, 2003. I'm twenty-nine years old and I'm in Grand Central Station interviewing my friend Diane Burns.

Diane Burns:

Hi, I'm Diane Burns. I'm an adult female. I'm in New York City. It's getting cold. So I think it's around winter. They tell me it's 2003. Not the temperature but the year.

JM:

Great. So first of all, I'm very interested in where you grew up. Can you tell me a little bit about that?

DB:

I was born in Kansas. I'm what they call a Haskell baby. My mother was Chippewa or Anishinaabe or Ojibwa. My father was Chemehuevi, from the desert between California and Arizona. They met in the middle of their territory, right in the center, in Kansas, and I was born there. Then we went to live with my father's people in California. We would go back and visit my mother's family and live with them for a while. My parents were child psychologists, which makes me a PK. It used to mean "preacher's kid," but now it means "psychologist's kid."

JM:

So you lived in two different places when you were growing up?

DB:

Yes, two very different places. My mother's people are forest people. And they have very well-developed three-dimensional brain concepts, which makes them very attractive to the military. They get recruited an awful lot. My father's people are desert people who also get recruited a lot because they have an incredible store of survival techniques.

JM:

Do you know much about any of your ancestors?

DB:

Oh yes. Yes, indeed. The "Burns" comes from a great-great-grandfather who was a Scot—from the same place that Robert Burns came from. Robert Burns came from Argyll, Scotland. Anyway, Charlie Burns, who's my great-great-grandpa, came from the same place. So perhaps they were related, I don't know.

JM:

And on your mother's side?

DB:

My mother's family name is Gaoshkibos. That was anglicized to Barber. The little compound she lives in now is called Barbertown, where all our relatives live. Not *all* of our relatives: I mean, "all our relatives" is the whole reservation and most of southern Canada and the northern United States. The clan that we belong to, the Whitefish clan, is particularly known for lawyers, politicians, religious leaders, and that sort of thing. Intellectuals, in other words. We're not particularly known for being warrior people. We're more known for sneaking around people. In fact, the Chemehuevi, my father's people, are also known for that. The Apache name for us was "those little short people." Those short, sneaky people. Most people think American Indians are just skulking around in the desert or wandering around in the woods or something like that. But my family are judges and lawyers and marine biologists and freshwater biologists and social workers. I mean, most people think Indians never have jobs. They think we're wandering around with bows and arrows in the woods.

Anyway, could I read a little bit of fiction? It's kind of making fun of the whole concept. It's from a novel I've been working on called *Tequila Mockingbird*. This is from chapter one, "Tequila's First Shot":

I am Tequila Mockingbird. Yes, I'm related to Isaiah Mockingbird. And yes, I'm the face in the moon on the cover of the Carson CD. And I'm the marshmallow beer girl. And that's me on every stick of North Lakes butter. You'll see me now and again on the backs of paperback novels, the kind you buy and lose in airports. You can see my screaming face dodging the sabers of the seven cavalry on westerns, romances, potboilers, spider-punk, Gothic romances, Western Gothic thrillers, bodice rippers, whodunits, and sci-fi.

But enough about me. How about yourself? What kind of white person are you? Substitute black, brown, or yellow as it applies. I can trace my lineage back to the beginning of time, when the world was nothing but a scrap of mud on the tip of a loon's nose. Knowing who my parents' parents' parents were does not, however, help me know any better than you just who I really am. All I can do is lay the pieces of the puzzle face up and try to figure out the pattern they make up. I am Anishinaabe, which means human being, female. Just a plain old creature of this earth. A humble name for people who call themselves Shnaabes for short, which rhymes with snobs by coincidence. I know this because everyone says so, even themselves. And I love them very much and wish I could be with them always. And I miss them very much in New York City, where I've lived for twenty years.

My name is the result of a long-ago powwow where I was conceived over, or under, a bottle of tequila. I suppose I should be happy my name is not Jose Cuervo, and things could be worse. My paternal grandfather was the famous Isaiah Mockingbird, that great old Indian fill-in-your-preference: writer, painter, poet, spy. Or, if you're more ethnically inclined: potter, silversmith, rug maker, totem pole carver. I'm not being facetious. We all at some time have done many different things to survive.

I, myself, besides modeling, have played the guitar and sung, painted lewd graffiti on the streets of the Lower East Side, read plays in the Village, and appeared in numerous bad movies and worse TV shows. The thing I do worst and am paid the most for is modeling my ethnically accurate face. My ethnically accurate body has never been in quite the same demand.

It all started when I became a young woman. My family, I believe, had a dream of me becoming the first Indian Miss America. The nearest town was Hayward, Wisconsin, the muskellunge capital of the world. A muskellunge is a big, huge freshwater game fish. Since Hayward was the nearest town, I would have had to enter the regional pageant first, before going on to the state competitions. And I worried about the future. "What could be worse than being a former Miss Muskie?," I asked my cousin Lucy. "Being runner up," she said. Well, that sure gets the competitive juices flowing. "Could always be worse," she reminded me. "Be glad you're not from Webster." "What's that? The big mouth bass capital?" "Nope." "Walleye?" "Worse, crappie."

I'd like to skip the sordid details of those glory days and fast-forward to my days in New York where no one knows or cares about my totemic relationship with the muskellunge. I'm sure my family, should you ever meet them, will fill you in on all the facts, adding that, although I no longer represent that big proud fish, I certainly drink like one now.

JM:

And that's what you've been working on lately.

DB:

Yes.

JM:

Wow. How did you get to New York City? When did you come here?

DB:

Well, when I was fifteen, I came to White Plains or Westchester or someplace like that. I attended an alternative school. Then I went to a boarding school in New Mexico when I was like sixteen, seventeen, eighteen. That was the Institute of American Indian Arts in Santa Fe. After that, I came back here to New York, to Barnard College and Columbia University. I was going to be a lawyer. But by the time I was entering law school, I knew so many lawyers, and I knew I didn't want to be like one of them. So I took a leave of absence and never went back.

When I was a kid, I always wanted to be a writer or an artist. I thought about comics as an in-between kind of thing. And I did a few things in that direction, like poetry in comic strip panels. I liked that a lot. I'm still doing a lot of art that has comic-y aspects to it. And my writing, unfortunately, also has that tendency to it. As a writer, I always admired the hard-boiled detective novels. I wanted to write like Raymond Chandler, Dashiell Hammett. But just like with my paintings, I would try to make them very realistic. Whenever I would paint a horse, for instance, it looked like a stuffed animal. The same thing happens with my writing, unfortunately. I would really like to be very realistic: a super-realist in writing, and to have a hard edge and a gritty kind of persona. Instead, I ended up with a stuffed animal and a silly grin on his face.

JM:

I'm going to go back to before you came to New York City, when you were growing up. Were there any memorable characters that influenced your life that you remember from growing up?

DB:

Most of the memorable characters were in my own family. For instance, my uncles. I had many uncles. My mother was the only female in her generation. I mean, now I have aunts because everyone got married. But to begin with, my uncles were a big influence on me. And my cousins, of course. I have one cousin who's a freshwater biologist. She's always running off to Russia, to Lake Baikal, to test the amoebas in the system. And she told me about this pyramid system, where you assume humans are at the top, amphibians at the bottom with the reptiles and everything like that. She was one of the first people to realize frogs in Minnesota and Wisconsin were suddenly being born with like three legs or five legs, or three eyes, or eyes in the back of their ears. When these "lower echelon" beings start having deformities like that, it means trouble for people—beings, I should say—higher up on the pyramid. I have another uncle, my Uncle Dick, who was like a spiritual leader, and my Uncle Buck, who was also a spiritual leader. But they're very different people. My Uncle Dick was a very quiet guy. And my Uncle Buck was a really bluff, hearty kind of guy.

JM:

You say that two of your uncles were spiritual leaders. How did that manifest?

DB:

Well, for us, the entire universe is our church. It's not like we go to church every Sunday and sit down and be religious. It's all the time and all the world. Every day is, for us, being in church and being spiritual. Every simple action we take has a religious significance to us, and a spiritual meaning. For instance, for thousands of years, we had to kill meat to eat. But we always thanked the animal for sacrificing its life for us so that we could eat. We also made it a promise that we would see that its offspring would be protected and grow up and reproduce. It was a reciprocal relationship. We all understood that. Even with the plants: we would tell them, "Well, we're harvesting you now, but we will spread your seed, and your offspring will grow." This is a part of our lives and something we always understood from when we were little, bitty babies.

JM:

How does that spirituality work in your community? Was it something that everybody pretty much believed in? Or were there different factions of it?

DB:

There were different factions. For instance, there were Christian Indians and there were some who were traditionals. When my great-grandmother died, she was a traditional but she'd been living in a Christian house, so the spiritual leader who was serving our family at that time, he wouldn't go in the house for the funeral because it was a Christian house. That was another of my uncles, my Christian uncle. He became a Roman Catholic, and he named all his chickens after saints. So there was St. Barbara and St. Catherine and St. Elizabeth. The rooster was St. John. St. John would always run after me. When he'd see me in the yard, he'd run after me and spur me in the ankles with his rooster claws. I was so happy when we chopped up St. John's head. We had him for Sunday dinner. I was so happy.

JM:

Are there any other funny or memorable stories you remember from your childhood?

DB:

Oh, I could tell you about the day we moved the outhouse, but my aunt made me promise not to tell that. Yeah, there's lots of funny stories. I mean, sociologists tell us that Native American Indians are people who laugh the most in a group together. And I've noticed that that's true. Whenever there's a bunch of us together, the jokes just fly back and forth. That sort of mentality is really prized—to be able to tell a good joke and a good story is something prized in our society.

JM:

Do you feel that influenced your writing, that component?

DB:

Yeah, I think it couldn't help it. Most people think, *Oh, you're the poorest of the poor, you have the highest suicide rate, the highest mental illness, alcoholism rate*. But those are just statistics. What they don't hear about is the fun and the jokes that happen there.

Oh, I can tell you about trapping. That might be interesting. We did a lot of trapping for pocket change when we were kids because if you could catch a fox, the tail would be $25, which was an enormous fortune for a kid. But usually we'd get like $2 for a little muskrat skin. Which would be like, say, if you got a New York City rat and skinned it. It would be that size. Anyway, my brother had this dog that was really stupid. His name was Wally. He walked into a trap. He got a muskrat trap on his foot. I saw him on top of the hay piles, you know, to feed the horses. And I'd say, "Wally, come here, come here." He wouldn't come here. I'd go up and I see the trap on his foot and the big chain hanging off of his leg. I can't get it off his foot. So I take it to one of my uncles' houses. Wally jumps into the couch, just like he's entitled to: *I'm injured, please take care of me*. My uncle pries off the trap, and he's got two toes that are kind of smashed. And my other brother had a pet frog named Gomer. So Wally walks over and eats Gomer. *I'm entitled, I'm sick*. Anyway, there was a battle between brothers after that.

JM:

Needless to say! I was hoping to talk a little bit more about spirituality. What does that term mean to you?

DB:

Well, this always reminds me, our term for Great Spirit is Gichi-Manidoo. Not Mani*tou*, which is the way it is spelled in most English translations, but Gichi-Mani*doo*. I remember I was a girl scout in California and they were reading [Henry Wadsworth] Longfellow: "By the shores of Gitche Gumee / By the shining Big-Sea-Water / Stood the wigwam of Nokomis / Daughter of the moon, Nokomis." And I went up to the leader and said it's not Gichi *Gu*mee. It's gichi-gum*ee*. She was saying to me, "Don't correct us. You're a little kid." I was saying "No, no, this is the way you pronounce it. My mother's Chippewa. That's her language. She knows what it's pronounced like. It's gum*ee*, not *gu*mmy." If you mispronounce something and say "bour-gee-osie" instead of "bourgeois," people are going to think you're stupid, but because it's a Native American language, when you correct them, they think it doesn't matter. That really upset me when I was a kid, that they would not take correction. They did not want to know what the real truth was, even in just pronouncing a word.

JM:

What do you think that was about?

DB:

Cultural imperialism and a snottiness that is kind of endemic in Southern California. But also this religious thing. I'm a third-generation boarding school kid. My parents went to Indian boarding school, I went to Indian boarding school, my grandparents went to Indian boarding school. When my grandparents went, they were literally rounding up kids from the reservations, taking them from their parents as young as four and five years old, shipping them in cattle cars hundreds of miles away to someplace where they didn't know anybody. They weren't allowed to speak their language. If you spoke your language to somebody else who spoke the same language, you were beaten, you were kicked, you were smacked and put into solitary.

My grandmother said, "I tell them what it was like, they look at me like I was crazy. They made us march in lines like we were in the army." These are little kids—five, six years old. They don't know any English. My grandma would describe some of the things that happened to her. Like sometimes some of the kids would misbehave so much, they'd have to be put in a hole. They were hoping to be sent home. But some of the funniest things she told me were when kids would rebel and they would start yelling at the matrons and the attendants, yelling at them with terrible Indian words. And all the other kids would be laughing because they all knew what they meant but none of the other kids did. You'd have kids from all different nations: Navajos, Apaches, Chemehuevis, Mojaves, Hopis. They all speak different languages. Even if you speak the same language—for instance, if you're Navajo, if you come from Shiprock, you're going to speak a little bit different than somebody who's from Tuba City.

JM:

So you feel there's a lot of ignorance on the part of outsiders?

DB:

Oh, absolutely.

JM:

How does that make you feel?

DB:

Well, it makes me feel like an outsider myself. But I'm the most inside here in the continent. On one hand, I feel like I'm the landlord of this continent, but it's not really me owning land, it's more like the land owns me. People who think they own the land here are really mistaken. I feel sorry for them in a spiritual sense, but in a physical sense I wish I had their money.

Everyone here is an immigrant except for me. My spirituality helps kind of hold me up. Because I know this isn't going to last forever. I mean, it's like my deep-down belief that Indians have been here, we always have been here, we always will be here. When everyone else is gone, we'll still be here. I used to live in this really multiracial, multiethnic house in Brooklyn. There were Indians, people from Nairobi, people from Colombia—all over the globe. We were sitting in the living room, and me and my Apache girlfriend were saying, "Well, we're just all waiting for you guys to go. You guys are going to be gone pretty soon. And all of us Indians will just be here." And everyone started laughing at me. The girl looked at me and asked, "Why do they always laugh when we say that?" We were wondering, *Why do they doubt us?* We know. It's not even something we Indians talk to each other about; we just know, no matter what, we're going to be here when everyone else is gone.

JM:

You use the term Indian. Is that a term that you're comfortable with?

DB:

It's a term that encompasses a bunch of people who aren't really related, but are all in the same continent. For instance, they call us all sorts of things. They call us red ankles and redskins and heathens and screaming heathens, and all sorts of things like that. Let's see, in Europe, there are three language families. In just the United States there are seven language families, with three hundred different languages being spoken. So it's not like we all understand each other to begin with. We were all different people to begin with. But as a pan-racial ethnic group, we all understand each other in the United States now. That is part of the consequences of colonialism. What happened was, the boarding school system forced us all to communicate between each other. All of a sudden, we were in a school. We were all Indians, but we were all different nations: Ponca, Cherokee, Chemehuevi, Cheyenne, Lakota, Chippewa. All together, not speaking any common language, and all of a sudden we're all speaking English because they forced us to. Once we started speaking English together, that became our common bond. So now we have Indian jokes that are in English. In fact, one of the main musical expressions we have is called a forty-nine song. It's an Indian song, but it uses English words, so everyone understands it.

JM:

Do you have any examples of something like that?

DB:

Sure. Okay, now this is a real old one. This comes from 1869. No, 1848. Now, in 1849, there was a big gold rush in Oklahoma. And the Indian men would tease the Indian girls about looking like forty-niner girls. That's how that term forty-niner came about. There's also a story that the forty-nine songs were made in honor of warriors. Fifty warriors went out and only one came back. The one made up the honor songs for the forty-nine who didn't return:

I don't care if you're married I still love you
I don't care if you're married
When the party's over
I will take you home in my One-Eyed Ford
Way yah hi yah, Way yah hi yo!

Modene!
the roller derby queen!
She's Anishinabe,
that means Human Being!
That's H for hungry!
and B for frijoles!
frybread!
Tortillas!
Watermelon!
Pomona!
Take a sip of this
or drag of that
At the rancheria fiesta
It's tit for tat!
Low riders and Levis
go fist in glove!
Give it a little pat
a push or a shove
Move it or lose it!
Take straight or bruise it!
Everyone
has their fun
when the sun
is all done
We're all one
make a run
hide your gun
Hey!
I'm no nun!
'49 in the hills above
Ventura
Them Okies got a drum

I'm from Oklahoma [claps rhythmically]
I got no one to call my own
if you will be my honey
I will be your sugar pie, way hi yah,
Way yah hey way yah hi yah!

We're gonna sing all night
bring your blanket

or

be that way then!

JM:

That was so awesome. Thank you. That was from 1869?

DB:

Well, yeah, those songs in particular were. There are all kinds of variations that go with it. That was my poem "BIG FUN," for my book *Riding the One-Eyed Ford* (1981). That incorporated two old forty-nine songs, one called "One-Eyed Ford" and the other one just called "Sugar Pie."

JM:

How has New York been? Thinking about the perceptions you had before you came here and what it's turned out to be, how do those differ?

DB:

People don't realize how much of New York is Indian country. For instance, I was in the 50s working for an accounting firm. I stopped in a bar to make a phone call. I turned around and this guy said, "You're an Indian, aren't you?" I say, "Yeah." He says, "I'm an Indian too." I looked around. He said, "We're all Indians here." And they were all Mohawk steel workers who are like, "Yeah, we're all working on the building across the street." I just had the greatest time connecting with other Indian people here. Not only the Mohawks, there's a lot of different nations who have representatives here. And it's not just because of the United Nations here.

JM:

Did you not expect that when you came here? Did you not expect to find solidarity in that way?

DB:

No, I actually expected more. I thought it would be a lot easier to connect with people. And I found it a lot more difficult. Now it's become a lot easier because there are just a lot more Indians now. For instance, in the Village, Eric Oxendine said, "It was you, me, Roland Moose, and Buffy Sainte-Marie. If you saw an Indian back then you'd run out down the street after them." That was a long time ago, but it was true. It was very unusual to see another Indian back then.

JM:

If you don't want to talk about this, that's fine, but I'm curious to ask you about drug use, actually. I'm curious what your first introduction to drugs was in general? What did you get out of them?

DB:

For me, drugs were something I was introduced to gradually, and it was more a result of me living in a certain neighborhood and having certain acquaintances than it was my ethnicity, for instance. Alcohol was actually the first drug I experimented with, but it became the biggest drug I experimented with.

I think that's everybody's experience throughout the world, since alcohol is the most addictive and long-term destructive drug on the planet. But it's also the drug Jesus worked his first miracle to produce. There's a lot of contradictions with alcohol that I don't feel qualified to address. But I find it very funny to contemplate all the different aspects of it. Especially when I'm drunk.

Even tobacco is a medicine. For us, it represents the physical manifestation of prayer. It comes from our hearts, inside our lungs, comes out of our mouth up to the heavens. It's a physical manifestation of prayer. That's why you always see the quote-unquote "peace pipe" being passed around. This is what we use to solidify or concretize prayer. It all depends on the respect you show the plant that it came from.

JM:

I know you've been living with the Krishnas lately. What is that like for you?

DB:

Well, it's part of their religion to believe that they really know what the answer is, and that it's their duty to proselytize. For me, I'm not sure the answer is anything so simple. Maybe it is. I don't have any trouble with thinking that words have power. For instance, in the movie *Dune*, Paul Muad'Dib discovers his word is a killing word and, funneled through a certain machine, it destroys things. By chanting the name of Krishna, they believe that this is one of the names of God, and this is a way of reaching [God] by chanting his name. It's pleasing to God, in other words. I don't have any problems with that. And I don't think that Gichi-Manidoo cares what I call him one way or another. I do think he objects to being called Manitou instead of *doo*.

JM:

I'll have to remember that.

DB:

It's like when people call me Diana instead of Diane—it's just a personal quirk.

JM:

Are there any other practices or beliefs that are part of your life at this point?

DB:

I think a respect for other beings and not thinking myself elevated because I'm a human being. I mean, I realize I really have to work on it. Because sometimes I can be as much of a racist as other people can be. I mean, one thing I used to always hurl at my husband, or ex-husband, is, "I know you're not a human being. But you could treat me better in this way or that way." I was trying to make allowances for him, which was really condescending.

JM:

And what was he, white?

DB:

Yes.

JM:

Do you have any regrets?

DB:

I talked about this with our mutual friend, Jade, whether we had any regrets. We both agreed that the big regret we had was hurting the feelings of people who meant only the best for us. Hurting people who loved us, or even just people who wanted good things for us. For one reason or another, we couldn't avoid hurting them. I know when I was younger, I was very oblivious to other people's feelings. But I mean, that's true of other people also, to my feelings. What goes around comes around. I just wish the wheel wouldn't turn on me.

JM:

I know, that's karma for you. Is there something about yourself that you think nobody knows?

DB:

Boy, I don't think so. I would hope so. I hope I have some mystery into my old age. For instance, I used to live on Perry Street, and there was this building across the street. The guy who owned the building wrote "Dog of the Ilk" on top of it. I think the building is owned by Virgin Records now, which is a weird thing to begin with. But anyway, he said he was the only person who knew what that meant, "Dog of the Ilk." Carl Jung also had an inscription on one of his buildings, and he was the only one who knew it. He said it was very important that each and every person had one secret that they never told to anybody else. I've always been trying to figure out what my secret is, and how I can keep it a secret.

JM:

What have you learned from life?

DB:

I have learned that no matter how good you are, bad things will happen to you. No matter how bad you are, good things will happen to you. I also learned that there's no one of us who has not eaten while another has starved. There is no one of us who has starved while someone else is eating and hasn't felt resentful. But there's no way around it. That's just the way the world turns. And you just try to live your life as well as you can, or as well as you think you can, and get through it. I'm just looking forward to the next level.

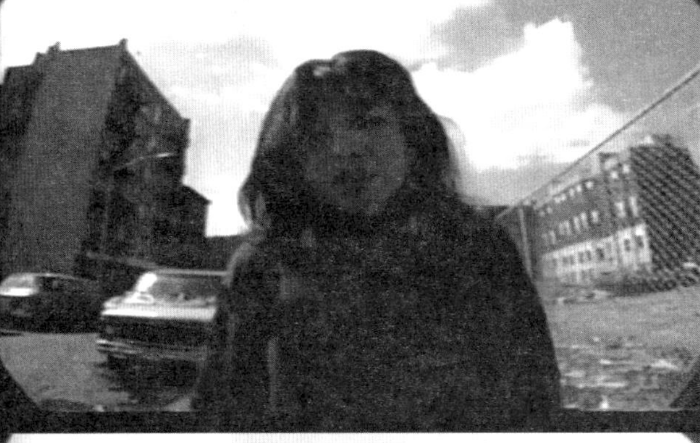

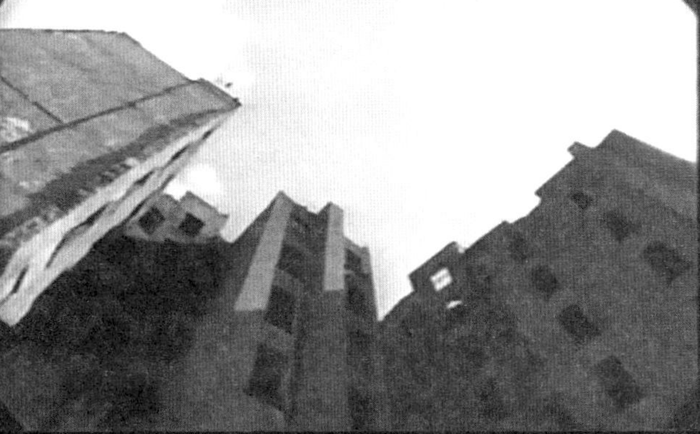

DIANE BURNS, STILLS FROM *POETRY SPOTS: DIANE BURNS READS "ALPHABET CITY SERENADE,"* 1989

This interview is excerpted from a conversation that took place in 2003. It was recorded as part of the launch of StoryCorps and was originally published in the magazine *A Gathering of the Tribes*.

Justina Mejias is a Boston Conservatory trained jazz & blues vocalist, slam poetry champion, and arts educator who was an originator of the StoryCorps project.

Traces of Ecstacy

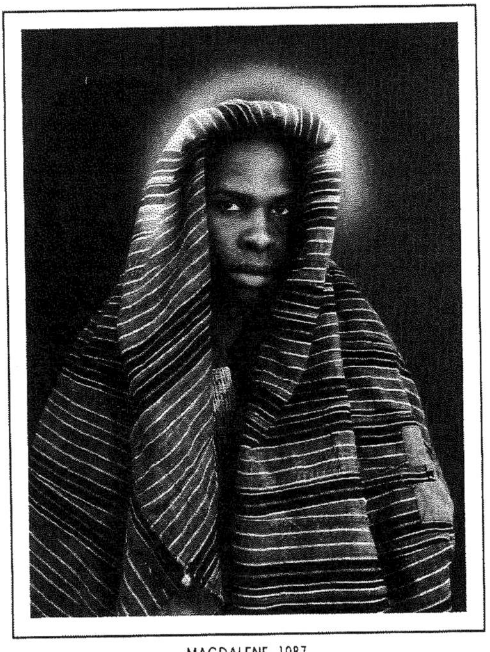

MAGDALENE. 1987.

Rotimi Fani-Kayode

It has been my destiny to end up as an artist with a sexual taste for other young men. As a result of this, a certain distance has necessarily developed between myself and my origins. The distance is even greater as a result of my having left Africa as a refugee over 20 years ago.

On three counts I am an outsider: in matters of sexuality; in terms of geographical and cultural dislocation; and in the sense of not having become the sort of respectably married professional my parents might have hoped for.

Such a position gives me a feeling of having very little to lose. It produces a sense of personal freedom from the hegemony of convention. For one who has managed to hang on to his own creativity through the crises of adolescence and in spite of the pressures to conform, it has a liberating effect. It opens up areas of creative enquiry which might otherwise have remained forbidden.

At the same time, traces of the former values remain, making it possible to take new readings on to them from an unusual vantage point. The results are bound to be disorientating.

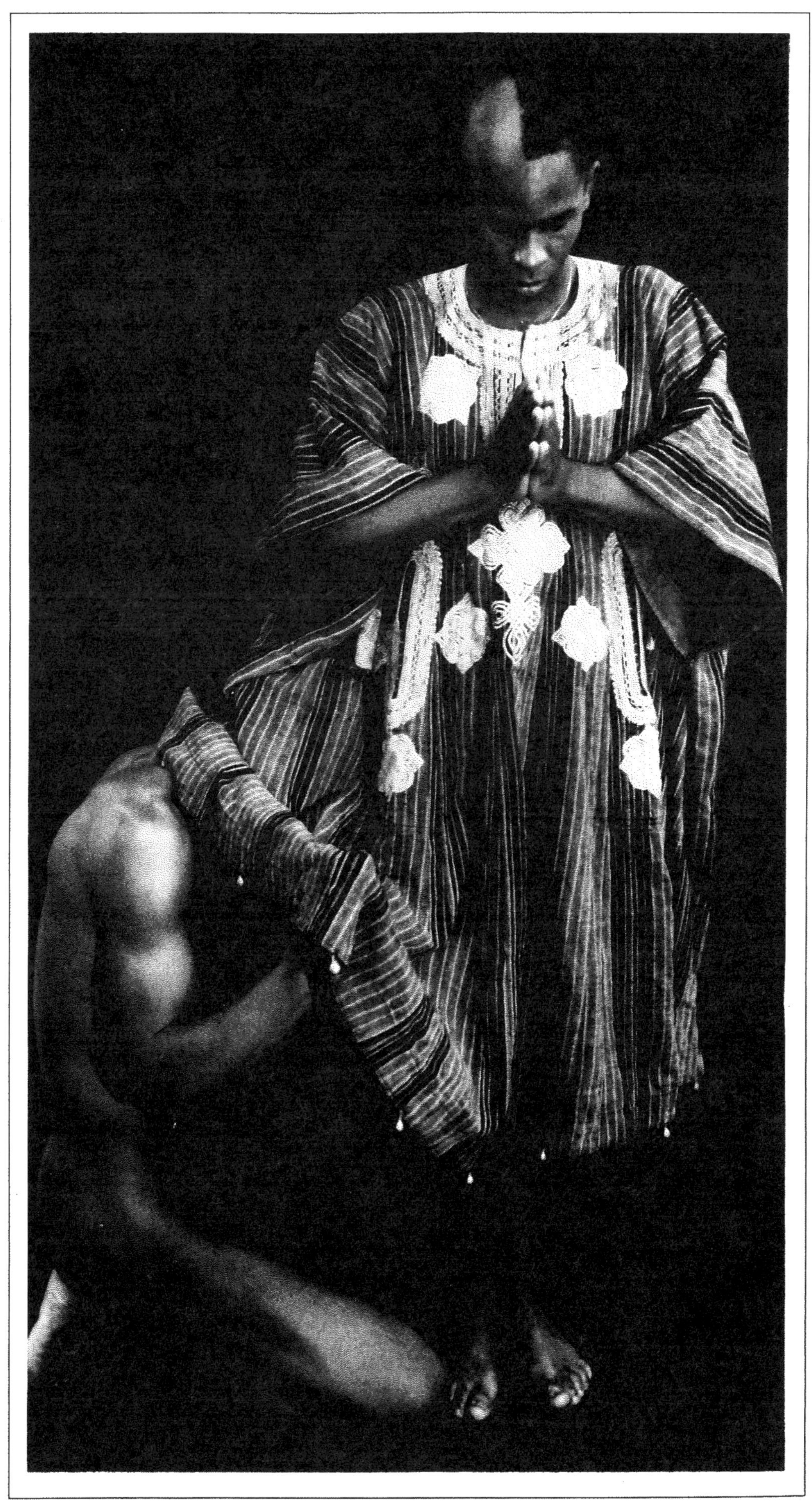

UNDER THE SURPLICE. 1987.

Rotimi Fani-Kayode, "Traces of Ecstacy," published in *Ten.8 International Photography Magazine* No. 28, 1988

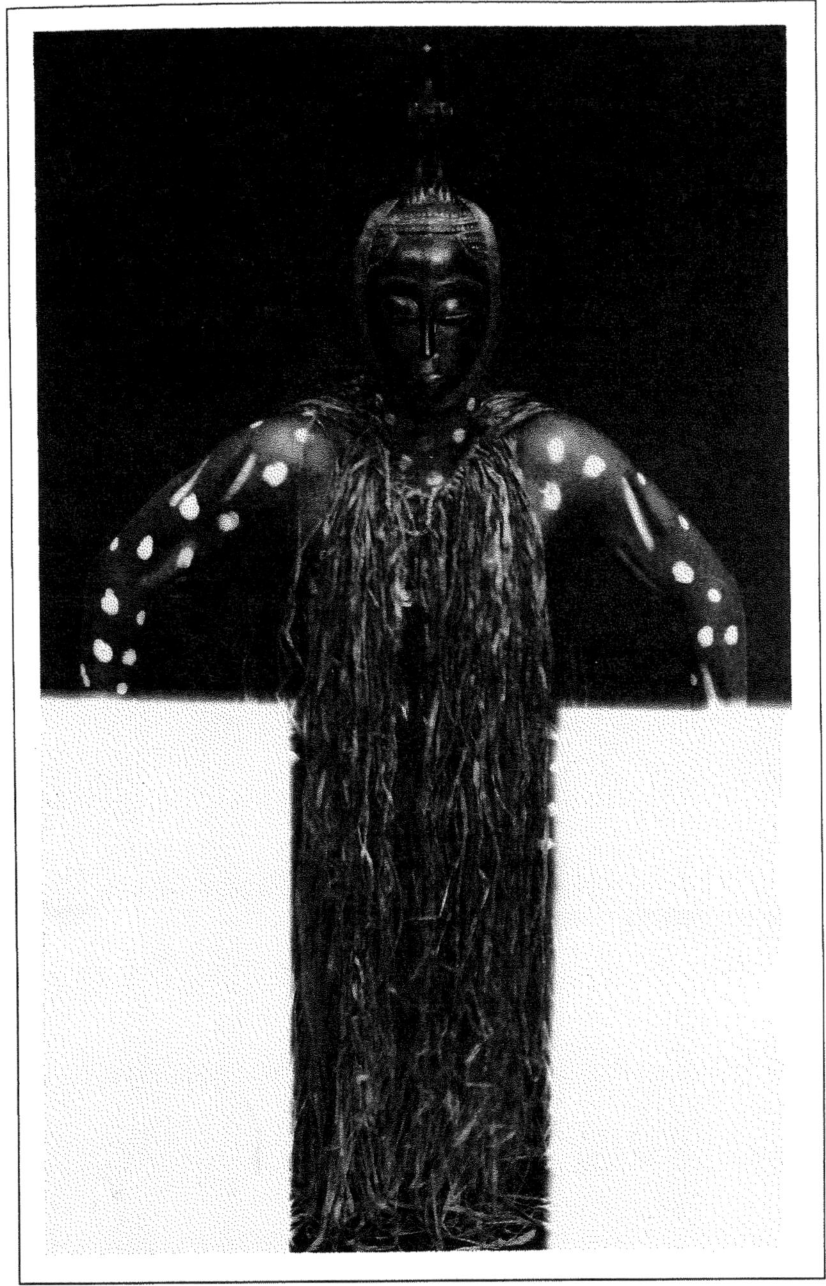

BABAOLUAYE (PRAISE-NAME OF THE SMALLPOX GOD). 1987.

In African traditional art, the mask does not represent a material reality: rather, the artist strives to approach a spiritual reality in it through images suggested by human and animal forms. I think photography can aspire to the same imaginative interpretations of life.

My reality is not the same as that which is often presented to us in Western photographs. As an African working in a western medium, I try to bring out the spiritual dimension in my pictures so that concepts of 'reality' become ambiguous and are opened to reinterpretation. This requires what Yoruba priests and artists call a 'technique of ecstasy'.

Both aesthetically and ethically, I seek to translate my rage and my desire into new images which will undermine conventional perceptions and which may reveal hidden worlds. Many of the images are seen as sexually explicit - or more precisely, homosexually explicit. I make my pictures homosexual on purpose. Black men from the Third World have not previously revealed either to their own peoples or to the West a certain shocking fact: they can desire each other.

Some Western photographers have shown that they can desire Black males (albeit rather neurotically). But the exploitative mythologising of Black virility on behalf of the homosexual bourgeoisie is ultimately no different from the vulgar objectification of Africa which we know at one extreme from the work of Leni Riefenstahl and, at the other from the 'victim' images which appear constantly in the media. It is now time for us to reappropriate such images and to transform them ritualistically into images of our own creation. For me, this involves an imaginative investigation of Blackness, maleness and sexuality, rather than more straightforward reportage.

However, this is more easily said than done. Working in a Western context, the African artist inevitably encounters racism. And since I have concentrated much of my work on male eroticism, I have also had homophobic reactions to it, both from the white and Black communities. Although this is disappointing on a purely human level, perhaps it also produces a kind of essential conflict through which to struggle to new visions. It is a conflict, however, between unequal partners and is, in that sense, one in which I remain at a disadvantage.

For this reason, I have been active in various groups which are

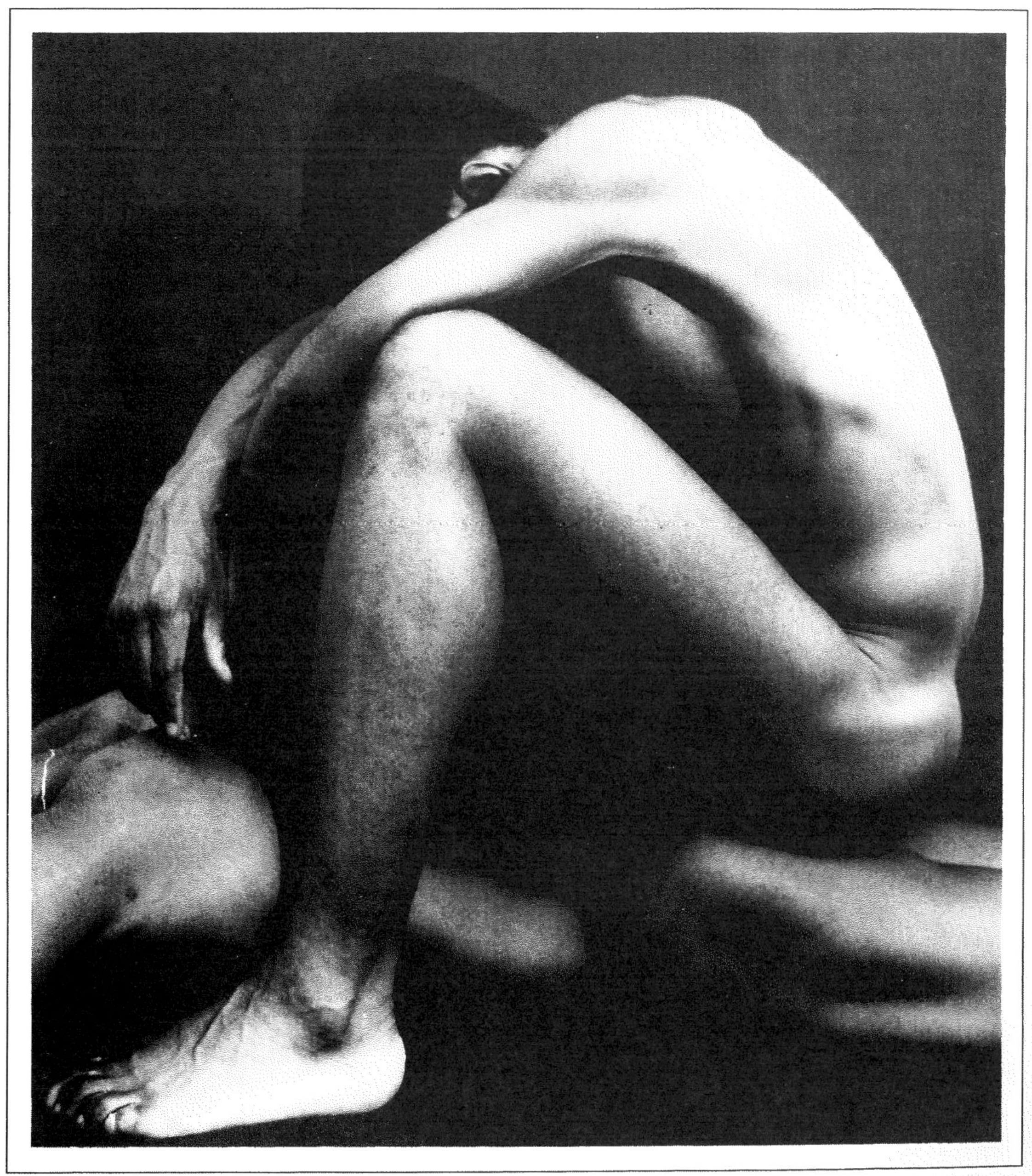

TECHNIQUE OF ECSTACY. 1987

Rotimi Fani-Kayode, "Traces of Ecstacy," published in *Ten.8 International Photography Magazine* No. 28, 1988

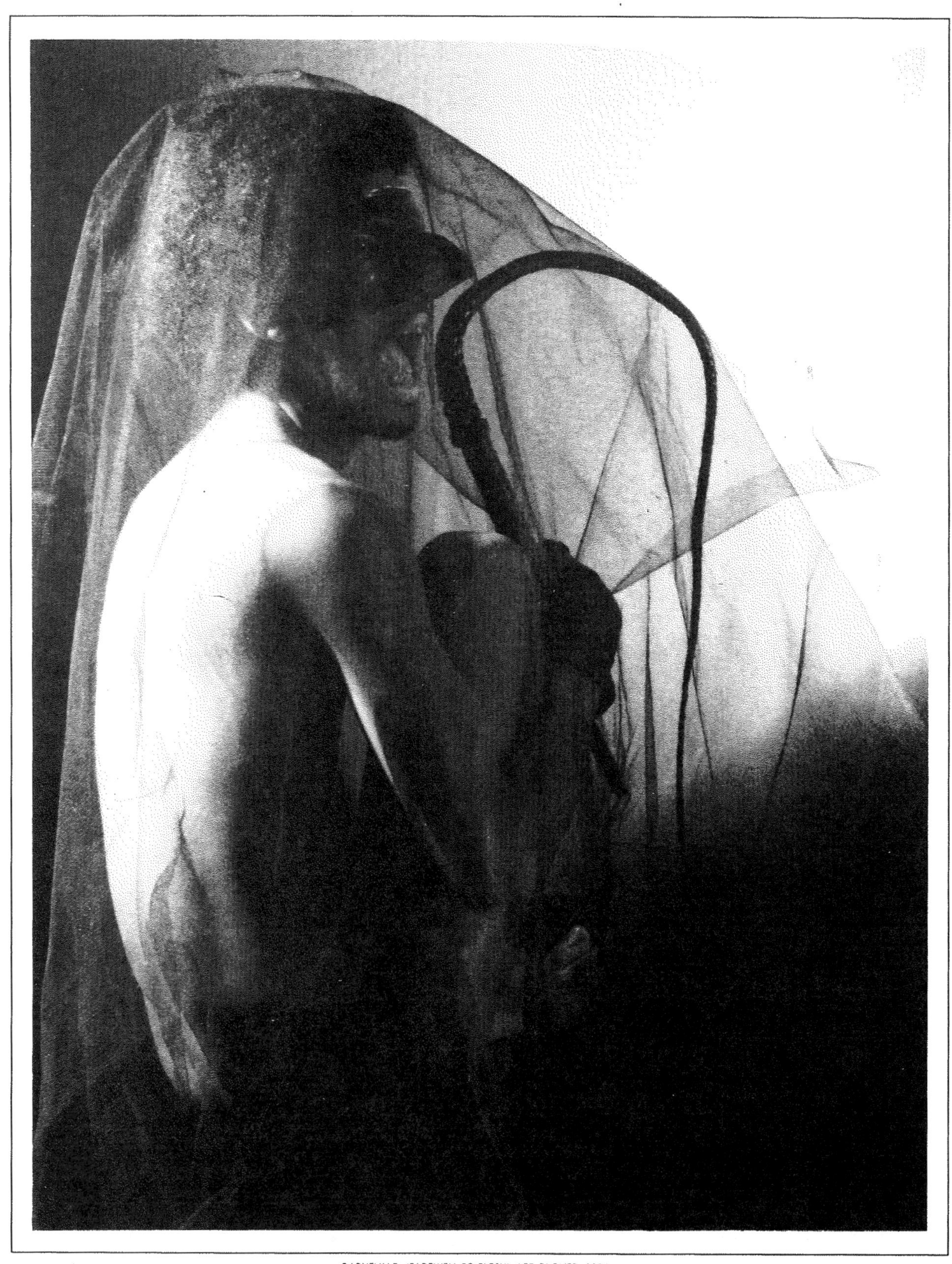

CARNEVALE, (FAREWELL TO FLESH), LEE CLOVER, 1984.

organised around issues of race and sexuality. For the individual, such joint activity can provide confidence and insight. For artists, it can transform and extend one's Westernised ideas - for instance, that art is a product of individual inspiration or that it must conform to certain aesthetic principles of taste, style and content. It can also have the very concrete effect of providing the means for otherwise isolated and powerless artists to show their work and to insist on being taken seriously.

An awareness of history has been of fundamental importance in the development of my creativity. The history of Africa and of the Black race has been constantly distorted. Even in Africa, my education was given in English in Christian schools, as though the language and culture of my own people, the Yoruba, were inadequate or in some way unsuitable for the healthy development of young minds. In exploring Yoruba history and civilisation, I have rediscovered and revalidated areas of my experience and understanding of the world. I see parallels now between my own work and that of the Osogbo artists in Yorubaland who themselves have resisted the cultural subversions of neo-colonialism and who celebrate the rich, secret world of our ancestors.

It remains true, however, that the great Yoruba civilisations of the past, like so many other non-European cultures, are still consigned by the West to the museums of "primitive" art and culture.

The Yoruba cosmology, comparable in its complexities and subtleties to Greek and Oriental philosophical myth, is treated as no more that a bizarre superstition which, as if by miracle, happened to inspire the creation of some of the most sensitive and delicate artefacts in the history of art.

Modern Yoruba art (amongst which I situate my own contributions) may now sometimes fetch high prices in the galleries of New York and Paris. It is prized for its exotic appeal. Similarly, the modern versions of Yoruba beliefs carried by the slaves to the New World have become, in their carnival form, tourist attractions. In Brazil, Haiti and other parts of the Caribbean, the earth reverberates with old Yoruba rhythms which are now much appreciated by those jaded Western ears which are still sensitive enough to catch the spirit of the old rites. In other words, the Europeans, faced with the dogged survival of alien cultures, and as mercantile as ever they were in the days of the Trade, are now trying to sell our culture as a consumer product. I am inevitably caught up in this.

Another aspect of history - that of sexuality - has also affected me deeply. Official history has always denied the validity of erotic relationships and experiences between members of the same sex. As in the fields of politics and economics, the historians of social and sexual relations have been readily assisted in their fabrications by the Church. But in spite of all attempts by Church and state to suppress homosexuality, it is clear that enriching sexual relationships between members of the same sex have always existed. They are part of the human condition, even if the concept of sexual identity is a more recent notion.

There is a grim chapter of European history which was not drummed into me at school. I only discovered much later that the Nazis had developed the most extreme form of homophobia to have existed in modern times, and attempted to exterminate homosexuals in the concentration camps. It came not so much as a surprise but as yet another example of the long-standing European tradition of the violent supression of otherness. It touches me just as closely as the knowledge that millions of my ancestors were killed or enslaved in order to ensure European political, economic and cultural hegemony of the world.

I see in the current attitudes of the British Government towards Black people, women, homosexuals - in short, anyone who represents otherness - a move back in the direction of the fascistic values which for a brief period in the 60s and 70s ceased to dominate our lives. For this reason I feel it is essential to resist all attempts that discourage the expression of one's identity. In my case, my identity has been constructed from my own sense of otherness, whether cultural, racial or sexual. The three aspects are not sepasrate within me. Photography is the tool by which I feel most confident in expressing myself. It is photography, therefore - Black, African, homosexual photography - which I must use not just as an instrument, but as a weapon if I am to resist attacks on my integrity and, indeed, my existence on my own terms.

It is no surprise to find that one's work is shunned or actively discouraged by the Establishment. The homosexual bourgeoisie has been more supportive - not because it is especially noted for its championing of Black artists, but because Black ass sells almost as well as Black dick. As a result of homosexual interest, I have had various portfolios printed in the gay press, and in February a book of nudes will be published by GMP. Also, there has been some attention given to my erotic work by the sort of straight galleries which receive funding from more progressive local authorities.

But in the main, both galleries and press have felt safer with my 'ethnic' work. Occasionally they will take on board some of the less-overtly threatening and outrageous pictures - in the classic liberal tradition. But Black is still only beautiful as long as it keeps within white frames of reference.

I have been more disconcerted by the response to my work from certain sections of the self-proclaimed avant-garde, however. At the recent MiSFiTS exhibition at Oval House (which happened to coincide with the unveiling of a plaque to commemorate the birth there of Lord Montgomery of Alamein) I was asked, along with other artists, to remove my work in case it attracted unfavourable publicity for Oval House. We refused, naturally. Unfortunately, the press were too busy paying homage to Monty so the national reputation of Oval House was saved, and we were denied some free publicity. It is perhaps gratifying that the inadequacies of Oval House's Equal Opportunities Policy have since been recognised by many of its erstwhile supporters. But given the new Government ruling against local authority funding for any form of 'promotion' of homosexuality, I assume that, in any case, community organisations will no longer be allowed to show my work.

As for Africa itself, if I ever managed to get an exhibition in say Lagos, I suspect riots would break out. I would certainly be charged with being a purveyor of corrupt and decadent Western values.

However, sometimes I think that if I took my work into the rural areas, where life is still vigourously in touch with itself and its roots, the reception might be more constructive. Perhaps they would recognise my smallpox Gods, my transexual priests, my images of desirable Black men in a state of sexual frenzy, or the tranquility of communion with the spirit world. Perhaps they have far less fear of encountering the darkest of Africa's dark secrets by which some of us seek to gain access to the soul. ■

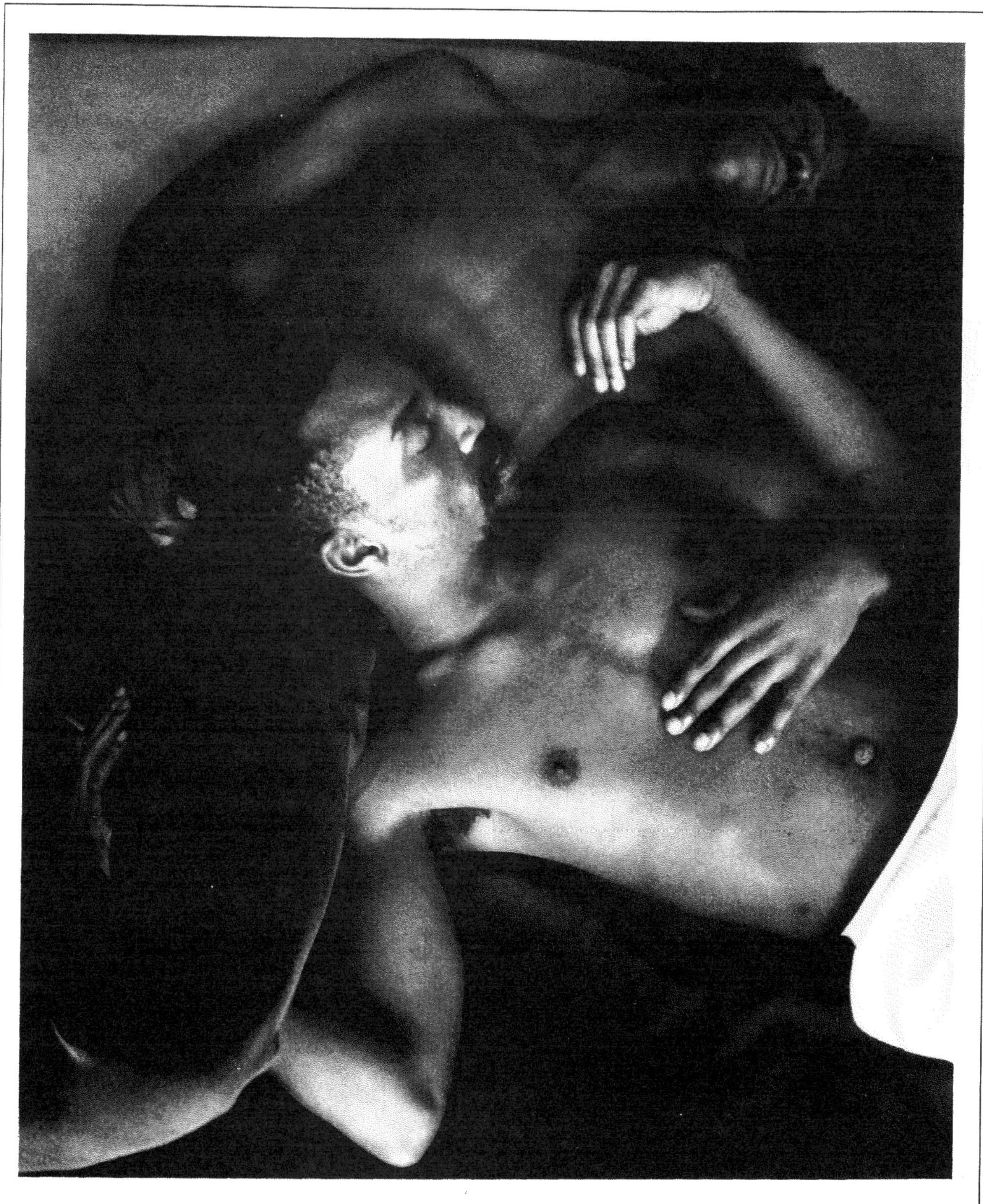

DENNIS CARNEY AND ESSEX HEMPHILL, 1986

Rotimi Fani-Kayode, "Traces of Ecstacy," published in *Ten.8 International Photography Magazine* No. 28, 1988

On a small patch
of hill in front of
the local dump is
where you can find friendship
The pastor says that a wise person Cemetery
celebrites
death it in the eye
and that the fool turns their back at it and looks away.
I think
about how being in
grief makes
me feel how I wish I felt on birthdays
That Im
suddenly wiser That a year has passed and Im a differ
My father would say the only thime he ever felt different Pers
was when he woke up on his 5th birhday

I feel like

I should draw Friendship Cemetery to show you how confusing the graves are here

It's as if someone said here its this dirt find any spot you can to hold your past

And people rushed to bury them

Some with no birthdate

Its funny across the street you can see Hollywood Cemetery its much nicer

Raque Ford, preparatory text drawings for *Hollywood Cemetery (I The Fool)* and *Friendship Cemetery (The Wise)*, 2021

The Doll Hospital

'When baby learns to walk keeps falling down. If never failed never tried.'

Hippie Runaway

Who am I

Engagement in World

Fracture -- Mirrors

Jamaica -- Stone -- Girl with Machete

A skill like a mechanical skill to learn how to operate a camera

A group of people stood outside a cage-like gate with iron bars 100 Yuan notes in their hands

Mud mountain roads + long narrow streams

My animal symbol is rabbit

When I asked Zhou -- an engineer -- what would he do if he could be anything in world he said be a tourist or journalist

Scared

Who I am

Refuge from suffering   Green chickens

Recovery -- rape group -- looking for self

Thailand Mickey Mouse shopping bags

Doing own thing

Anthropologists

Journalists

Literary writers

Poetry

Music

Actress

Photographers

Beautiful children

Radio people

Psychologists

TV news people

Humanitarian aid workers

Dead Boys   Richard Hell

Sonic Youth   wandering

A dangerous unpredictible world

What's my story

I watch a white boat named Pink Lady with all the happy people perched on deck

Who would my child have been?

A man whistling as he walks barefoot to the hut . . .

Pig toilets herbal

Medicine overland

Sleeping on a

mattress on the

floor of the

bus nightmare ride

from hell -- don't

want my pockets

picked

Looking for

solitude

Excerpts -- New York, December, 1996

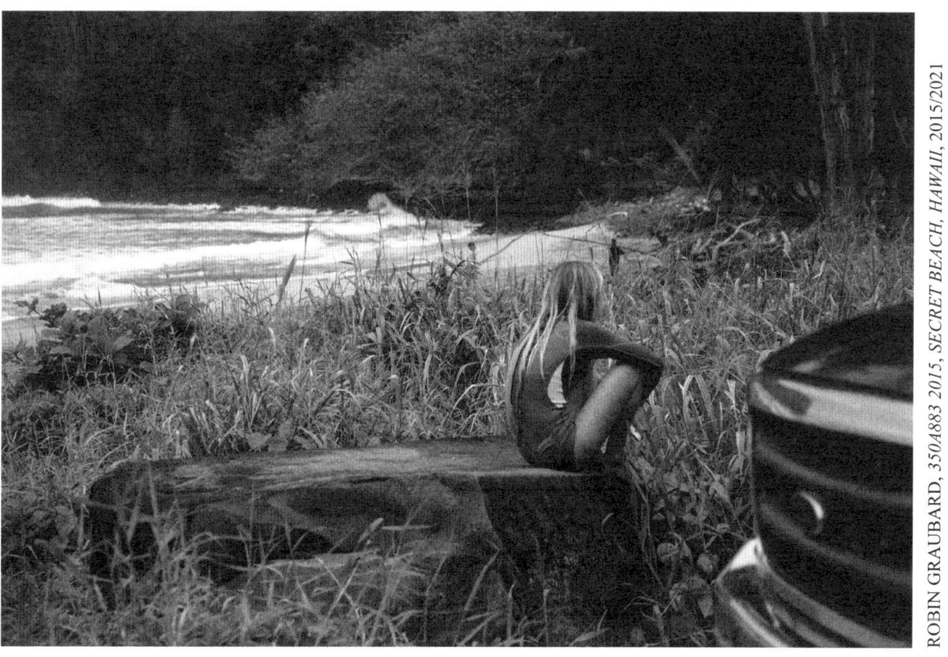

ROBIN GRAUBARD, *350A8883 2015, SECRET BEACH, HAWAII*, 2015/2021

ON SIMILITUDE
STEFFANI JEMISON

1. From when I was eight years old until I was about eleven, I thought I would grow up to be an actor. I would be pretty good if somebody would give me a chance, I thought. I often astounded even myself with my reckless capacity to identify with others. When I heard a sad song, I grieved inconsolably. When I watched a film starring a kid my age, I felt what she felt.

Moreover, I was never all that comfortable in my own skin. My self-conception—mostly shaped by the girls I read about in books like *Anne of Green Gables* or *Little Women*—didn't quite align with what I saw in the mirror. The first actress in whom I recognized a bit of myself was Rudy from *The Cosby Show*. Later, I studied Ashley from *The Fresh Prince of Bel-Air*. I could do that, I thought, as she sang, danced, and was showered with affection.

It didn't hurt that I liked to write and was a confident reader. This seemed important, since my conception of acting was fundamentally literary, textual, discursive. But there was a problem: when I spoke, I didn't know what to do with my hands.

2. The more I thought about my body, the weirder it became. When I raised a hand to emphasize a point or illustrate an idea, it felt forced, excessive. My hands, my elbows, my shoulders, my torso, my whole body felt dis-integrated from my thinking and speaking self. In some ways, this wasn't a surprise—I knew that my mind and my body didn't match up the way I wanted them to, which is why it was so easy for me to imagine myself as another person, as an actor. But this same misalignment led me to feel impossibly self-conscious about how I used my body when I talked.

3. With some dismay, I accepted that even when I didn't like what my body was doing, it was still doing something. The angle of my neck, the hunch of my shoulder, the strain at the edge of my mouth, the stiffness of my brow, the softness of my spine, the rigidity of my wrists—so many tics and gestures and tensions, too many to track, too wild to manage, and they all spoke as clearly as my voice. My eleven-year-old body felt inert and oppositional in relation to the possibility of some clearer and more streamlined ideal.

4. I wanted to act, but my body was in the way. How can a body be in the way? Bodies are the physical, biological origin of speech and language. But they also provide the friction through which language operates. I know, logically, that there is no voice, no thought, maybe even no language without the body to produce and contain them. So why does the body feel so much like resistance rather than ease? How can I find an easy body, an agile body, an agreeable body that can go anywhere or do anything? Can I slough off my excesses, my bents, my habits? Can I find within myself a neutral position?

5. The nineteenth-century movement instructor François Delsarte began sessions with exercises for achieving deactivation, release, or what he called "decomposition." His students included politicians, preachers, singers, stage actors, and other orators. The sessions were transcribed as follows:

- Let fingers fall from knuckles as if dead; in that condition, shake them. Vital force should stop at knuckles.
- Let hand fall from the wrist as if dead; shake it in that condition forward and back, up and down, sideways, rotary shake.
- Drop forearm from elbow as if dead; shake it. Vital force arrested at elbow.
- Raise arms above head, decompose them; in other words, withdraw force. They will fall as dead weights. Arms still hanging decomposed from shoulders, agitate body with a rotary movement. The arms will swing as dead weights; now change and swing body forward and back, allowing your knees to bend. The arms will describe a circle in their sockets. They must be decomposed.
- Drop head to one side decomposed; it will gradually describe a half-circle, moving from its own weight as you have seen persons asleep nodding.
- Beginning with the head, drop torso sideways decomposed. The head will draw the shoulder, and by degrees, with no conscious effort, the torso will fall. Do this first on one side, then on the other.
- Lifting foot from the ground, agitate it as you do the hand. Be sure the foot falls from the ankle decomposed.
- Decompose lower leg as forearm; agitate from knee.
- Lift leg from ground as a horse does in pawing, then drop it decomposed.
- Standing with your weight on back leg, bend that knee while bending your torso forward. Withdraw the will from back leg. The body will drop to the ground.
- Let eyelids fall as if going to sleep.
- Let jaw fall so you feel its weight; i.e., decomposed.

6. I am always unsettled to encounter the word "decomposition" in close proximity to a clinically detailed description of the cross-sections and bones and pieces of a person. Falling, nodding, dropping, hanging, withdrawal: these feel like steps and stages of ending, rather than ways to begin.

7. Delsarte's decomposed body is neutral insofar as it is mobile. As if all bodies are neutral—of equal value. As if all movements are available to all people at all times. If neutrality means something like available for or open to any action, the neutral body is a precondition of freedom.

There's another dimension to the ideal of neutrality in the actor's body: portability. An artwork—a painting, for example—can move between a gallery in New York City and a museum in Paris and the living room of a collector in Arkansas. With training, any body can learn to inhabit any gesture. The actor's body is like an artwork, portable. And it's also like a gallery, an arena that can host any character at all.

8. Last spring, I read an article in the *New York Times* that described the pernicious effects of Botox on empathy and memory: without the ability to physically mimic the expressions of others, our capacity to identify with them is degraded. (Is freedom the capacity to identify?) The report confirmed what we already know: that our bodies are in a constant dialogue, and that it is primarily through the activity of mirroring the actions and movements of others, whether consciously or unconsciously, that we come to understand them.

9. The twentieth-century acting instructor Jacques Lecoq was interested in imitation and yawning, both of which are infections, contagious, "catching." "When two individuals are having a pleasant conversation, they share behavior: side by side, they walk in step; when they begin to disagree, each one starts to walk at his own pace," he writes in *Theatre of Movement and Gesture* (1987). "If I cross my arms, or my legs, my interlocutor, without realizing it, will copy my gesture as he becomes more attentive and all the more so if he finds me hard to understand."

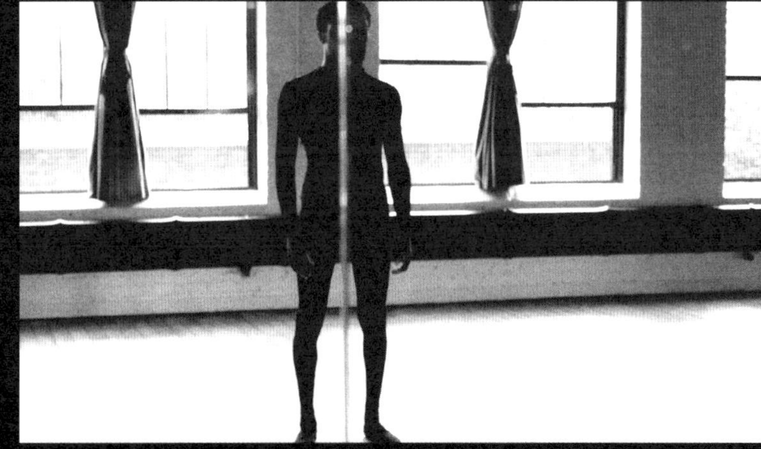

There is a classic acting exercise—also a popular children's game—called the mirror, in which two partners face each other. One is designated as leader, the other as mirror. The leader improvises movements carefully, slowly, and the mirror follows with absolute concentration. Such play can be amusing or absolutely maddening, depending on your perspective. But this use of the body is about something deeper than the endless reflection of surfaces and effects. After all, as Lecoq writes, quoting Aristotle's *Poetics*, "Man is, of all animals, the one most drawn to mime and it is through miming that he acquires all of his knowledge."

THE GOOD TERRORIST
MARIE KARLBERG

Alice:
I wonder if they'll accept us.

Jasper:
The question is not whether they will accept us, but if we will accept them.

Alice:
Jasper, stop it. It hurts.

Wow, Jasper! Look at this place. I mean, I never stayed in such a nice place before! I can't believe that we're squatting this. I mean, it's just standing here empty anyway. It should be given to the people that need it.

Jasper:
You don't seem to understand the value of property. You haven't even read Marx's "The Law of Value."

Alice:
They're motherfucking fascist pigs! They're fucking assholes! They did this to this place! They pulled out the cables, locked the gas, and filled the lavatory bowls with concrete! I don't understand how anyone would obey an order and destroy a house, especially when they're working class themselves! They did this.

Jasper:
We're not here to make ourselves comfortable. You're just like your mother. You gotta let go of those bourgeois inclinations.

Alice:
I just don't understand why we choose to live like this, not when it's so easy to organize in a better way.

Jasper:
Where's Burt?

Jasper:
Burt!

Burt:
Comrade Jasper, Comrade Alice.

Alice:
We spoke to him in there.

Burt:
Oh, Jim. Look, the situation has changed. My analysis was incorrect. I understand the political maturity of the cadres and when I put the question to vote, they decided against it. They left here at once.

Jasper:
Good riddance. Then they would have proven to be unreliable.

Alice:
Why did they leave? What was the question?

Jasper:
You know what the question was. I told you. We've decided to join the Anti-Imperialist Army, the AIA.

Burt:
That's correct. We're now offering our services to the AIA as the New York–based branch.

Alice:
That's why the others left.

Burt:
No, but look, this has been discussed and decided upon. We've had enough with the CCU and the soft politics. We've decided to reach out to the AIA, the military terrorist group, because we've decided that we need to take action into our own hands.

Alice:
But...that trash pile over there is a health hazard.

Burt:
That's what the police said. They were here last night.

Alice:
That's why the others left.

Burt:
No, they left because we're turning this into a militant squat, and they ran out shit-scared like little rabbits.

Alice:
So what did the police say?

Burt:
Well, they gave us four days to leave.

Alice:
Then why don't we go to the city council?

Jasper:
Here she goes again.

Pat:
Hey. I'm Pat. Burt told me about you two. Mm, brother and sister?

Jasper:
No, we're not.

Alice:
Thanks.

Why don't we go to the city council? We could pay for electricity and stay here.

Pat:
Well, everyone else in this house prefers this, um, romantic bohemianism.

Alice:
Romantic? You gotta be kidding me.

Burt:
It does go against the grain, negotiating with the establishment.

Jasper:
So does this mean that the commune is breaking up?

Alice:
Where did you get electricity to make that coffee?

Burt:
The squat next door.

Alice:
In Baltimore, a group of seven of us went to the city council over a house scheduled for demolition. We ended up paying for water, electricity, and gas, and stayed there for thirteen months.

Pat:
Hmm, good for you.

Alice:
And in Portland, I was in a negotiated squat for six months. It started out as a squat, but then the city council came to terms with it, and now, it functions as a student house. Why don't we go to the city council, ask them if we could pay for electricity and water, and then stay here rent free?

Pat:
I would, but I'm out. Like, I'm leaving. What the fuck did you expect? Basic meeting like that, these two, from the outside? We don't know shit about them. We don't know shit about the two from last week. Jim's here, he's not even CCU. I mean, when we started, we decided we would take individual approaches to each person. We said we would be careful. Is that what this is?

Burt:
It wasn't sudden, and anyway, you changed your mind. You were the one that decided working with the AIA was the logical thing to do.

Pat:
Look, I haven't changed my mind, but if I'm gonna work with the AIA, or anyone else, I better fuckin' know who I'm working with, right? Like, no offense, sis. Good old Burt here met you, what, at the CDU rally last Saturday? And two days later, you're here! I mean, sorry, that's just...and I do shit correctly.

Alice:
I understand, yeah, you don't know us and here we are, but let's get back to the house. Do I get a confirmation or not to ask the city council for electricity and gas?

Burt:
Alice, the lavatories are filled with concrete. The pipes are smashed and electricity is torn out.

Alice:
We can fix that. We did that in Baltimore.

Burt:
And who is going to pay for that?

Alice:
We are.

Burt:
Out of what?

Pat:
Shut the fuck up for once and be reasonable. Like, do the math. The money we spend on takeout or gym fees just to take a shower costs more than electricity and water, if we paid for it.

Alice:
There's one problem. In this borough, we need someone who's employed in order to guarantee expenses. Anyone working with a salary?

Pat:
Oh, yeah, the comrades who left last week.

Burt:
Comrades! The only thing that I would describe them as is opportunistic little shits.

Pat:
They happened to be very good, fine, comrades. They just didn't wanna work with the AIA.

Alice:
I mean, I could ask my mother.

Jasper:
Ha! Her mother, the bourgeois pig? Take the rich middle class for everything you can. Bleed 'em dry, that's my line.

Alice:

She's my mother and we stayed there for four years, remember? Why wouldn't she help me?

Pat:

No need to ask mine. I mean, I haven't spoken to her for years.

Burt:

Listen, are you fucking staying or are you leaving? Make up your mind.

Pat:

We have to talk about that.

Jasper:

So, you're really gonna ask your mother? I mean, to be the guarantor.

Alice:

Yes, and I'll get the others to contribute as well.

Jasper:

What if they refuse?

Alice:

Some will, some won't, but we'll manage, won't we?

Jasper:

And who's gonna do all the work?

Burt [in the background]:

Oh, comrade.

Pat:

Ohhh. [moaning]

Burt:

Oh, fuck. [moaning]

Alice:

Hey, Jim, if I go to the city council and we get permission to stay here, would you share expenses with us?

Jim:

They say I can't stay here.

Alice:

Why not?

Jim:

I've been here for eight months, eight months. I've been keeping my head down, keeping my nose clean, and then suddenly, I'm not politically involved enough to continue living here. I have no money. I've been looking for a job for weeks and months, and still nothing. You know that saying "first fired, last hired?" That applies to people like me, not Burt. It's here, otherwise I'm on the street. To get kicked out of the little nothing I have in the name of your system doesn't make a shred of sense to me. Clearly, I'm to be included or excluded, and it makes more sense to kick me to the curb than it does for us to figure out how to live underneath the same roof.

Alice:

Hello, Mom? Hello? Mom, please answer. Mom, it's Alice. Mom, are you there? Mom, look, I know you're angry with me, but please, just hear me out this once. You see, there's this squat, and we could do just what we did in Baltimore in getting the city council to agree on controlled squat basis. No, no, no, no, no, no, you don't have to pay for anything. Hello? Mom? Mom, are you there? Mom! Mom! Mom, I know you're angry with me. Yes, I know, yes, I know. I know that the last four years, having me and Jasper stay in your house, ruined you financially, and that you can't pay for anything. Yes, I know, Mom, but look, you have all those rich friends! Fuck, why can't you be more like us? We help each other out when we're in trouble. Mom! Hello, Teresa? Hello? Yes, I need to speak to Teresa. I don't care if she's in a conference meeting. Tell her Alice is calling. Get her on the phone now! It's an important matter. Hello, Teresa? It's Alice. Look, I need you to guarantee expenses. For a squat. No, no, no, no, you don't have to pay for anything, ever. It's only your signature we need. To guarantee for electricity and gas so we can stay there. I don't care about your shitty conference meeting! This is more important! What? Jasper's so good. He's a revolutionary. He's not selfish and bourgeoisie like you. Yeah, so what if we don't have sex? That's all you care about, is having sex with your shitty boyfriend and money to spend. No, I don't want your 500 bucks. No. I need your signature to guarantee for electricity and gas at the squat! $500. You spend $500 on a dress or a meal. No, I'm not being silly. Have you ever seen me spend $500 on a meal? You bunch of rich shits! Why's the door locked? Let me in! Jasper! Ow, ow! Let go of me! Ow, don't be stupid!

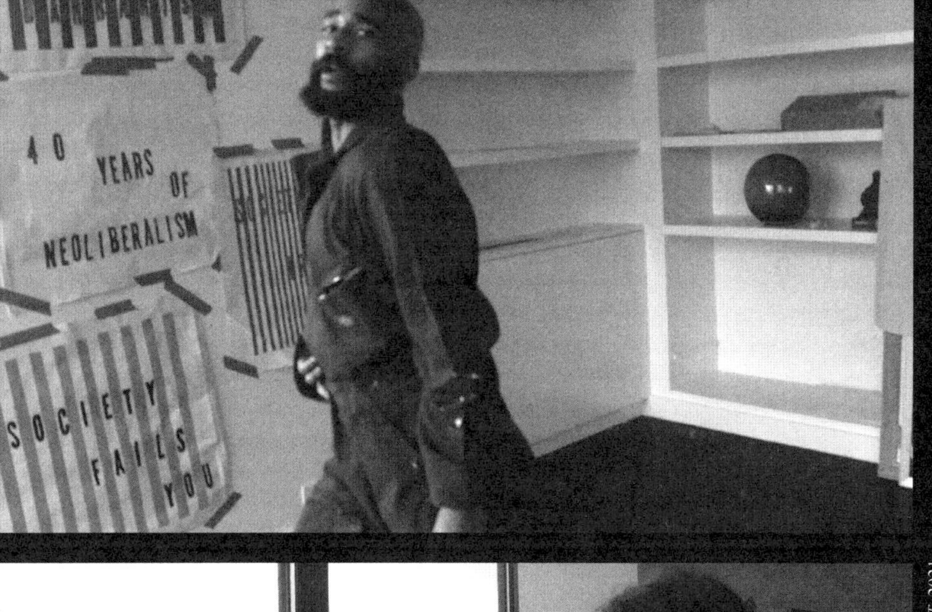

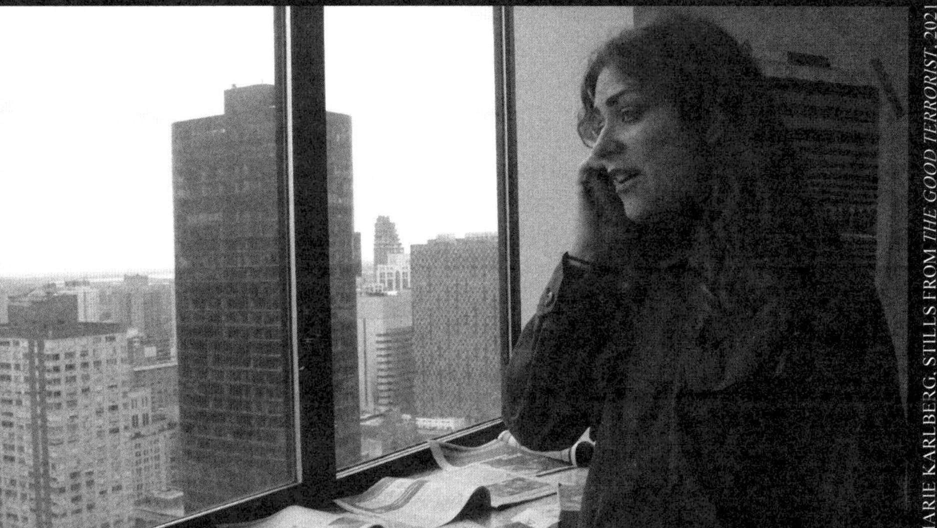

MARIE KARLBERG, STILLS FROM *THE GOOD TERRORIST*, 2021

This dialogue is excerpted from the script for *The Good Terrorist* (2021), a film by Marie Karlberg based on a 1985 novel of the same name by Doris Lessing. The book, set in 1980s Thatcher-era London, follows a young woman named Alice as she joins a group of radical leftists living together in a squatted apartment and negotiating how to practice collective politics.

RED LIGHT PROBLEM

MATTHEW LANGAN-PECK

Car door slams, engine starts, radio begins to play "Butter" by BTS]

First stop of the morning down, Dunkin'

Sings] Smooth like butter...

Sometimes I think I'm going to Dunkin' too much. So, today, I order my coffee on the Dunkin' app, I walk in, and my order's not sitting there in the pickup counter. So a guy I've never seen before—a night shift guy, I don't know—comes up to me and says "How can I help you, are you waiting for pickup?" Uh, and at this point my regular girl Mariam comes out the back and says to this guy, "Oh you don't know him yet? He comes here every day."

So, I might be going to Dunkin' too much. What can I say, I run on Dunkin'.

Sings] Sidestep right left...

Gotta go to Chase, gotta go to Home Depot, pick up a package at the post office, personal package, not work related. Luckily my boss is cool about that, I can run little errands for myself if it's on the way or like I'm going to Home Depot to get keys cut for him or something, I might pick up a few things for myself. You know, you gotta be efficient in this business because taking care of properties is a ton of work and you're basically on call all the time in case something goes wrong. And you gotta be an independent thinker, you gotta think on your feet, because there are so many random problems that come up. Really, you would be shocked at some of the stuff I have seen in my time working for this guy, seven years.

Anyway, I deal with some crazy people, and some cool people Uh, you really find out that people are like, so disgusting, and, let me put it this way, oftentimes in my job, you're not really seeing the best side of people because by the time they call me they're pissed off, they're stressed out...

Ok, what do we need today Peck? Uh, Home Depot we've got LED light bulbs, spackle, china white, and a bolt lock for Joey.

We've got the Fire Inspector at three.

We've got to go ask for rent again from Sixty-Seventh Street...

New toilet handle at Stratford Road. You know I tell this joke a lot, but it's true, if I had a nickel for all the times people told me their toilet handle is broken, like "The toilet is not flushing," and then I get Joey to go over there and it's the chain has come detached? I would be rich.

And, if it were my building, I would be happy to talk the tenant through it over the phone, say you know, open the top of the toilet? Is the chain still attached to the handle? Hook it back on. And then you are teaching a man to fish, you know, and shockingly, many people do not care to learn this type of stuff And really this stuff is all online, it's not like I'm a genius who knows how to do all this stuff without looking it up, but you gotta have the desire for knowledge and you gotta believe you can, you know, at least start these projects. And I think that confidence starts small and then it grows from there.

[Sings] Sidestep right left to my beat, high like the moon rock with me…

Vacation rentals, you know, that's where it's at in terms of real estate. Ok, so you get paid in advance, you don't have to deal with problem people long term, everybody is out of there in a week. If you get an agency or something like that, that handles part of it, it's basically passive income.

My uncle's friend, my boss, a couple of these real estate guys I talk to, they're like, "Ah you're still young, don't worry, you'll get that deal of a lifetime that will come your way. When you deal comes in front of you, you will know. Don't be impatient."

It's hard, I see myself more as a go-getter type guy. And I am saving for that first downpayment, but for now I'm kinda stuck a little bit.

[Slurps]

I finish one of those coffees and I want another one, and I want another one. Probably get one with lunch.

[Sings] Smooth like butter, like a criminal undercover, smooth like butter...

Ok, what is going on here? There's gotta be something wrong with this light, This light has been red for like five minutes. Come on.

[Car honks]

We've got one asshole going around me there, ok, good for you, have fun with that... I am not getting that ticket.

You know sometimes I've noticed the timing on these lights gets a little out of whack, and they change eventually, after whatever, a couple minutes. And this has actually happened to me where I've been waiting behind people, and maybe a light is taking a little longer than usual, and these people get so impatient, it's hilarious. I see them inching forward, inching forward, inching forward, and they turn on red! Which is no allowed in New York, and, I'm sitting there, two seconds later the light turns green.

Sometimes, you know, it's these people in from Long island or Jersey hitting these right-hand turns on red, and they don't even know that you're not allowed to do that here.

[Truck honks]

Ah shit, we got a truck, come on you can get around me, pull your mirror in. Come on.

[Truck honks twice, several cars honk]

It's a red light! What do you want me to do?

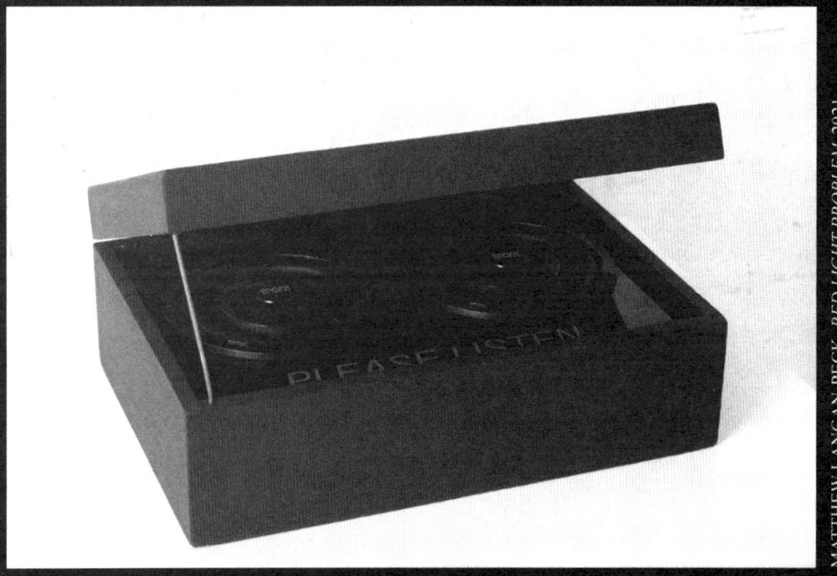

MATTHEW LANGAN-PECK, *RED LIGHT PROBLEM*, 2021

[Cars and truck honk together]

Ah, shit. He's not gonna do it, he's not even gonna try. What should I do?

[Truck honks, several cars honk]

Everybody is telling me to go through. Everybody is telling me that I should go through. I guess I should go through.

This text is a transcription of a monologue presented in *Red Light Problem* (2021), an artwork by Matthew Langan-Peck.

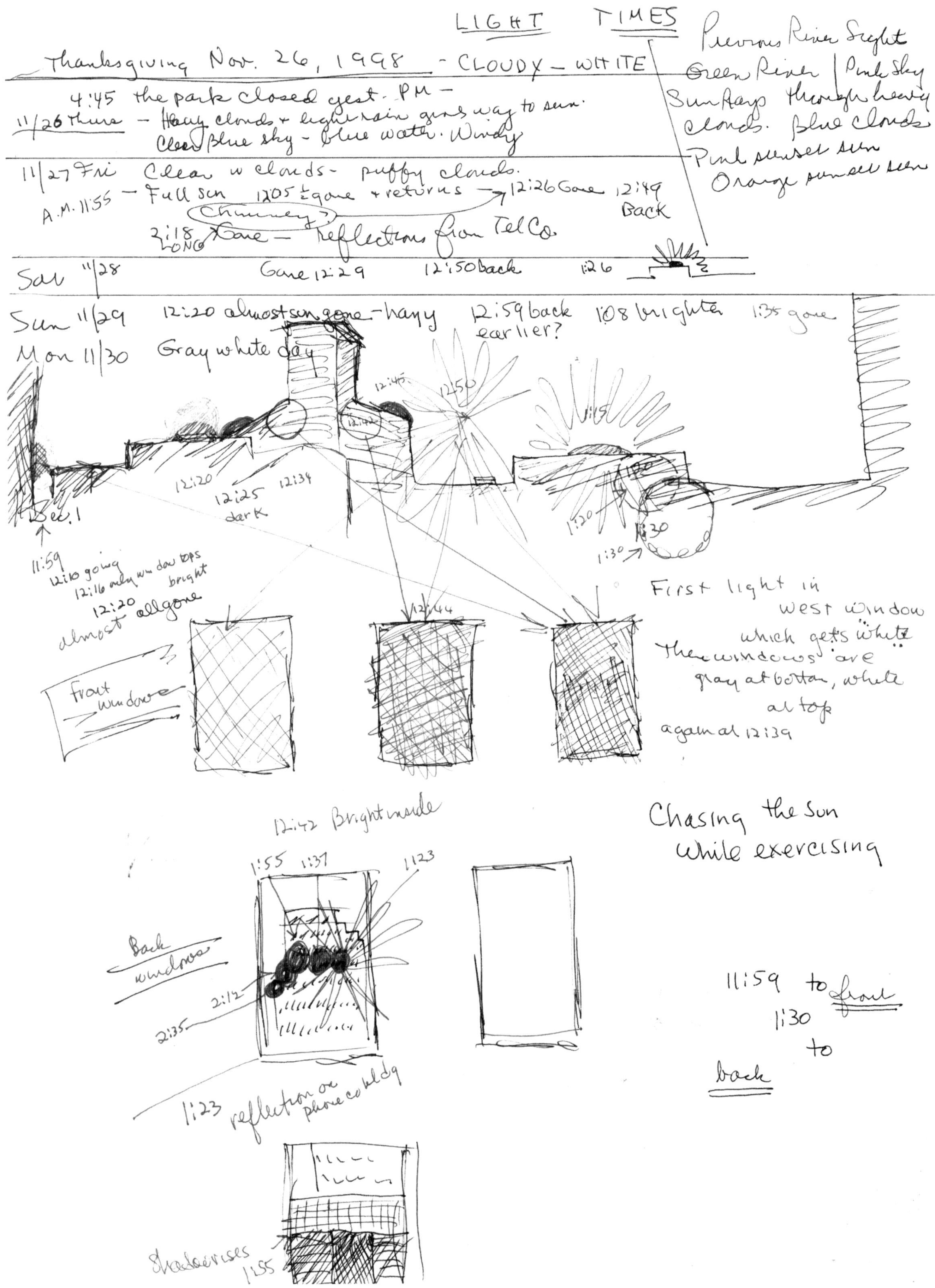
LIGHT TIMES
Thanksgiving Nov. 26, 1998 - CLOUDY - WHITE
4:45 the park closed yest. PM -
11/26 Thurs - Hazy clouds + light rain gives way to sun.
Clear Blue sky - blue water. Windy
11/27 Fri Clear w clouds - puffy clouds.
A.M. 11:55 - Full sun 12:05 gone + returns - 12:26 Gone 12:49 Back
Chimney?
2:18 LONG Gone - reflections from Tel Co.
Sat 11/28 Gone 12:29 12:50 back 1:26
Sun 11/29 12:20 almost sun gone - hazy 12:59 back earlier? 1:08 brighter 1:35 gone
Mon 11/30 Gray white day
Green River
Pink Sky
Sun Rays through heavy clouds. Blue clouds
Pink sunset sun
Orange sunset sun
12:20
12:25 dark
12:34
Dec. 1
11:59
12:10 going
12:16 only window tops bright
12:20 almost all gone
Front window
12:44
First light in west window which gets white
The windows are gray at bottom, white at top
again at 12:39
12:42 Bright inside
1:55
1:37
1:23
Back windows
2:12
2:35
1:23 reflection on phone co bldg
Chasing the Sun While exercising
11:59 to front
1:30 to back
Shadow rises 1:55

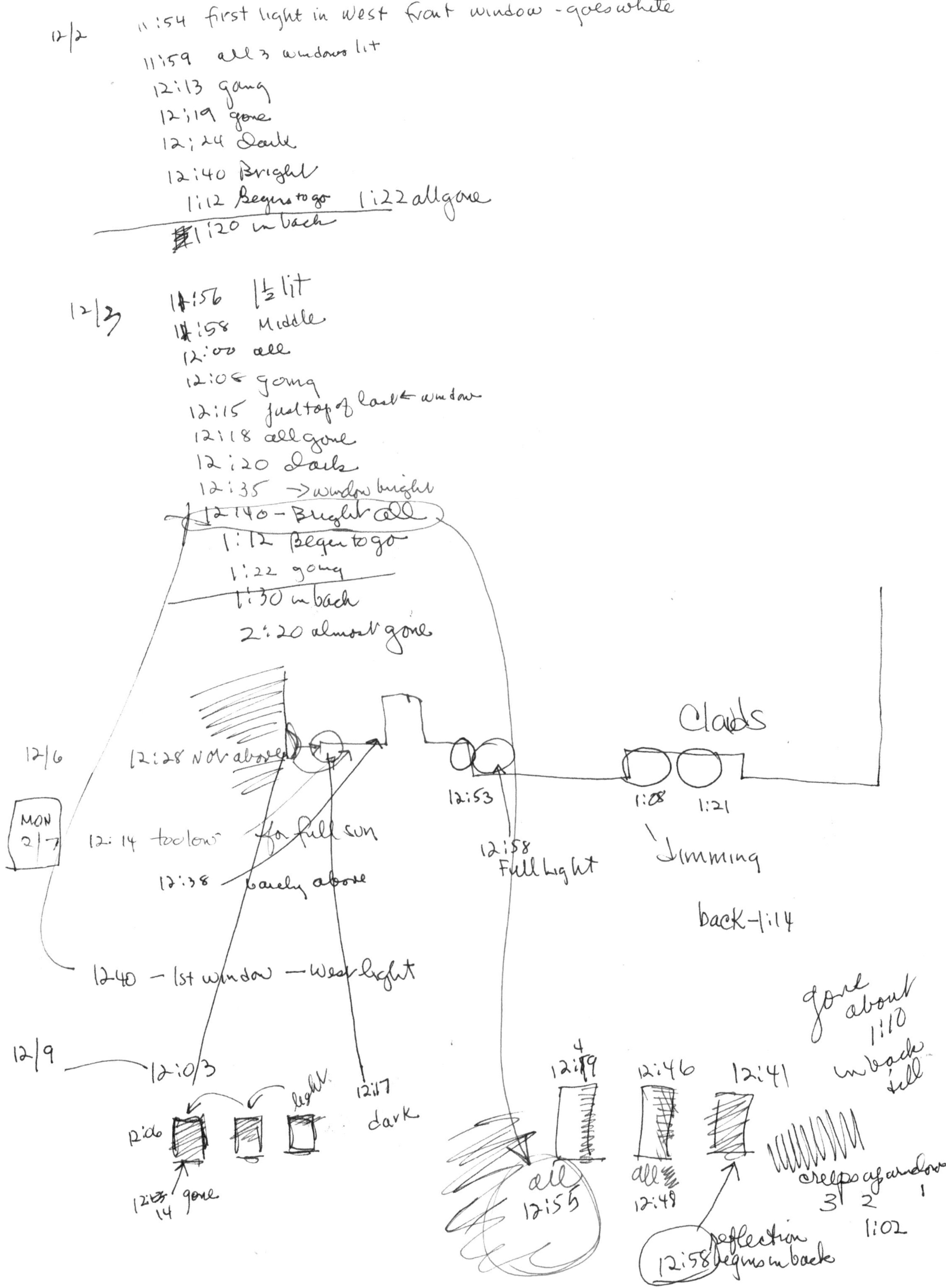

Rosemary Mayer, pages from sketchbook, 1998–2001

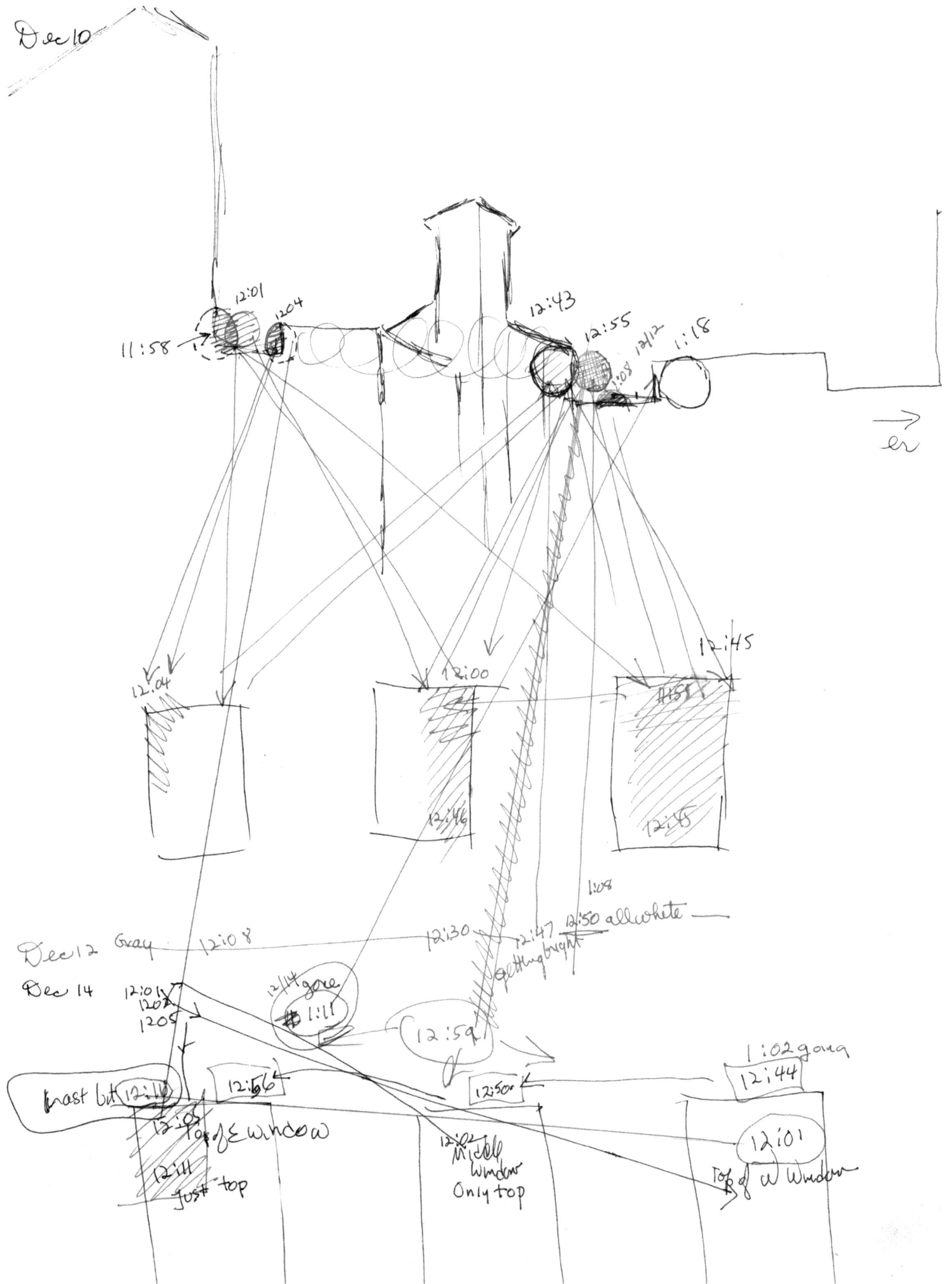

Dec 10
11:58
12:01
1204
12:43
12:55
1:18
12:04
12:00
12:45
12:46
1:08
12:50 all white
Dec 12 Gray
12:08
12:30
12:47
getting bright
Dec 14
1205
12:14 gone
1:11
12:59
1:02 gone
12:44
12:56
12:50
last bit 12:11
12:05 Top of E window
12:11 just top
Middle window Only top
12:01
Top of W window

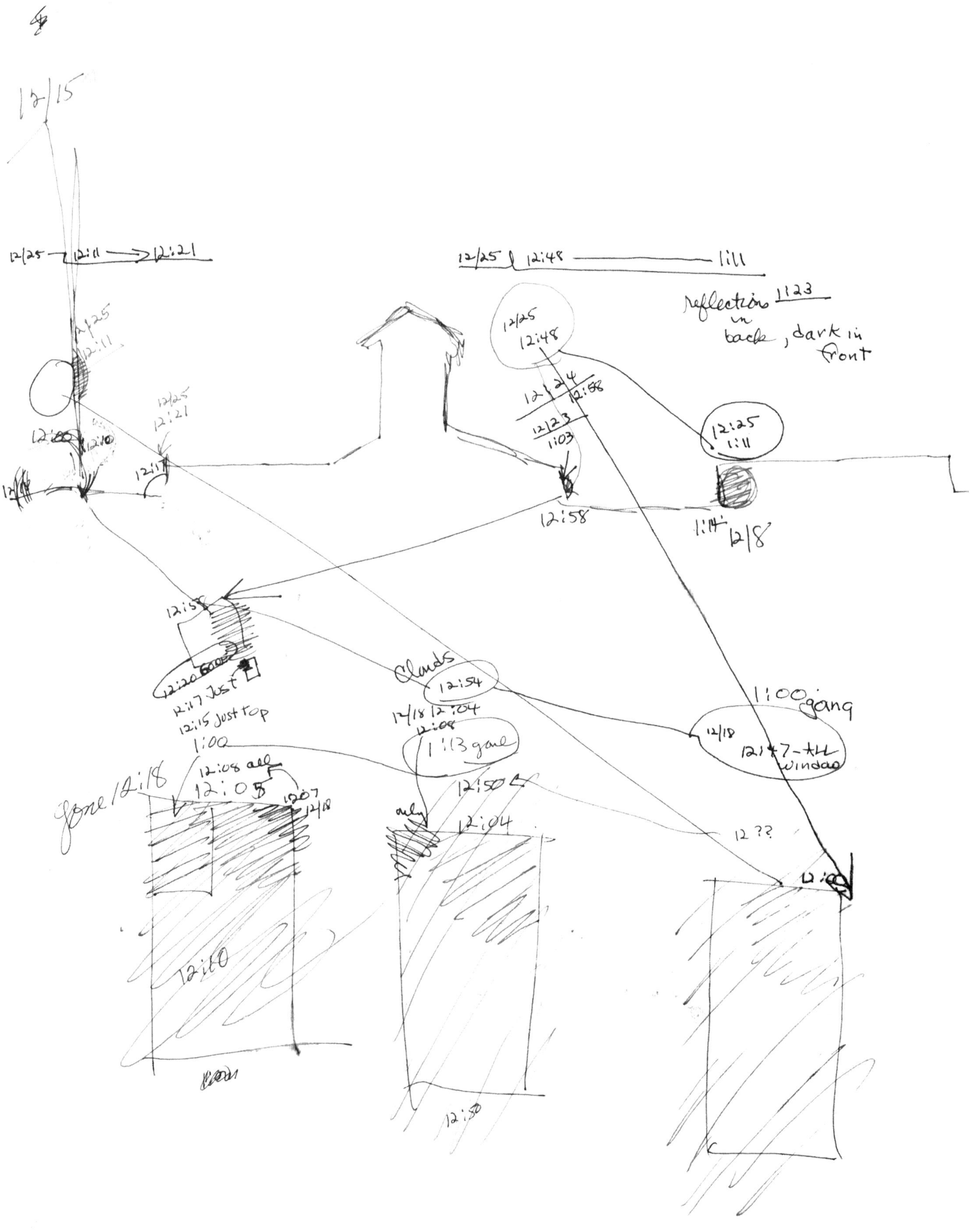

Rosemary Mayer, pages from sketchbook, 1998–2001

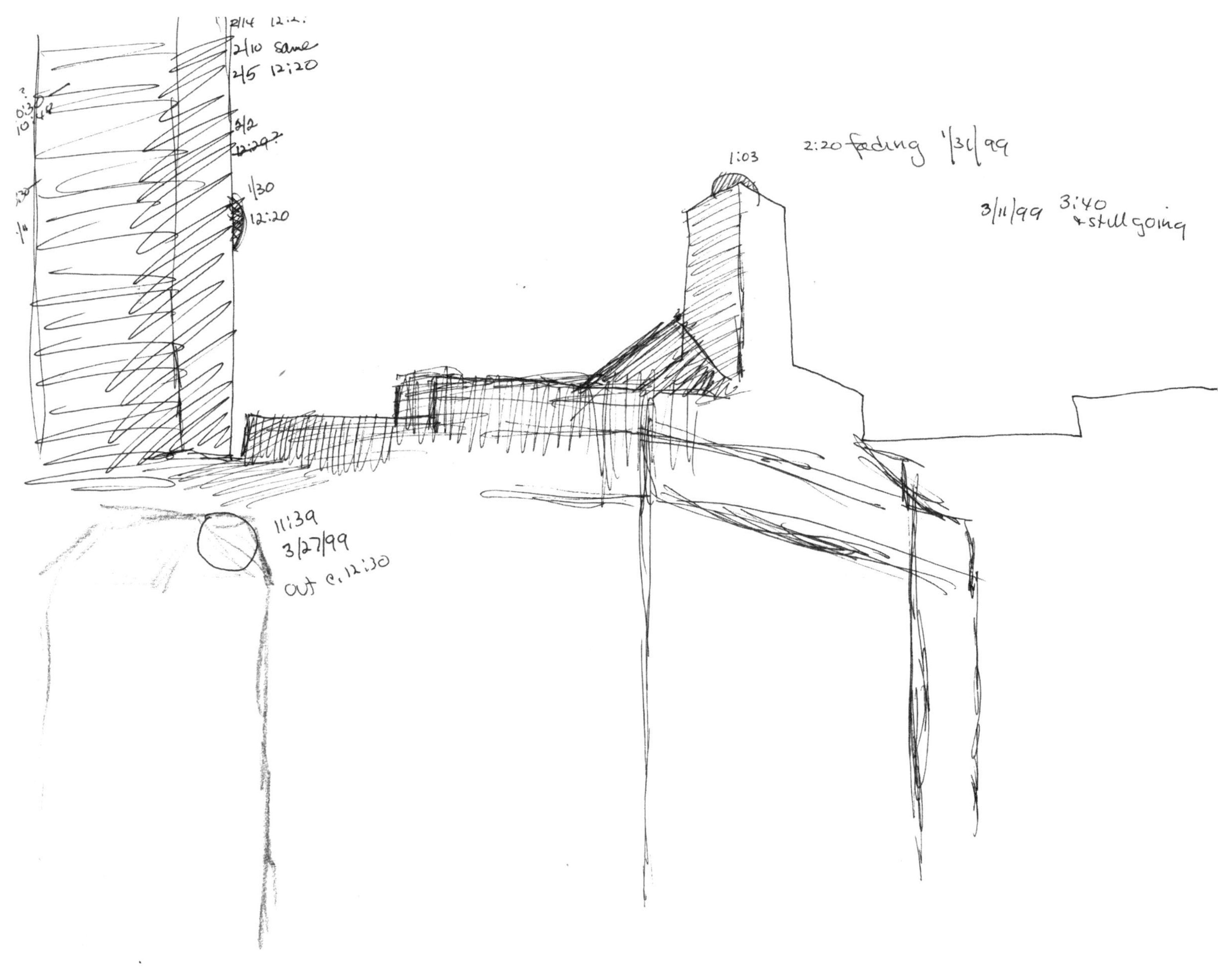

Rosemary Mayer lived in a loft space on Leonard Street between Church and West Broadway in Tribeca. Her studio was in the front of the building because it was southfacing and she often timed her work to coincide with the periods of brightest light. During the winter of 1998–1999 and then again in 2001, Mayer charted the diminished light in winter. These diagrams and notes record the movement of the sun in relation to neighboring buildings and how it illuminated the windows and entered her studio.

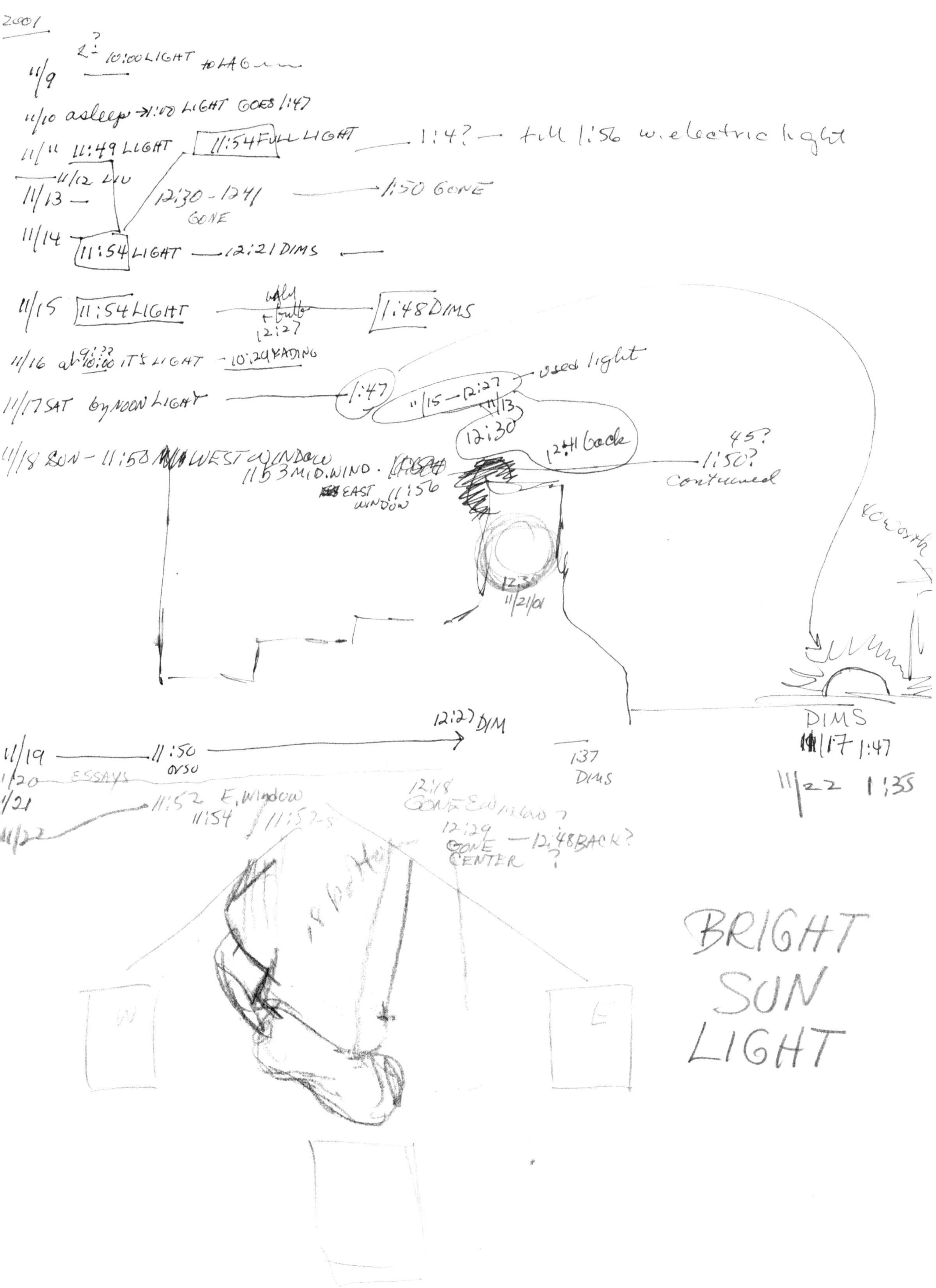

Rosemary Mayer, pages from sketchbook, 1998–2001

294 E. 48TH ST., NY 10017

1
My advice to those wishing to live in Manhattan
if they fear the pursuit of Death,
crouching in corners, in abandoned apartments,
in the dark labyrinths of washing machines,
in the elevator:
Don't look for a house built before the war.

2
Death lives there among the tenants,
moves about under a mask
that looks like the masks of others
waiting at subway stations.

3
One of the neighbours said,
while I was trying to throw out last week's newspapers
for recycling:
"Would you believe it?
Larry's dead."
It seems my face did not reflect
the expected expressions of grief
and she started talking about Larry
and his wife Linda:
"They were on the West Coast
escaping the perishing cold of New York.
On the way back,
before reaching the gate
he dropped dead on the terminal floor
holding the boarding cards."

4
You usually hear someone – a neighbour – has died
but you never hear a widow weeping
or even know where they've been buried,
if it really mattered to you that is,
and over time I forgot about Larry.

5
I usually get up with the dawn.
After taking a shower, I walk like an automaton
to the locked and bolted door
and fetch the daily newspapers.
Every day I saw him waiting for the elevator
to go for his regular daily jog
before the streets of Manhattan woke up.

6
Larry drank, every evening,
a bottle of French wine.
He wasn't a drunkard
but he loved life.
He frequented the cinema
he frequented restaurants with Linda
like two young lovers, despite the bent back,
the hoarse and cracked voice,
the blonde hair dye.
Did it disguise Linda's real age?

7
The bottles are no longer lined up at midnight
empty as in one of Morandi's still lifes.
No longer does that good man, our neighbour, rise
in the half-light of dawn
to run alone in a city that never sleeps –
a pregnant woman screaming orgasmically
during contractions, morning and night.

8
His wife returned in mourning, without makeup,
though she kept
the dyed-blonde colour of her hair,
determined to defy
the snares of Death
who did not know her address in New York.

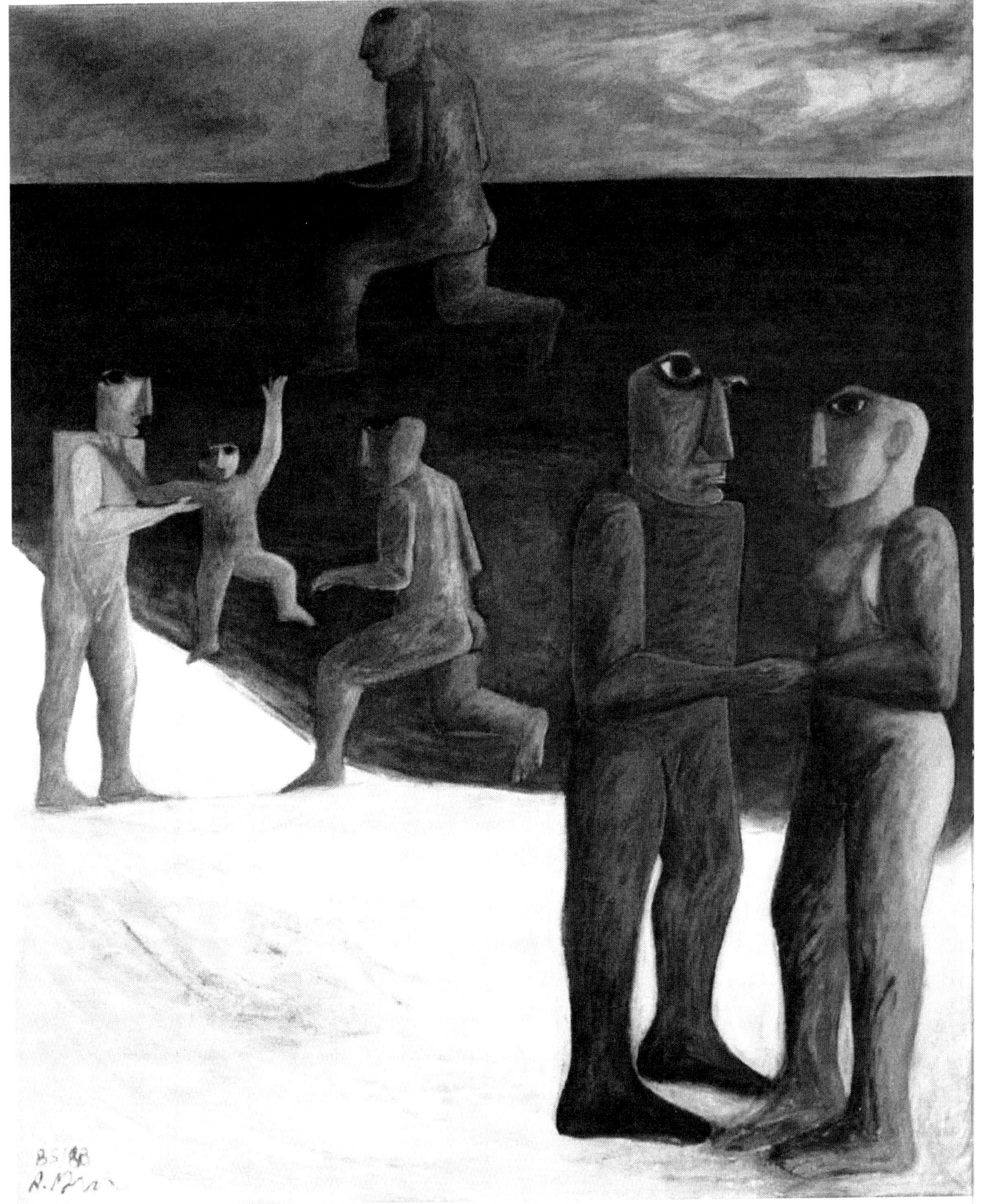

Summer by seaside. Acrylic on canvas, 175cm x 155cm, New York City 1985-88

9

The days of mourning did not last long.
It seems Larry had bequeathed his wife Death.
Six months later
she died on another airport floor.

...

My advice to those wishing to live in Manhattan,
if they fear the pursuit of Death,
crouching in corners,
in abandoned apartments,
in the dark labyrinths of washing machines,
in the elevator:
Don't look for a house built before the war.

New York, 1996

THE ROAD TO MANHATTAN

1

From the car that morning Manhattan
loomed in the distance
like tall Giacometti figurines
plucking the fins of fish
submerged in the clouds.
A crazy idea possessed me:
the image had fallen
from my mind onto the ice.

Manhattan was shackled in ice.

2
The picture wasn't bright in any case.
The highway from Queens
crossed neighbourhoods besieged by cities of the dead
strip joints
and brothels advertising Paradise in neon,
admission not by good deeds
but by dollar bills.

Here and there a crumbling church
bears a sign: For sale or to rent.

3
Manhattan slithers forward
stretching dragon hands, smashing drawers
out of which the secrets of poets fall,
like eyeballs in urns of sand and water
and on the threshold of the horizon, skyscrapers
procreate in boredom,
brazenly.
Manhattan approaches naked,
without dyes or masks
to hide her sallow face
in the middle of the day.

4
Long Island City was a shock,
a poke in the eye to a new immigrant.

It was not the gateway to Manhattan,
the Lady of the Atlantic Ocean
the repository of twentieth-century art
exile for Guernica
exile for Les Demoiselles d'Avignon and Max Beckmann
where Marcel Duchamp adopted
a urinal that entered history.

I witnessed for the first time
how neighbourhoods die
and years later
how they come back to life.
The streets, the housing projects,
and hospitals
are the signs of a city of ghosts
abandoned by its inhabitants.
The car slowed down near Queens Bridge.
"Isn't it Sunday?" I wondered.

The bridge was jammed
with cars, and with cyclists
even though they had their own little lane,
but the heralds of Fall
and the brightness of September turned
the rumble of engines
into a choir of singers –
as if all the people
were marching on Manhattan
each in search of something lost.

Was I too
searching for something lost?

5 April 1997

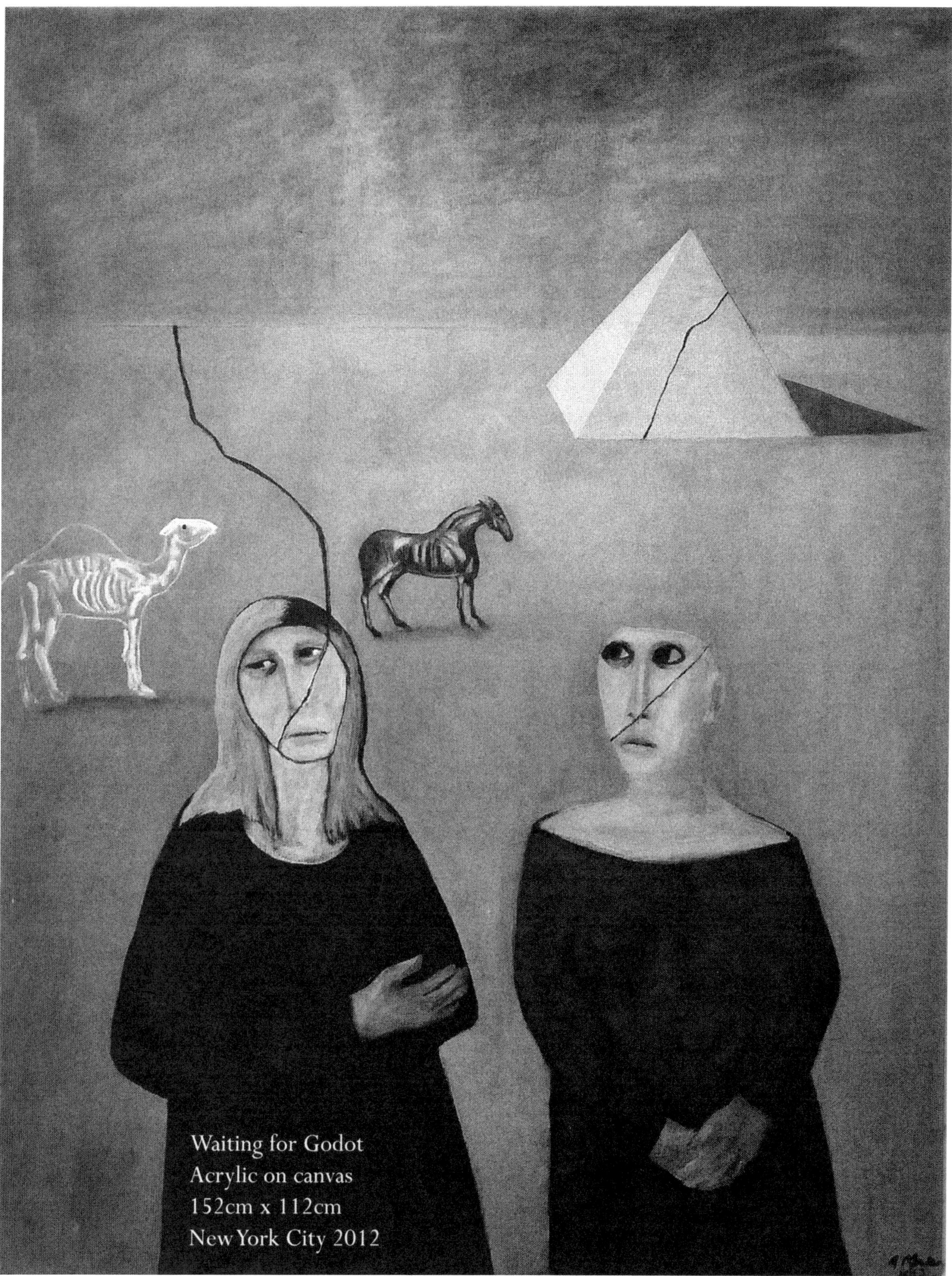

Waiting for Godot
Acrylic on canvas
152cm x 112cm
New York City 2012

MY ALEXANDRIA

1
My first city
I lost
like I lost
my true image
in a secret suitcase
that I forgot to take
with me into exile,
should I say,
or did I bury it deliberately
underground
to draw a new image
without features
to live with in exile
like a false prophet
or a secret fugitive
from a life sentence
in the prison of nothingness
in limbo between silence and wordlessness?

2
My other city
New York
where I've spent a third of a century

with a changeable mask
without features
without identity
has not made me forget my first city,
the one I lost.

3
Alexandria of revelation
and concealment
Alexandria of fragments
in the blood.
My Alexandria,
I rebuilt inside me
all that vanished –
its lighthouse, its treasures –
so it could all vanish
with me for ever.

26 November 2007

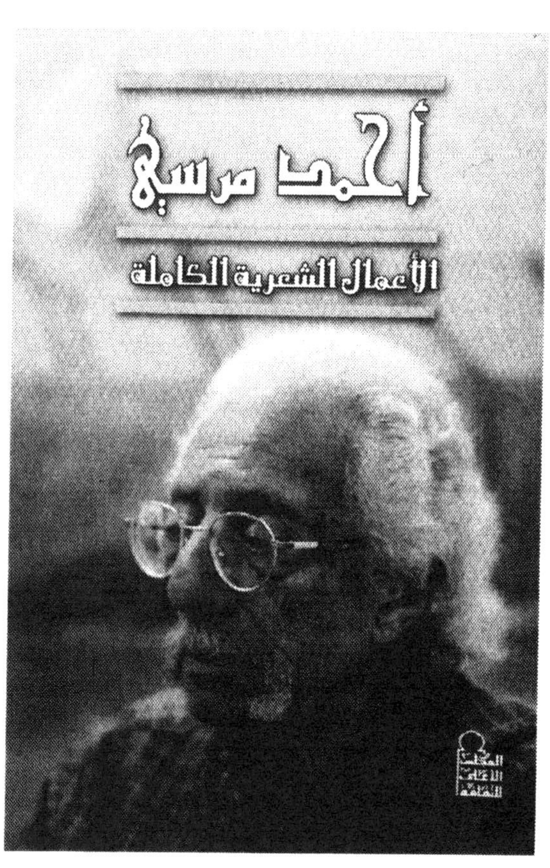

Selected and translated
from the collection
Photos from the New York Album,
published in Ahmed Morsi's
Al-'Amal al-Shi'riyya al-Kamila
(Collected Poetic Works),
by the Supreme Council of
Culture, Cairo, 2012.
ISBN 978-9774799520.
www.scc.gov.eg

THE MUTANT INTERNATIONAL

NICOLAS A. MOUFARREGE

Vision invasion in varying landscapes defines the need for integral survival.

In taking that traditional backward look over the season, the art/artists and the shows, presented (or not presented), I realize that there are few occupations so interesting, so attractive, so full of surprises and revelations for a critic, a critic as artist and an artist as critic, one whose mind is given to generalization as well as to the study of details, to contradictions, to accomplishing a revaluation; or to put it better, to the idea of a mobile universal order and hierarchy—as a comparison of the nations and their respective products. When I say 'hierarchy', I have no wish to assert the supremacy of any one nation over another. All I wish to do here is to assert their *equal* utility and value, and the miraculous way in which they come together to one another's aid in the harmony of the universe.

The International is a nomadic wanderer, on land and in mind. Everywhere and a lot of places are home, because the International becomes them. I write for myself, for strangers, and for my dead father. It was while watching the fireworks, this Fourth of July, that I believed the American I am more intensely than before. Here, and now it was to be my birthday too. Another birthday, the same as Bastille Day, the 23rd of March and the 22nd of November, the latter being coincidentally the date John Kennedy was assassinated, Lebanese Independence Day, *and* the date I left Beirut for Paris in 1975!

I, confusing the issues of art and criticism, aim to chronicle my impressions. By virtue of my descent, I am granted an eye beyond all merely local, merely nationally conditioned perspectives; it is not difficult for me to be a 'good American'. On the other hand, I am perhaps more Lebanese than present-day Lebanese, mere citizens of Lebanon, could possibly be; I, hyperhybridized before birth and after, have many racial instincts in my body. I am an interpreter who will not give *the* interpretation. I do not claim to see anything as it really is—all is purely subjective.

This is now a little of what I love and how I write it. I deal with art not as expressive but as impressive. I am content to feel, and beg pardon of the academics of all kinds who occupy the various workrooms of our artistic factory.

There is tension on the borders as we prepare for total planetary and self-extinction. Yet a unity of the human mind exists; we have to realize the collective life of the race: it is only thus that we are absolutely modern, in the true meaning of the word modernity. And as long as war is regarded as wicked, it will always have its fascination. When it is looked upon as vulgar, it will cease to be popular. It is through art and through art only that we can realize our perfection. Art, however, does not address itself to the specialist. Art is universal and, in all manifestations, one. Wherefrom the need for the International, the universal, trans-Atlantic and trans-Pacific, a mutant existentialist whose imagination is concentrated and collected racial/cultural experience.

And where the concern gets more planetary and cosmic, the International's voice gets louder and clearer. One is an individual being; everyone then is like many others always living; there are many ways of thinking of everyone. Alain Jacquet's pacifier (on the roof of an abandoned warehouse) frames the buildings of a New York skyline; cyclic, it is all-memory without a passport. Hervé Di Rosa's green door opens on a parallel world; out in a magic space, vast and strange, it is life itself. As E'wao Kagoshima's rock, the mossy rock of God's Isle, heaves under the bright red sunsphere. François Boisrond stereotypes a cipher of daily existence, a normal existence, coded, decoded, recoded, epigrammatic, and semiotic. Chuck Nanney looms a giant red and green creature afore a gray *Dead Planet.* The shelters along Milan Kunc's highway are human organs, the brain, the heart, the eye and the ear, and at the horizon, pointing up into space, a hand. David Bowes' is Beauty, incredible, larger than death, but for the appleglow of the Tree of Wisdom. Different, very different, *but* as palpable as the marblestone nutcracker Angela Ho hews is immaterial.

The International is spirit, sponge, and mirror. The artist, incorporating elements from the near and distant past, the present, and an ambitious future. Mutagenic changes, chromosomes adrift in a plasma of color. Personal, social, political, and fantastic commentary blends East and West, the Sheikh of Araby, Coca Cola, the Eiffel Tower, and Mount Fuji. Edgar Allan Poe meets Alice in Wonderland. Gertrude Stein is in my collection; Baudelaire, Nietzsche, and a lot of Jack Kirby and Steve Ditko comics.

The comic books I had as a child are not the same as the ones the public has access to today. The Downtown Branch of the Whitney surveys cartoon culture and its influence from 1900 to the present in "The Comic Art Show: Cartoons in Painting and Popular Culture." I anticipated this reaffirmation of Pop; I also applaud the show and catalogue. The cartoon and the International go hand in hand. In the early Sixties when Warhol and Lichtenstein, among others, exploded Pop into painting, across the Atlantic, in France, Alain Jacquet was doing his "camouflage" pieces. Superposing two drawings, a third reality was created. Jacquet found meaning in the characters of the Flintstones and used them in one piece. Another piece was the camouflage of an actual Lichtenstein; a month after the piece was shown, Jacquet camouflaged by superposition Lichtenstein's *Hot Dog*. Transformed into a giant perforated stampsheet, Jacquet's holes punned, visually, Lichtenstein's enlarged dot pattern. Meanwhile, popular comic books received the creative jolt of Jack Kirby and Steve Ditko's collaborations with Stan Lee at Marvel Comics.

For a new generation different superheroes took on a more vulnerable cast. The conflict between good and evil and the code sparing the taking of life played an important role in epic sagas that covered a broad and exotic territory. Injected with the spirit of the Sixties—man's actual ventures into outer space, drugs, flower-children, and the occult—the heroes, while possessing a range of super-powers, remained recognizably human. Jack Kirby's *Fantastic Four* is a husband/wife, brother/sister, and college roommate team. Steve Ditko's *Spiderman* is really Peter Parker, a freelance photographer; orphaned at the age of six, shy and somewhat of a social outcast, he acquired his spider-like abilities after a bite from an irradiated spider. An already mutated spider, its blood contained radioactive, complex mutagenic enzymes now functioning and triggering changes in Peter Parker's body. Another famous Ditko hero, *Doctor Strange*, an ex-neurosurgeon, studied magic in the Himalayan Mountains, trained by The Ancient One. His training developed powers of mesmerism, astral projection, teleportation, thought-casting, and energy projection. He also lives on Bleeker Street in Greenwich Village. For these heroes, a vast array of villains, of almost equal powers, were also created; and oftentimes these villains proved more indestructible with every encounter or combat. Twenty years after their original creation these characters live on, in multilingual editions around the world and on the corner newstands.

Each in their idiosyncratic, personal and individual approach, Hervé Di Rosa, François Boisrond, E'wao Kagoshima, Chuck Nanney, Milan Kunc, Keith Haring, Kenny Scharf, Angela Ho, Jim Nutt, David Wojnarowicz, Alexis Smith, and various innumerable artists, painters, sculptors, and graffiti writers select and transmute the Pop influence. Video games and frisbees play an important role in Alain Jacquet's recent paintings. Di Rosa and Nanney quote freely from Kirby and Ditko. The Flintstones and Jetsons, the backbone of Kenny Scharf's earlier and continuing work, are now mated with Felix the Cat, calling into being El Fredix. In subtle or unsubtle ways, Pop embraces the cosmos and vice-versa as the works and paintings of these art-

Alain Jacquet, Flintstone Camouflage, 1963.

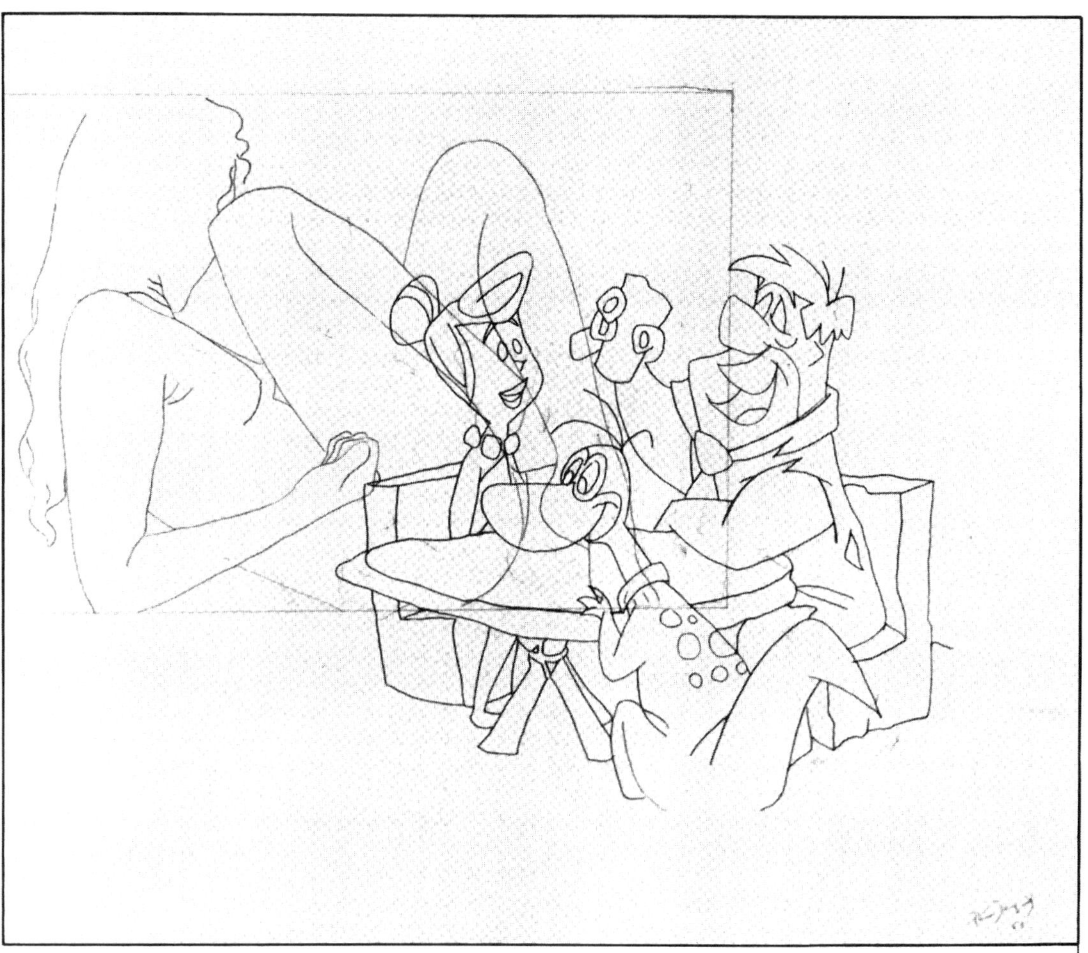

ists comment on the planet, this world, as we know it and what we have yet to find out about it.

Before I go more into how Pop and/or comic book culture is assimilated in current contemporary art, it is interesting and ironic to recall Steve Ditko's macabre tale, "The Painting" (*Where Creatures Roam,* #6, 1971). The narrative moves from artists' studios in different countries where Mr. Simon Squeed, art dealer, buys paintings cheaply only to resell them for personal and enormous profit. One day Mr. Squeed hears of a priceless work owned by a gypsy in Bessarabia; a jet flight takes him to the gypsy who refuses to sell the painting. But Mr. Squeed is used to having his way, so he has the gypsy unjustly arrested and proceeds to steal the painting. The next day the gypsy is set free because Mr. Squeed is nowhere to be found and cannot press charges against him. Back in his caravan, the gypsy realizes the painting is missing, but he knows what he shall find. The painting is back in Squeed's hotel room and Squeed, himself, an imprint on the canvas.

Hervé Di Rosa is the chief proponent of the duality and overlap of comic art and painting. His imagination has bred an extravagant number of characters who people his canvases. New ones appear every day and a narrative unfolds, a necessity of life, where conflicts and torments are essential elements of the immutable uncertainties in the parallel world his characters inhabit. Even within this parallel world another reality exists, a realm of spirit and mystery, of comic fear and layman psychology. Di Rosa's is an extreme position, its ethics, the philosophy of desirability: that things ought to be different, that they shall be; in realizing the dissatisfaction that is the germ of ethics, he reaches into the essence of strength. Di Rosa's is the aesthetic of revolt.

Painting makes a choice. It *isolates* and this is its way of unifying. The landscape isolates in space what is normally lost in perspective. The painting of scenes isolates in time the gesture that is normally lost in another gesture. Di Rosa's images give the impression that the fixation has just taken place, as if the projector had suddenly stopped.

The frame freezes on a generous vista. A synthesis of the total narrative, the painting also resembles a poster, an announcement, its power manifold. The first encounter with Di Rosa's paintings flings one into the adventure. The characters slowly become more alive, moving in eccentric spirals from one work into another as one learns these characters, their names and their traits. Time equals zero: it is night or day, or neither. A landscape of the ridiculous, a telescopic invasion of vision, magnifying and magnificent. And the ever-present *Question Marc.*

The name is innocence, knowing and not-so-innocent. A prominent nose, more like a stick, is the mystery feature in a rounded stele-shaped head atop a stereotypical male physique. The character of *Question Marc* is conjoined in Di Rosa's kaboodle of 'heroes' by an X triumvirate: *Dr. Tube, Monsieur Plat,* and *Professeur X.* In a recent sequence of paintings, an episode in the life and adventures of Di Rosa's cast, *Question Marc* is assailed by various forms which are crude renderings of body parts related to sex. Sex, a central theme in Di Rosa's oeuvre, is organic and romantic. It is also sad and scary, *bistrot*-vulgar, kinky and comic. Pop Freud and primary, the real and the symbolic merge. The series begins with the creation of the mystical space, the magic parallel world where the action takes place.

There is the premise of two worlds, one free-floating, antigravitational, the other, more or less as we know the world to be. One is made up of those who live there and the other of those who visit the former. A Ditko/Dr. Strange influence teleports Di Rosa's characters from one world into the other. A vaginal opening, a kind of green door leads into the *alter*, where the characters have doubles. But not all of Di Rosa's characters possess the mystical powers that enable some to visit this world. The 3 X, Question Marc, the Hindu, and the Egyptian are some of those with the mystic power. The occurrences are equally strange, revelatory, and off. The viewer is voyeur, looking into and at the complexity of an existential quest, multi-faceted, and in spite of its personal, egocentric uniqueness, exemplary of plebeian vitalism.

The mood is of dramatic optimism. Di Rosa reserves the right to do what he wants and to change his mind whenever he chooses. He feels that his life is inextricably meshed with his

Nicolas Moufarrege, "The Mutant International," published in *Arts Magazine*, September 1983

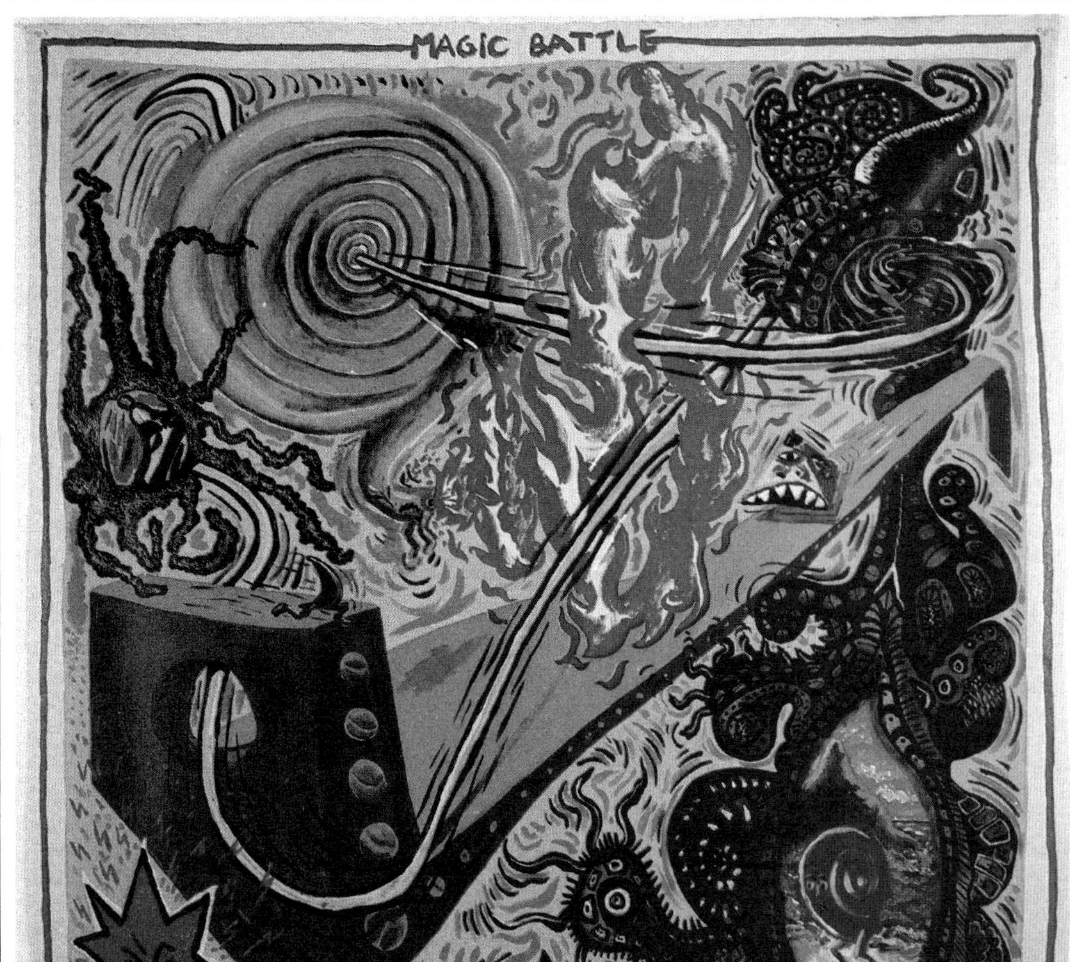

Hervé Di Rosa, Magic Battle, 1983. *Acrylic on canvas, 73 x 72". Courtesy Tony Shafrazi Gallery.*

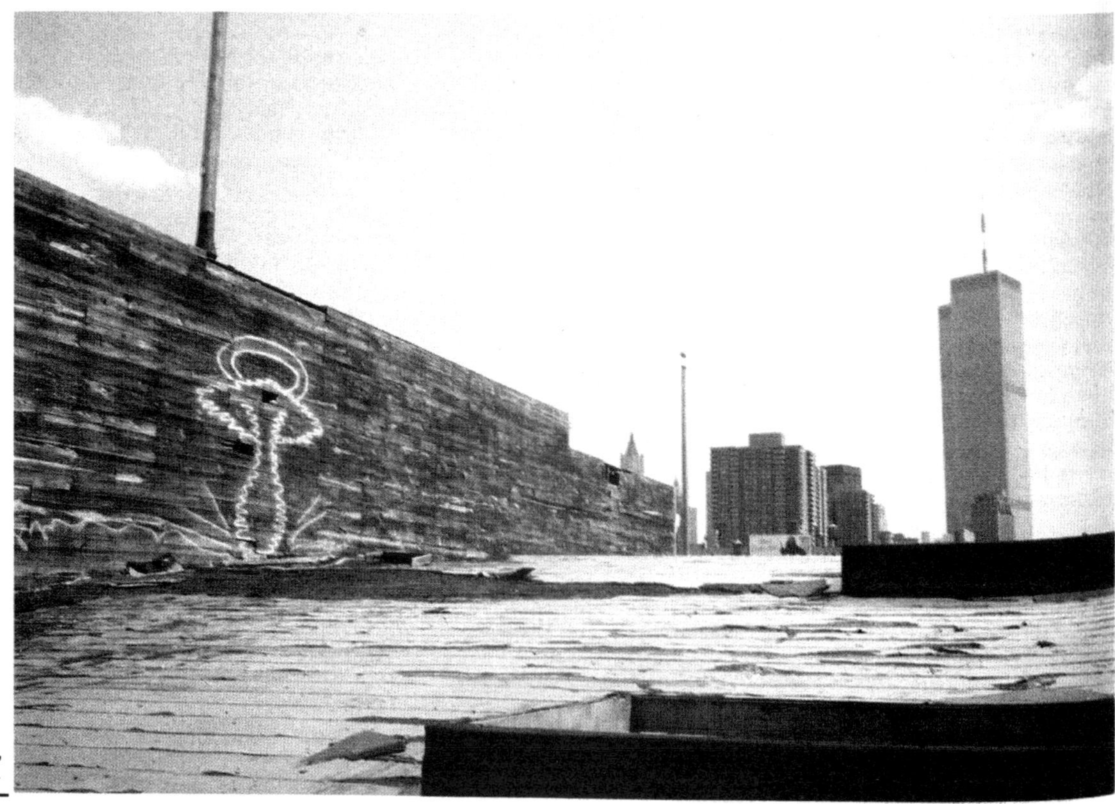

Alain Jacquet, First Breakfast, 1972. *Oil on canvas.*

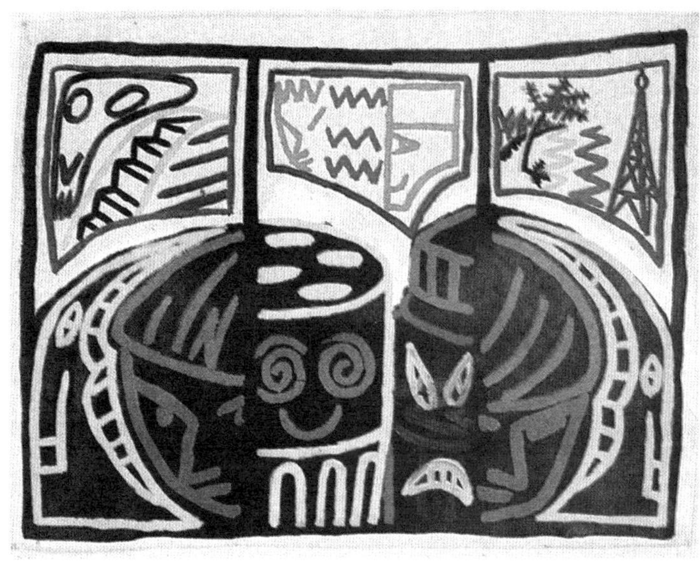

François Boisrond, Untitled, 1983. *Acrylic on canvas, 52 x 74". Courtesy Annina Nosei Gallery.*

François Boisrond, Untitled, 1983. *Acrylic on canvas, 125½ x 74". Courtesy Annina Nosei Gallery.*

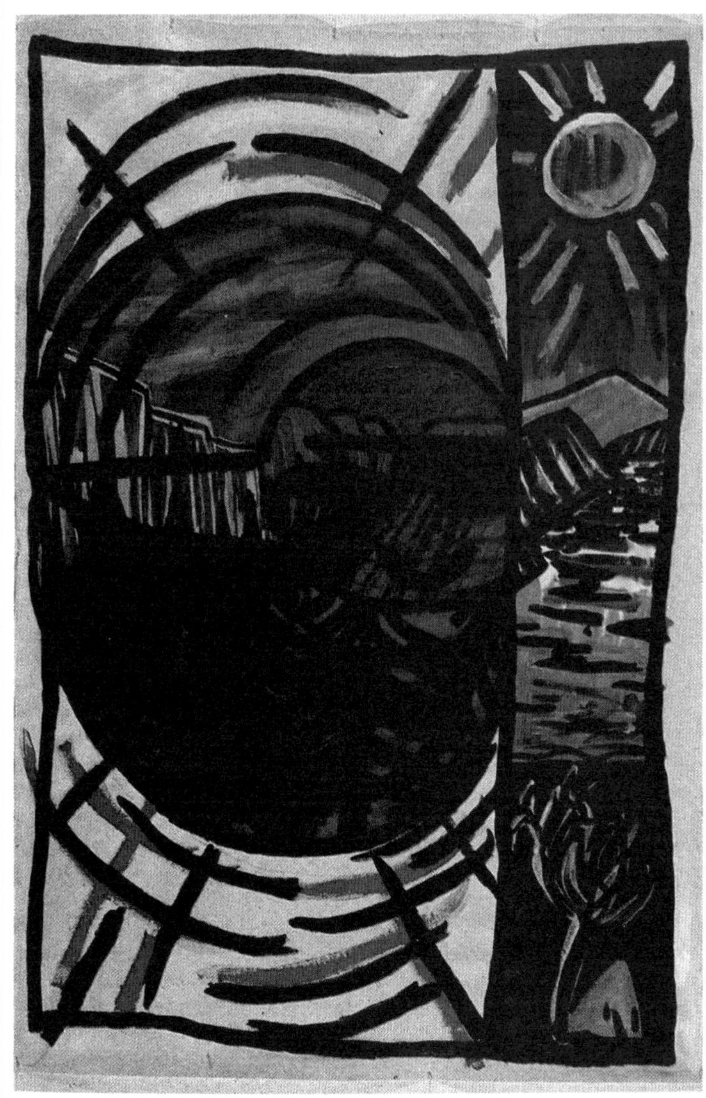

characters—they are his reason and shelter. A reason that defies reason: the revaluation occurs and in only very few cases is the demarcation between good and evil definitive. More usually it is a combination of both. Di Rosa's map of the world divides the land into the country of normal people, the country where everybody is the same, and that where everybody is different. A spiral-shaped mysterious island floats in the southern region.

Raymond, Raoul, Raphael, Rene. Mique, the immigrant laborer from the land where everybody is the same and all work in a factory (the Land of Miques), who went to work for Dr. Tube and is now rich, is a symbol of the working class; with his character social commentary enters the oeuvre. One of the two main leading ladies is now dead. But the ghost of *La Peteuse* is still around for guest appearances; it is she who farted and died whereby she sinned, shitting blood. *La femme a tête plate,* the woman with the flat head, is a sexpot. Ruthless, a whore and a bitch, she has slept with all of the guys and was the cause for the separation of the original 3 X. Her passionate life and secret biography is a future project of Di Rosa who does not tire in his exploration of sex and love and male/female relationships. Another major character is the green monster; originally a woman who changed forms, the monster is now the male character, Raphael, a seedy, shabby person, a *minable.* As a woman he used to be married to another hero, *Jean Claude Quiquette.* The latter was sent out into space, but again, while it has been a while since he made an appearance on canvas, will remerge as central to the action. But Di Rosa will not give all his secrets away; one must wait for the painting to see the continuation of the tale. The approach is both methodic and empiric; Di Rosa decides the fate of his characters along the way.

But what is art and what is painting? In 1981, Di Rosa's text for a museum catalogue read: "With his two hands like a bird of prey's claws, he spread the fresh buttocks of the young girl. On all fours, she started to squirm on the gallery floor. He thrust his throbbing dick, hard as steel, in the moist pussy and proceeded to screw following the rules of art. With an animal gasp she asked: 'What's painting to you?' 'Stop asking stupid questions,' he breathed, his face dripping with sweat, 'the pleasure of doing things is what is important, the rest is lies, hypocrisy and without great interest.' She said no more and he continued to fuck silently." The text was rejected, but Di Rosa, imperturbable, continues the session in other gallery catalogues. Rude? Perverse?

I like it. Di Rosa is genuine; his work causes an upset in long established valuations and establishes him as a personal favorite. True, sex is universal and international, but it is not always as traumatic as Di Rosa depicts. There is no escape from it as subject matter, the International perceives that. It is the mask of God, the mystery and reality of life everywhere.

François Boisrond dissects the anatomy of conjugal bliss, the memories and the landscapes, the days of wine and roses. E'wao Kagoshima's mist clears on a ritual of blood and death, crimes that cross saints and fuckers. An infinite number of babies converge radially into a point behind a kissing couple in a painting by Milan Kunc—a point that is the focus, the beginning/end of the concentric spirals of Alain Jacquet's truth.

Man/womankind is the focal point through which the universe of matter and mind is surveyed. Not the objective, the rational, the subconscious, the cybernetic nor man-as-machine; rather man in his flesh and spirit, in his universality, rather than man as a *measure* of things. It is the transformation of a visible reality into an imaginary, poetic, and subjective representation dependent on intellect, but more importantly on intuition, instinct, and the inner impulse and urge to create and represent life. Art is the obsession with life, and after all, as human beings, our greatest obsession is ourselves and our surroundings. We and the planet then become the subject.

The paintings, however silent, still speak. Alain Jacquet's pacifier between my lips silences the child's crying. To see is language, and the blind touch. Who was that born just the other day? Boy or/and girl? A ring (halo? donut?) and a nipple. As the retina welds itself on the image surface, I see female and male, lingam and yoni; my eye becomes radiated, the wave activity a spirit factor. I slip in as a ghost. From a landscape into a sun, I exit into the stratosphere.

The child is ready for his first meal. I exit facing Jacquet's *First Breakfast* (1972). The ultimate landscape: the earth viewed from outer space, spinning superposed by a concentric spiral reading. As the projector fixes on the waltz, Jacquet intervenes with visions and multiple horizons—visions of the earth and the elements. Alchemy and the globe becomes crystal ball; the continents on the earthsphere become faces, figures of men and women, androgynous, holy, animal and plant. The vision sums up a history of time and space; the game unifies mythologies and the concern is life. A spool of thread lies on a drape in *La Dentelliere* (1978-80); it unravels the mysteries of a thimble as it weaves the subject of a symbolism that defines our existence.

The breakfast menu is a sculpture piece made of three eggboxes in a row. It hangs on the wall of Jacquet's studio. The wrappings originally contained both brown and white eggs and in actuality are half-boxes (six-packs). Installed from left to right, different portions, eggforms, are punched in: sculpture is touch and the blind read. Jacquet's code is Braille: the letters spell GOD. As I discuss it with him, I cannot but remark on the cosmic egg, the yin and the yang, and the symbolism viewed in context within the artist's total oeuvre. Dice on the table, the backgammon board, the *jeu de jacquet*, and another roll of the dice as the game proceeds.

The dimple, the nipple, concave/convex. The hole, *le trou,* the whole, *le tout; et les etoiles qui font des trous pour faires des trous. Les toiles, la toile:* the canvas on which Jacquet signs/shines a star. Alain Jacquet penetrates both the whole and the hole. The union of the male and female principles carries through in the more obvious *Hot Dog* to the *Flintstones Camouflage* (1963), where their prehistoric pet Dino's nose and eyes become the male sexual organs superposed on the female organ of a nude pinup pose. The cartoon is now tantric and pop goes the universe. The vision is equally vast, magnified and concentrated as the reality of animated and animate life and sight. As the vision concentrates in the cyclopean heads of E'wao Kagoshima's cartoon heads (1982), and the elements of air, fire, water, and earth are viewed in full perspective, the artist's ethereal element wafts its elastic vibrations.

Le dejeuner sur l'herbe has turned car bumper into car bumper: the artist delves into integral myth and layered levels of awareness. Jacquet stresses the need for the evolution beyond geography into a different landscape, the need for planetary consciousness. His is a chaos of symbols, a mosaic of messages rich in humor, romantic irony, and analogy. There is an added dimension beyond the literal and allegorical: a naked madonna's bust becomes penis and testicles, the orbs of the breasts and the extension of the neck—the idea of entity merges with that of place. With life so much at stake, the discourse between it and death is an insistent recurrence in the *tantra.* Jacquet's *Madonna with Child and Skull* (1981) revitalizes and sublimates; in the embrace of shadow comes light that has the power to startle. Inseparable from the perfection of beauty, the incomprehensible anomaly of still lurking melancholy.

The sea never sleeps. Space is a pier. Columns of incense spiral upwards. Three phantoms appear: the phantom of love, that of rebellion, and that of freedom, the manifestations and expressions of the universe. Dawn will come to the people of Orphalese; Jacquet quotes Khalil Gibran. He transforms with his vision the gross sexual energy of man and woman into superpotency by total integration of opposing polarities. The primal state of oneness is attained; human art can do no more in the delineation of superhuman beauty.

Sex is seen neither in the context of morality nor as an inhibiting act nor as indulgent or permissive. Liberation is a change of perspective; no code of social ethics holds the body. It is a vital energy capable of acting with force on the mental plane, which in turn reacts on the spiritual plane and realizes the free original *and* planetary awareness. All is nevertheless cipher, close to the concept of, if not identical to, zero.

I am merely the spectator. I become participant and what I see is mine alone. Your associations function as laws wherein every partial representation recalls the total representation of which it had been a part. The composition awakens in each element the power of recalling another. I believe in sight, in the *regard.* There is something in seeing that encompasses more than its comprehension. What does 'understand' mean? A solution to a mathematical equation? The molecules of the reactants in a chemistry, analytic or synthetic, bonding and breaking? I relate to what I feel. The inner is outer, the outer is inner—do we ever really understand?

The beautiful is always strange; it is the touch of strangeness that is its endorsement. Painting, not its formulae, is an evocation. Feeling is a common but individual sensation among peoples of the world. Feeling is communication, and consciousness develops only under the pressure of the need to communicate. The subtlety and strength of consciousness are proportionate to man/woman's capacity for communication; and this capacity is in turn proportionate to the need for communication.

Love makes the world go round. The theme from *Carnival;* the lights of Times Square spin; Pigalle, Barbès; call it cliché, call it hoi polloi, but remember it is you and I. It is E'wao Kagoshima pouring ketchup on the *Shinjuku;* it is Angela Ho's stone pinball machine, red and blue, prehistoric and futurist. It is very definitely François Boisrond and B-movies; Ophuls' *Madame de;* also Milan Kunc's *Rubic Cube,* with the map of the world atop, sending messages through cloud rings to a brain-shelter in the space around a green planet. The idiot, primitive pop and explosion of Chuck Nanney's gawk and its sugar-in-the-blood mutant colors reincarnate Elvis Presley on T-shirts and in dreams. Di Rosa's sequential wonders, densely populated with dazed characters in frenetic dramas, aren't merely about remembering what's happened to whom and how or why.

As an engendered species, man needs help and protection. He/she needs consciousness, the need to know him/herself, the feelings and the thoughts. The International, like every living being, thinks continually without knowing it. What rises to consciousness is a small part, signs of communication which in fact uncover the origin of consciousness. The human being inventing signs is at the same time the human being who becomes ever more keenly conscious of himself. Boisrond develops an incomparably personal, unique, and infinitely individual language, a day-to-day diary of signs, writing that translates into its antithesis: the average/normal.

Boisrond's is an ordered confusion in a videospace that chronicles his life and its simple activities and his friends (in particular, his girlfriend, Françoise Lavole). He sleeps and reads and watches television. Françoise and François on a beach, in bed, kissing and fighting. A mythology, personal and familiar. The very French, very *intimiste,* François/Françoise couple is the exact opposite of *Monsieur et Madame.* Di Rosa's couple is unreal! *Madame* is crazy about money, her head is like an artichoke, while *Monsieur,* potato-headed, is possessed and goes graveyard hunting. They live in a hacienda in the middle of the desert. The artist's studio, his bedroom, the tradition of painting (here I refer to the landscape and the portrait as well as the abstract/figurative duality) occupy the space and spirit of Boisrond's oeuvre.

Within deconstructed partitions Boisrond stereotypes with a line. A semiotic comic strip and an assemblage and superposition of family Polaroids and drawing, his work is integral calculus: normality and nature and an encompassing definition of the noun figure that includes form, outline, person, and diagram through syllogism, pattern/design, evolution, theme, and composition. The figure is numeral, becomes cipher, waxes and wanes abstract. Simultaneously objects earn faces: the can of paint, the cocaine straw, or the form with the yellow lightbulb-like face, simply named *Monsieur Jaune,* the circles with eyes, nose, and mouth. Though humanized, these objects relate no more than their functions and have no story other than their ties to the painter and the painting.

It is not how things are in the world, but that they are. Boisrond's journal reiterates and counterpoints the imagination as a prime agent of human perception and a repetition in the finite mind of the eternal act of creation in the infinite *I am.* The familiar resembles me; I know it—it is my room, the bed. I can enter its outlined space/scape. I can wear a skin and have a shape and volume: I am something. I am the writhing and the repose. Interchanged momentum and force, weight and location, direction or position. The passage within the passage.

Boisrond's untitled triptych (1983) describes a triplicate of passages, parallel and crossing lines and a sun. The three panels are partitioned lengthwise in an approximate 2:1 ratio; the central one is over 10 feet high, the sidepieces less than a couple of feet shorter. The work relates the artist's transformations upon arriving in New York. It formally separates into 'the portrait', 'the landscape', and what Boisrond refers to as 'the mystic'. Three figures, personnages of Boisrond's iconography, describe the various metamorphoses. In the left panel, *Monsieur Jaune,* a kind of Mr. Peanut shape, changes into a red and orange deformed monster; an autoportrait is superposed on both images, regular and somewhat flipped out. In the narrow right partition of the panel the idea of portrait is spelled out. Similarly in the middle panel, the narrower right partition reiterates the landscape theme. In the last panel, the narrow partition is now on the left with a skull and bones, elongated and odd on a red background; to its right is the can of paint. Religion comes in: the larger French can of paint has a cross scrawled atop; the smaller, more designed American package has a more styled cruciform. While the can of paint diminishes in size, in the Paris/New York shuttle, the personnage of the middle panel, a round face, representing the landscape, grows larger with forward momentum. There is an electric immediacy to the dynamism operating around Boisrond's lines. The contrast of the small-scale, tree-lined French countryside landscape to the Grand Canyon, giant boulder, American vast space combined with the total landscape of sun/sky/earth/water/submarine slice stuns. Boisrond's logic sums, lists, and permutates; in words they become the pages of the diary. Boisrond lays his composition out, a personal repertoire. He manipulates a *mise en scène* and a philosophy of rebellion that is traditional, scientific, endlessly repeating the same images, always in the plural—rhymes, metaphors, and different complements, crystallized time in perpetual motion within the inner and outer space of identity.

Boisrond defines at least three passages toward abstraction, even while it is a figurative form undergoing the defined processes of lineup and support, superposition or breakage and shattering. In these passages imagination, memory, and perception exchange functions; Boisrond uses the implements of a free dialectical logic for the fusion of opposites to produce the anatomy of living. Memory is desocialized; it discovers the unknown being, the sum of all the elements that make up the soul of a child. Boisrond's paintings possess the right tension of reminiscence; the memories become great images, magnified and magnifying; they are associated with the total season, reposing in perfection. Beautifying, as one goes off dreaming to the bottom of their simplicity into the very center of their value, the seasons of childhood that are the seasons of the poet.

Boisrond finds the means to be singular while remaining universal. A homology exists between the box partitions and the psychology of secrecy. The artist, nevertheless, applies his talent to making us feel this identity of intimacy. Similarly the enclosed room and the open landscape are the intimate and the exterior, encouraging each other in their growth. Within Boisrond's normalcy, the normal notion of spatiality is disturbed. His spontaneous mythology wants to be both visible and hidden. Boisrond, through a principle of correspondences, receives the immensity of the world, which he transforms into the intensity of intimate being.

The consciousness of this immensity is common to the International. It offers an extremely diverse range of styles and media. Another war has begun (they say that tales of war are like serpent's tails: they grow). This time the war is different; we're really winning. Today's art is displaying an awareness of the human condition on a planetary scale. We are on the threshold of profound discoveries within our own nature and in external nature. The world of abstractions and concepts, the world of immediate experience and objective observation, and the world of spiritual insight are brought together in an integrated point of view. The artist draws on all: fine art traditions, popular media, foreign culture; he wills life and moves mind and hand for it.

The artists I have mentioned are all characters in the planetary scenario. Future articles will shed more light on their work and intentions. A quirky soap opera, it is art working with life. Why is a snail climbing up E'wao Kagoshima's Doric column? What new beauties will unfold in David Bowes' mannerist dreamspace? How come two nymphets toss a frisbee at a madonna in Alain Jacquet's portrait of Marcel Duchamp? And now that we have seen how Di Rosa's cast loves, we will next learn how they fight. Boisrond's lines will continue to compile and layer a simple quotidien and a complex metamorphoses of personal poetics. How does Chuck Nanney deal with being an *Absorbing Man* and what are Sue and Reed of *The Fantastic Four* doing in his painting? Myriad faces, multiple personalities, Kagoshima's line drawings of heads become writing and lettering. An accordion shape unfolds Patrick Raynaud's cut-outs of primordial man; children play in the virgin forest.

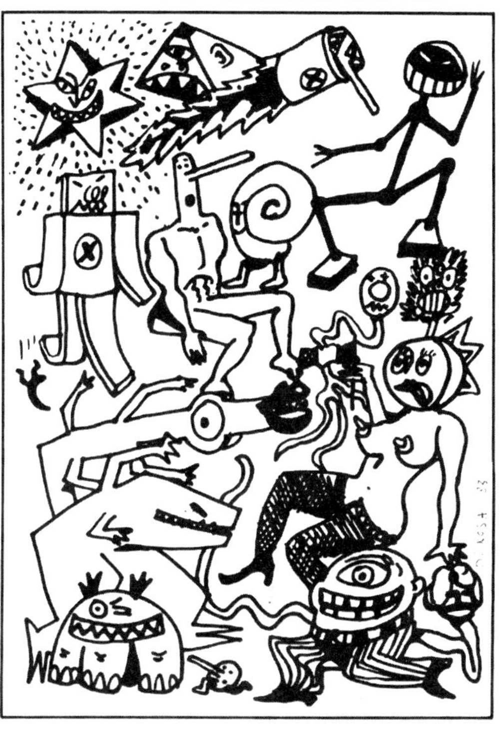

Hervé Di Rosa, Professeur X, the Egyptian, Dr. Tube, Mique, Monsieur Plat, Question Marc, Hank, Monsieur et Madame Raoul, La femme a la tête plate, Raphael, Raymond, Rene, the Hindu, 1983.

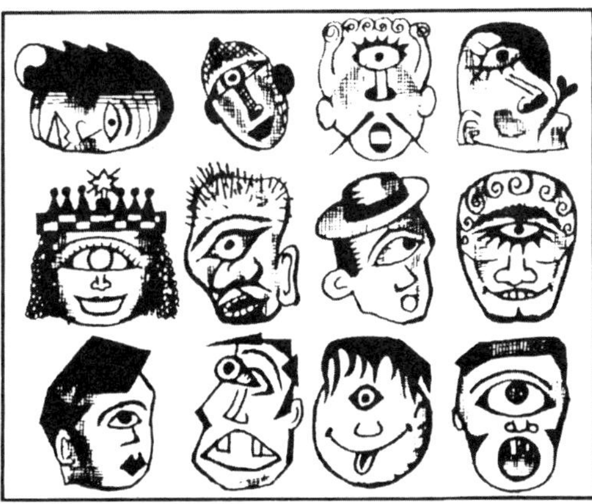

E'wao Kagoshima, Heads, 1982.

Jack Kirby's *Silver Surfer* soars; a solitary who observes the affairs of mankind, naive, otherworldly and tinged with sadness, he also possesses the cosmic power to revitalize life energies and heal the wounded. He can restructure molecules to create other configurations, but he cannot transmute elements. The *Silver Surfer* does not need to eat or breathe—he absorbs life/cosmic energy through his skin—and while his body does not require sleep, his mind still does in order to dream.

Meanwhile an international team, *The New Mutants,* makes its appearance on the pages of Marvel Comics. Trained by Professor Charles Xavier, who had previously trained the famous *X-Men,* their current adventures find them discovering a Nova Roma, hidden in the Andes, near the waterhead of the Amazon. Past, present, and future blend classical, pop, and original nature in the comic strip; a reflection of the state of the fine arts where individualism and spontaneous association of men and women of like spirit are the only honest possibilities. The mountain shepherds explore the countryside.

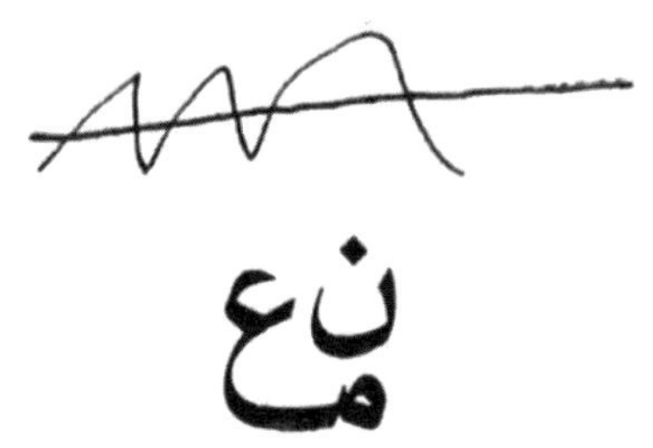

THE WORD ABOVE MEANS YES IN ARABIC
THE LETTERS FORM MY INITIALS
I BELIEVE IN THE UNIVERSE
I BELIEVE IN ETERNITY
IN WATER AND IN EARTH
IN THE SUN AND IN THE MOON
IN MARCH AND IN JUNE
THE MONTHS AND THE SEASONS
IN THE PYRAMIDS AND THE SPHINX
IN NEW YORK AND IN MAN.
MAN. MY INITIALS ARE NAM
PRONOUNCED AS IN ENGLISH IT SOUNDS LIKE
THE IMPERATIVE FORM OF SLEEP IN ARABIC.
SLEEP ... I BELIEVE IN SLEEP
IN DAY AND IN NIGHT
IN WHAT BRINGS THEM TOGETHER
IN WHAT BRINGS US TOGETHER
THE SUNSET AND THE DAWN
THE RED AND THE BLUE
THE BLACK AND THE WHITE
IN TIME AND IN YOU.

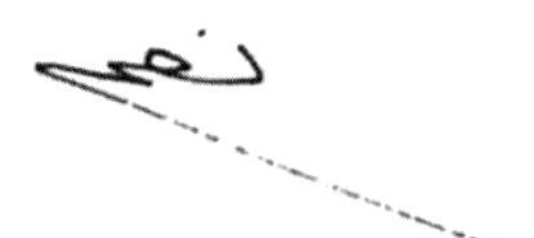

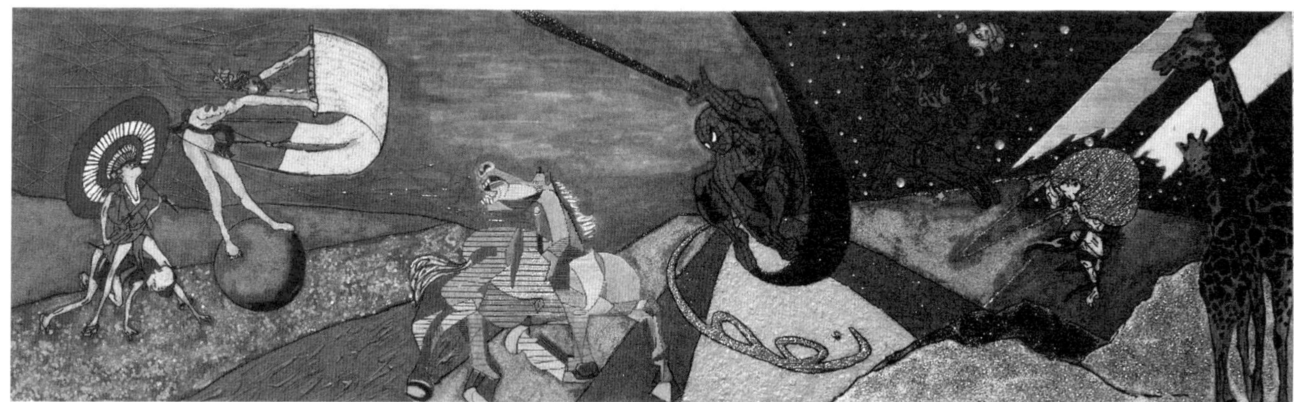

NICOLAS MOUFARREGE, *WORRY WAR RID*, 1983

THE WISE AND FOOLISH

so, writing all in sands of time
    all winds blow hot and then go cold
    the sands to sweep all hurts of birth
    to pulverize the rocks to mend the soul

so, all is life, it's wine, and spice
    that frankincense and myrrh, the
    magi-c of life's awesome chemistry

so, all is life, those threaded
    threatened spools of time then
    become hour-glassed glassined in
    as death unwinds its nether polyglot

so, all of life is s-and
    is s-pools of threaded
    threatened thought; at
    times the spring's too
    taut to hold the "real"
    to return from dying out

so, all, then, are the foolish
    virgins of the night's delight;
    all must gain their oil of light
    all must clean their lamps of life,
    all must clean; all must clean their lamps

so, the pulverizing sands of time
    become in thought great bulwarking
    foundation stones for that eternal
    building of the temple as the soul
    foundation s-tones sea-meant-ed there
    for life to buffet down agan to sands,
    to sands of time forever cleaning lamps

TIME IS THE MOMENT.

the moment is the fact of it, the tract of thought,
the incident inheld as memory, the breathing in and
the breathing out, the layering of co-incidental
laminations of the soul, the stitch in and it out,
the encircling square geometrically opposing
triumvirate archings of limit, and capacity
of expanding out; and then, just what
is it, that moment that is in-out?

the moment is the foot and the head; it is the
laugh and the cry overarching and intermingling
for its chemical residue known as the mood of it;
it is the love and the necessary reacting
negation; it is the birth and its ever
on expansion and contraction, its
exhaling out and its inhaling in
as a seed germinates to be plant.

it is the soul within, that enfolds its morrows
in its stem embraced and laced in dewy members
as membranes inter and cross-weave as life
inter-acts and outer-reclaims its residuals
of twining intermittent chimes of trunks
and limbs enfolding and arching of bent
elbows as knees hinged as verbally with
commas and semicolons and question marks.

it is the re-forming seed becoming itself as its
trunk and its truncated shelf leavened and leafly
activating blooms becoming seeds again to gain
overflowing boweries by thoughts not germinable
making the still of brew lying and sodden in; as
thought is the moment, and the moment is its sad
punctuation trinitously glacing in froth of its
expletives, they being its periods of punctuation.

DIAMOND

sensitivity, sentiment, sensation;
three esses- as a diamond clear faceted-
refractive, vortive, reflective, sential- and
sensual- as sentiment detailing life's lustre!

sartorium, saturation, suturnian-
sentiment, sentence, sententious,
separate, senescent- as stereoscopic.

diamond of mind- perfected and lustered,
life enanescent and everlastic, saturate-
diamond miner, cutter of facets of ego;
deliberate, conglomerate- the human mind!

lessons metamorphose as
cocoon in hardening- to
soften- in order to probate
the will, and to live by fact of
diaphanous- metamorphic glow!

all life is that diamond- with its
facets refacing- supersaturately declining-
while reminding its mining for glitter-
shining- rough-centerred and crystalline-
within its manifold facets- tangible withal!

THE POOL OF TEARS

I had stood
looking down into
the pool of tears
lying dormant at my feet
and by upward and by
sideward vision I saw
great elder beings
making their strides
passing me by

I was looking downward but my sight was upward to
the right and to the left, and my head was bowed

the beings were of stature great
I stood beneath their kneecaps

I know that I had wept and
had prayed in vain making that
pool of tears for ages long;
the pool of tears lying
dormant at my feet
was crystalline clear
for mirroring the vacuous
numbness of me, dormant as
the time of weeping had passed
for wisdom to emerge; for, in
spite of my numbness I saw
beings of stature great;
I saw!

I was looking downward
but my sight was upward
to the right and to the left
and my head was bowed;
as time came to pass
the vision stayed
for later reckoning

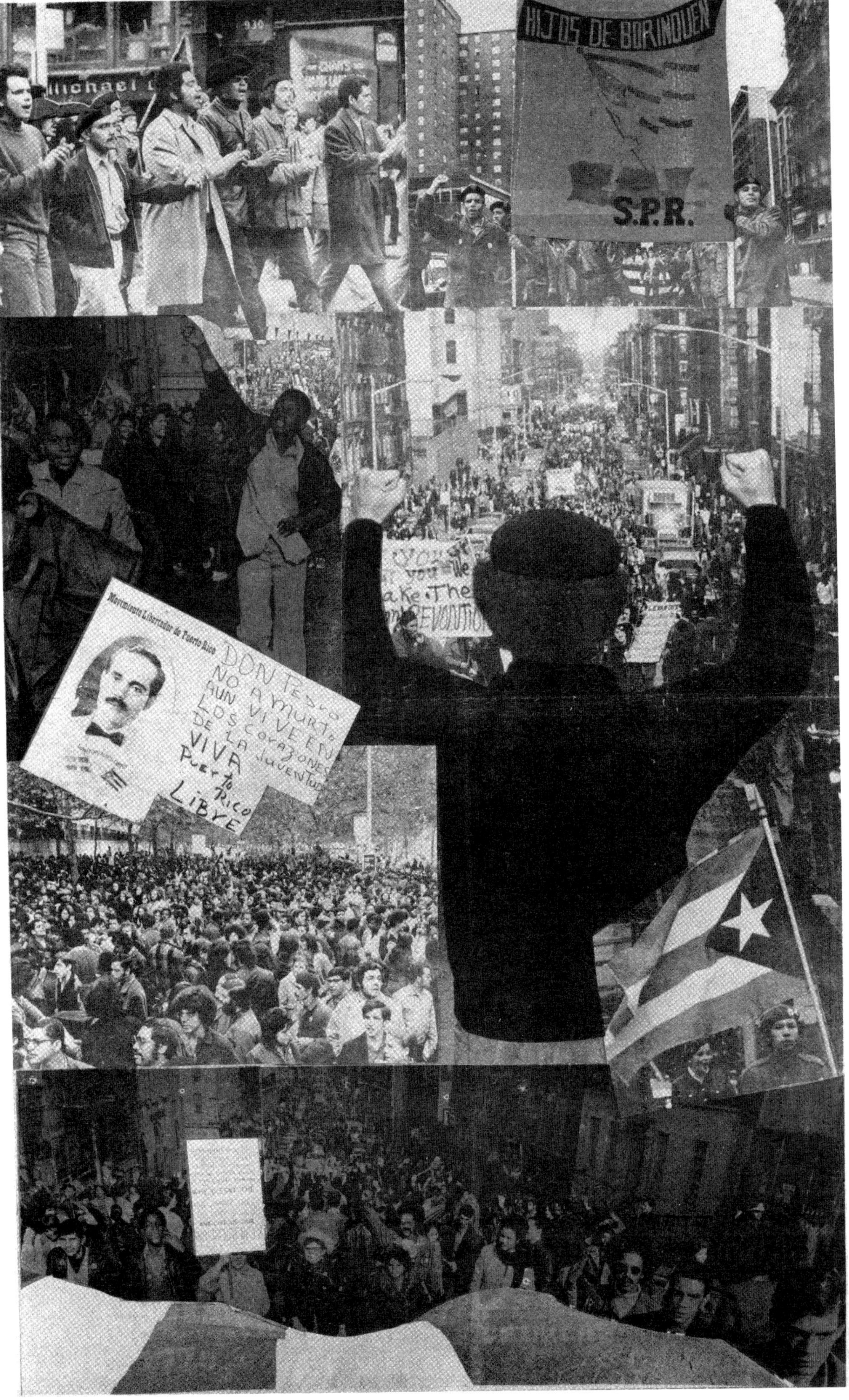
HIJOS DE BORINQUEN
S.P.R.
Movimiento Libertador de Puerto Rico
DON Pedro
NO A MURTo
AUN VIVE EN
LOS CORAZONES
DE LA JUVENTUD
VIVA
Puerto Rico
LIBYE

YOUNG LORDS PARTY

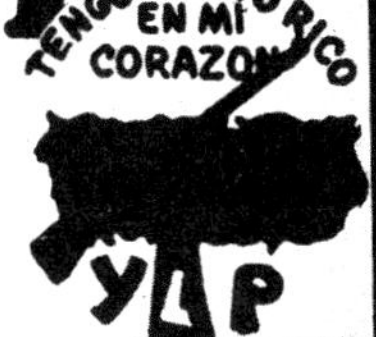

13 POINT PROGRAM AND PLATFORM

THE YOUNG LORDS PARTY IS A REVOLUTIONARY POLITICAL PARTY FIGHTING FOR THE LIBERATION OF ALL OPPRESSED PEOPLE

1. WE WANT SELF-DETERMINATION FOR PUERTO RICANS, LIBERATION ON THE ISLAND AND INSIDE THE UNITED STATES.

For 500 years, first spain and then the united states have colonized our country. Billions of dollars in profits leave our country for the united states every year. In every way we are slaves of the gringo. We want liberation and the Power in the hands of the People, not Puerto Rican exploiters. QUE VIVA PUERTO RICO LIBRE!

2. WE WANT SELF-DETERMINATION FOR ALL LATINOS.

Our Latin Brothers and Sisters, inside and outside the united states, are oppressed by amerikkkan business. The Chicano people built the Southwest, and we support their right to control their lives and their land. The people of Santo Domingo continue to fight against gringo domination and its puppet generals. The armed liberation struggles in Latin America are part of the war of Latinos against imperialism. QUE VIVA LA RAZA!

3. WE WANT LIBERATION OF ALL THIRD WORLD PEOPLE.

Just as Latins first slaved under spain and the yanquis, Black people, Indians, and Asians slaved to build the wealth of this country. For 400 years they have fought for freedom and dignity against racist Babylon. Third World people have led the fight for freedom. All the colored and oppressed peoples of the world are one nation under oppression. NO PUERTO RICAN IS FREE UNTIL ALL PEOPLE ARE FREE!

4. WE ARE REVOLUTIONARY NATIONALISTS AND OPPOSE RACISM.

The Latin, Black, Indian and Asian people inside the u.s. are colonies fighting for liberation. We know that washington, wall street, and city hall will try to make our nationalism into racism; but Puerto Ricans are of all colors and we resist racism. Millions of poor white people are rising up to demand freedom and we support them. These are the ones in the u.s. that are stepped on by the rulers and the government. We each organize our people, but our fights are the same against oppression and we will defeat it together. POWER TO ALL OPPRESSED PEOPLE!

5. WE WANT EQUALITY FOR WOMEN. DOWN WITH MACHISMO AND MALE CHAUVANISM.

Under capitalism, women have been oppressed by both society and our men. The doctrine of machismo has been used by men to take out their frustrations on wives, sisters, mothers, and children. Men must fight along with sisters in the struggle for economic and social equality and must recognize that sisters make up over half of the revolutionary army: sisters and brothers are equals fighting for our people. FORWARD SISTERS IN THE STRUGGLE!

6. WE WANT COMMUNITY CONTROL OF OUR INSTITUTIONS AND LAND.

We want control of our communities by our people and programs to guarantee that all institutions serve the needs of our people. People's control of police, health services, churches, schools, housing, transportation and welfare are needed. We want an end to attacks on our land by urban renewal, highway destruction, and university corporations. LAND BELONGS TO ALL THE PEOPLE!

7. WE WANT A TRUE EDUCATION OF OUR AFRO-INDIO CULTURE AND SPANISH LANGUAGE.

We must learn our long history of fighting against cultural, as well as economic genocide by the spaniards and now the yanquis. Revolutionary culture, culture of our people, is the only true teaching. JIBARO SI, YANQUI NO!

8. WE OPPOSE CAPITALISTS AND ALLIANCES WITH TRAITORS.

Puerto Rican rulers, or puppets of the oppressor, do not help our people. They are paid by the system to lead our people down blind alleys, just like the thousands of poverty pimps who keep our communities peaceful for business, or the street workers who keep gangs divided and blowing each other away. We want a society where the people socialistically control their labor. VENCEREMOS!

9. WE OPPOSE THE AMERIKKKAN MILITARY.

We demand immediate withdrawal of all u.s. military forces and bases from Puerto Rico, VietNam, and all oppressed communities inside and outside the u.s.. No Puerto Rican should serve in the u.s. army against his Brothers and Sisters, for the only true army of oppressed people is the People's Liberation Army to fight all rulers. U.S. OUT OF VIETNAM, FREE PUERTO RICO NOW!

10. WE WANT FREEDOM FOR ALL POLITICAL PRISONERS AND PRISONERS OF WAR.

No Puerto Rican should be in jail or prison, first because we are a nation, and amerikkka has no claims on us; second, because we have not been tried by our own people (peers). We also want all freedom fighters out of jail, since they are prisoners of the war for liberation. FREE ALL POLITICAL PRISONERS AND PRISONERS OF WAR!

11. WE ARE INTERNATIONALISTS.

Our people are brainwashed by television, radio, newspapers, schools and books to oppose people in other countries fighting for their freedom. No longer will we believe these lies, because we have learned who the real enemy is and who our real friends are. We will defend our sisters and brothers around the world who fight for justice and are against the rulers of this country. QUE VIVA CHE GUEVARA!

12. WE BELIEVE ARMED SELF-DEFENSE AND ARMED STRUGGLE ARE THE ONLY MEANS TO LIBERATION.

We are oppose to violence - the violence of hungry children, illiterate adults, diseased old people, and the violence of poverty and profit. We have asked, petitioned, gone to courts, demonstrated peacefully, and voted for politicians full of empty promises. But we still ain't free. The time has come to defend the lives of our people against repression and for revolutionary war against the businessmen, politicians, and police. When a government oppresses the people, we have the right to abolish it and create a new one. ARM OURSELVES TO DEFEND OURSELVES!

13. WE WANT A SOCIALIST SOCIETY.

We want liberation, clothing, free food, education, health care, transportation, full employment and peace. We want a society where the needs of the people come first, and where we give solidarity and aid to the people of the world, not oppression and racism. HASTA LA VICTORIA SIEMPRE!

The Young Lords, "13 Point Program and Platform," published in *Palante* Vol. 2 No. 15, November 20, 1970

PARTIDO DE LOS YOUNG LORDS

PROGRAMA Y PLATAFORMA DE 13 PUNTOS

EL PARTIDO DE LOS YOUNG LORDS ES UN PARTIDO POLITICO REVOLUCIONARIO QUE LUCHA POR LA LIBERACION DE TODOS LOS PUEBLOS OPRIMIDOS.

1. QUEREMOS AUTODETERMINACION PARA TODOS LOS PUERTORRIQUENOS --- LIBERACION EN LA ISLA Y DENTRO DE LOS ESTADOS UNIDOS.

Hace 500 anos que nuestra isla ha estado colonizada: primero por espana y luego por los estados unidos. Billones de dolares en ganancias salen todos los anos de nuestra isla hacia los estados unidos. En todo sentido somos esclavos de los yanquis. Nosotros queremos la liberacion y el poder en las manos del pueblo, no en las de explotadores puertorriquenos. QUE VIVA PUERTO RICO LIBRE!

2. QUEREMOS AUTODETERMINACION PARA TODOS LOS LATINOS.

Nuestras hermanas y hermanos latinos, dentro y fuera de los e.e. u.u., son oprimidos por las empresas norteamerikkkanas. El pueblo Chicano construyo el sur-oeste de este pais, y nosotros apoyamos su derecho a controlar sus vidas y su tierra. El pueblo Dominicano continua su lucha contra la dominacion yanqui y sus generales titeres. La lucha armada en Latinoamerica forma parte de la guerra de todos los Latinos contra el imperialismo. QUE VIVA LA RAZA!

3. QUEREMOS LIBERACION PARA TODOS LOS PUEBLOS DEL TERCER MUNDO.

Tal como los Latinos trabajaron como esclavos, primero bajo espana y luego bajo los e.e. u.u., los pueblos Negros, Indios, y Asiaticos han laborado como esclavos para crear la riqueza de este pais. Por 400 anos estos han luchado contra la injusticia y la indigidad impuesta sobre ellos por esta babilonia racista. El Tercer Mundo ha dirigido la lucha por la liberacion. Todos los pueblos oprimidos y de color forman una nacion bajo la opresion. NINGUN PUERTORRIQUENO SERA LIBRE HASTA QUE TODOS LOS PUEBLOS NO SEAN LIBRES!

4. SOMOS NACIONALISTAS REVOLUCIONARIOS Y NOS OPONEMOS AL RACISMO.

Los pueblos Latinos, Negros, Indios, y Asiaticos dentro de los e.e. u.u. son colonias en lucha por la liberacion. Reconocimos que washington, wall street, y city hall trataran de convertir nuestro nacionalismo en racismo, pero los puertorriquenos somos de todos los colores y resistimos el racismo.Millones de personas pobres blancas se estan levantando a exigir su libertad, y a estas tambien nosotros las apoyamos. Son estas las que son pisoteadas por el gobierno y los dirigentes de los e.e. u.u. Cada cual organiza su pueblo, pero la lucha contra la opresion es una y unidos venceremos. PODER A TODOS LOS PUEBLOS OPRIMIDOS!

5. QUEREMOS IGUALDAD PARA LAS MUJERES. ABAJO CON EL MACHISMO Y CON EL CHAUVINISMO MASCULINO.

Bajo el capitalismo, la mujer es oprimida por ambos elementos, la sociedad y el hombre. La doctrina del machismo es usada por el hombre para desenvolver sus frustraciones en las esposas, hermanas, madres, y en los hijos. El hombre debe pelear a lado de sus hermanas en la lucha por la igualdad economica y social y debe reconocer que la mitad del ejercito revolucionario se va a componer de hermanas: las hermanas y los hermanos somos iguales, luchando jumtos por nuestro pueblo. ADELANTE HERMANAS EN LA LUCHA!

6. QUEREMOS CONTROL COMUNAL DE TODAS NUESTRAS INSTITUCIONES Y TIERRA.

Queremos que nuestras comunidades sean controladas por el pueblo, y exigimos programas que garantizen que todas las instituciones sirvan a las necesidades del pueblo. Queremos que el pueblo controle la policia, los servicios de salud, las iglesias, las escuelas, las viviendas, el transporte, y el bienestar publico. Queremos que se ponga fin a los asaltos que sobre nuestra tierra llevan a cabo la "eliminacion" urbana, la "destruccion" de carreteras, y las universidades y corporaciones. LA TIERRA PERTENECE A TODO EL PUEBLO!

7. QUEREMOS UNA EDUCACION VERDADERA DE NUESTRA CULTURA AFRO-TAINA Y EL USO DEL LENGUAJE ESPANOL.

Tenemos que aprender la historia de nuestra lucha contra el genocidio cultural y economico impuesto sobre nosotros por el yanqui. Cultura revolucionaria, la cultura de nuestro pueblo, es la unica ensenanza verdadera. JIBARO SI, YANQUI NO!

8. NOS OPONEMOS A LOS CAPITALISTAS Y A LAS ALIANZAS CON LOS TRAIDORES.

Los gobernantes puertorriquenos, titeres del opresor, no ayudan al pueblo. Aquellos son pagados por el sistema para que dirijan a nuestro pueblo por callejones sin salida. De la misma manera miles de alcahuetes contra la pobreza son pagados para que apaciguen a nuestras comunidades para el beneficio de los negociantes. Del mismo modo los trabajadores sociales deviden a nuestras gangas y las mantienen peleandose entre si. Queremos una sociedad en la cual el pueblo controle su labor de un modo socialista. VENCEREMOS!

9. NOS OPONEMOS AL EJERCITO NORTEAMERIKKKANO.

Demandamos la retirada inmeidata de las fuerzas militares norteamerikkkanas de Puerto Rico, Vietnam, y de todas las comunidades oprimidas dentro y fuera de los e.e. u.u. Ningun puertorriqueno debera inscribirse en el ejercito norteamerikkkano para luchar contra sus hermanos y hermanas oprimidas. El verdadero ejercito de un pueblo oprimido es el ejercito popular, el cual combatira a todos los gobernantes. ESTADOS UNIDOS FUERA DE VIETNAM! QUE VIVA PUERTO RICO LIBRE!

10. QUEREMOS LA LIBERTAD DE TODOS LOS PRISIONEROS POLITICOS Y DE TODOS LOS PRISIONEROS DE GUERRA.

Ningun Puertorriqueno debe estar en la carcel, primero porque nosotros somos una nacion y amerikkka no tiene ninguna reclamacion con nosotros; segundo, porque nosotros no hemos sido tratados por nuestra propia gente (nuestros semejantes). Tambien queremos a todos los luchadores de la libertad fuera de la carcel, porque ellos son prisioneros de la guerra de la liberacion. LIBERTAD A TODOS LOS PRISIONEROS POLITICOS Y PRISIONEROS DE GUERRA!

11. NOSOTROS SOMOS INTERNACIONALISTAS.

Nuestro pueblo es enganado por la television, el radio, los periodicos, las escuelas, y los libros para oponer a nuestra gente en contra de otros pueblos que estan luchando por su liberacion. Muy pronto ya no creeremos estas mentiras que todos estos medios han impuesto en nosotros, porque habremos aprendido quien es el verdadero enemigo y quienes son nuestros verdaderos amigos. Defenderemos a nuestras hermanas y hermanos alrededor del mundo que luchan por la justicia y que estan en contra de los duenos de este pais. VIVA EL "CHE" GUEVARA!

12. CREEMOS QUE LA AUTO-DEFENSA Y LA LUCHA ARMADA SON LOS UNICOS MEDIOS PARA LOGRAR NUESTRA LIBERACION.

Nos oponemos a la violencia --- la violencia de ninos hambrientos, adultos analfabetos, viejos enfermos, y la violencia de la pobreza y las ganancias. Hemos pedido y peticionado; hemos ido a las cortes; hemos menifestado pacificamente y hemos votado por politicos llenos de promesas falsas. Y todavia no somos libres. Ha llegado el momento en que nos tenemos que defender contra la represion. Tenemos que iniciar una guerra revolucionaria contra el negociante, el politico y el policia. Cuando un gobierno oprime al pueblo, el tiene el derecho de abolirlo y crear un gobierno nuevo. ARMEMONOS PARA DEFENDERNOS!

13. QUEREMOS UNA SOCIEDAD SOCIALISTA!

Queremos liberacion, alimentos gratis, ropas, viviendas, educacion, atencion medica, transporte, servicios de gas, luz y otros servicios y empleos para todos. Queremos una sociedad en la cual las necesidades del pueblo se antepongan a todo; una sociedad que de a los pueblos del mundo solidaridad y apoyo, no opresion o racismo. HASTA LA VICTORIA SIEMPRE!

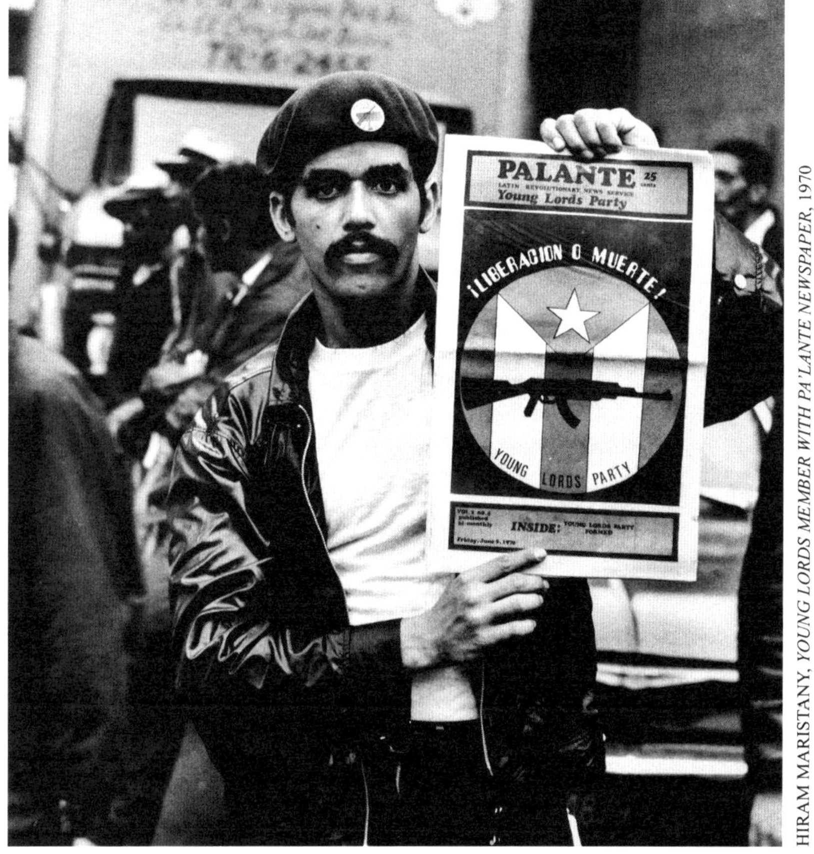

HIRAM MARISTANY, *YOUNG LORDS MEMBER WITH PA'LANTE NEWSPAPER*, 1970

Mei Hua

"EFEND DIGNITY COPYAND ORIGINAL"

:)

SMILE

TIME TEACMES ALL TMINGS HIM WHOMAVE WITHIN
ALOTED PLANTAS VEOME ORTE SALIMAE

C E IL I N E

FASHION
STOLE
MY
SMILE

The best time
New bcginning
Right now

Persistent

THE FUTURE IS BEHIND YOU

TO HELL
WITH
EVERYTHING

EVERYONE: AVOID LARGE
GATHERINGSTODREVET THI
SPREAD OFCORONAVIRUS

SB HEADS:

CARPE DIEM
THISTOSHALL
PASSAWAY

WEAINUNGLESS WASTE, TINE DOES NOT
Only the tone

Money is my mood

KEEP >>
MOVING
FORWARD

I'll be back
I'll be back

Riches
Unspecified
Fame, liquor,love,gioe it to
me slowly.

What is normal anyway?

LV

Louis Vuitton.
CHALLENGER RACES FOR
THE AMERICA S COP
FOR THE AMERICA S COP

hi.

don't be racist.

thanks.

Anything

M
FAS

YOUNGFASHION

Do you dream of month
n the United S duri
license whenyou
but it fees like yo
that day comes he
During th

DESNDNED IN THE UK FC
WILL
E
PROTECTION DURM
LOOK AFTER YOUR WETS

T
WASH THOROUGHLY IN C
STORE ON A HANGER TH
STORE IHSIDE AWAY FRC
KEEP AWAY FROM GREA
SHARP CEJECTS MAY CU

90% NEOPRENE 100% NE

No

YORK
NEW
CITY

NO
PE

New York
New York is a state in the
Northeastern and Mid--

idiot world

)UNG

FREEDOM

ALONG

TONIGHT
NEED YORK

CANAL

Art is a way of survivel.
fashion sport
ther your

YOU'RE
CUTE. CAN
I KEEP
YOU?

Eithout you? I'd be a
so
With e a
art
sdriver with m
a
e ut
a m,

Reflect

ARE U
READY 4

In spite of everything, I still bieiv epeopleare really good at heart,
-- ANNE FRANK (1929 - 1944)

SA utluise tunducee it
thousands of dollars ha
stolen from Gulf shores
uniploues allegedly soid
mes and owner clai
s a victim
AMY
DRBMER
cd
tunduce it
of dollars have been
Gulf Shores agercy
legedly sold bogus
owner claims she
im
se tunduce it
dollars have been
ulf Shores agency
edly sold bogus
wner claim s she

duce it

been t
f shores agercy s
bogus e
wner claims she p

SOLD
OUT

When I was afre ding
afriend come on while will be long
hugry as machine
what do you thinking unber highyer
be too afraid
so I is bigger from mewyorker
"good lucky"
someones wad toother

When I was afre ding
afriend come on while will be long
hugry as machine
what do you thinking unber highyer
be too afraid
so I is bigger from mewyorker
"good lucky"
someones wad toother

Glamour
HYSTERIU
ARGRL!

IT

ER BY

R USE
IDE OUTI
O DRY
DUCTS
ETSUTT

AND THE
SCREEN
THAT CIRCLE
YOU LIKE
NUTERFLIES
NOW//
ALL YOUR
EOMORROWS
TURNED
TO ELECTRIC
WATERFALLS
MODERNISM
IS A
DREAM
OF FALE
TAYATION
AND GENDER
QUATELITY
AND OF TEALIY
I I WATENESS
DREAM OF
LOVE.
A FROMISE
OF OVIUSINO
ZHUOWA STYLESTUDIO

OFF MIRACLES

:)
HERE
any enquiries relating to
advertising on our online or
print edition please contact
info@imutemagazine.com
iMUTE

WHEN I WAS LITTLE
I NEVER THOUGHT
EYEBROWS WOULD
BE THIS IMPORTANT.

Www.shift ,and ctrl tab caps look And So What
May Be You re No

ARTIST
STUDY

SCHOOL

RUINED

HONESTY

Shanzhai Lyric, "Incomplete Poem," 2015–ongoing

GUANGZHOU
ANERJIMER

I'm so fancy

STAND!
EVASIOY
vioent,uncohtrollble anger.
"her fase was distorted woth rage"
LOST GENERA TION
Lakeof Fire (1994)
"Forecer for hiehr hole"

UNCONDITONA
NEW YORK STOCK EXCHANGE

Eng soen yod andao moosm yodao addr
fesh costma costm daldcytal dyoscay yoad

pudlatl cfshion so

BE YOUR
MUSE

NUIVERSAL

ALWAYS BE
DIFFERENT.

FASHION
RSCESSWE
WEENANGEYU

WE
SHOUL
ALL B
FEMENIS

BEIBI

1992
I'm so tired of Love
I'm still more tired of Rhyme
But moner gives me pleasure all the timc
Lack of money is the roo of all evl

100% Happ
comus from y
not trdm youf su

AF 88
Lovetoma
LOVEHC
<3 <3 <
Please always
that I love yo
than anylhi

in thc w

sklayie jiabyeti aybe oasth klab ylesat h
m,ek atybeot iyaith k
jakj alyib skali atyovbse hkalbi asot yalb
seut uatkseutv asot y

ajkiwi qyt oasis tybvse tjmk laybioastik s
amnl kbsy let lk; sal eyib

qwiy iso ybsai otkla pi bshel kasl iyb eis

Discarded may be able to grow,
cliff might be able to be reborn…
Hello kitty

W
FC
EV

Anther.
Anther.
"Never Mistake"
Anther.

RIHANNA
@Rihanna

Alcohol is the devil and i need chinese food.
6:49 PM-5.Jan

163K COMMENT 41MM LIKE

YOU CAN ONLY
DE AS GOOD
AS YOUR TASTE

SINL IM BDFY
AND CHA JR THE DNA
TOG H IDEASTAR
OERH HOLDE RNEC-
CISA
NANE AEWGR LNE FOL GUYS MHF

GIRLS ONCE OFHNX RITH IT
NJHTX R WNWR IE
VNHOUTIT HRU HFG NSFOREVER

MY PERSONALITY
CREATING AND LEADING FASHION

Indulge your fantasies this season with sexy sithouettes and luxurionus lace
PHOTOGRPAHY LSE ZNCO FASHION NEW SIWZHE

AREA OF A
TRIANGLE

DISTINGTIVE
LOOK

STAY
FOCUSED

BOOM!

NEW PRODUCTS ON THE MARKET IN WINTER
THE EXPLOSION THE
DIS TRIBUTION AND PROMOYION THE
TLARGE DERONATIOG

In The Height of Fashion Into The Depths
In The Height of Fashion Into The Depths
In The Height of Fashion Into The Depths
In The Height of Fashion Into The Depths
In The Height of Fashion Into The Depths
In The Height of Fashion Into The Depths
In The Height of Fashion Into The Depths
In The Height of Fashion Into The Depths
In The Height of Fashion Into The Depths
In The Height of Fashion Into The Depths
In The Height of Fashion Into The Depths
In The Height of Fashion Into The Depths
In The Height of Fashion Into The Depths
In The Height of Fashion Into The Depths
In The Height of Fashion Into The Depths
In The Height of Fashion Into The Depths
In The Height of Fashion Into The Depths
In The Height of Fashion Into The Depths
In The Height of Fashion Into The Depths
In The Height of Fashion Into The Depths
In The Height of Fashion Into The Depths
In The Height of Fashion Into The Depths
In The Height of Fashion Into The Depths
In The Height of Fashion Into The Depths
In The Height of Fashion Into The Depths
In The Height of Fashion Into The Depths
In The Height of Fashion Into The Depths
In The Height of Fashion Into The Depths
In The Height of Fashion Into The Depths
In The Height of Fashion Into The Depths
In The Height of Fashion Into The Depths

I'M ALRI COOL
EADY THE LAST
SEASON ' S
GREATING
LEGENDS ARE
ARE BORN
IN OCTOBER
BROOKLYN
EGE LEAGUE
LEGENDARY TEAM
CO.
TEAM
QUALITY

G

N

E R
R FOR-
REVER

Shanzhai Lyric, "Incomplete Poem," 2015–ongoing

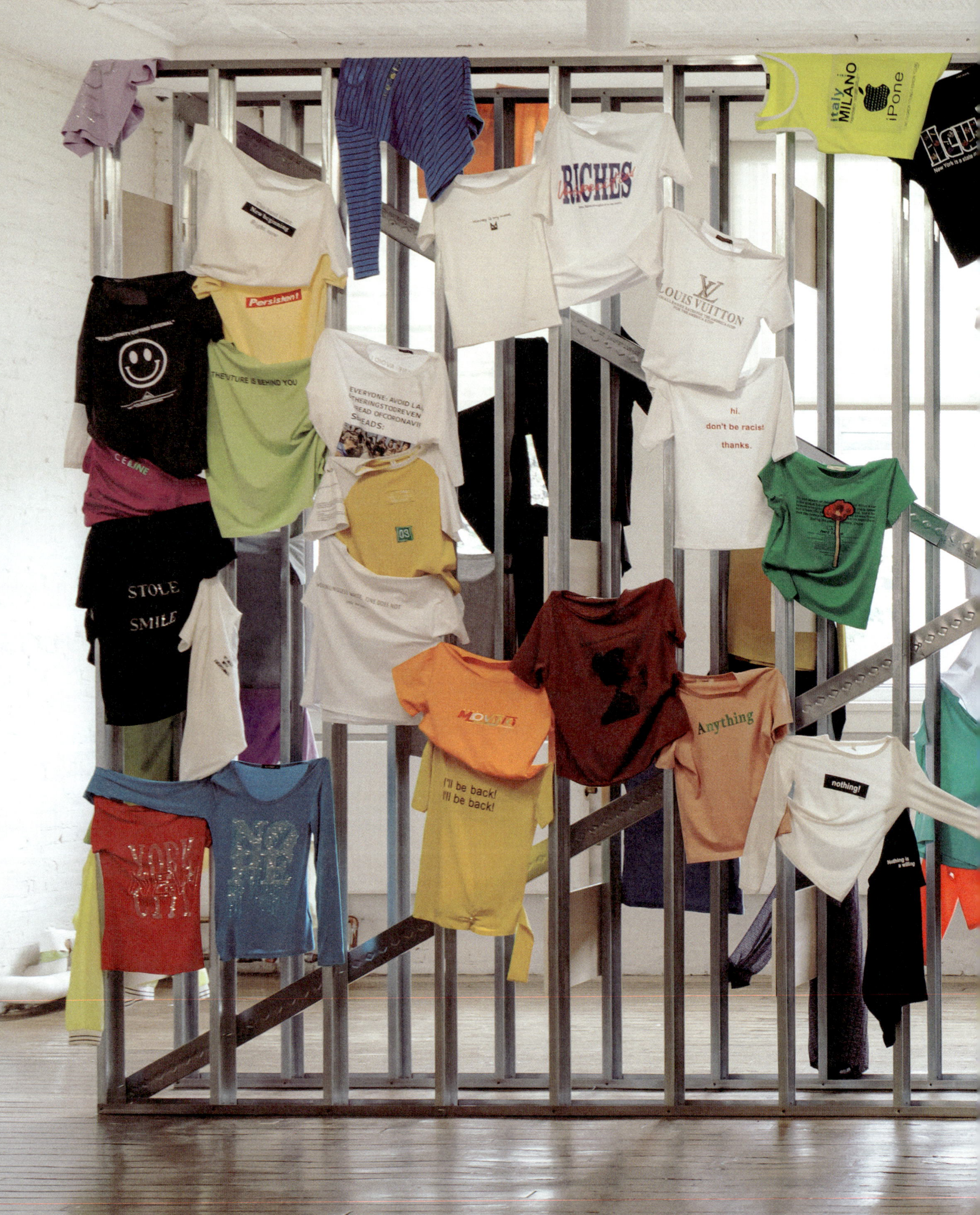

Shanzhai Lyric
Incomplete Poem, 2015–ongoing

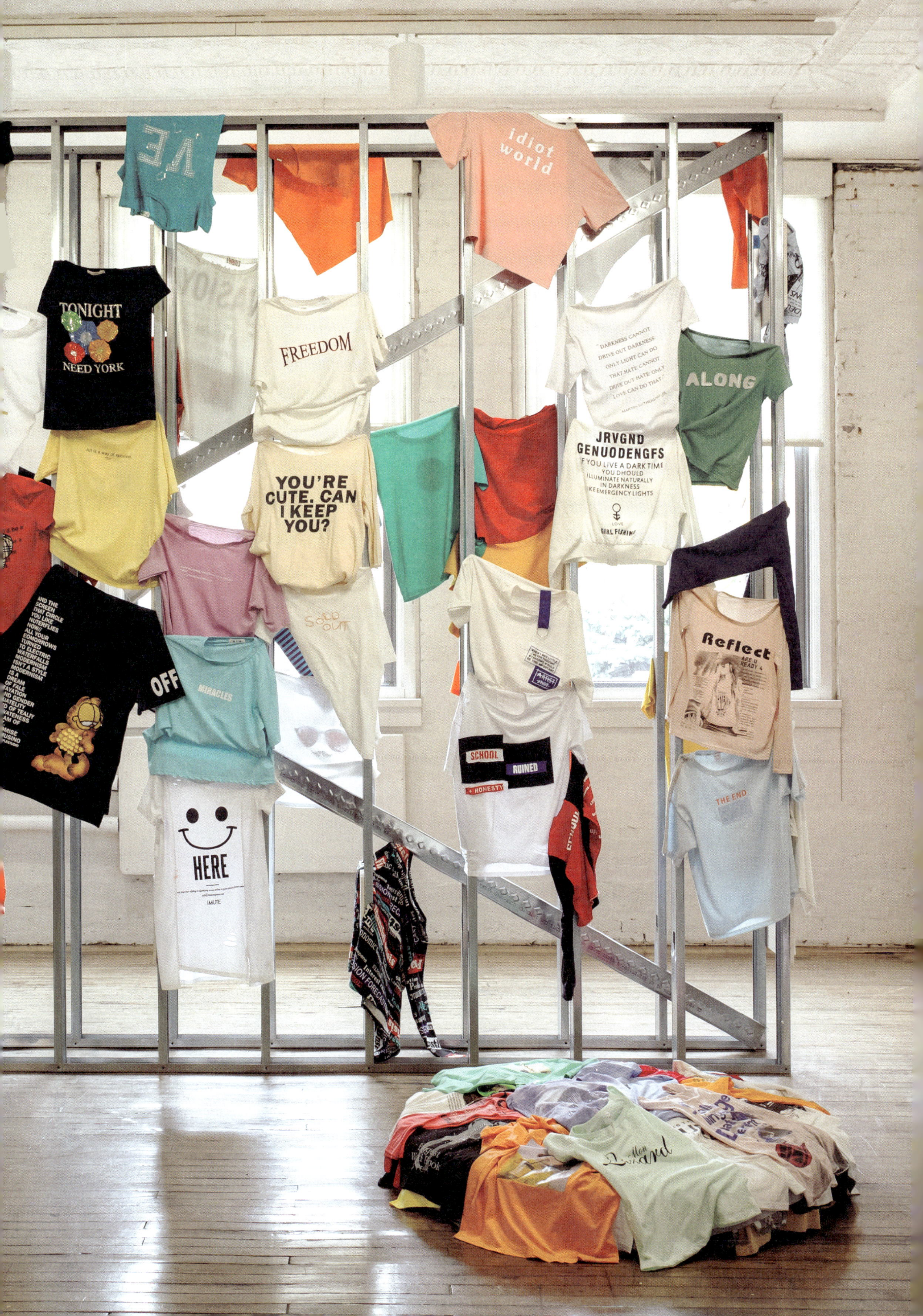
idiot world
TONIGHT
NEED YORK
FREEDOM
DARKNESS CANNOT DRIVE OUT DARKNESS ONLY LIGHT CAN DO THAT HATE CANNOT DRIVE OUT HATE ONLY LOVE CAN DO THAT
ALONG
YOU'RE CUTE. CAN I KEEP YOU?
JRVGND GENUODENGFS
IF YOU LIVE A DARK TIME YOU DHOULD ILLUMINATE NATURALLY IN DARKNESS
LOVE
GIRL FISHING
SOLD OUT
Reflect
ARE U READY 4
OFF
MIRACLES
SCHOOL
RUINED
HONESTY
THE END
HERE

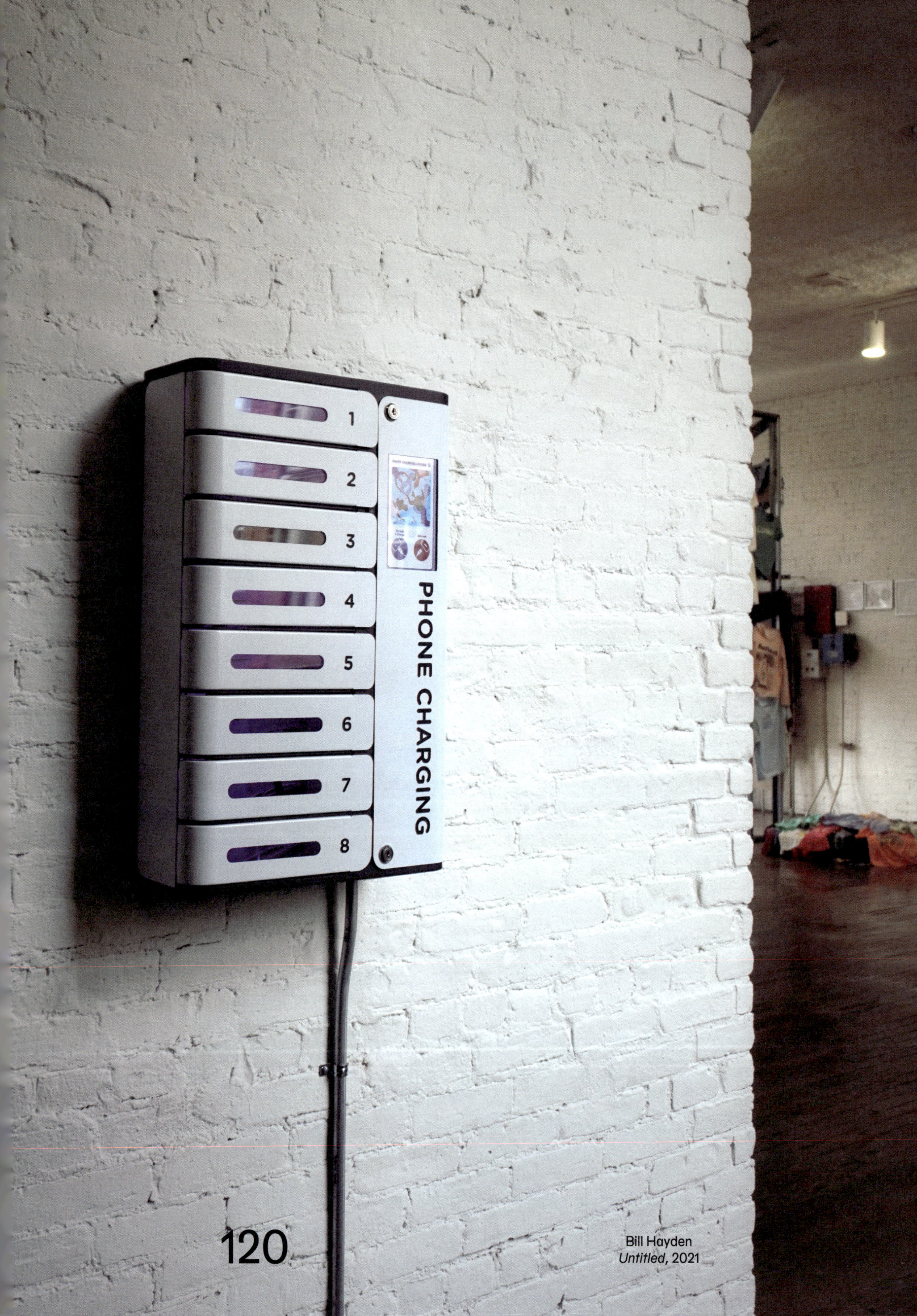

Bill Hayden
Untitled, 2021

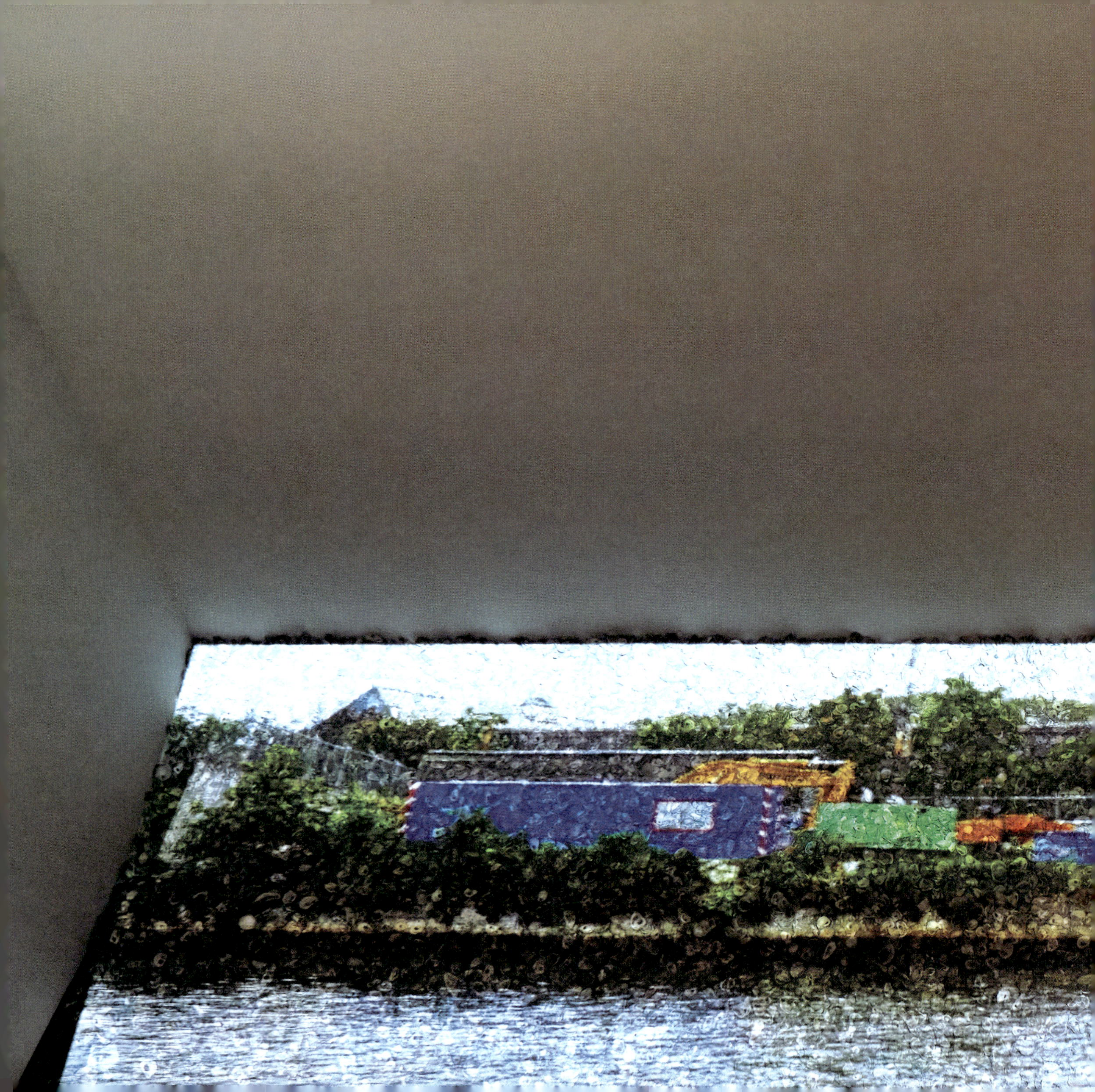

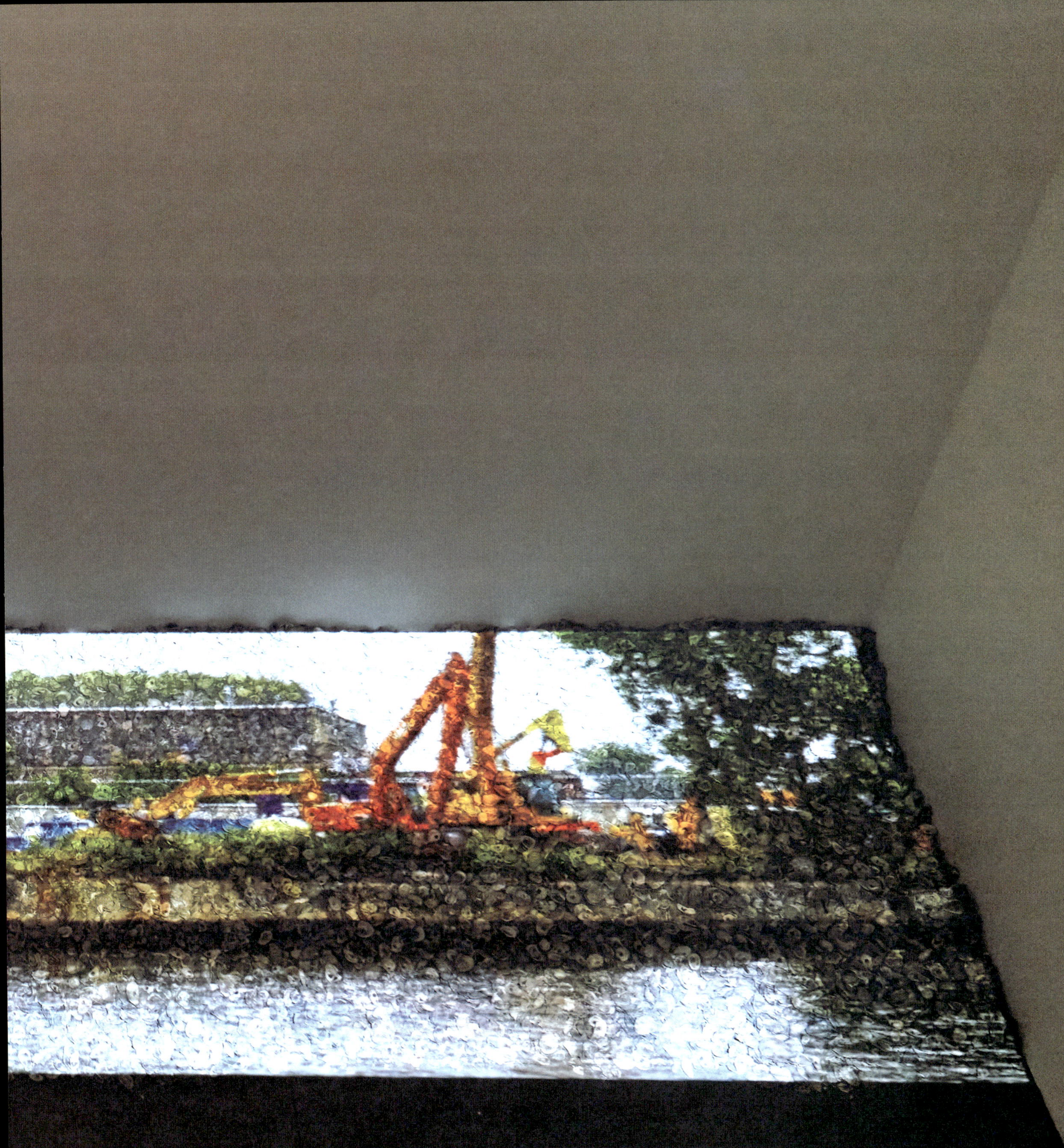

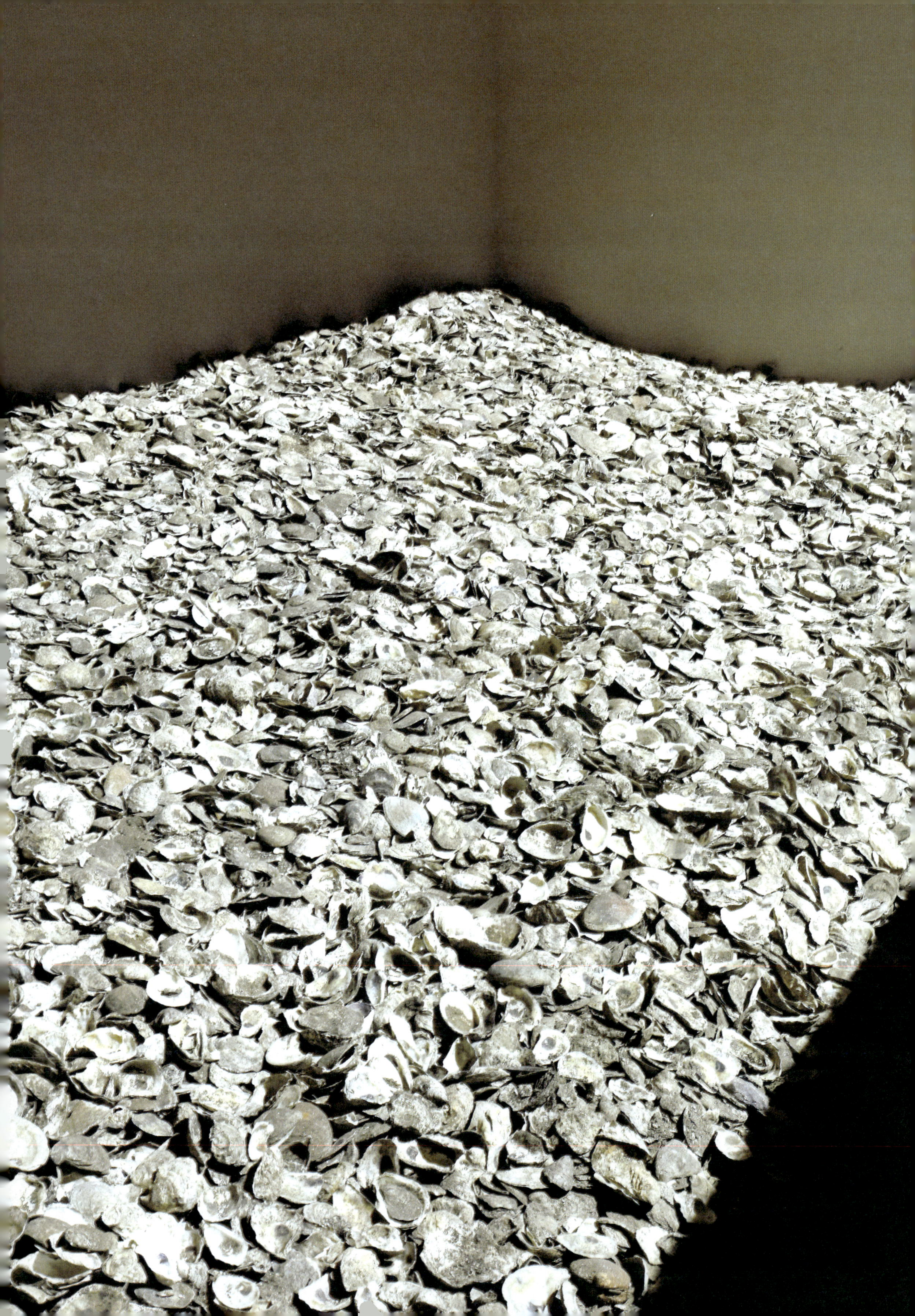

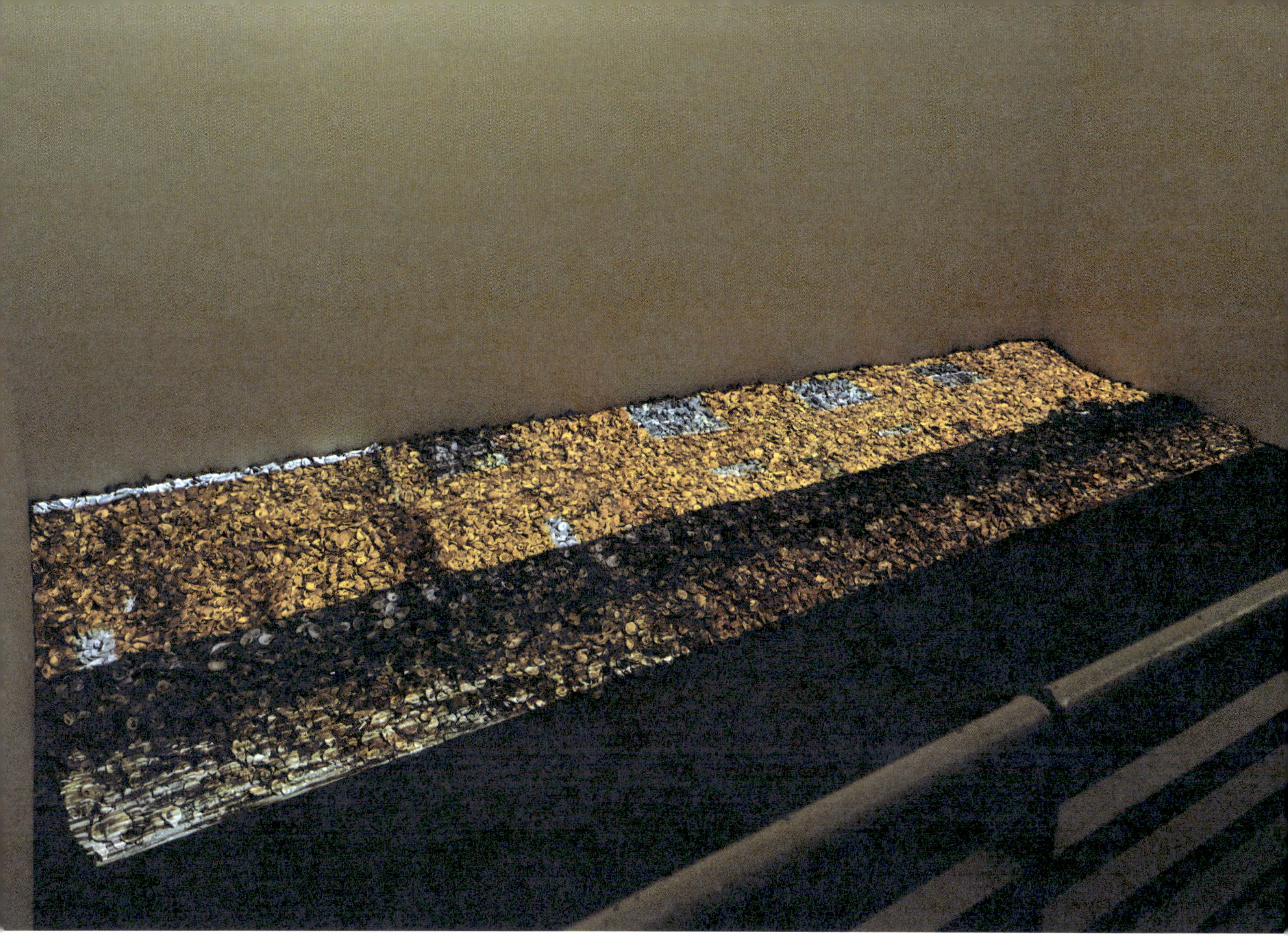

Alan Michelson
Midden, 2021

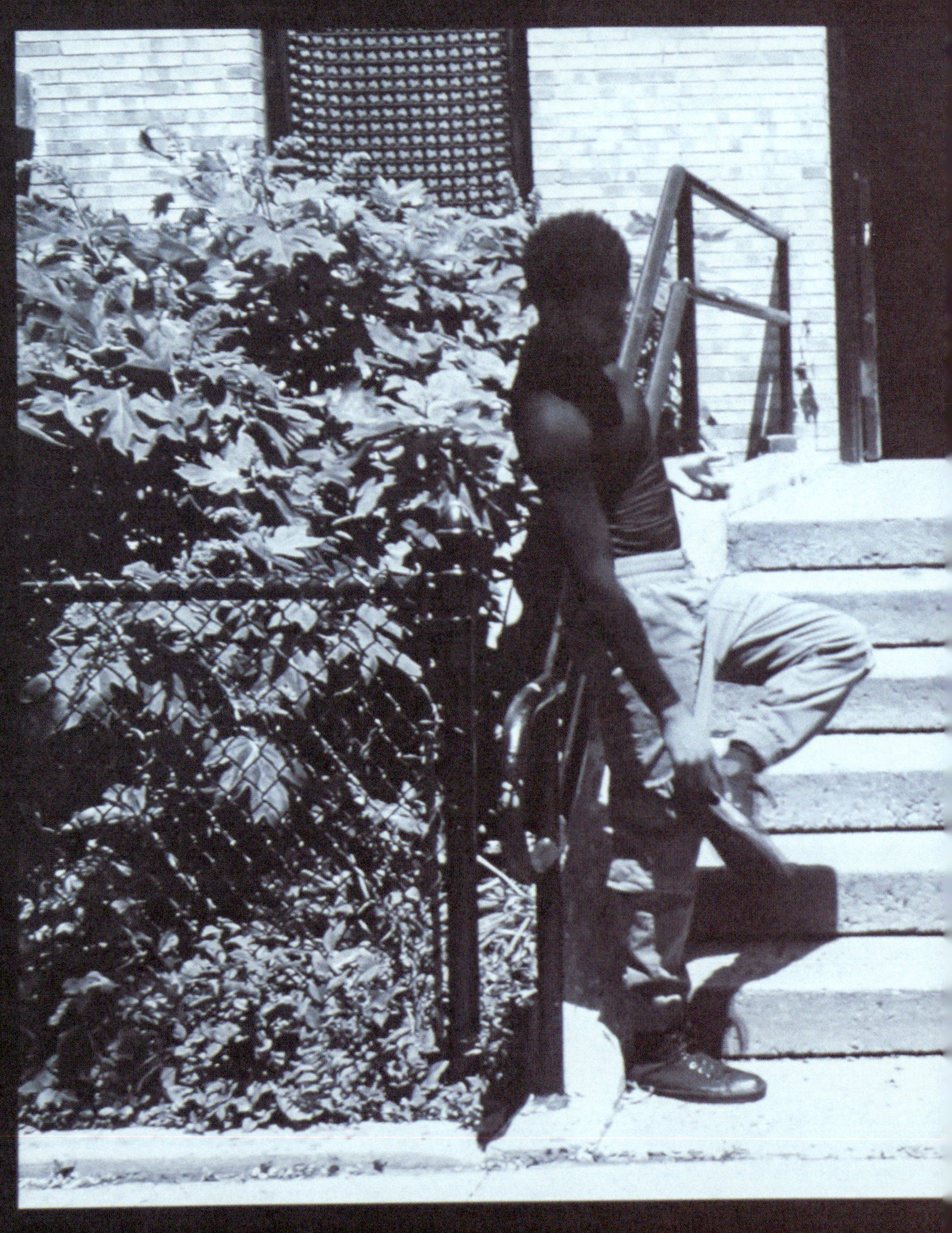

Steffani Jemison
Similitude, 2019

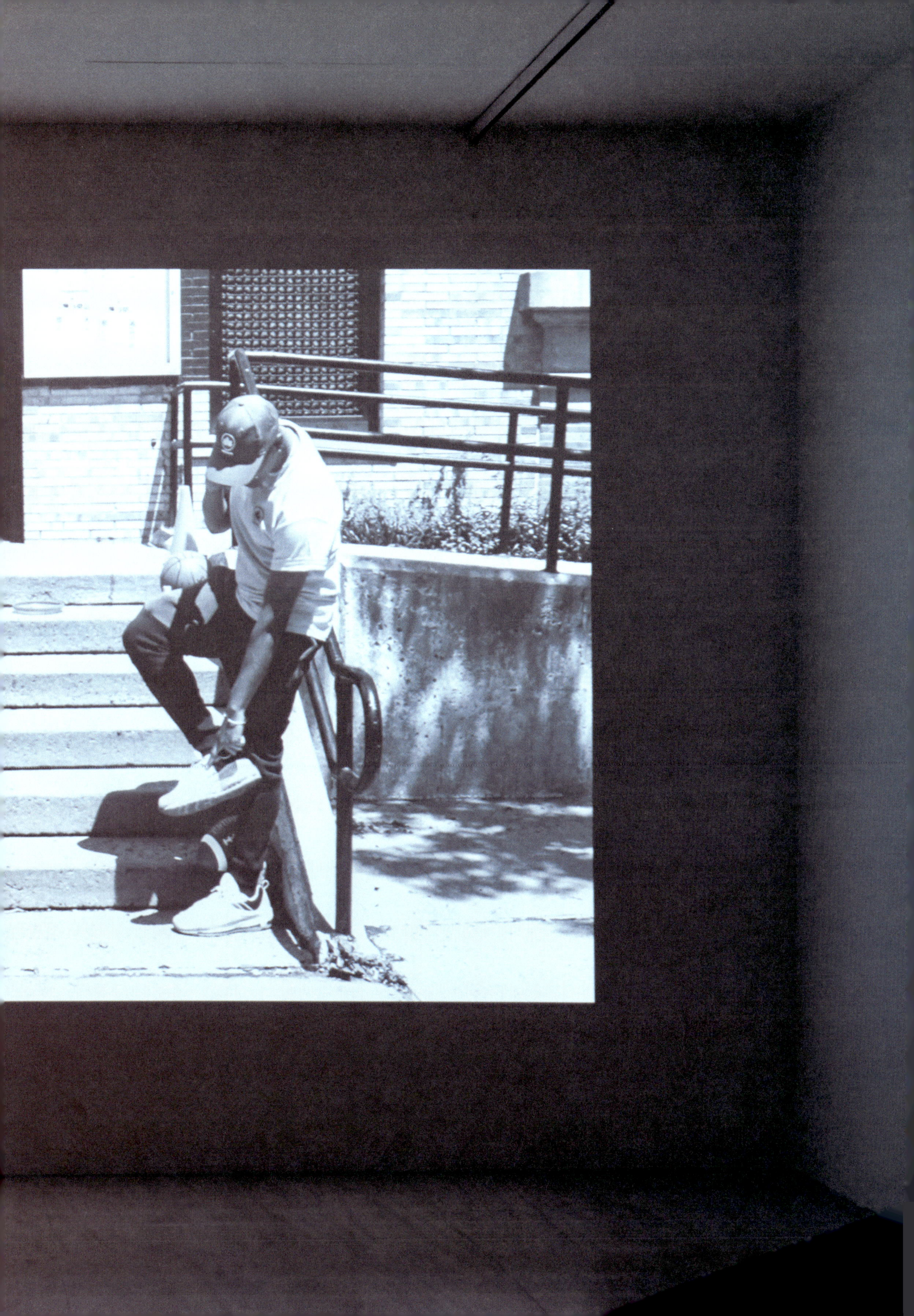

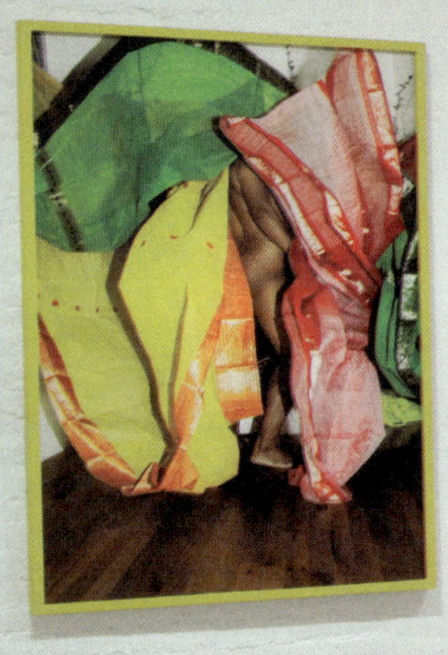

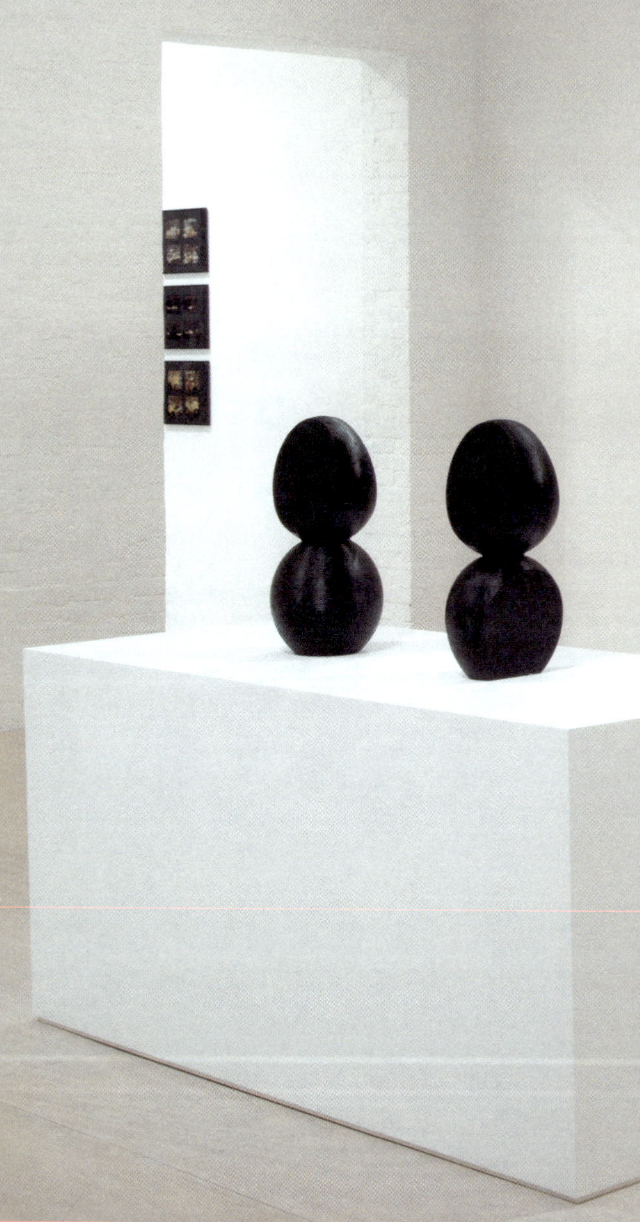

Left to right
Avijit Halder, Nadia Ayari

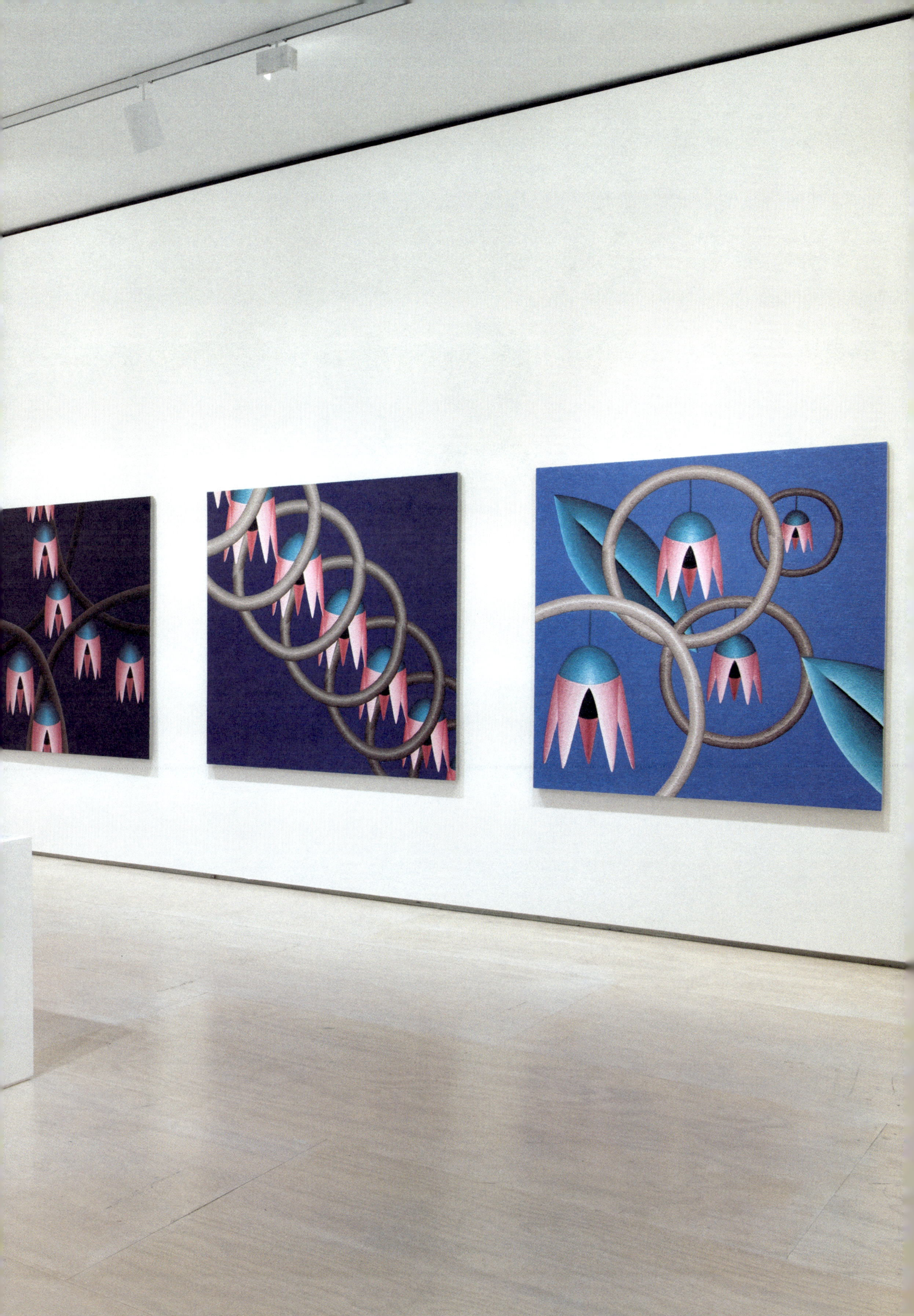

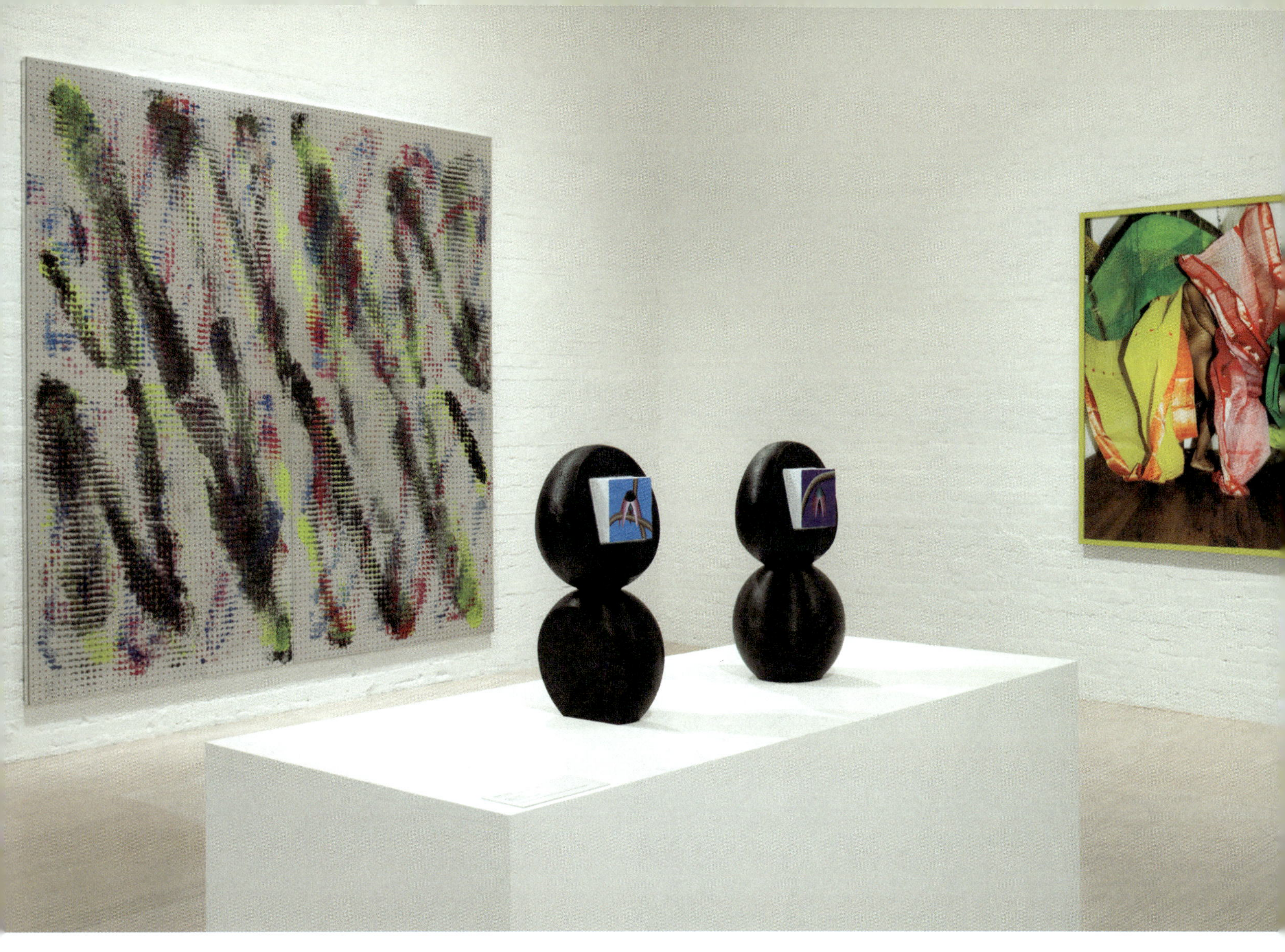

Left to right
Servane Mary, Nadia Ayari, Avijit Halder

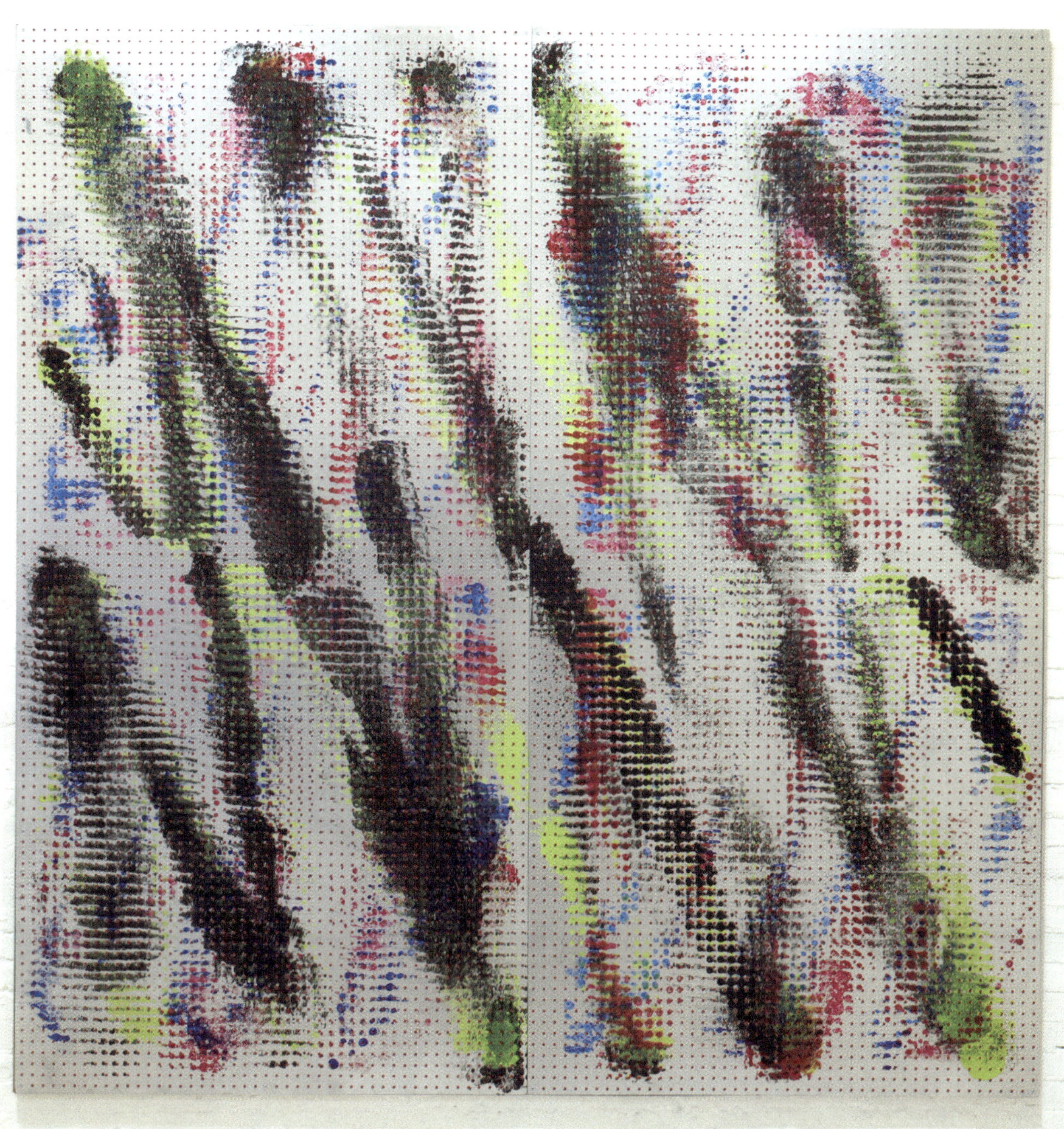

Servane Mary
Stay in the middle two lanes, 2020–2021

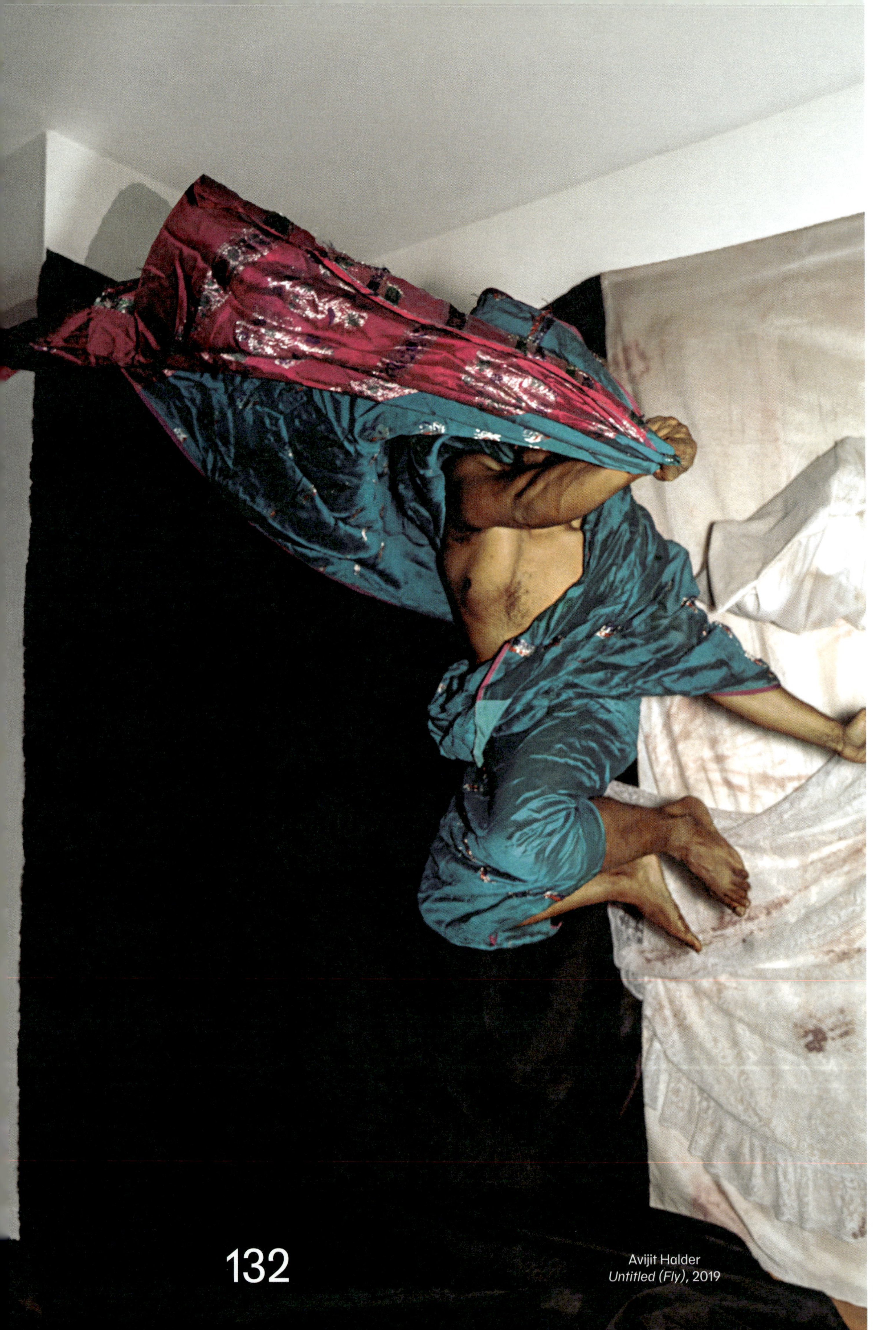

Avijit Halder
Untitled (Fly), 2019

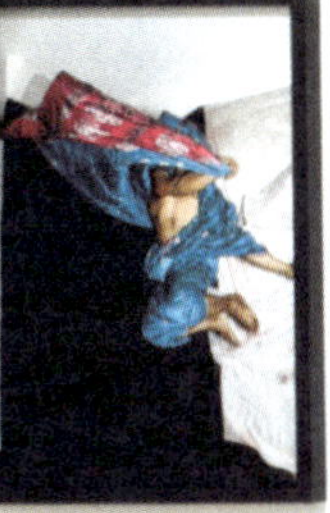
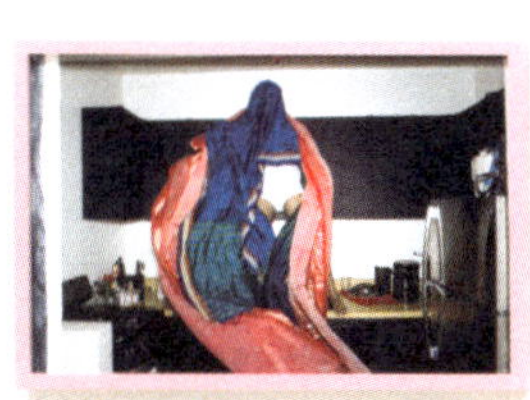
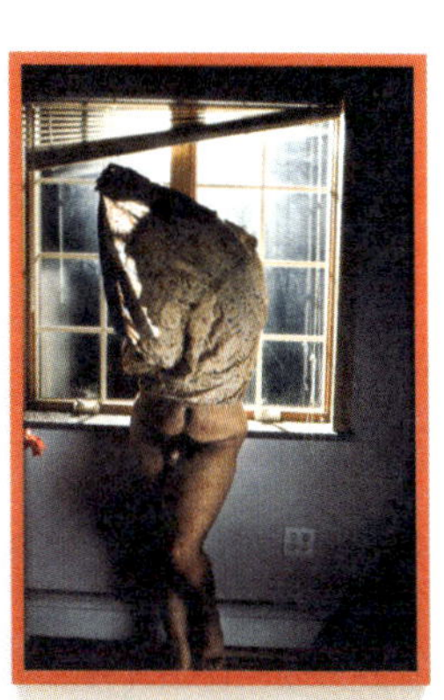
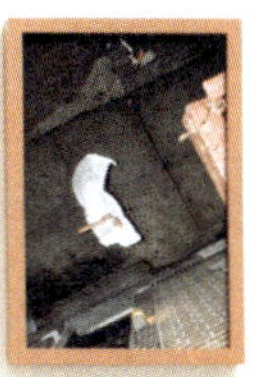
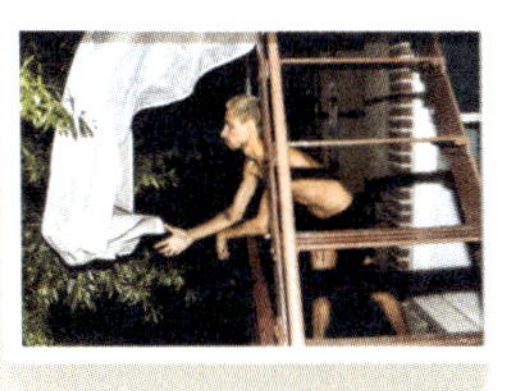
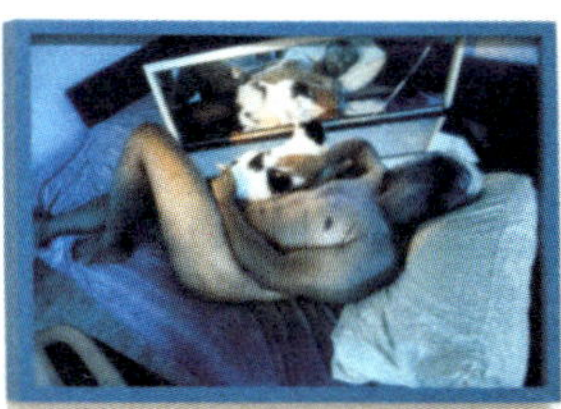

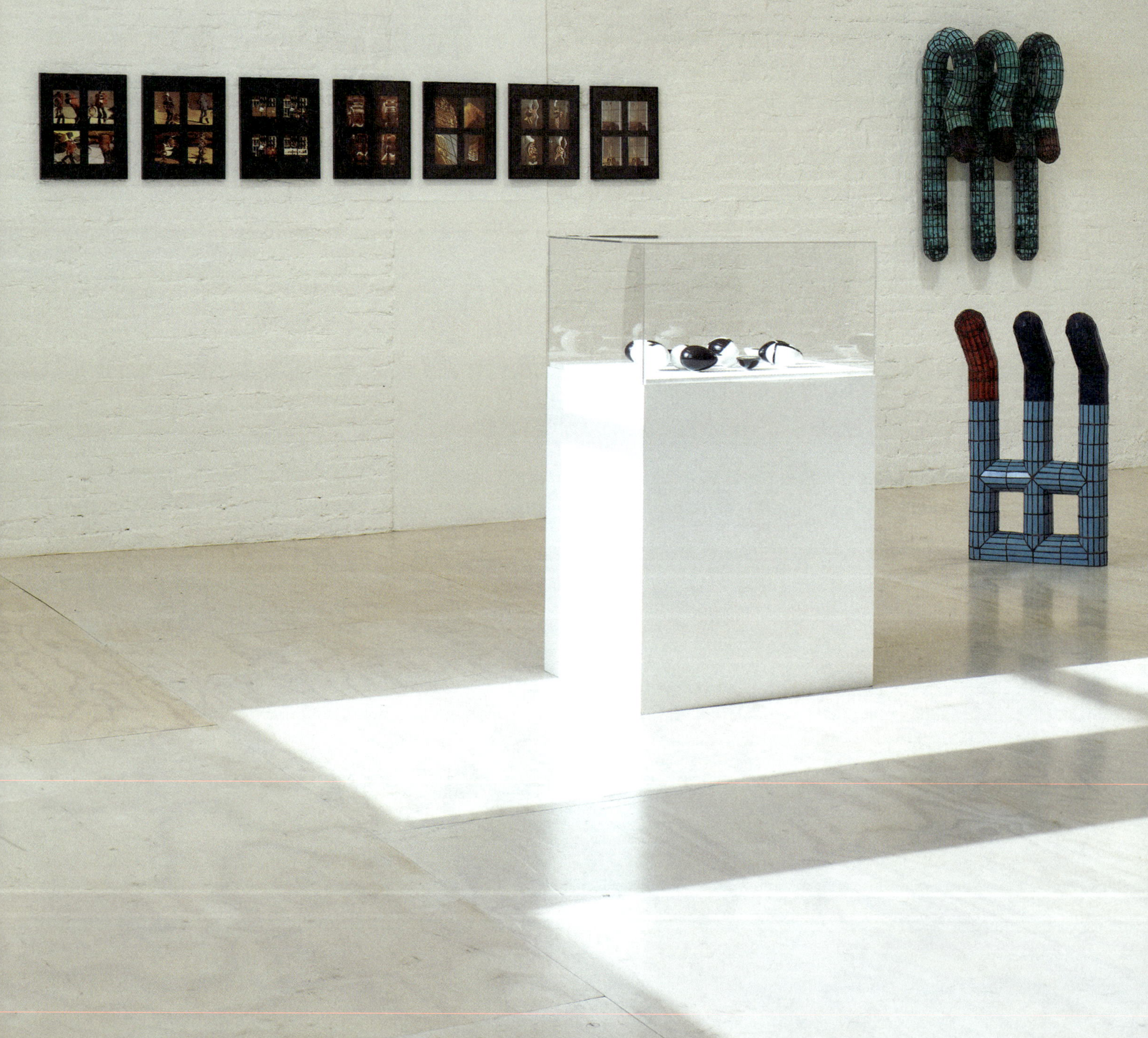

Left to right
Bettina Grossman, Kristi Cavataro, Hiram Maristany

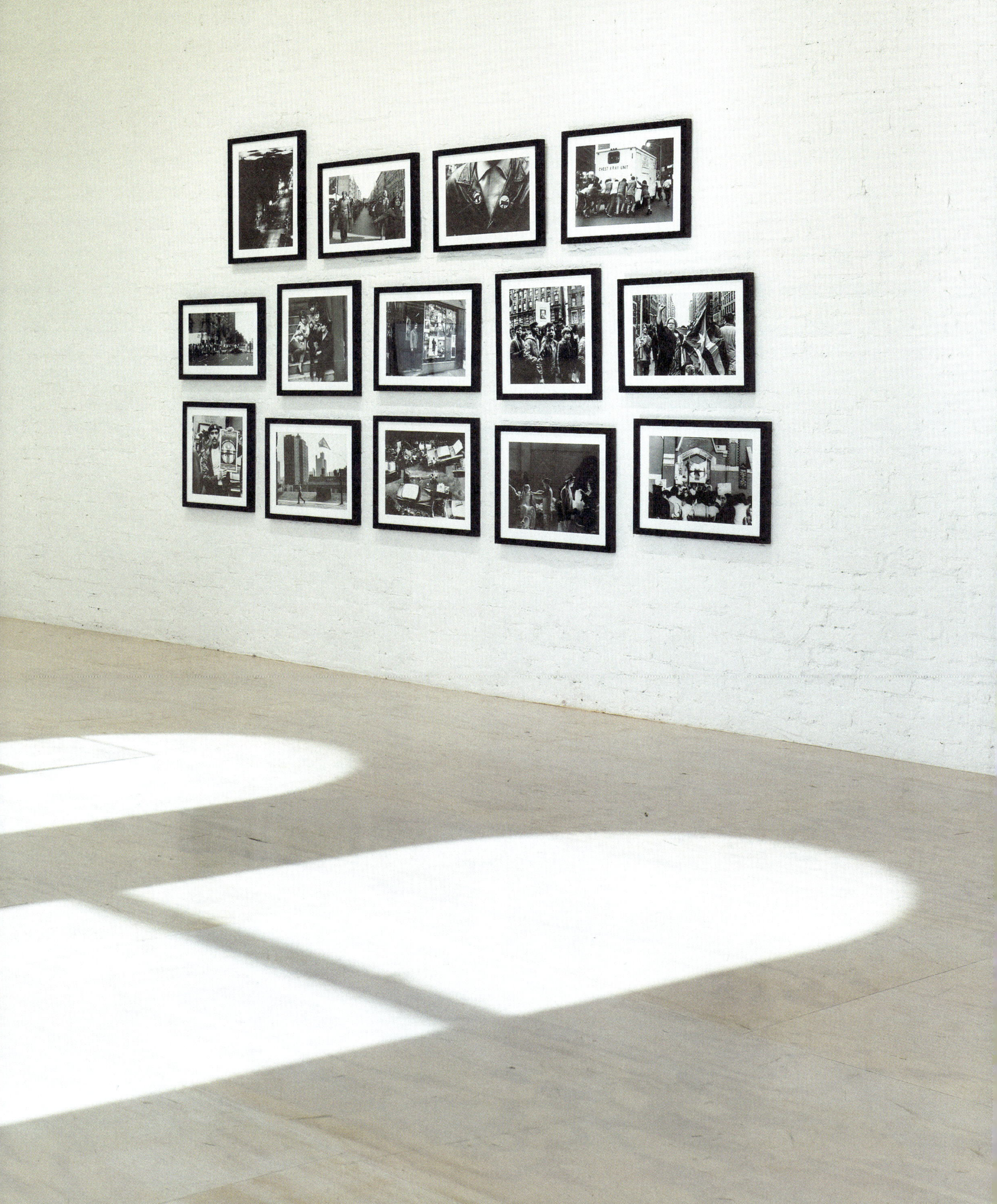
CHEST X-RAY UNIT

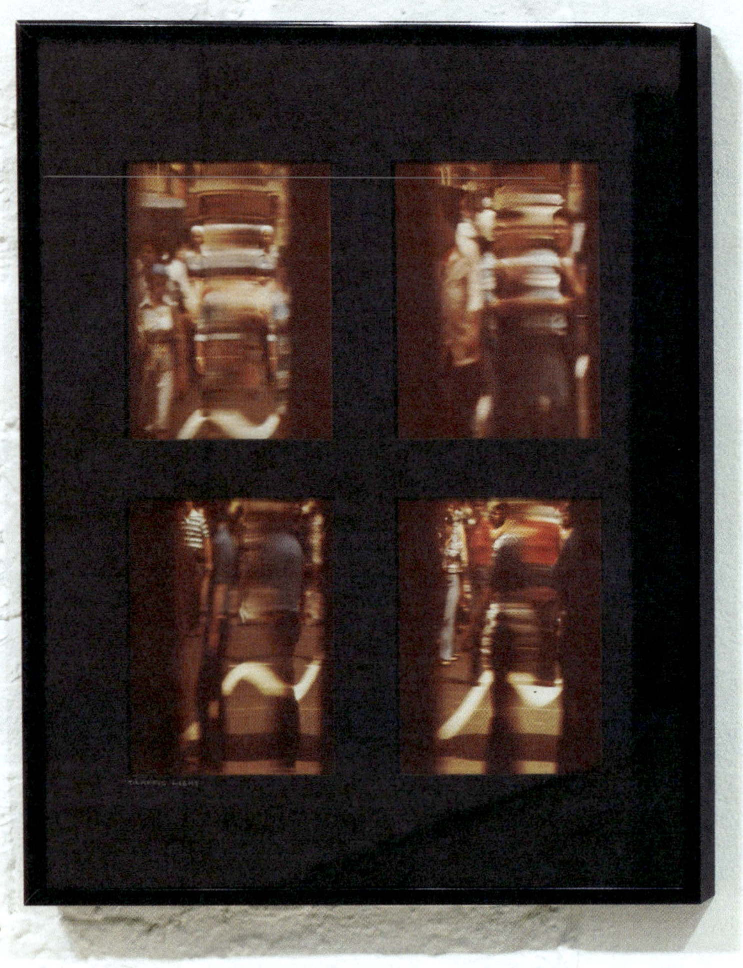

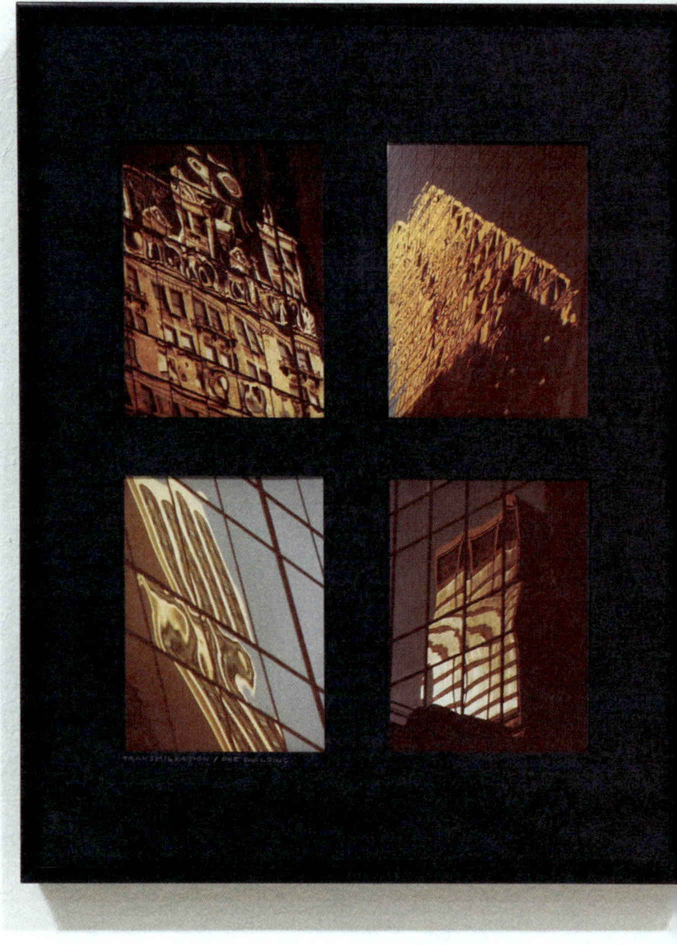

Bettina Grossman
Detail, *Phenomenology Project*, 1979–1980

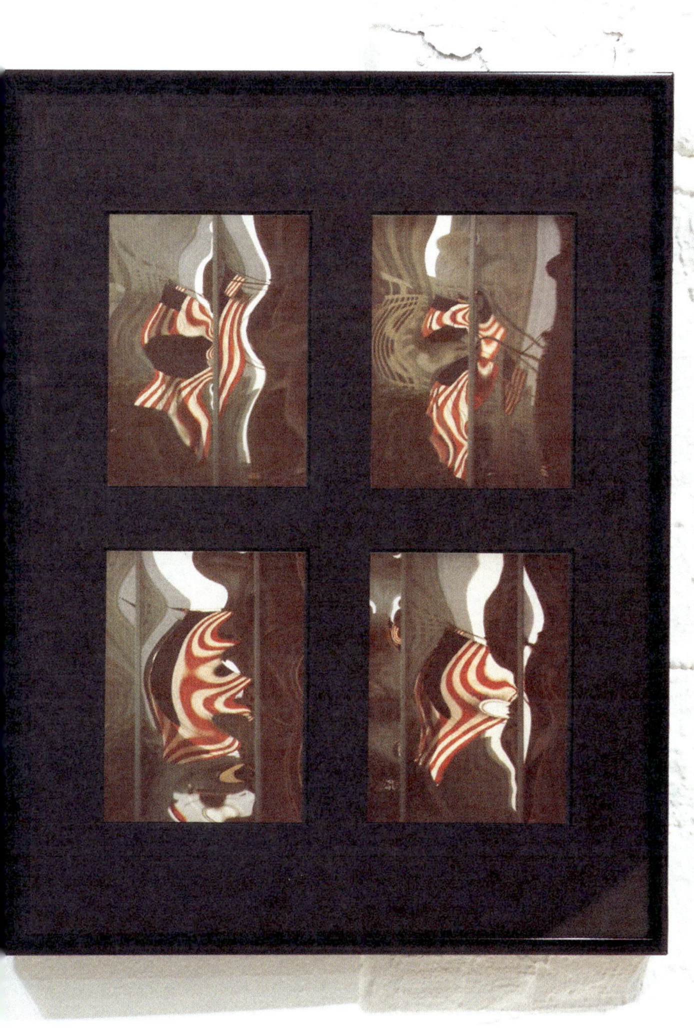

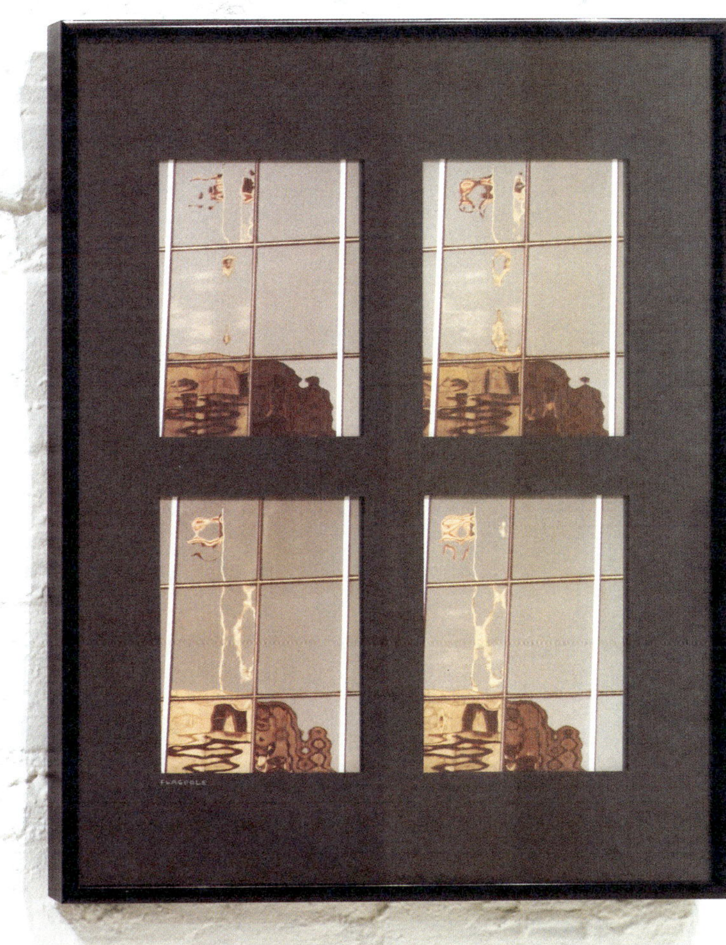

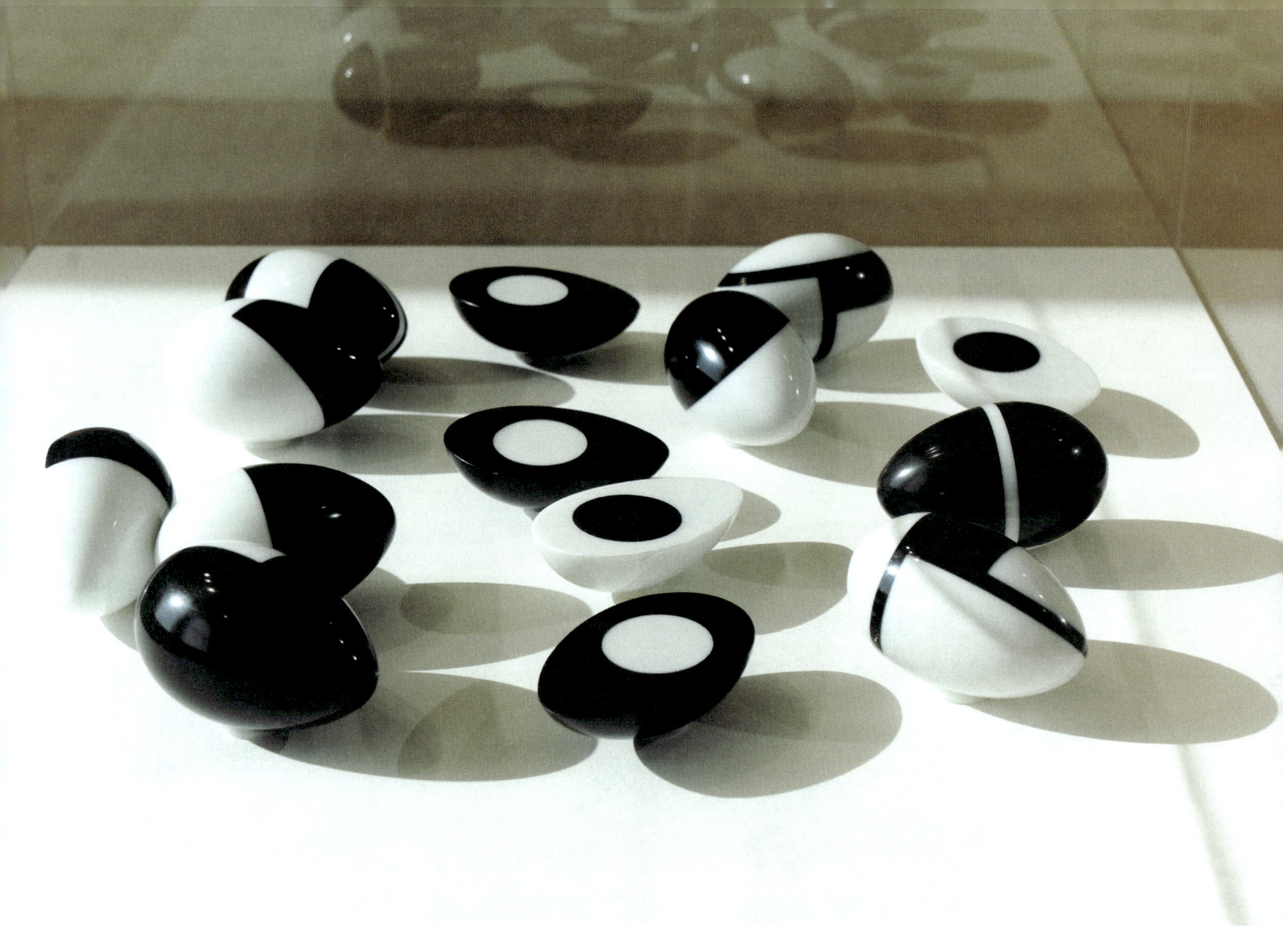

Bettina Grossman
options for an angle, 24 inconstants from one constant, 1971

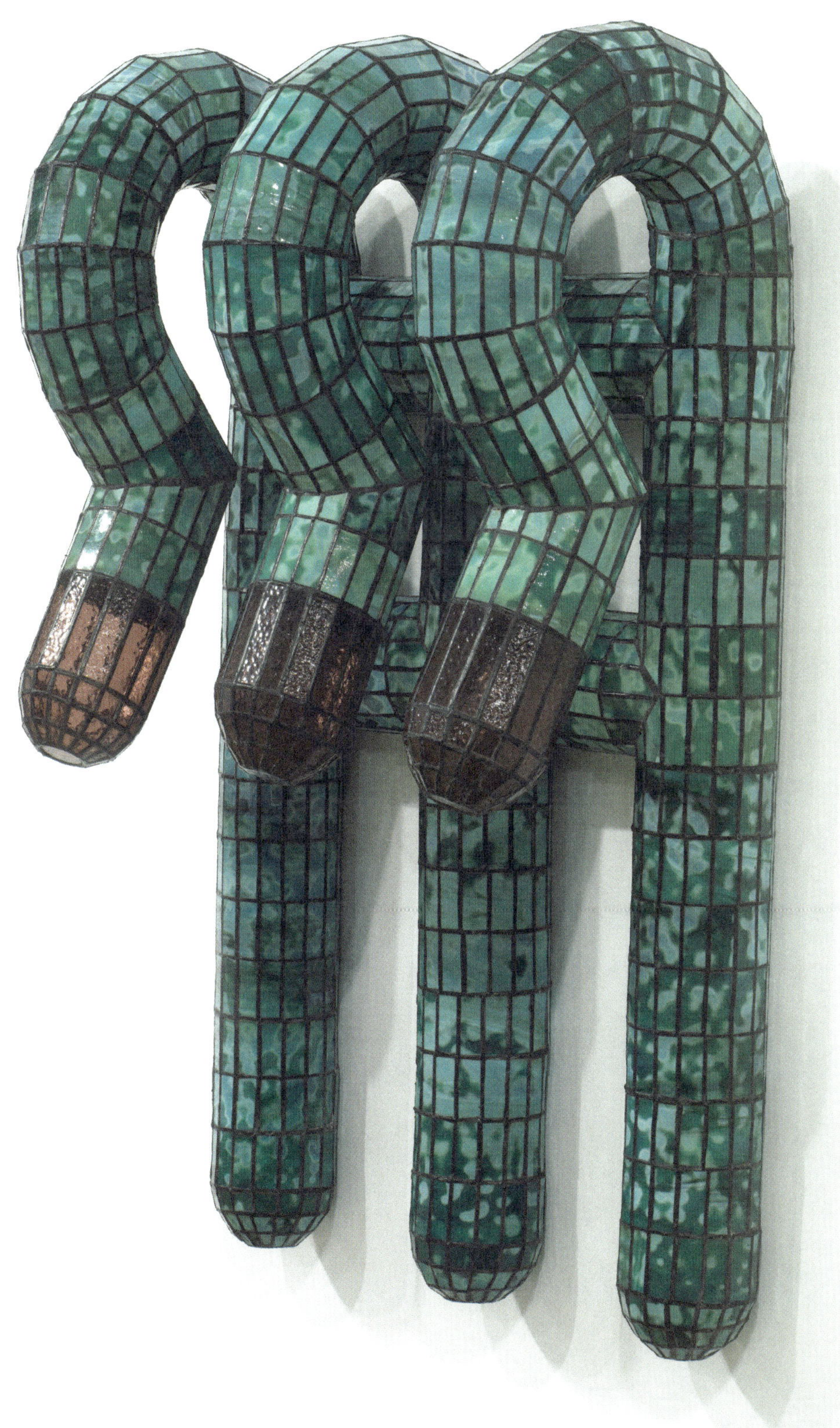

Kristi Cavataro
Untitled, 2021

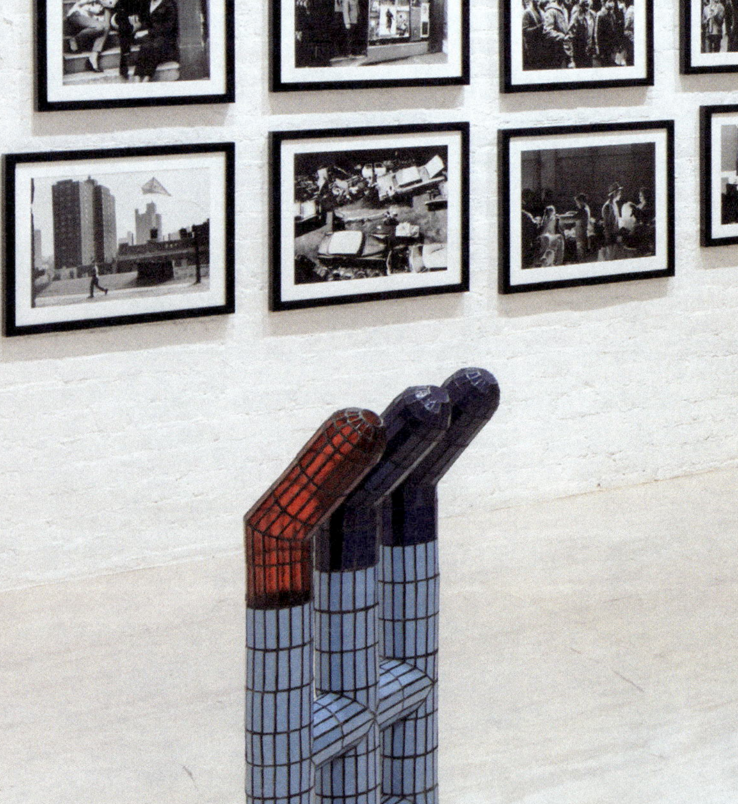

Left to right
Hiram Maristany, Kristi Cavataro
Bettina Grossman, Ahmed Morsi

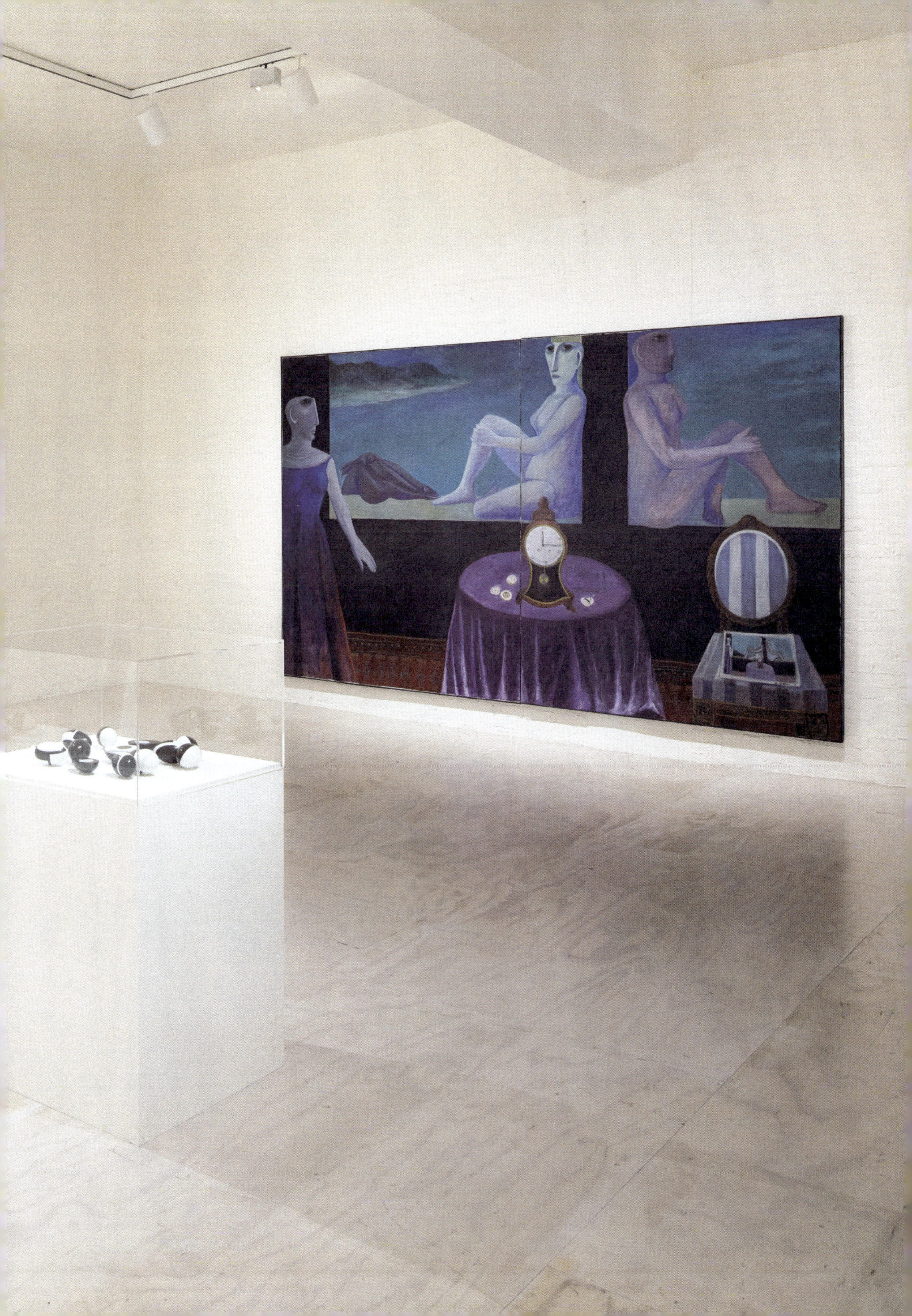

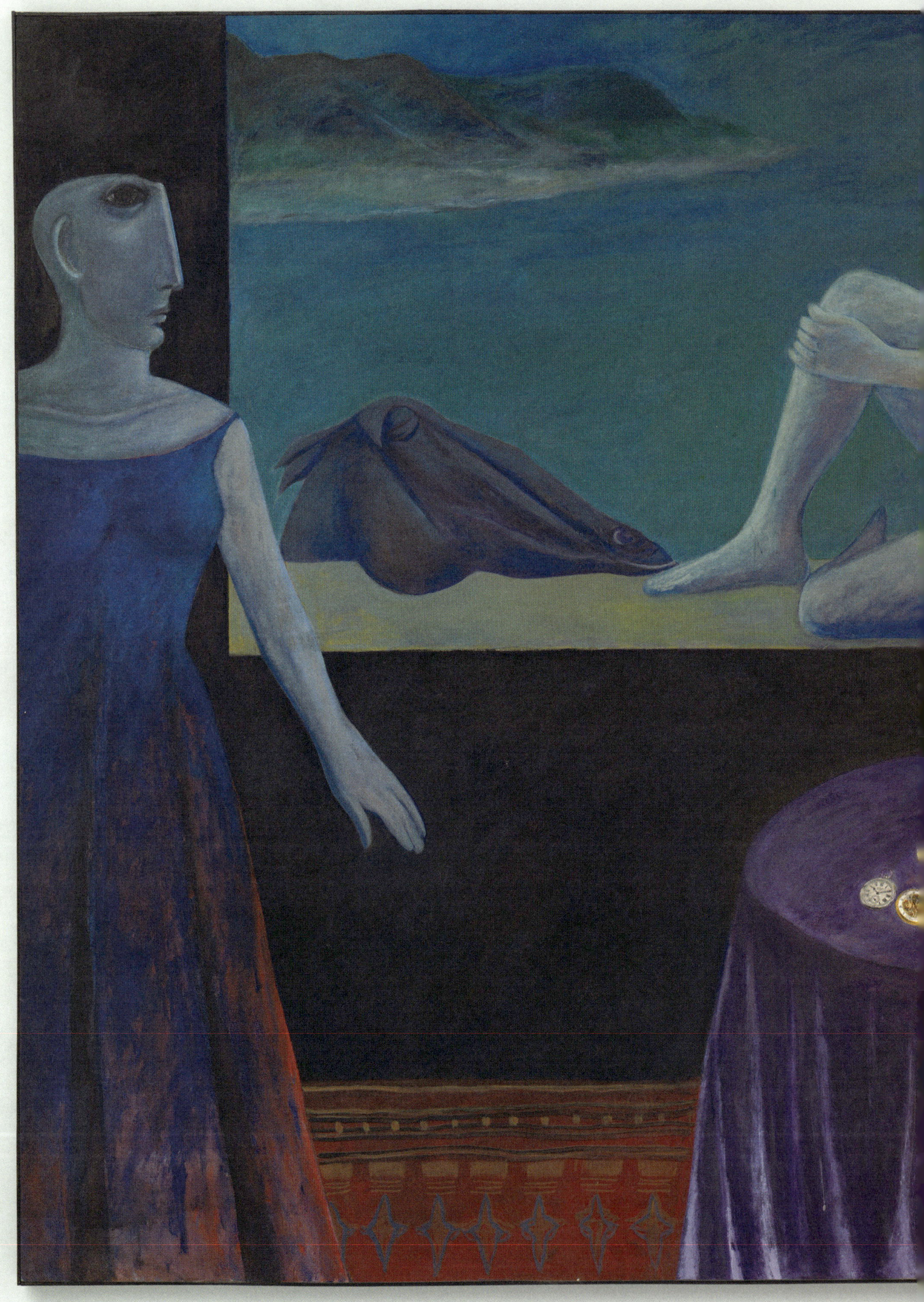

Ahmed Morsi
Clocks, 1996

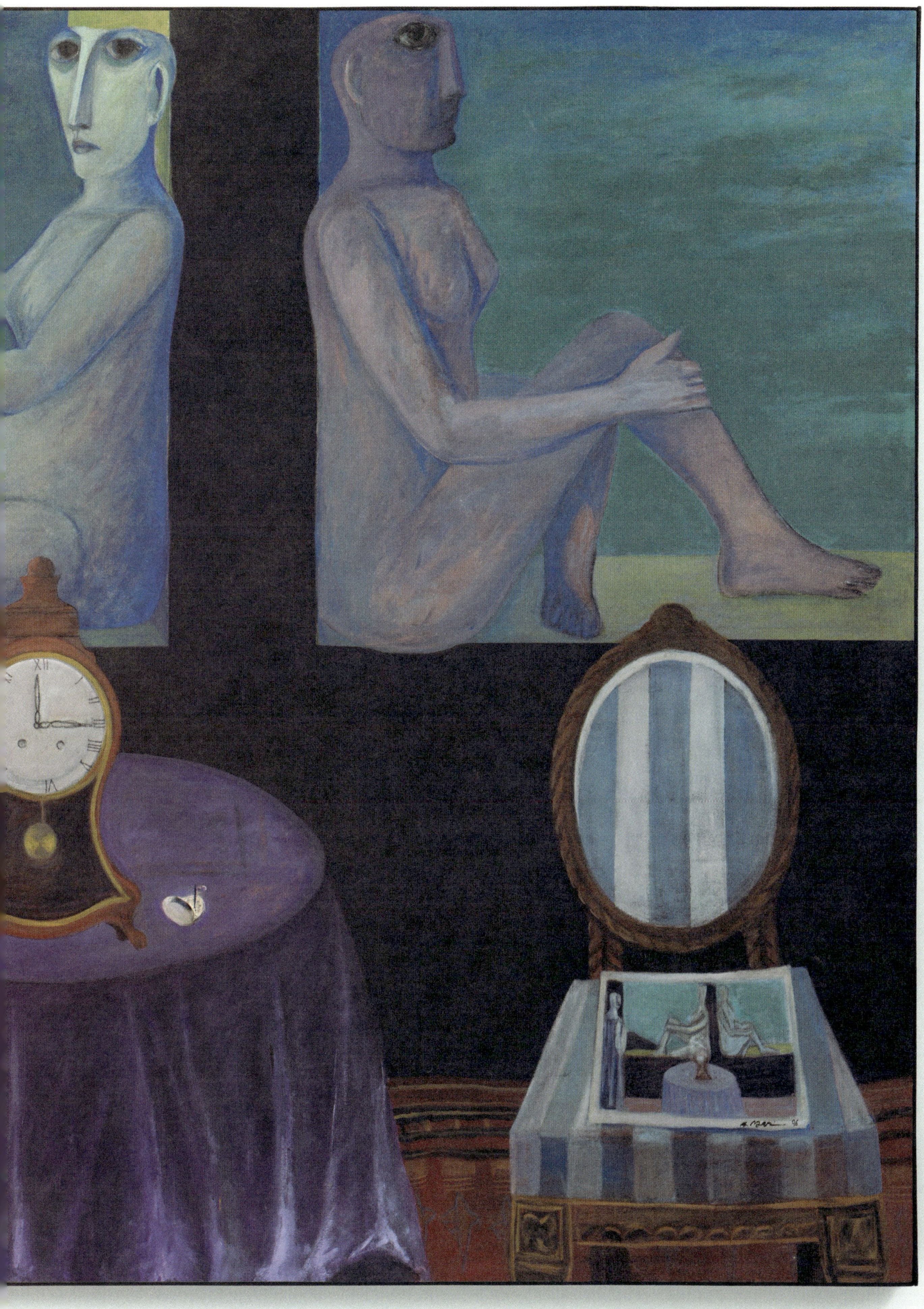

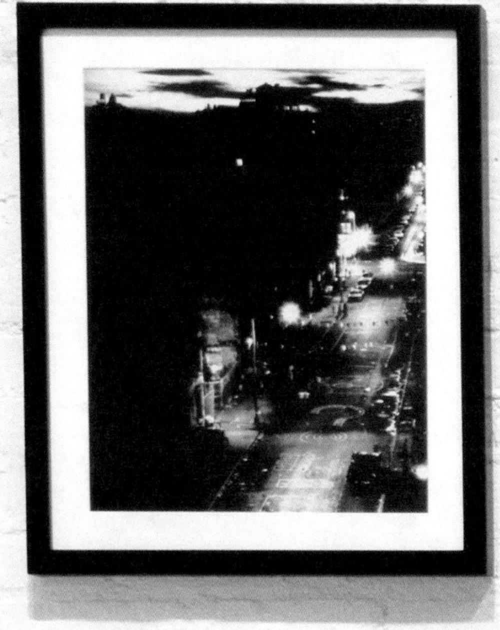
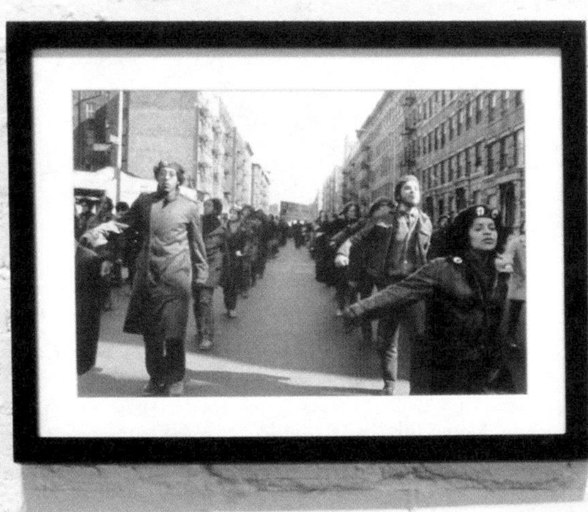
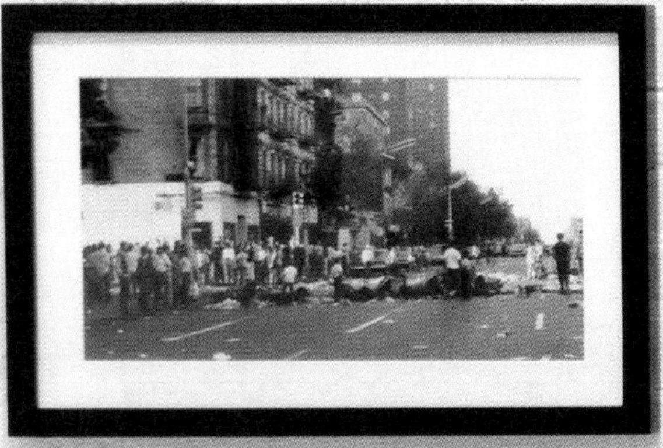
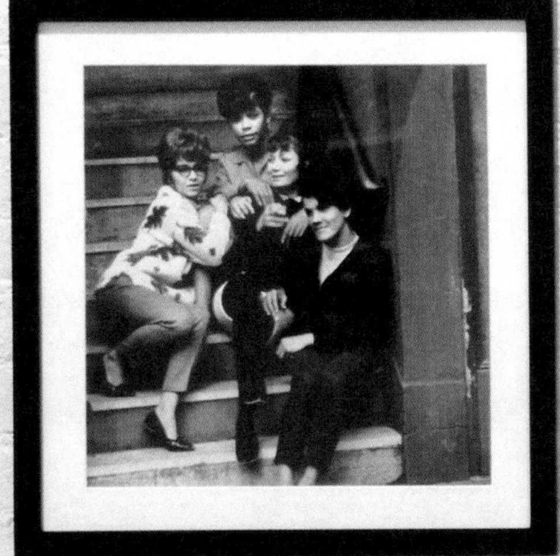
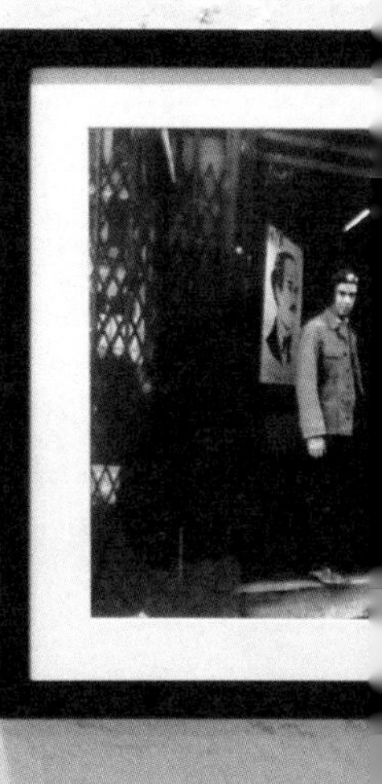
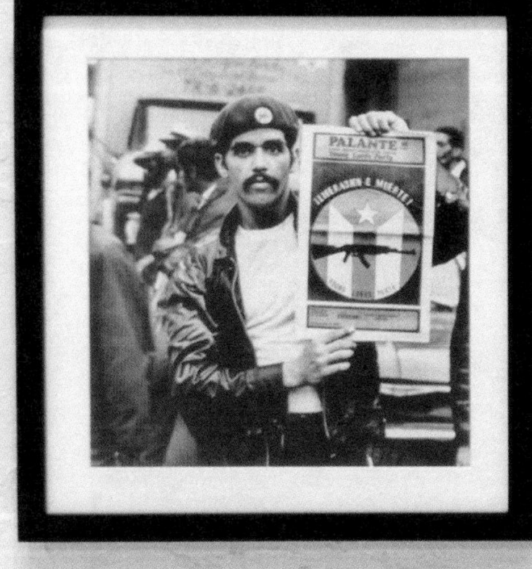
PALANTE
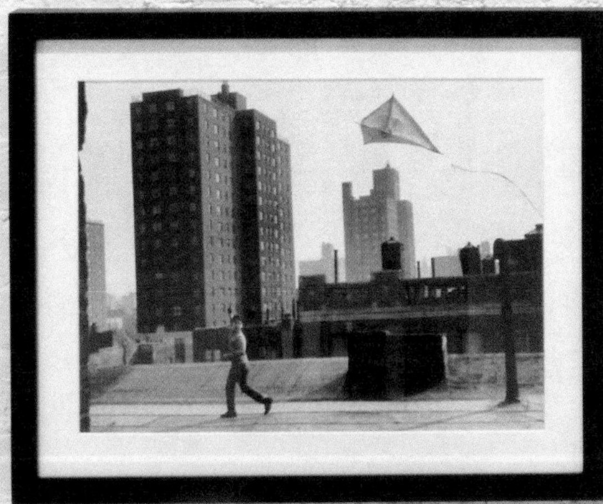
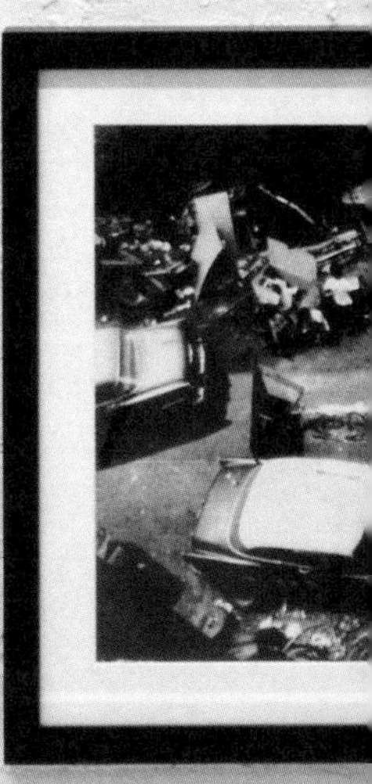

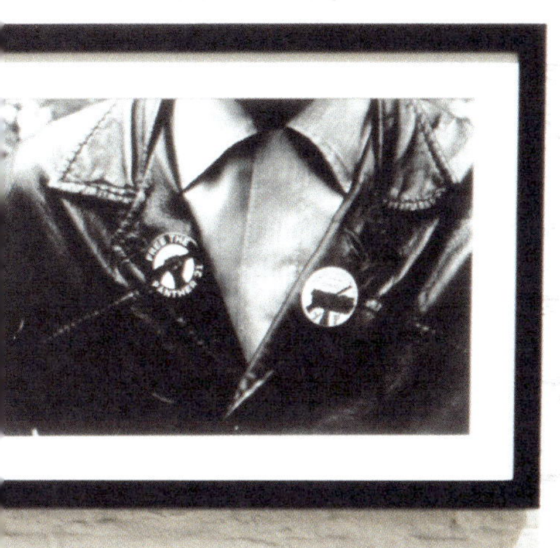

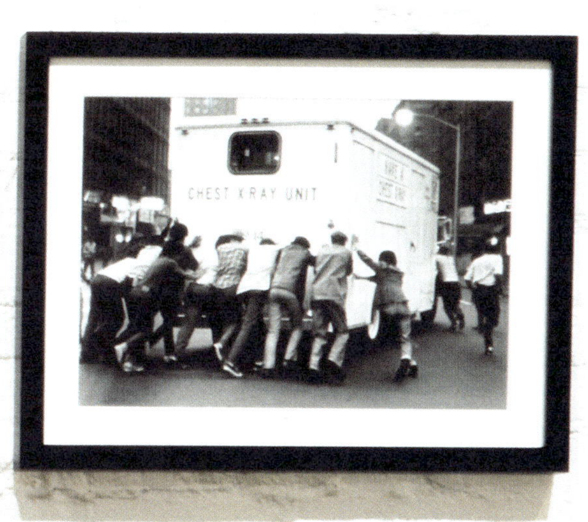
CHEST XRAY UNIT

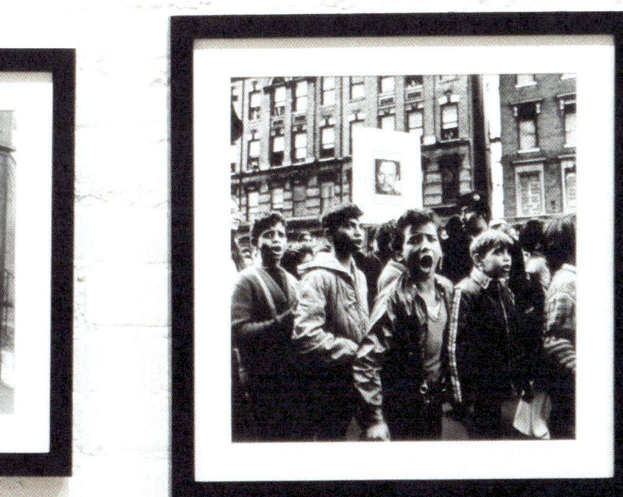

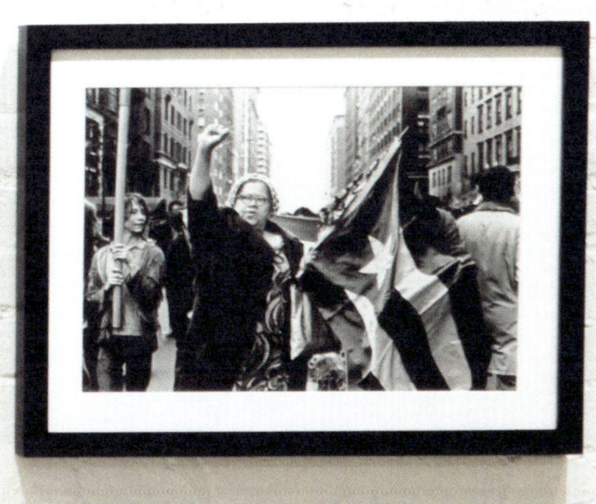

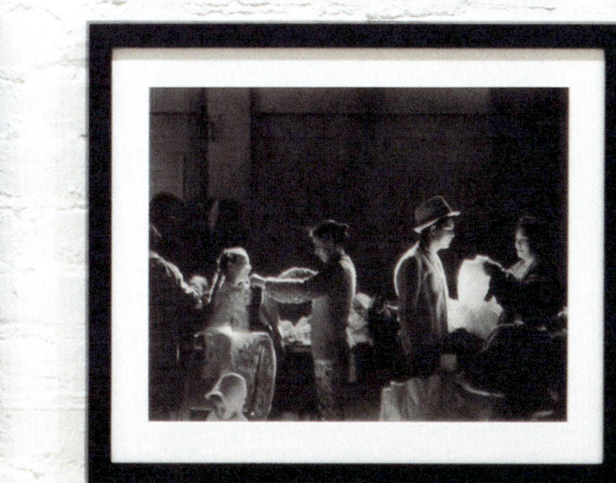

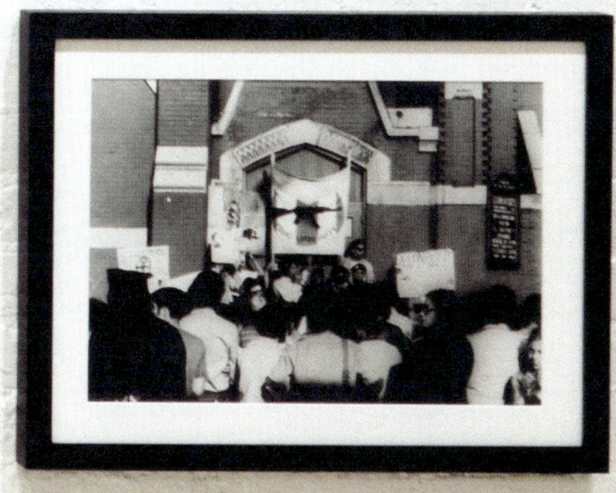

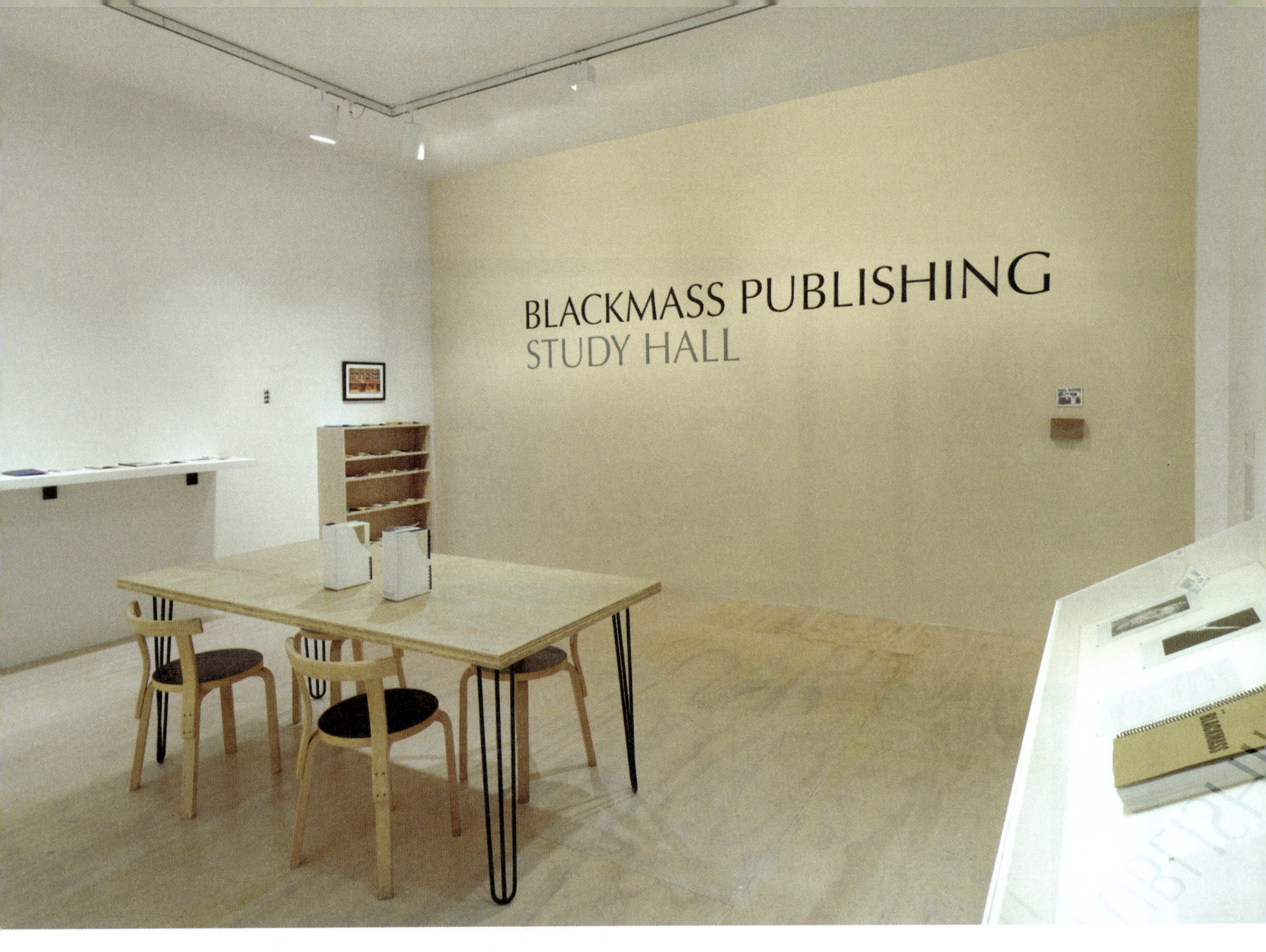

BlackMass Publishing
Study Hall, 2021

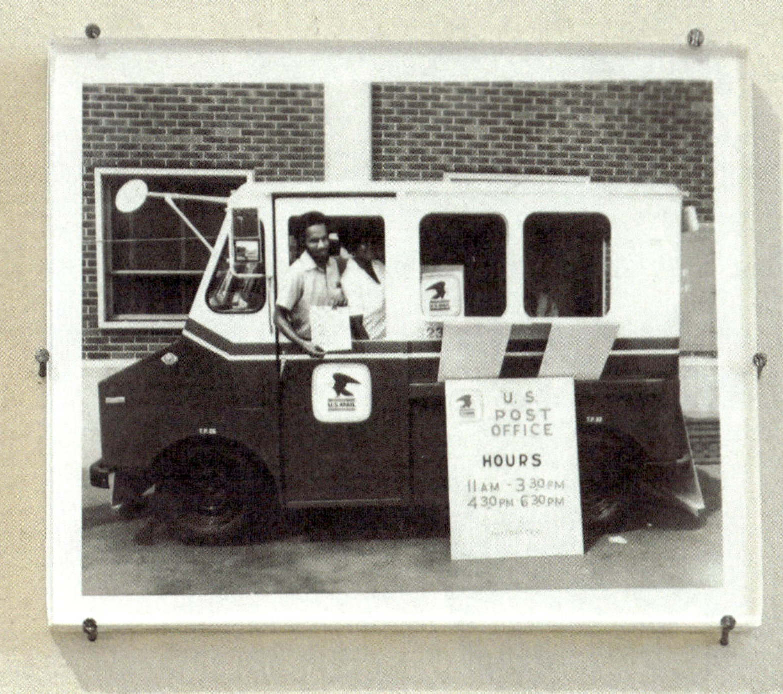
U.S
POST
OFFICE
HOURS
11AM - 3:30PM
4:30PM 6:30PM

BLACKMASS PUBLISHING
P.O. BOX 311277
JAMAICA, NEW YORK 11431

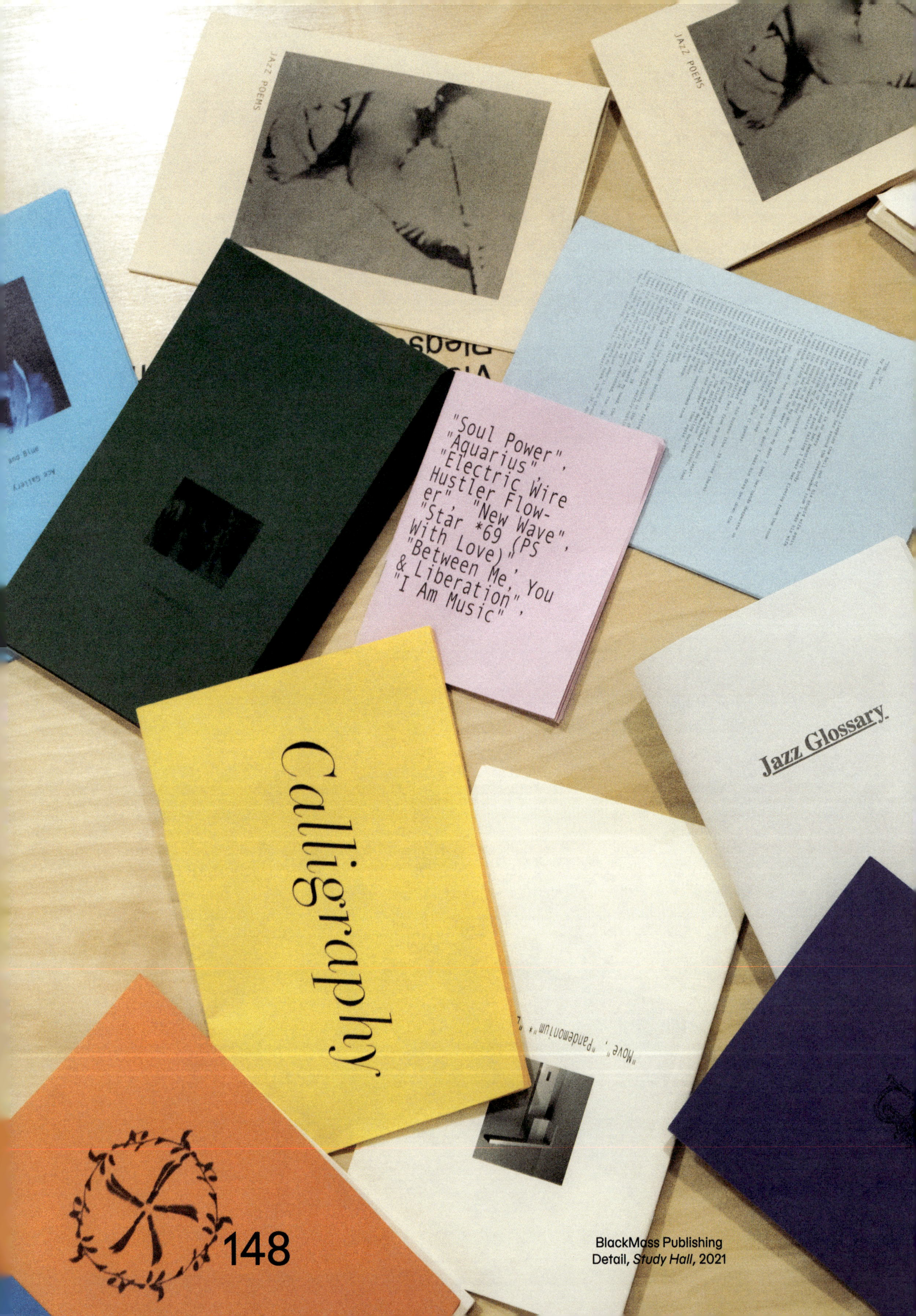

BlackMass Publishing
Detail, *Study Hall*, 2021

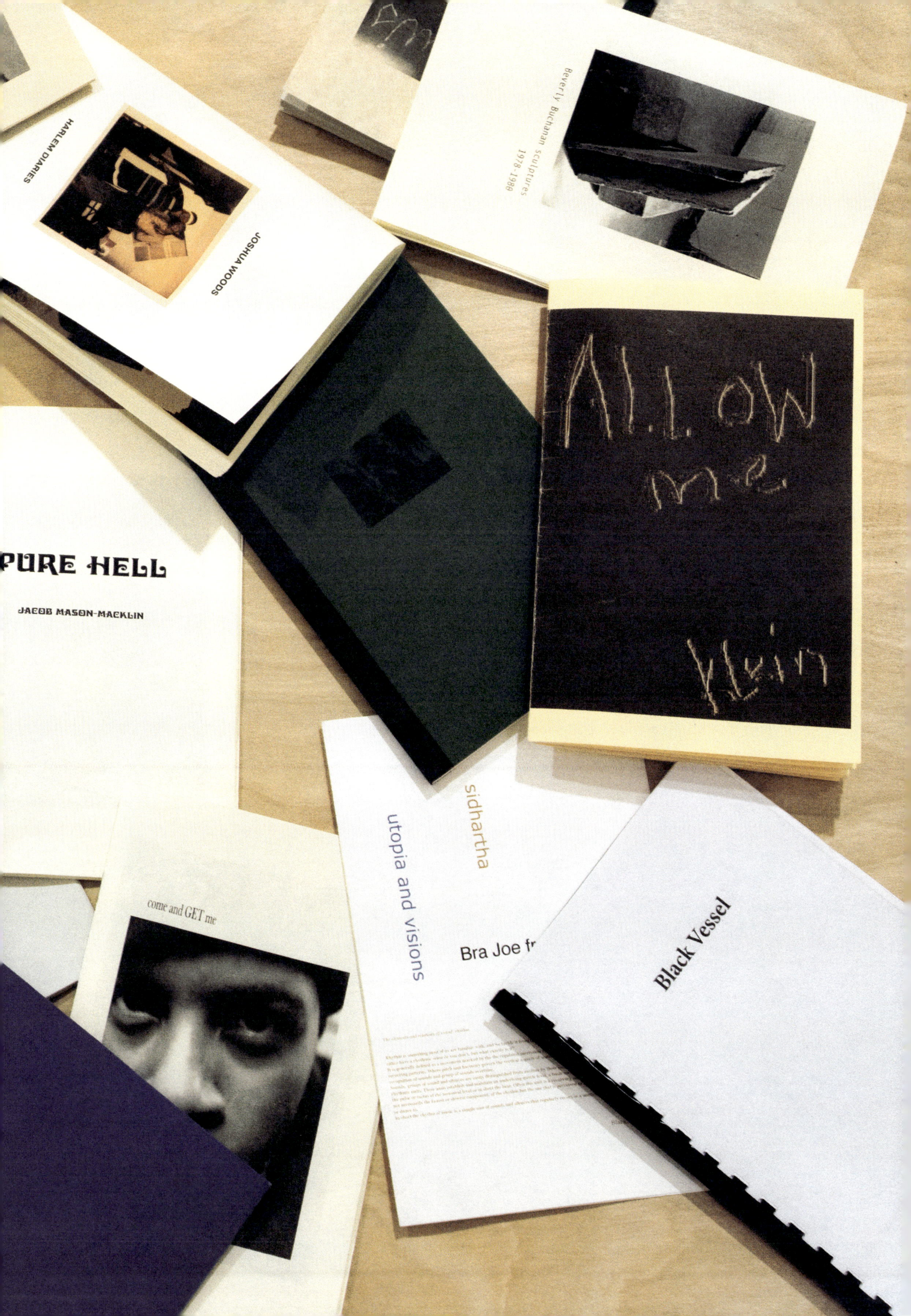

HARLEM DIARIES
JOSHUA WOODS
Beverly Buchanan sculptures
1978-1980
ALLOW me
klein
PURE HELL
JACOB MASON-MACKLIN
sidhartha
utopia and visions
Bra Joe
come and GET me
Black Vessel

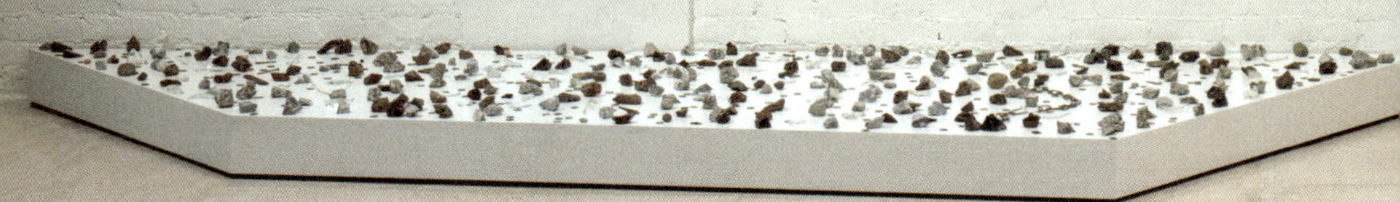

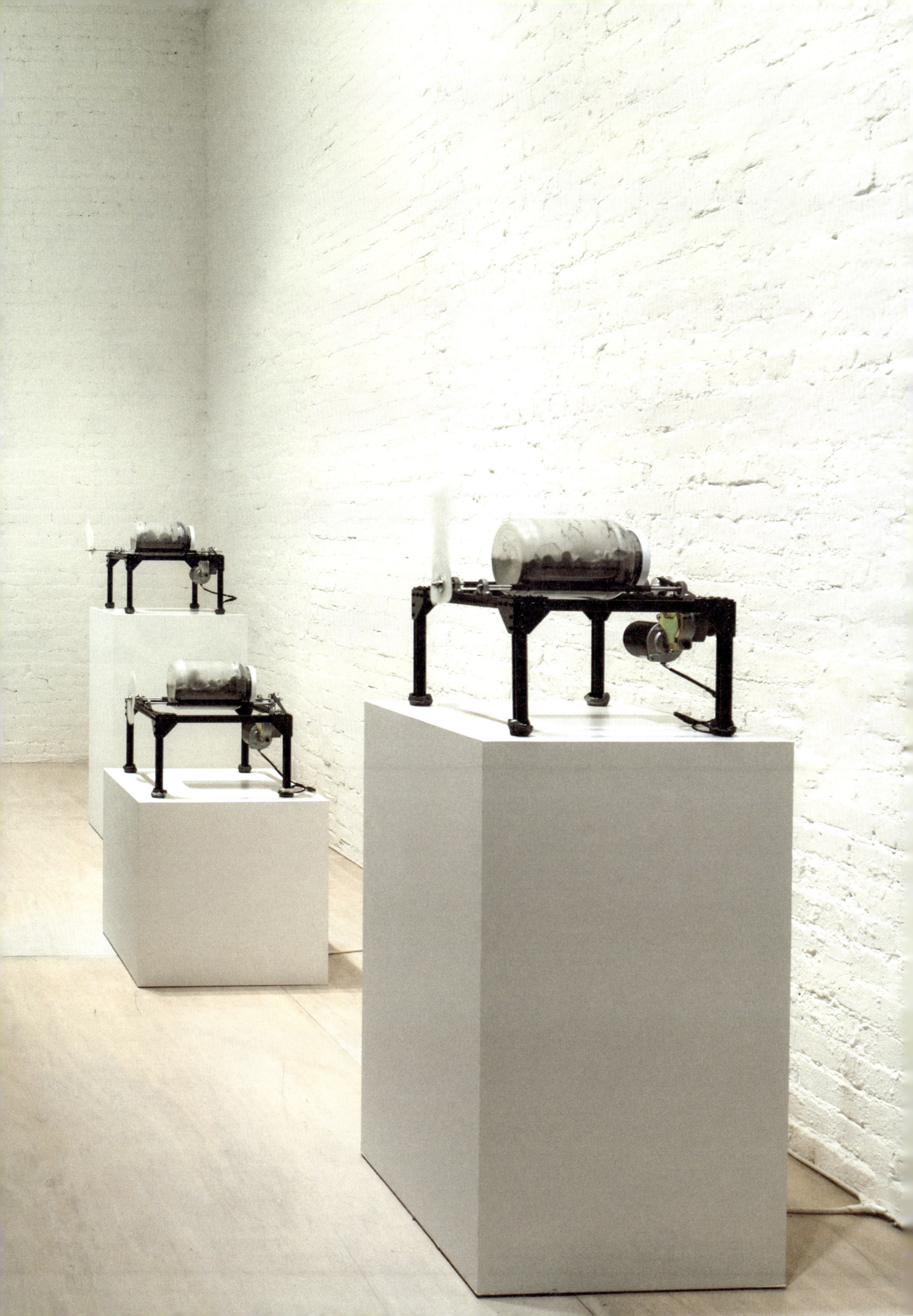

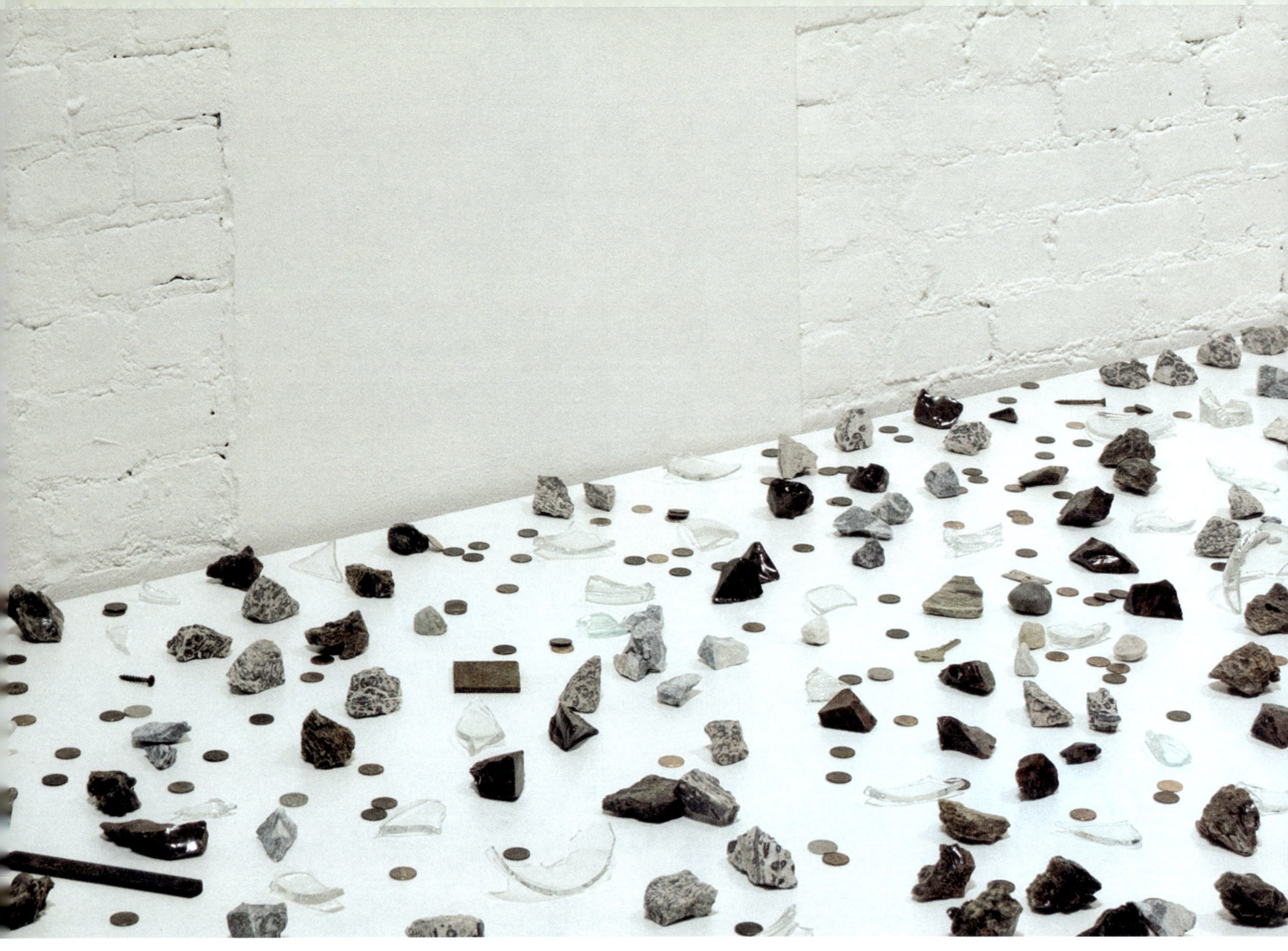

Steffani Jemison
Detail, *Tumblers*, 2021–2022

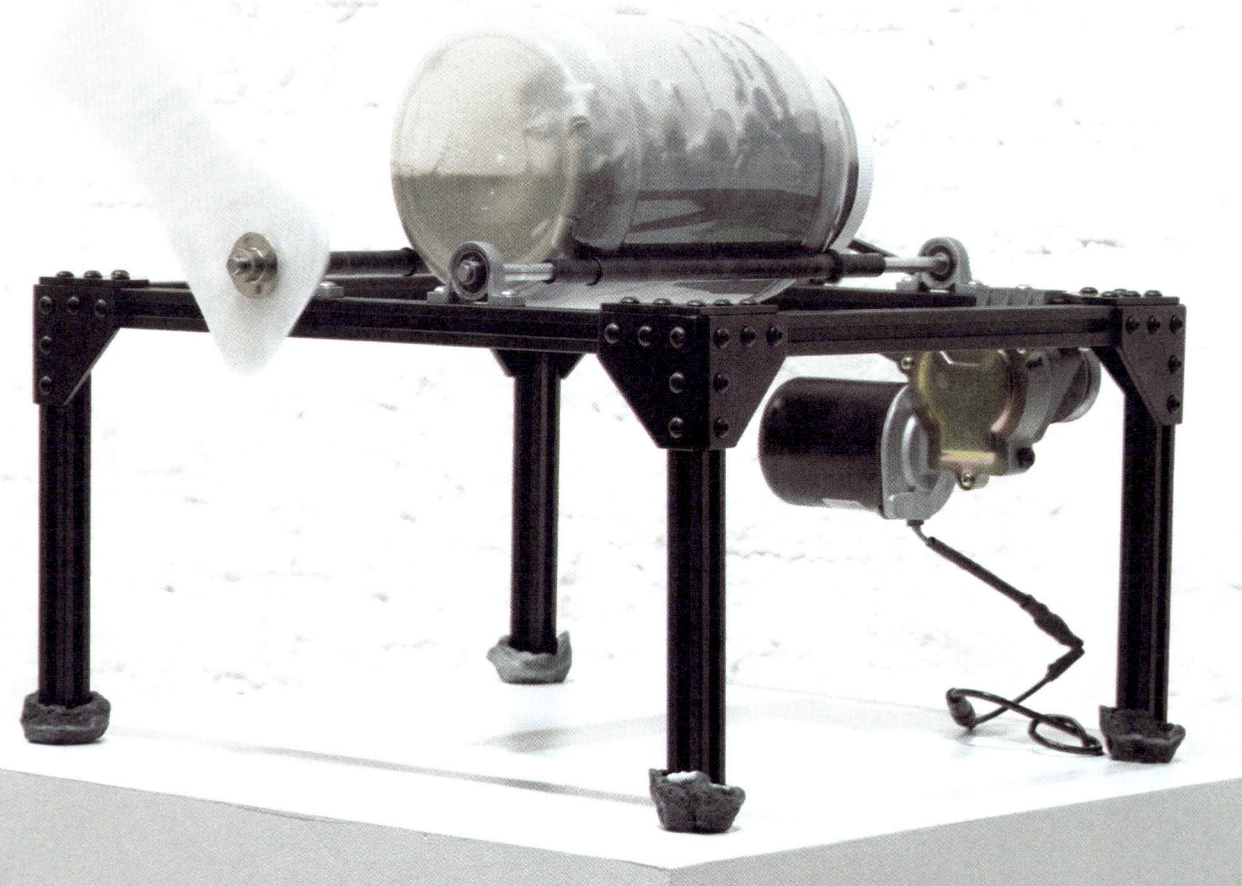

Steffani Jemison
Tumbler, 2021

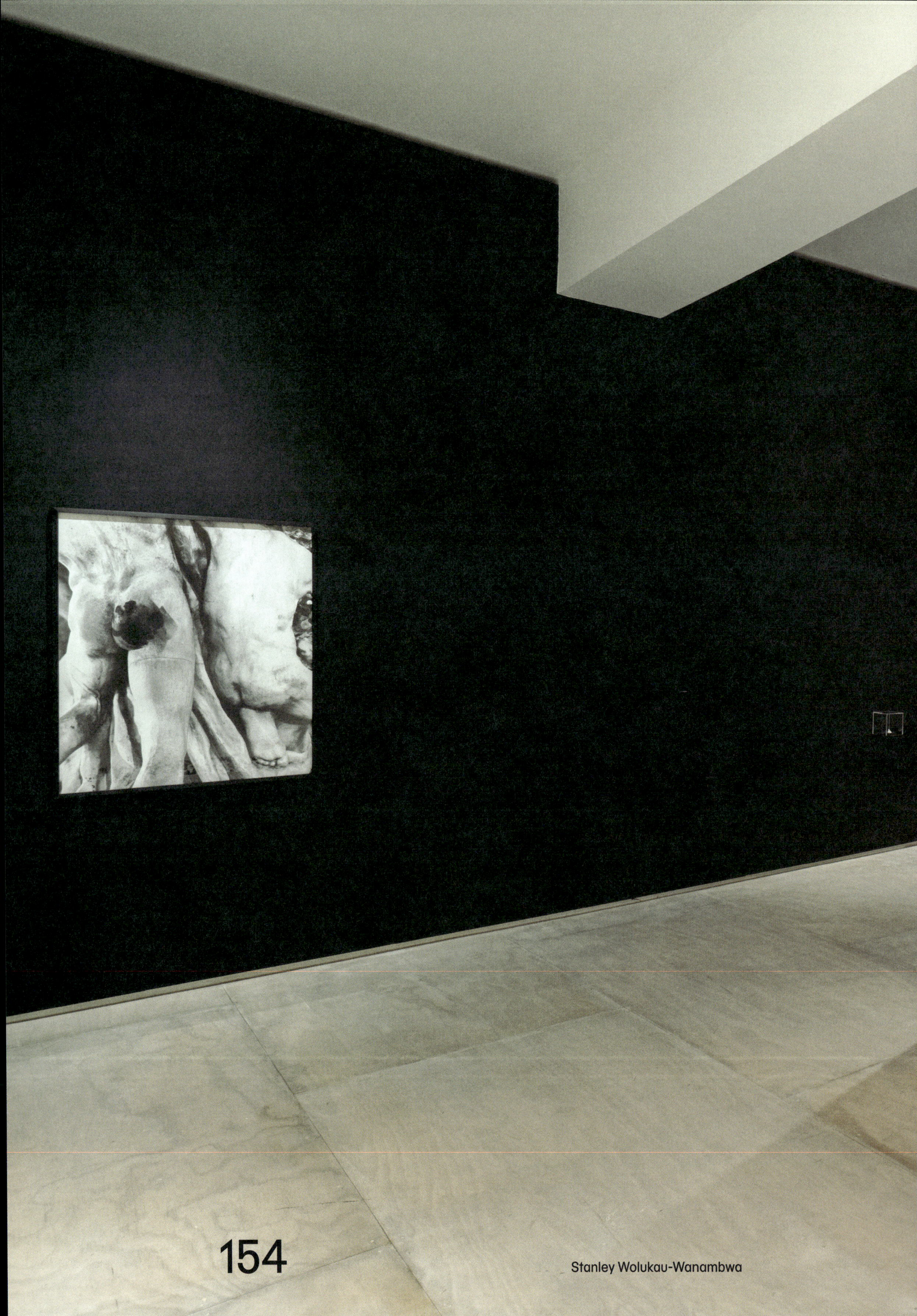

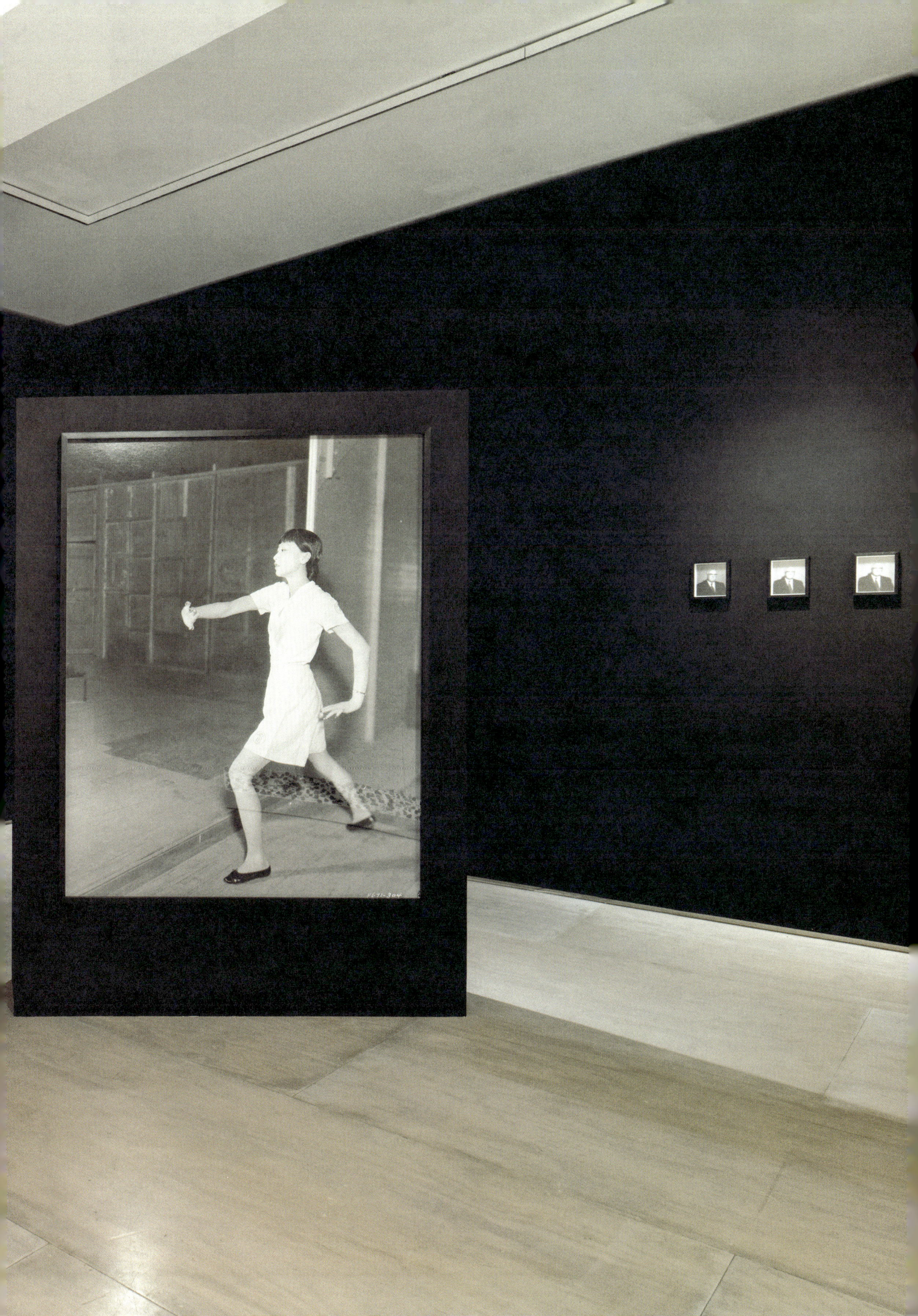

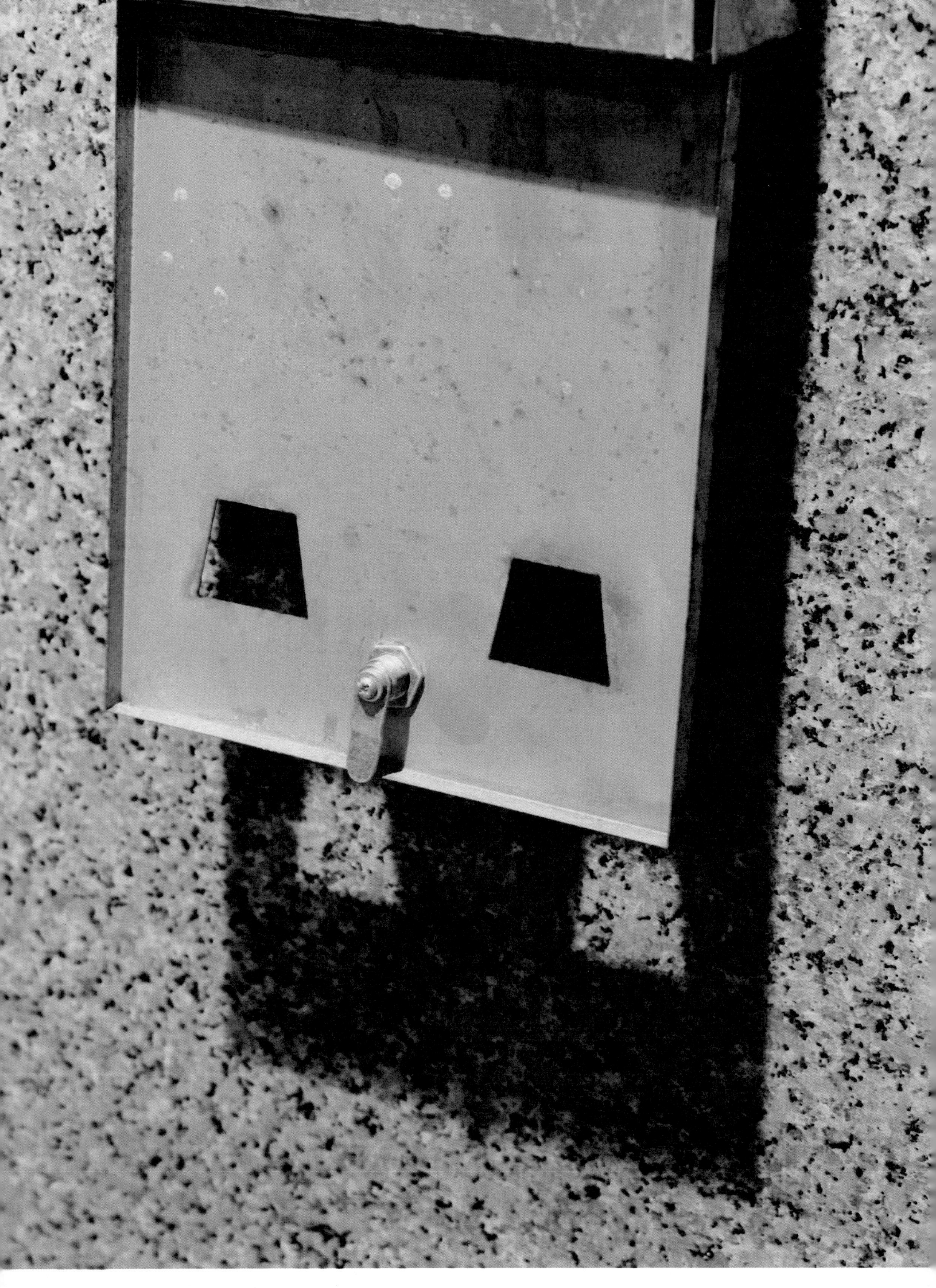

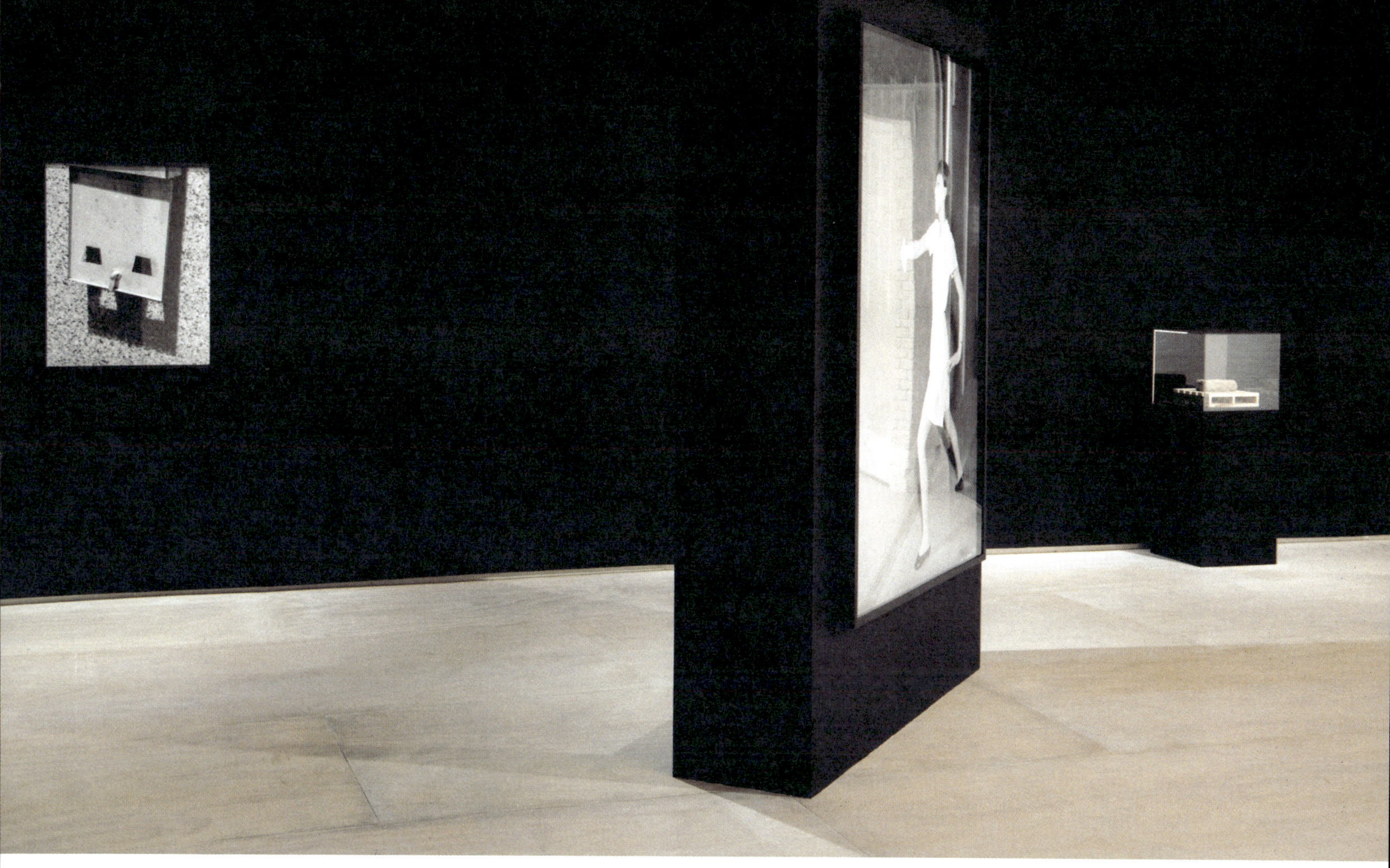

Opposite page
Stanley Wolukau-Wanambwa
Mask(s), 2021

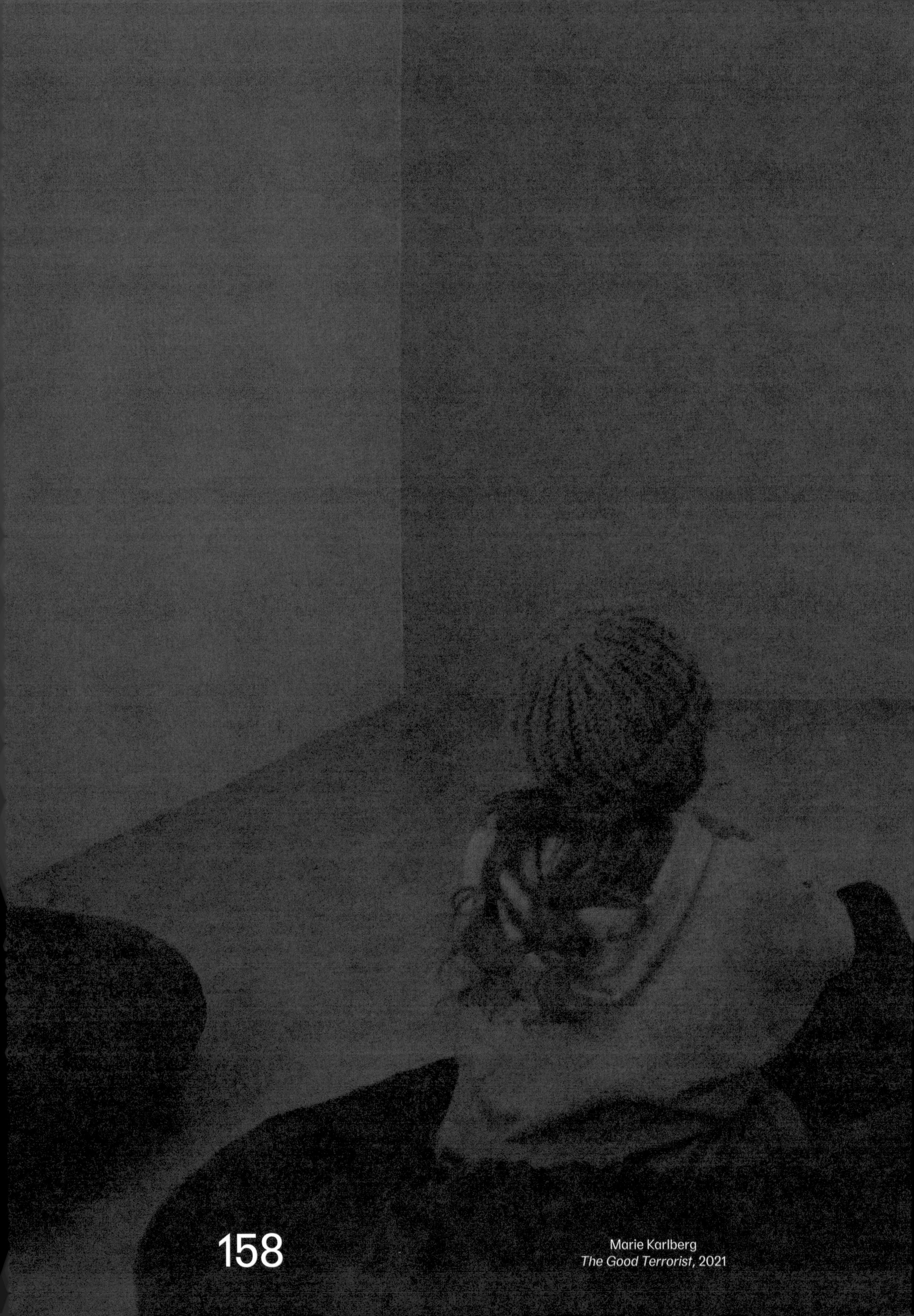

Marie Karlberg
The Good Terrorist, 2021

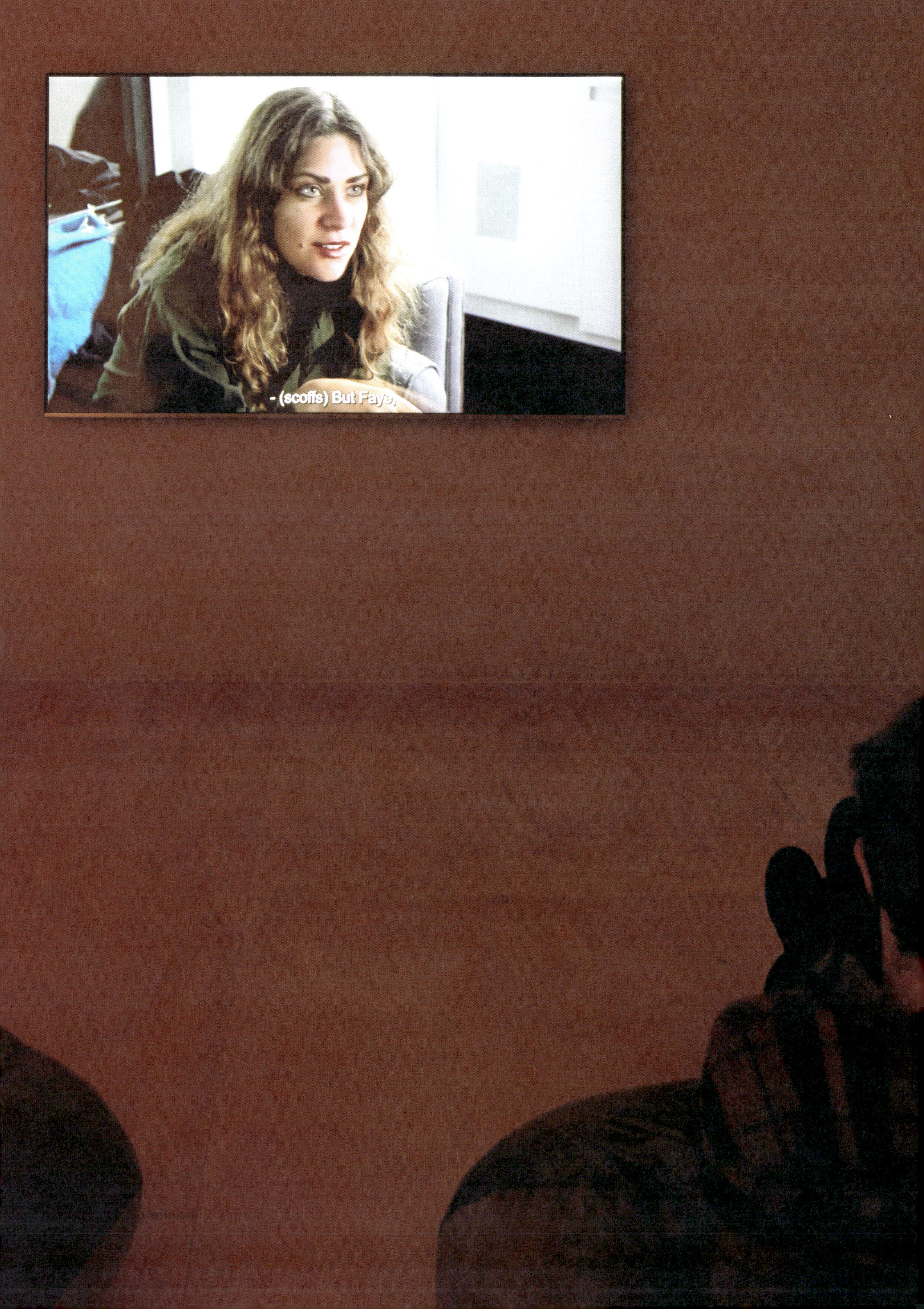
- (scoffs) But Faye,

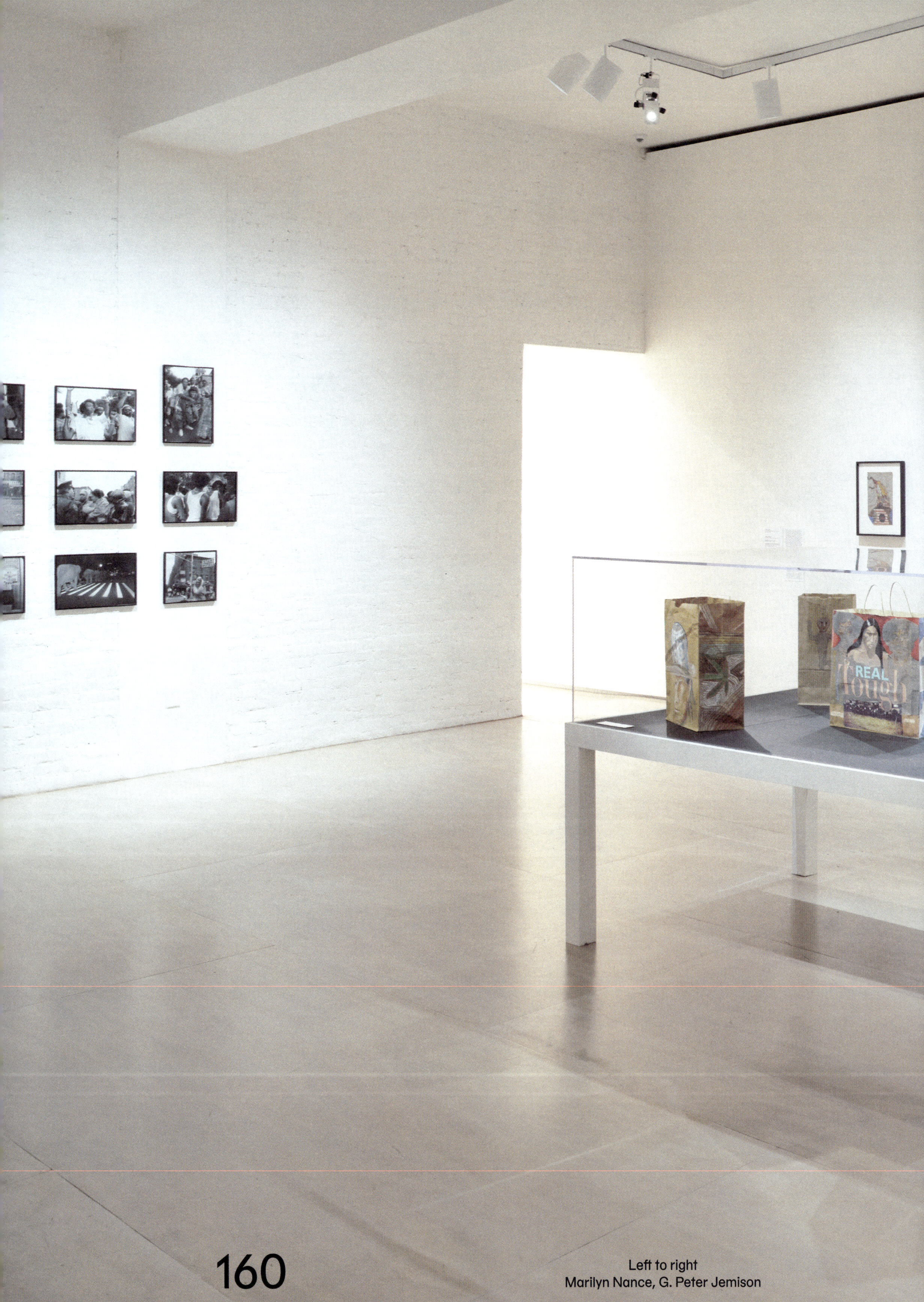

Left to right
Marilyn Nance, G. Peter Jemison

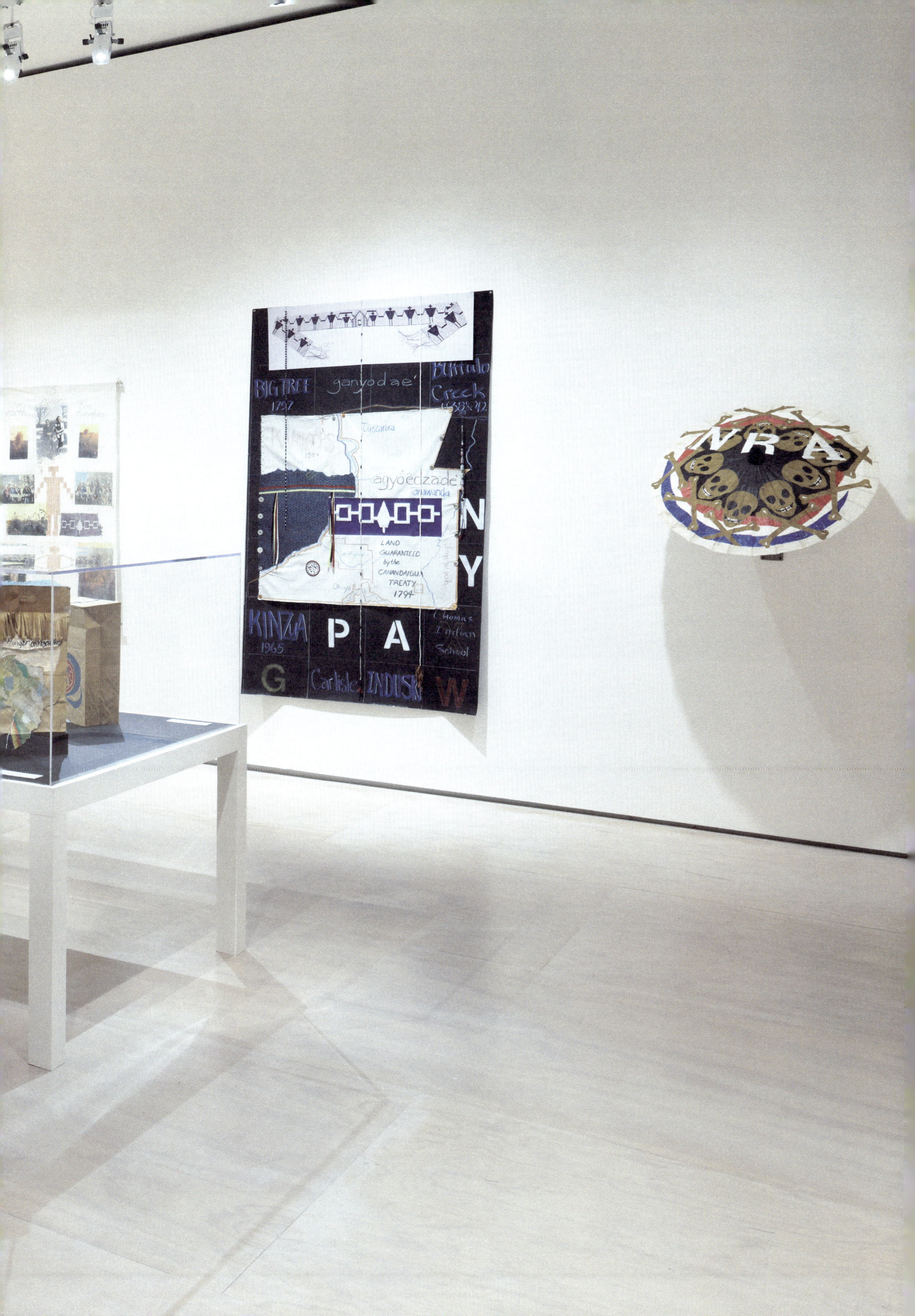

BIG TREE
1797
ganyodae'
Creek
Tuscarora
agyoëdzadé
Tonawanda
LAND
GUARANTEED
by the
CANANDAIGUA
TREATY
1794
N
Y
KINZUA
1965
P A
School
G
Carlisle
W
NRA

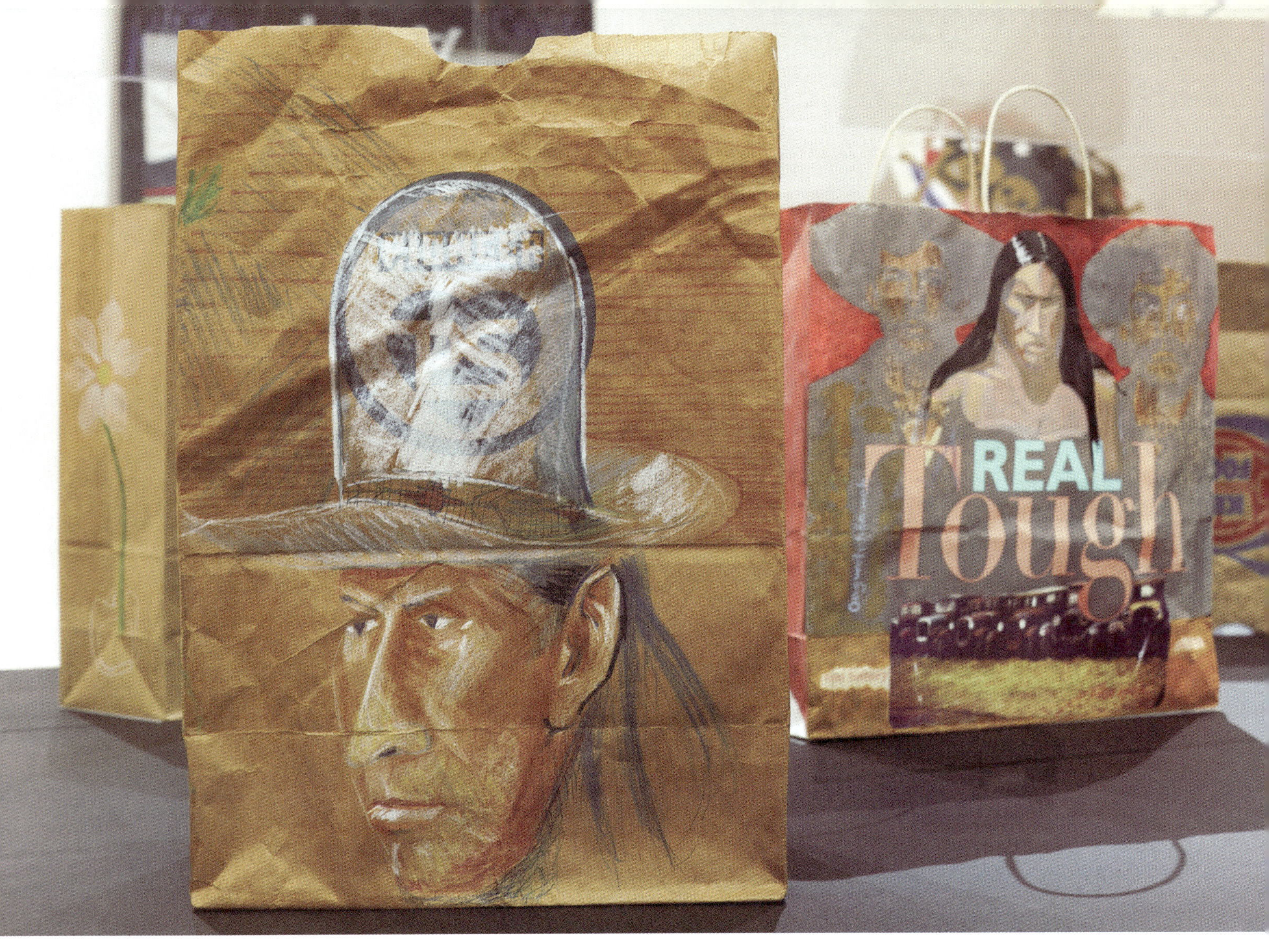

G. Peter Jemison, *Party Bag*, 1982 (left)
G. Peter Jemison, *Real Indian Land Claims*, 2000 (right)

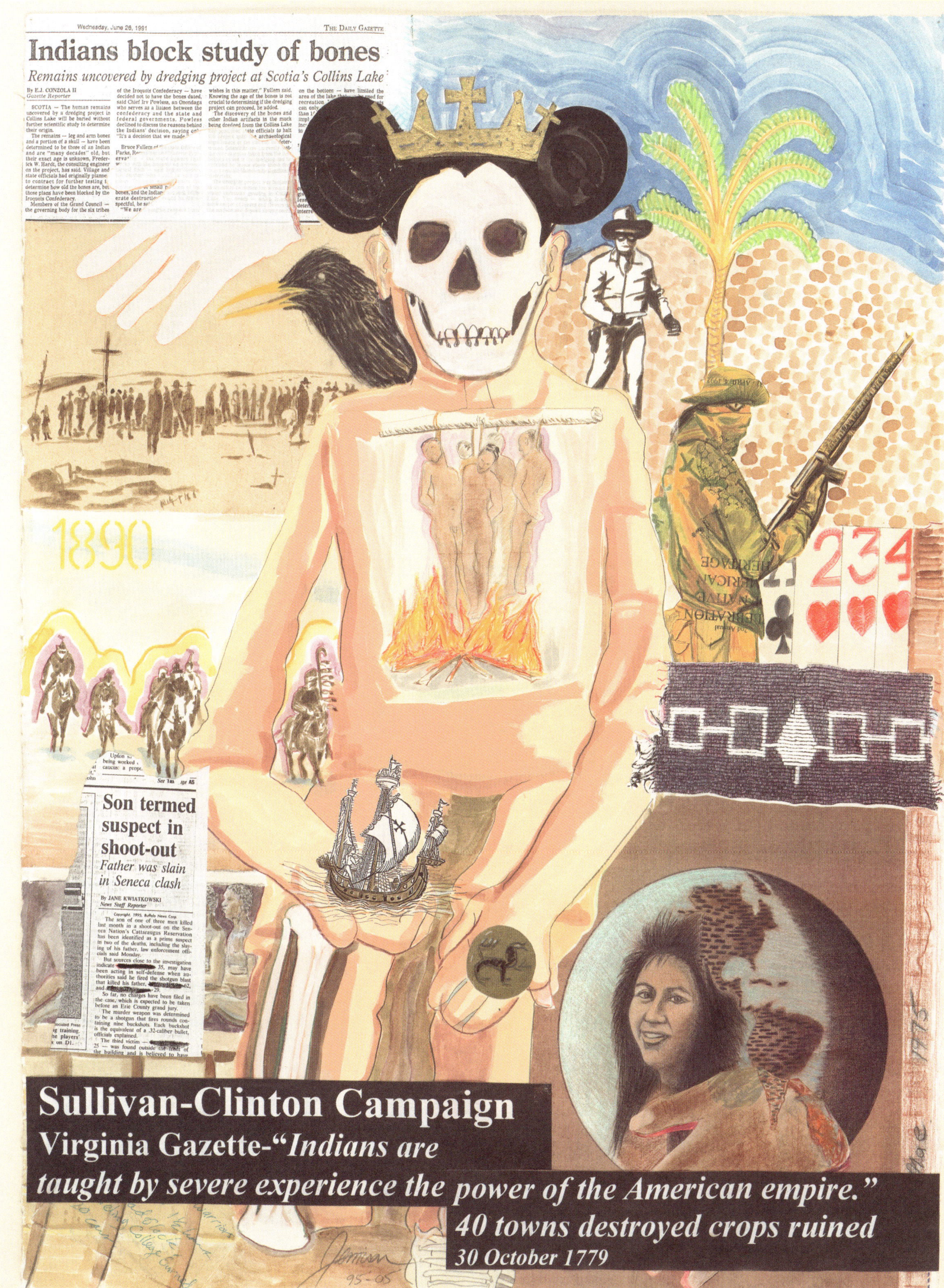

G. Peter Jemison
Indians Have Always Paid The Price, 2005

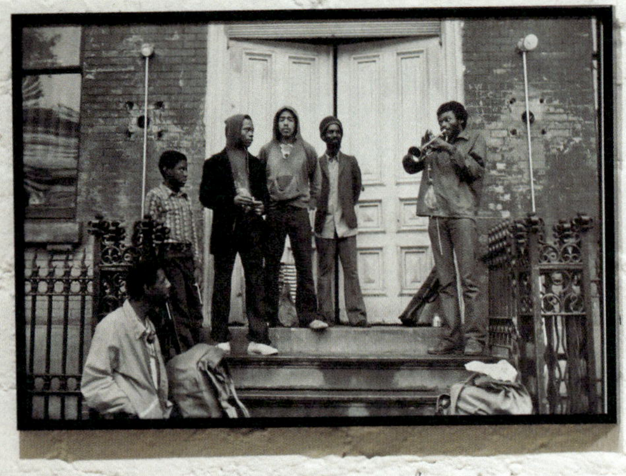

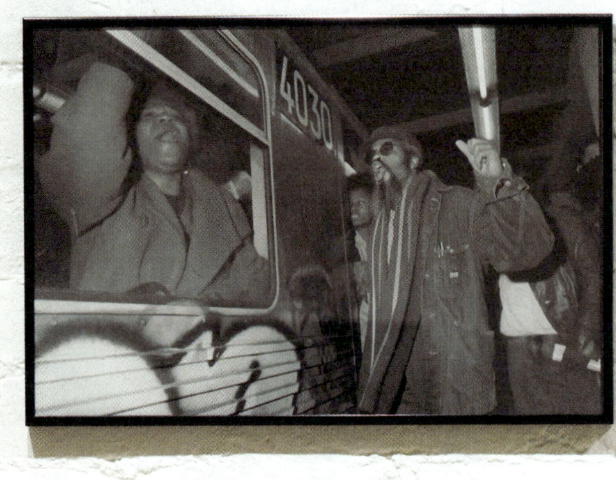
4030

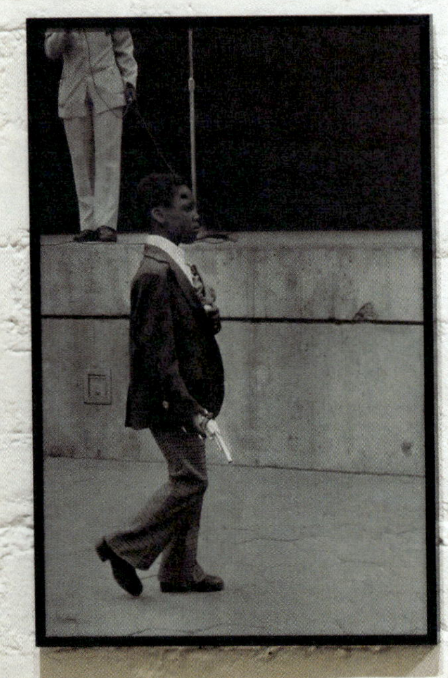

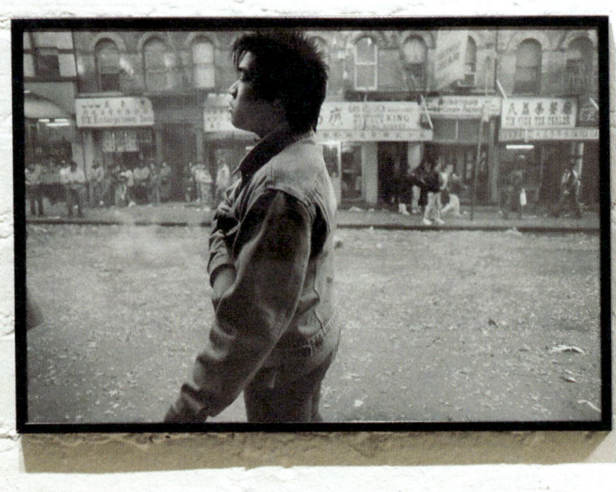

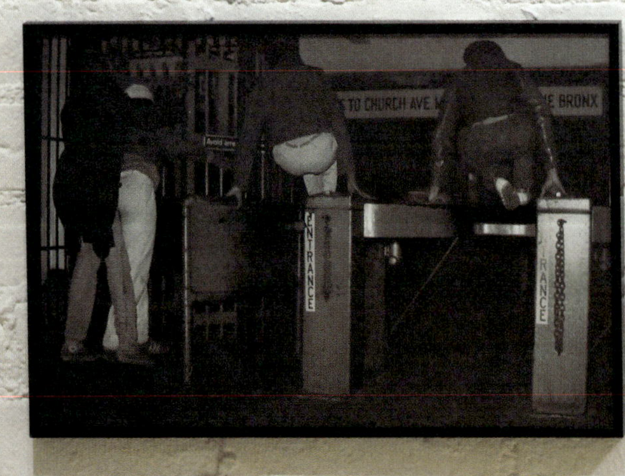
TO CHURCH AVE
ENTRANCE

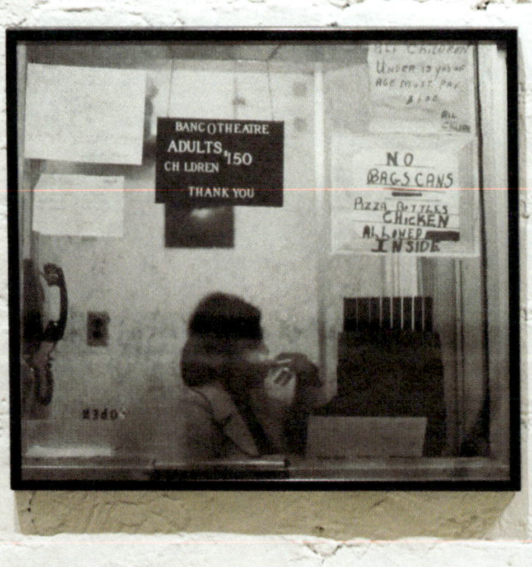
BANCO THEATRE
ADULTS 1.50
CH LDREN
THANK YOU
NO
BAGS CANS
CHICKEN
INSIDE

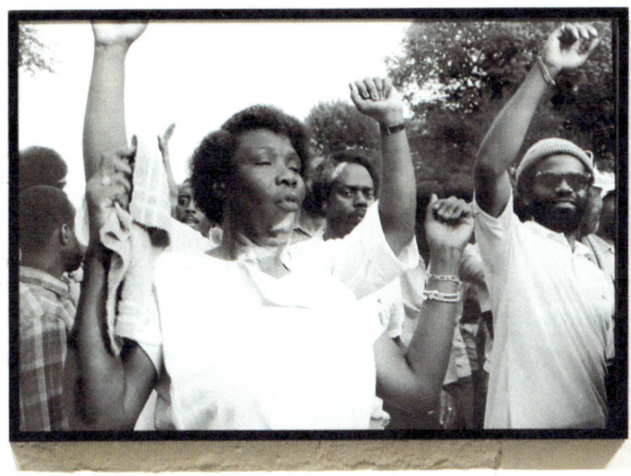

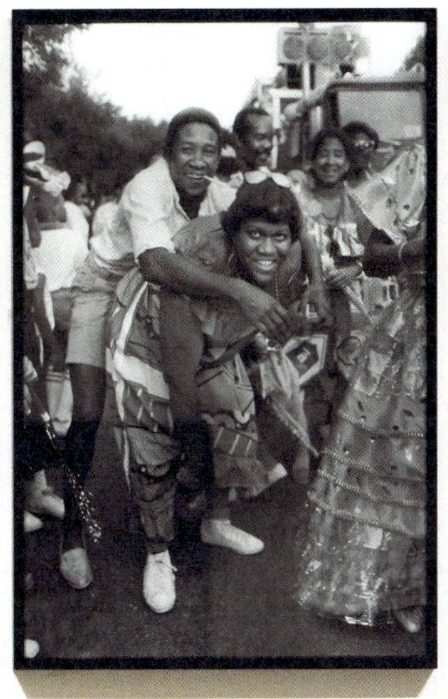

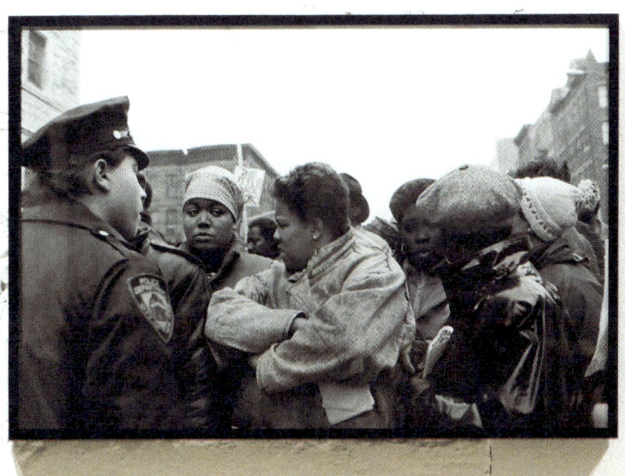

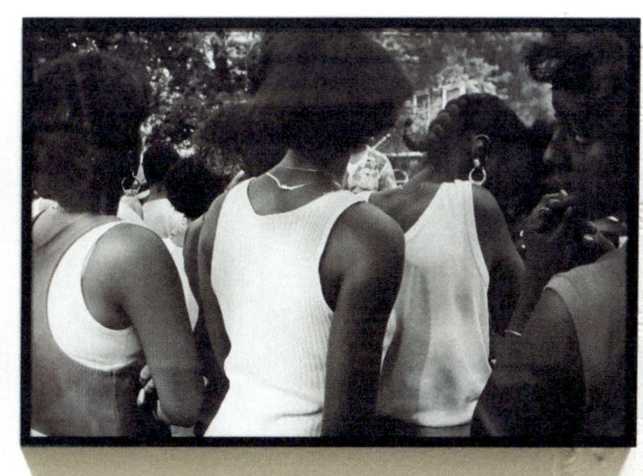

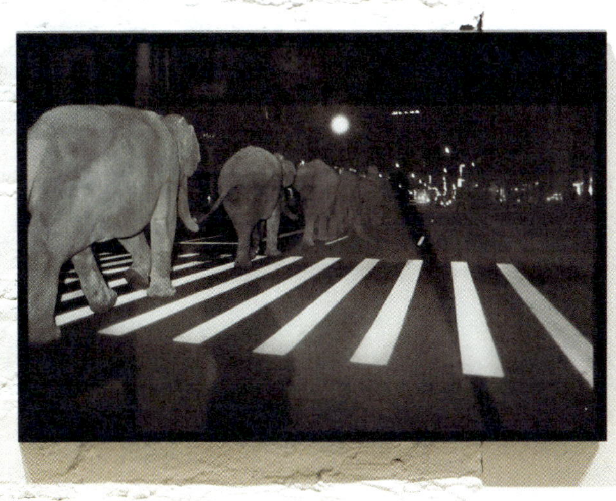

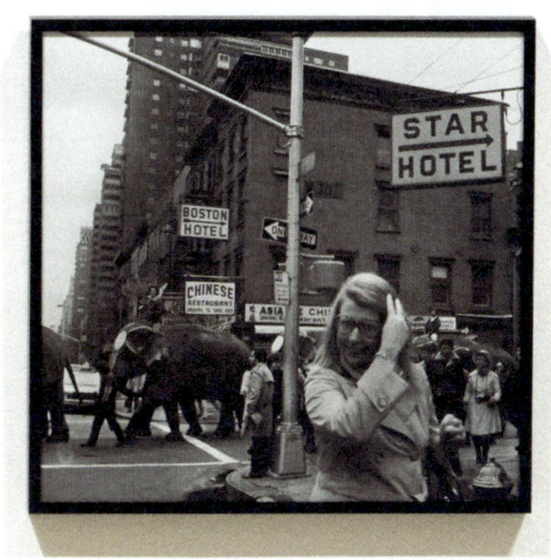
STAR
HOTEL
BOSTON
HOTEL
CHINESE

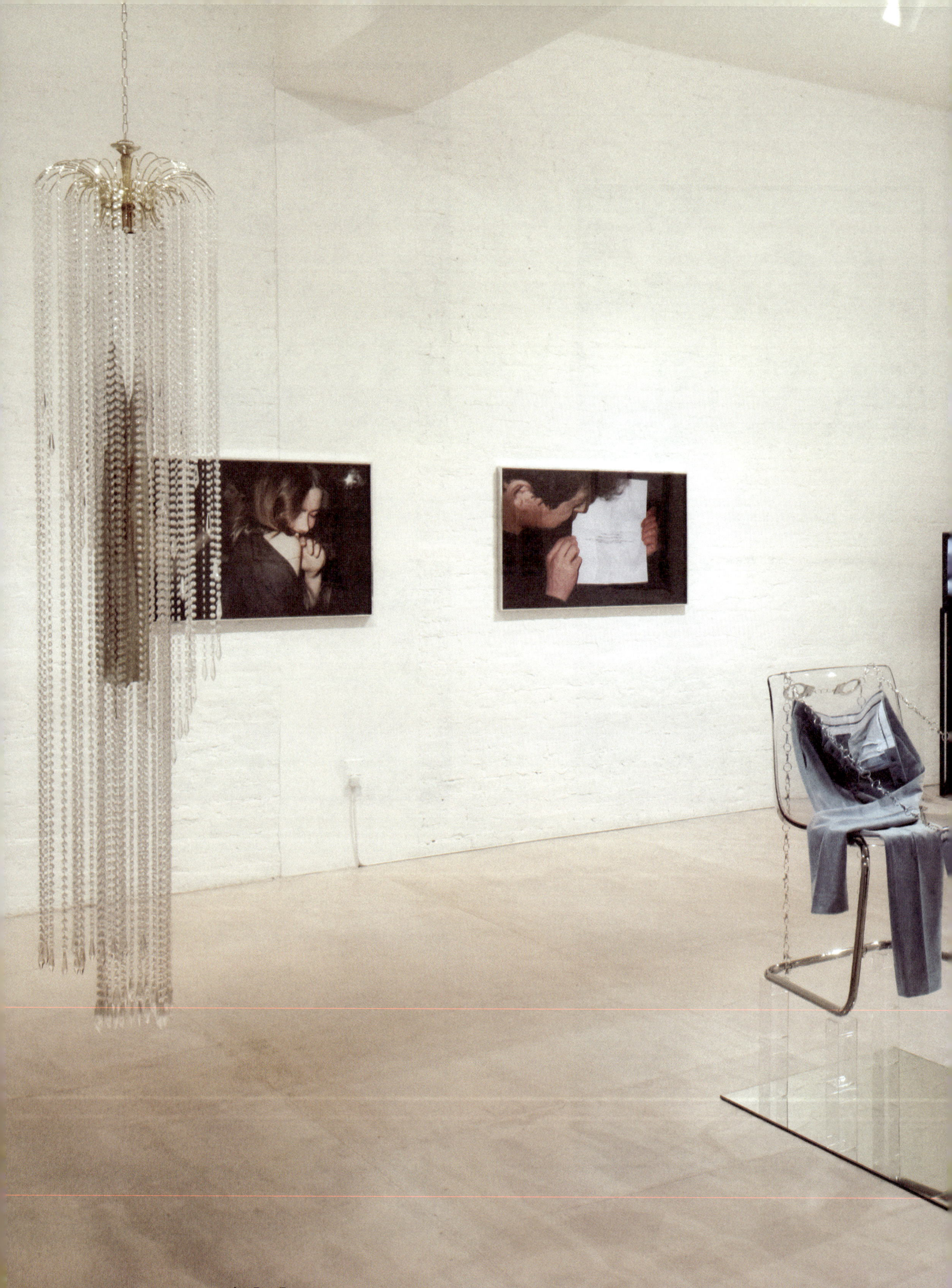

Left to right
Kayode Ojo, Regina Vater, E'wao Kagoshima

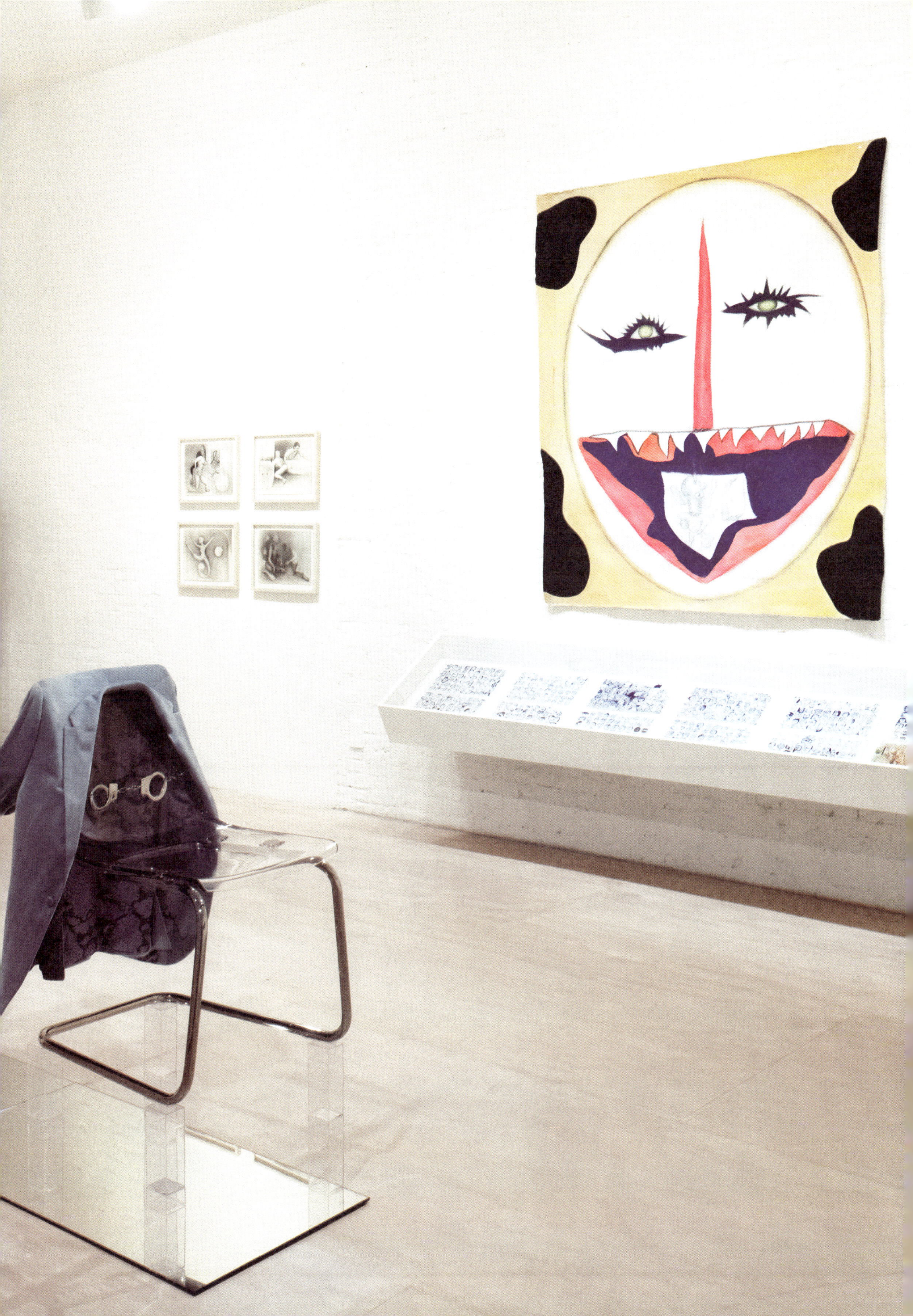

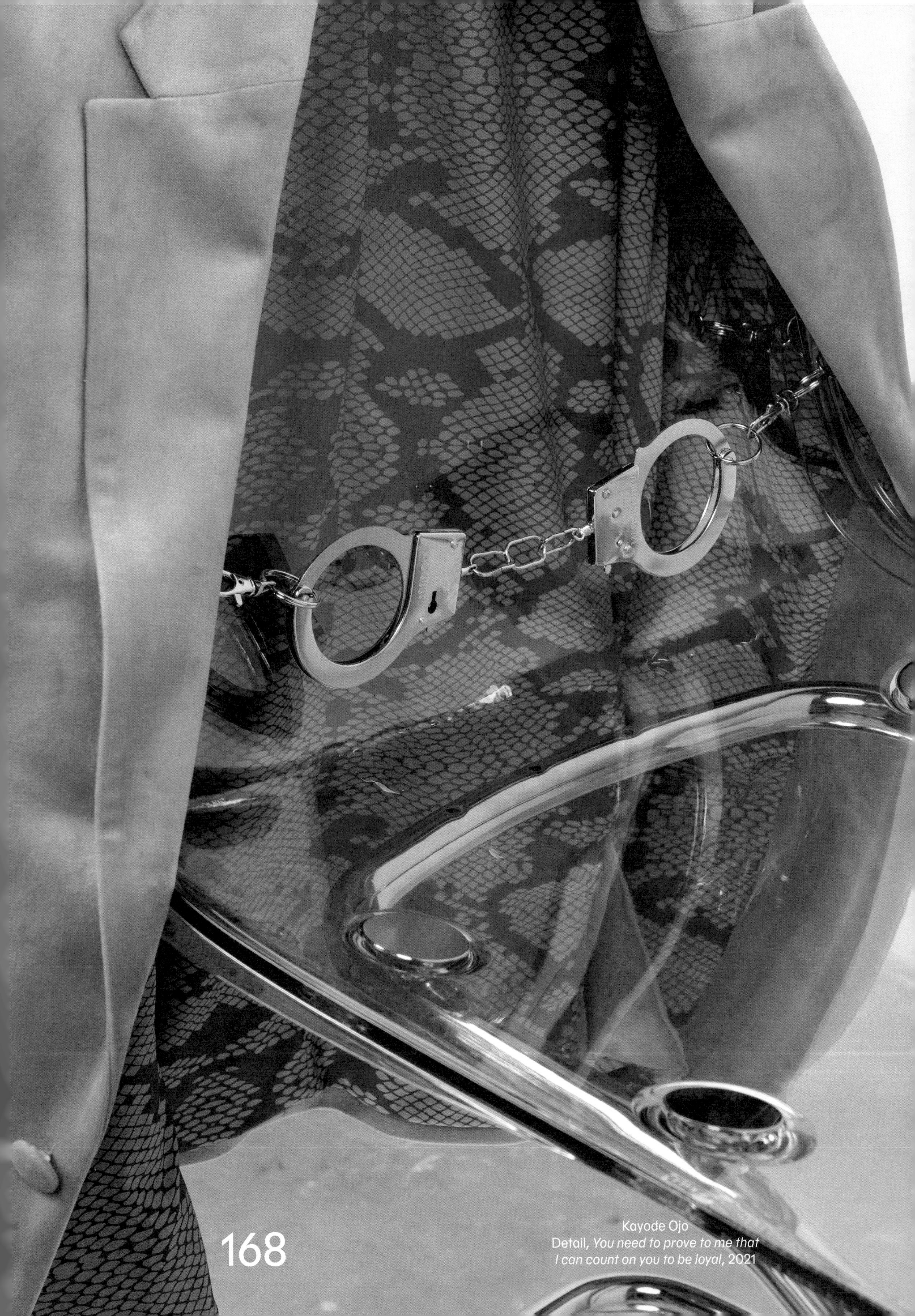

Kayode Ojo
Detail, *You need to prove to me that I can count on you to be loyal*, 2021

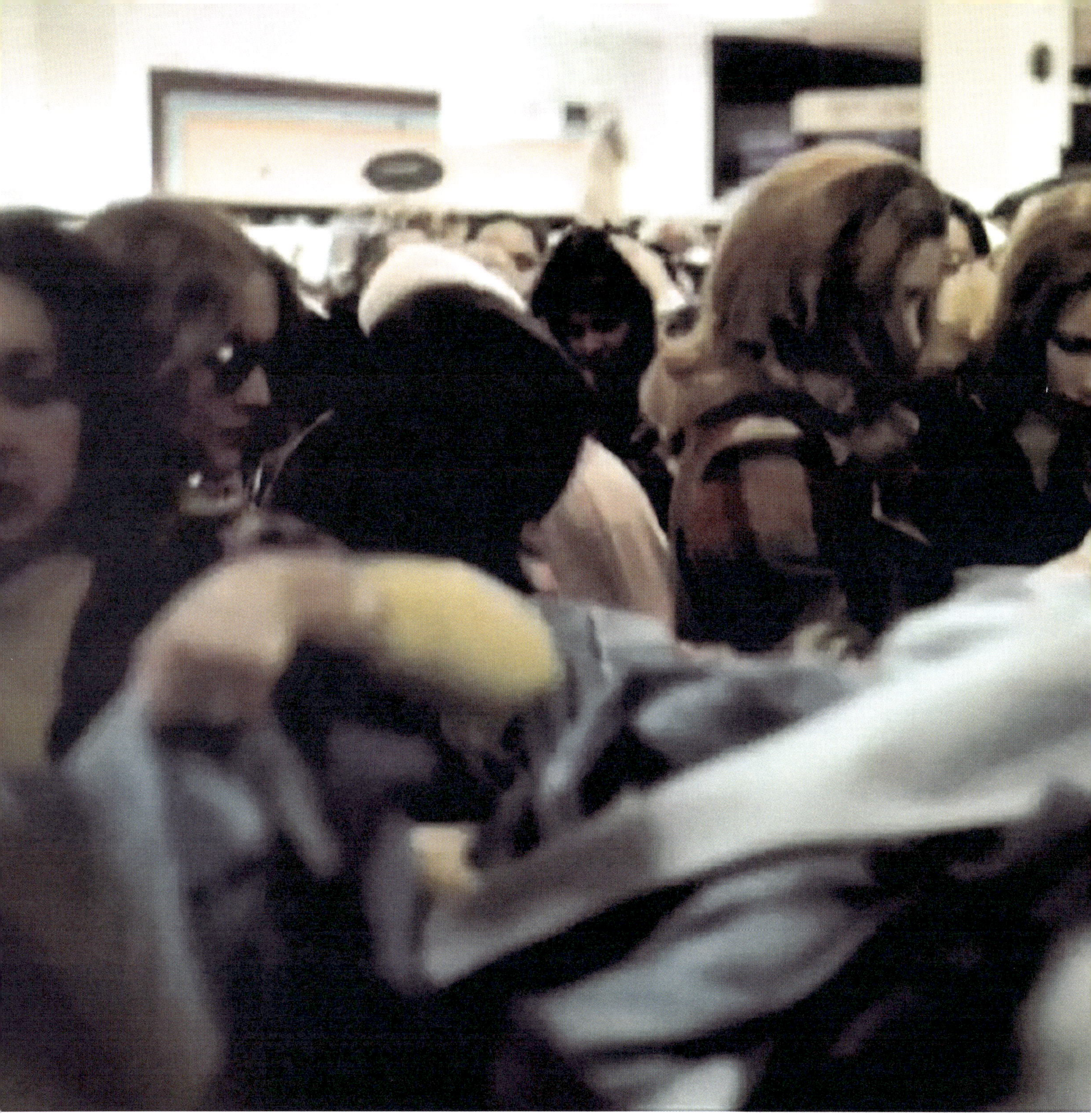

Regina Vater
Still from *LuxoLixo*, 1973/1974

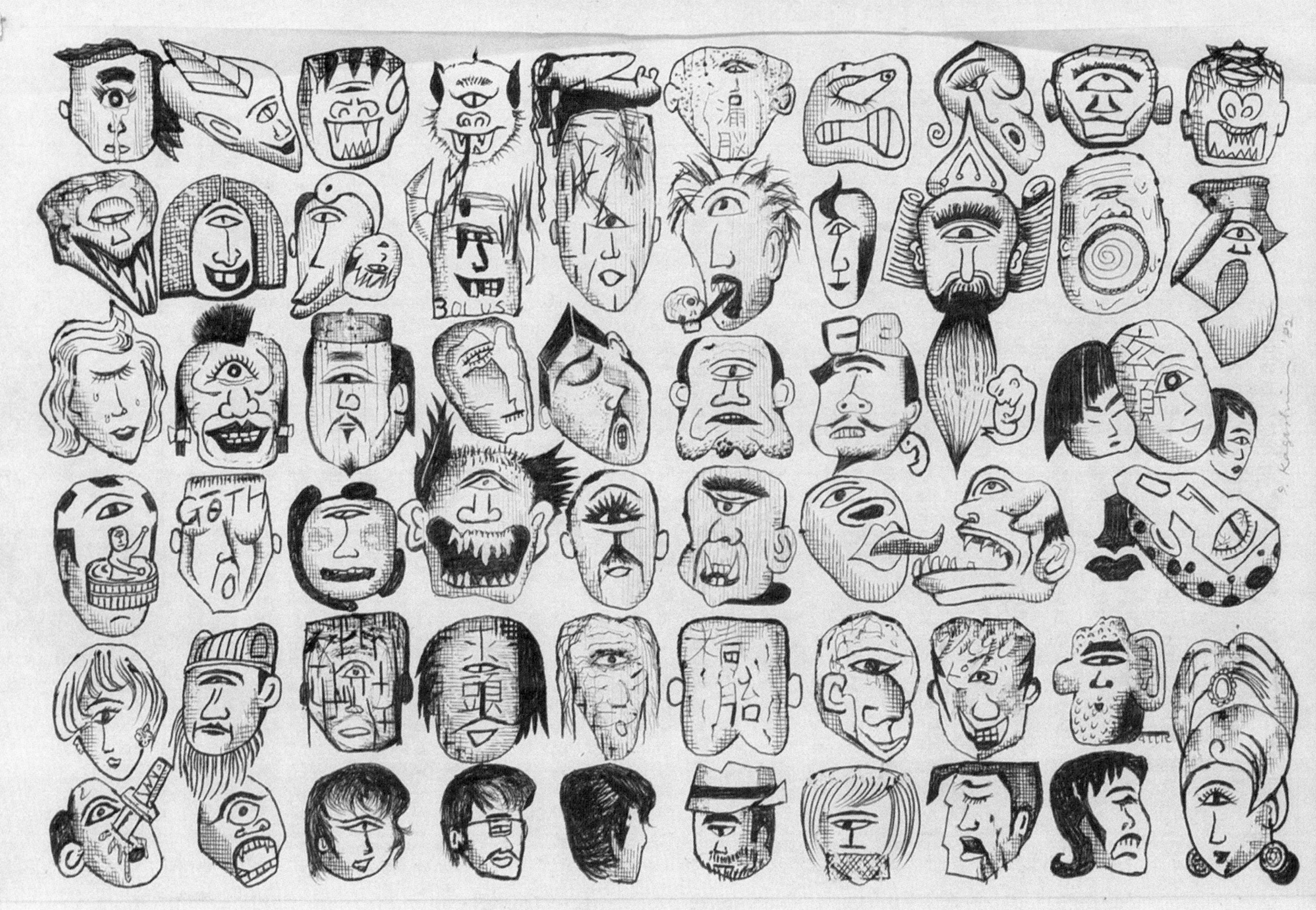

E'wao Kagoshima
Stick Together, 1982

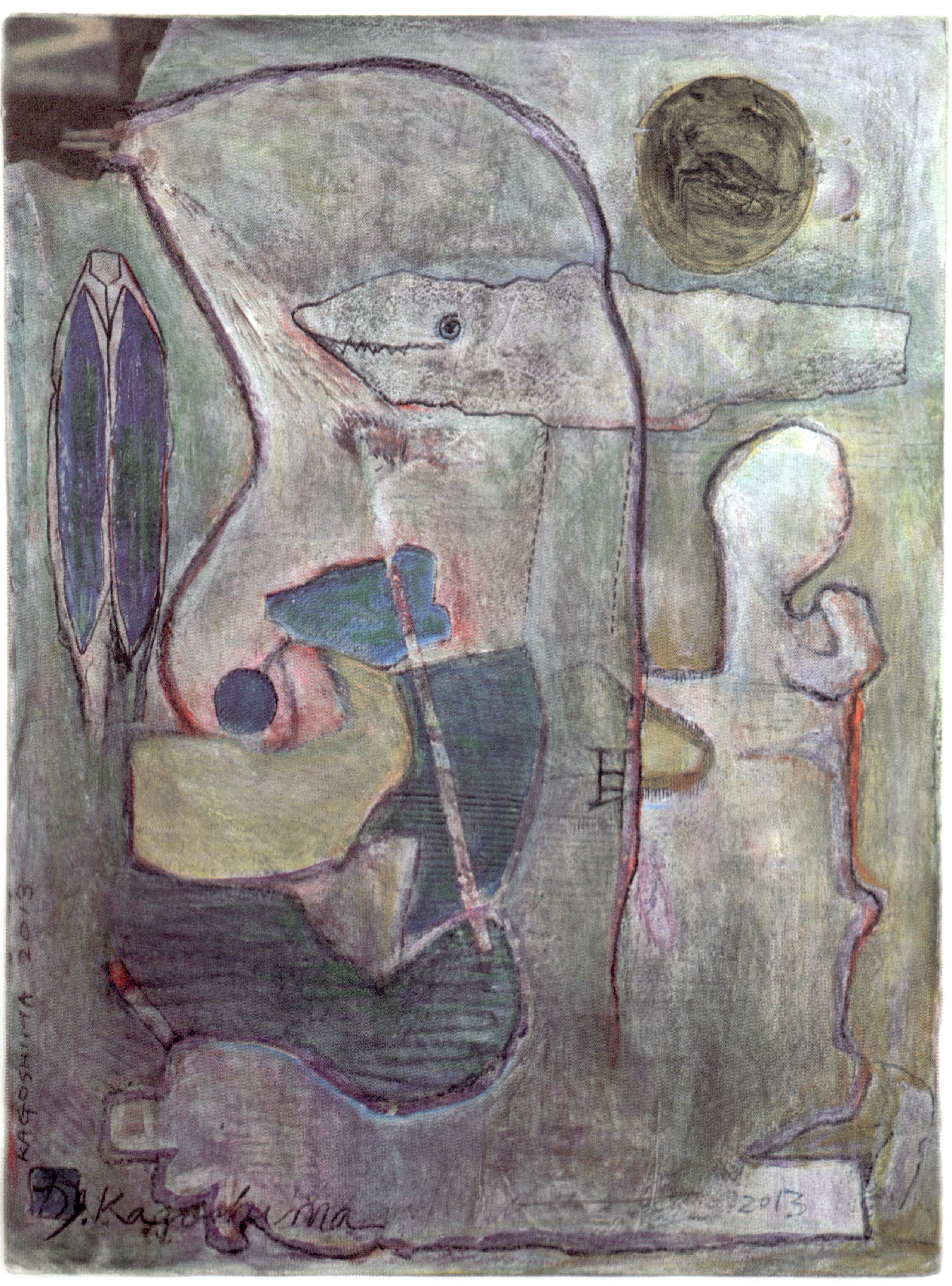

E'wao Kagoshima
Loop Hole, 2013

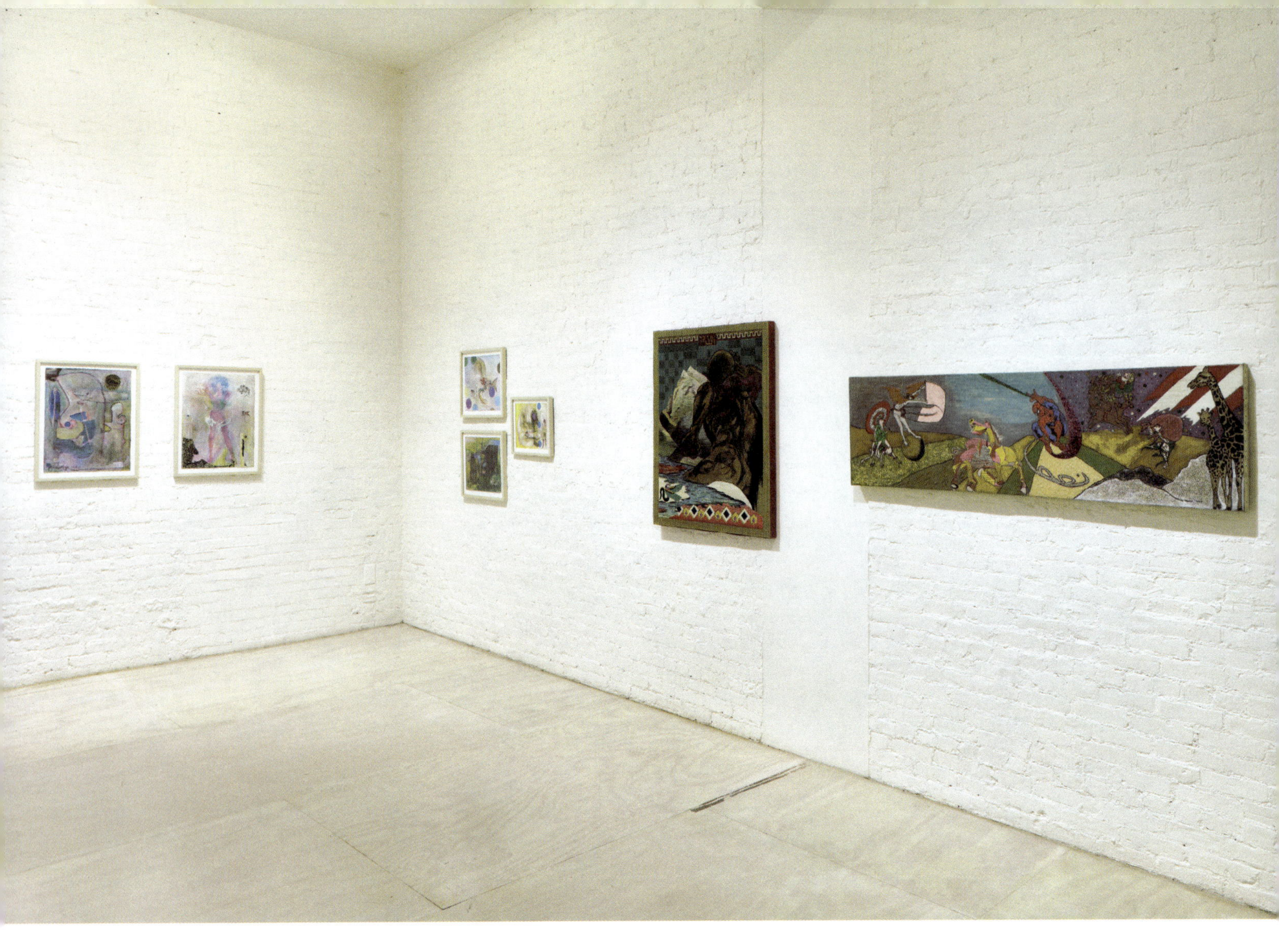

Left to right
E'wao Kagoshima, Nicolas Moufarrege

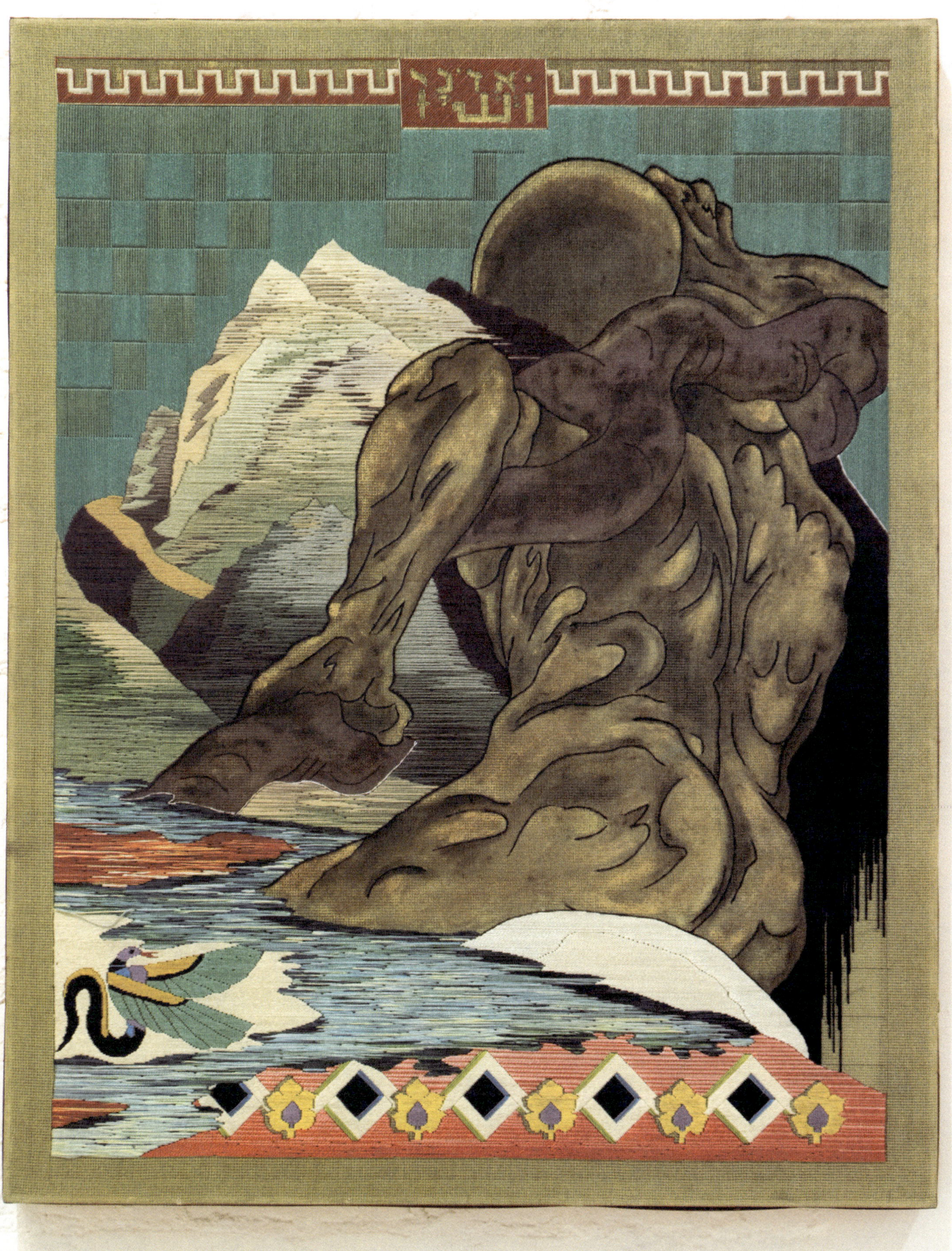

Nicolas Moufarrege
Laocoon Quest #2, 1980

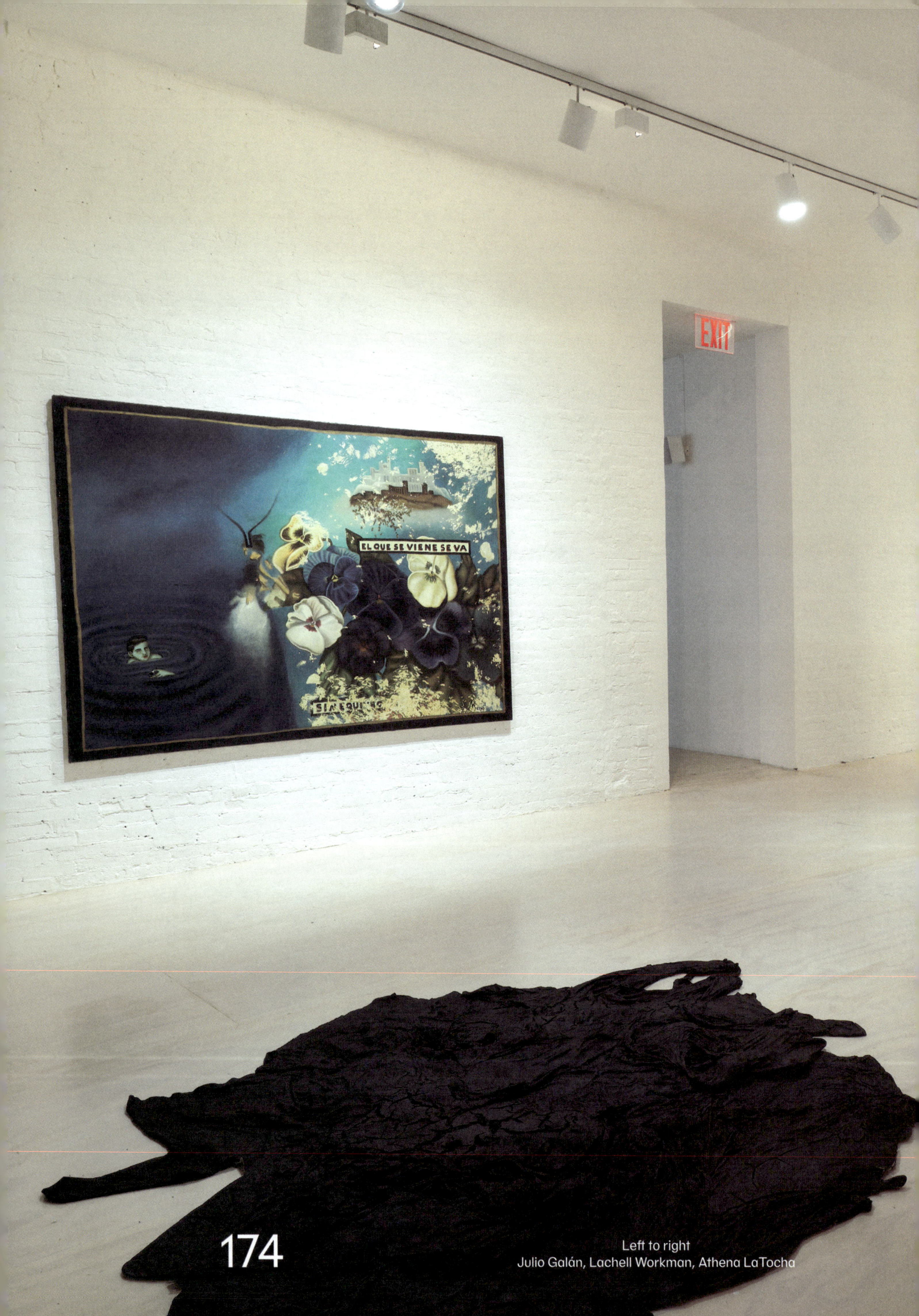

Left to right
Julio Galán, Lachell Workman, Athena LaTocha

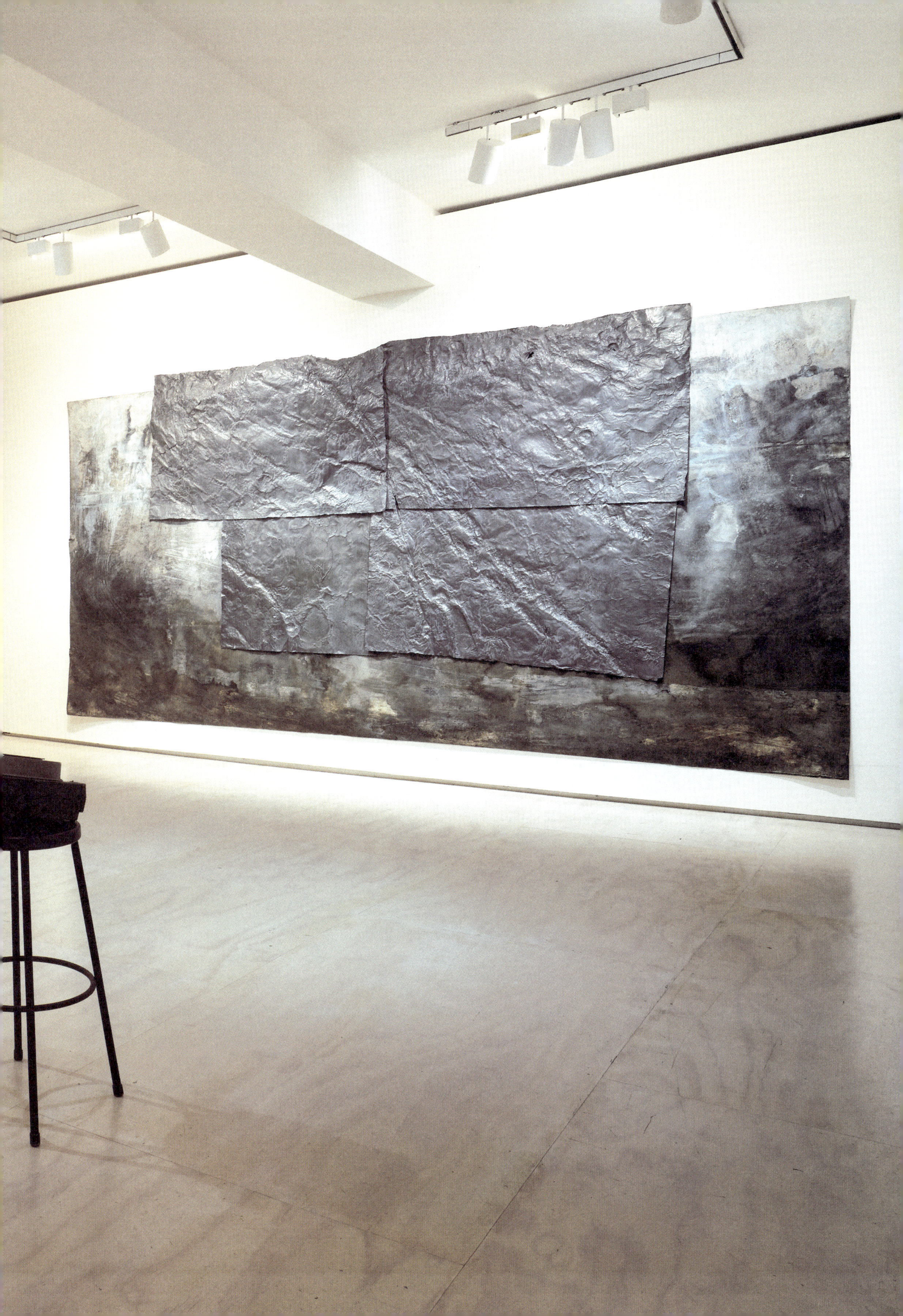

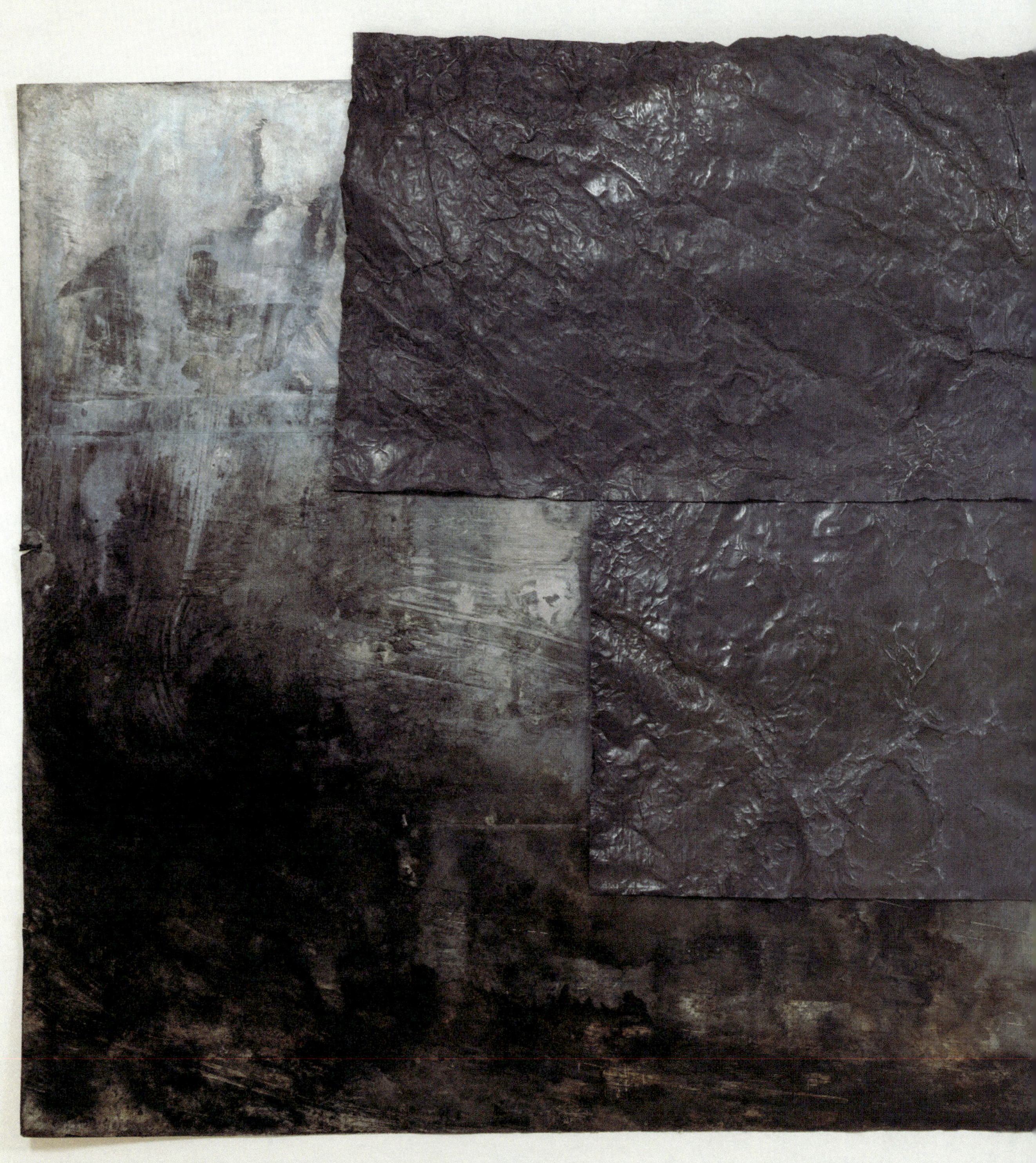

Athena LaTocha
It Came From The North, 2021

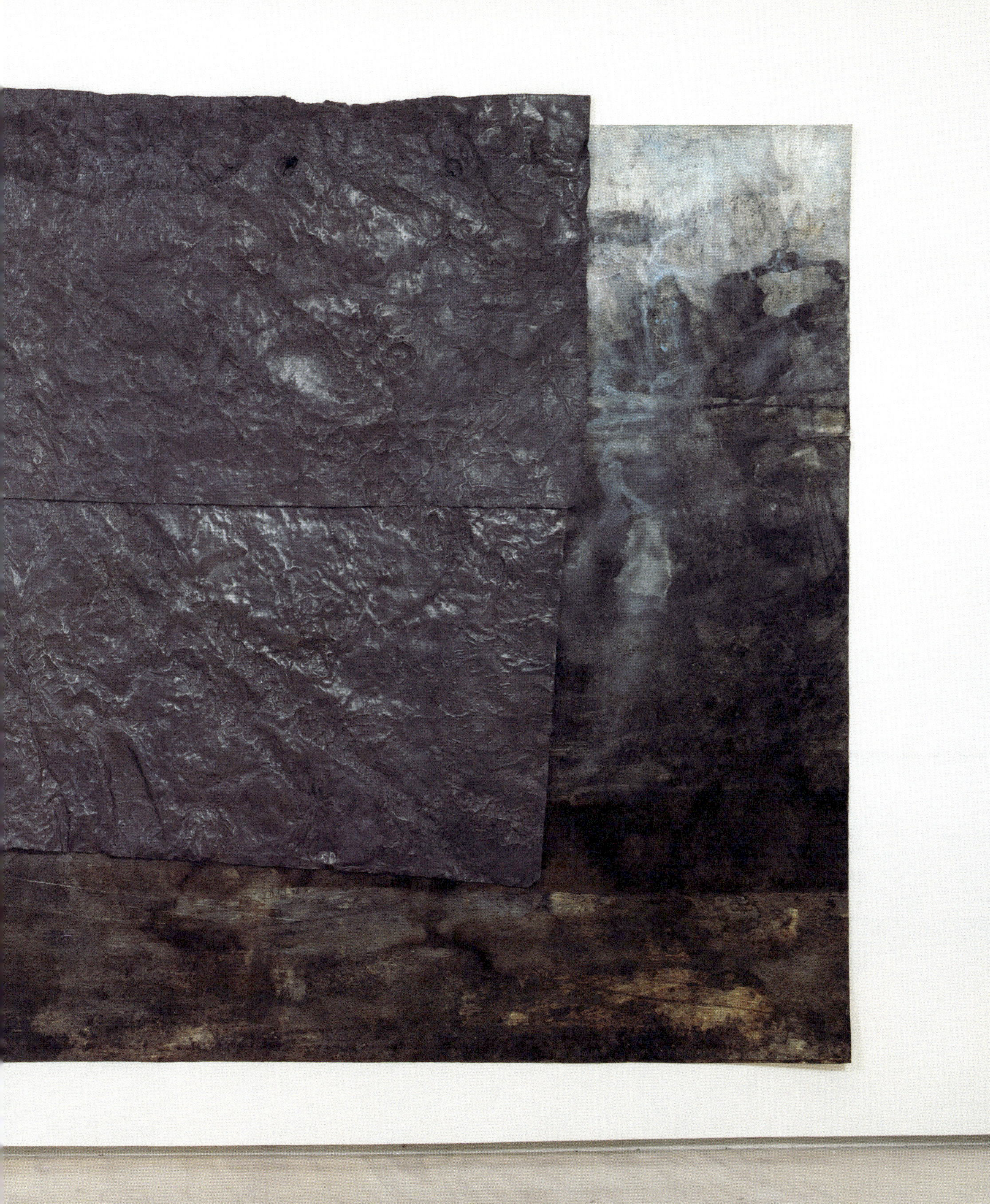

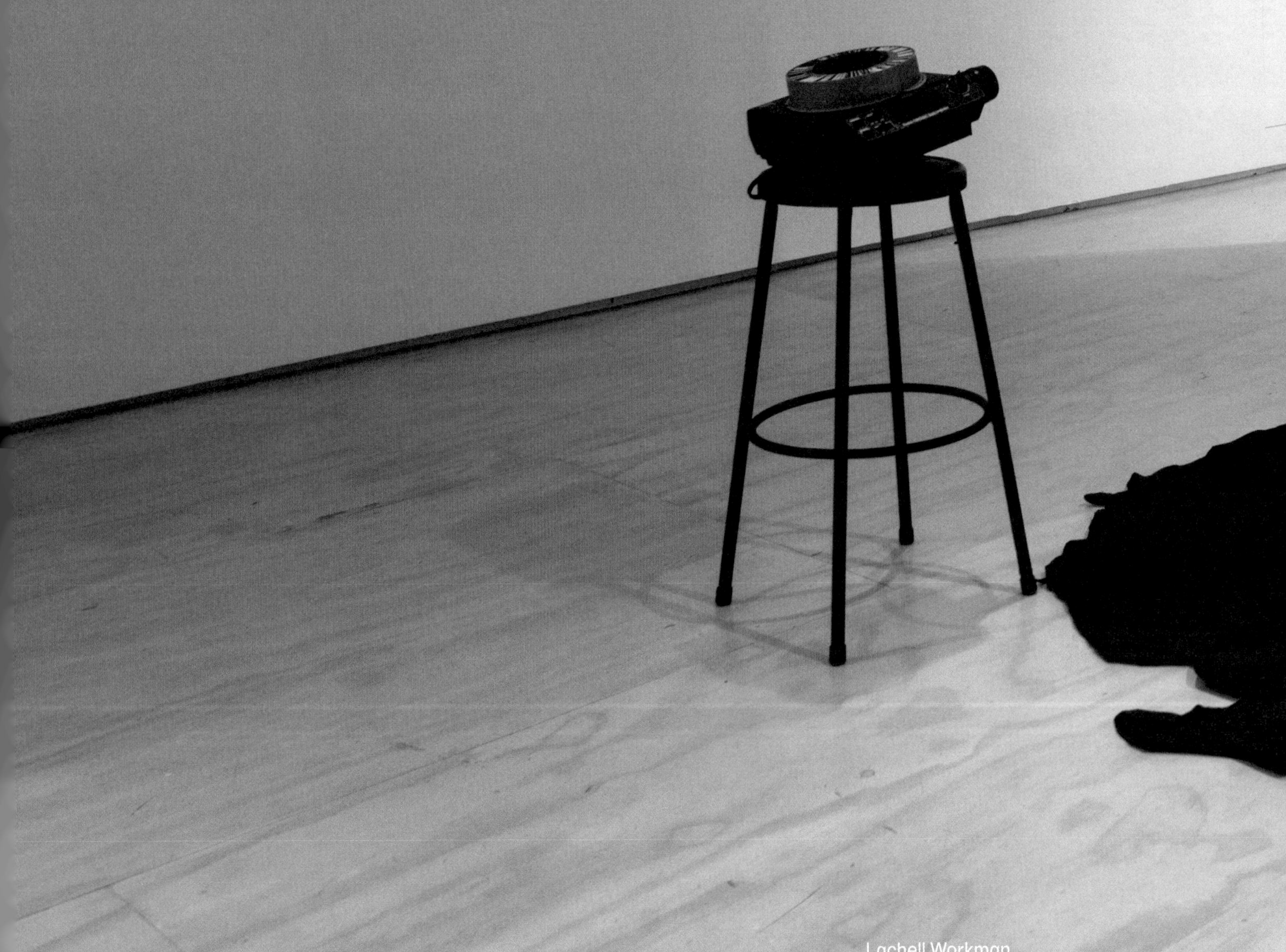

Lachell Workman
The Cenotaph Won't Hold, 2021
A Sartorial Monument, 2021

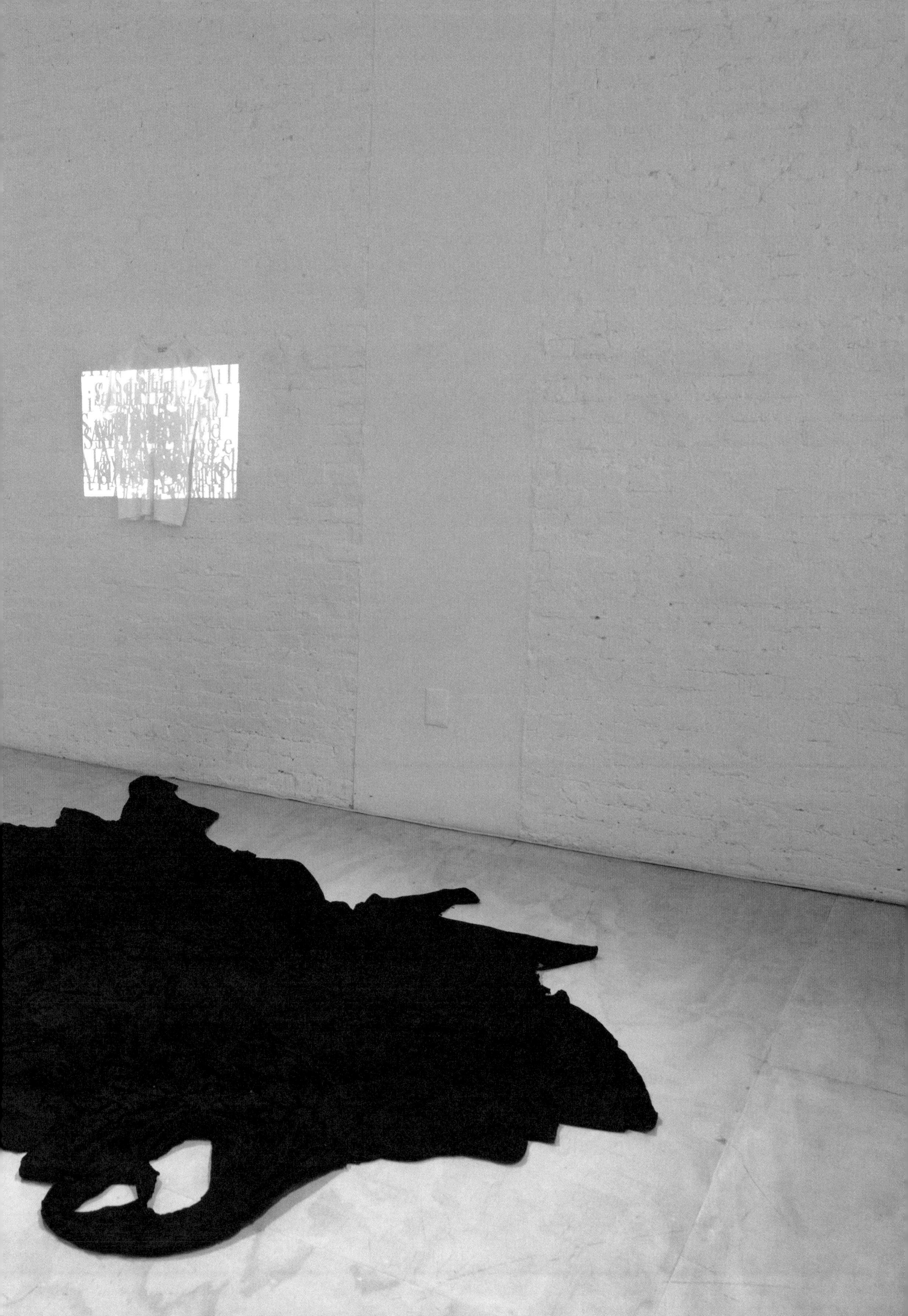

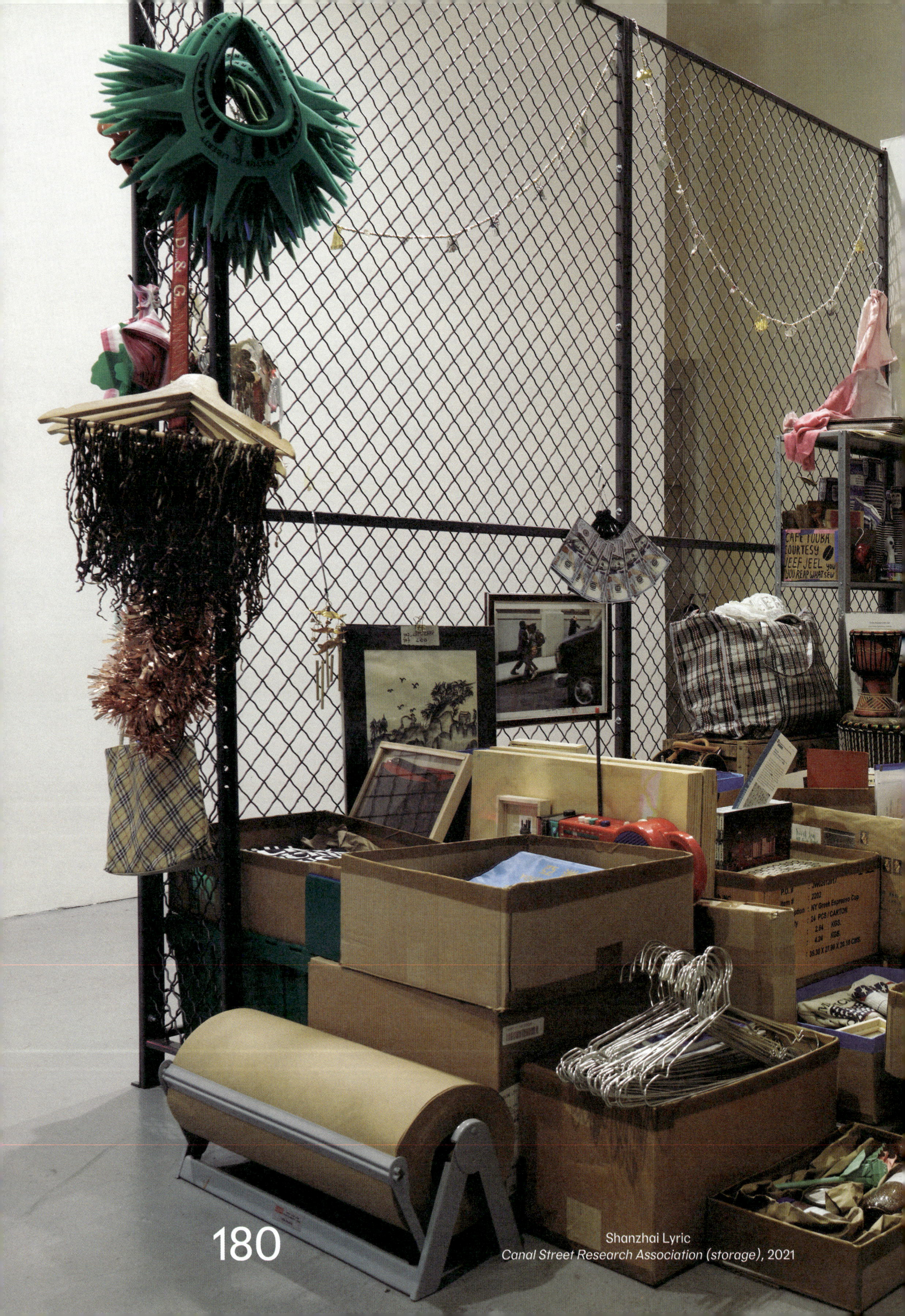

Shanzhai Lyric
Canal Street Research Association (storage), 2021

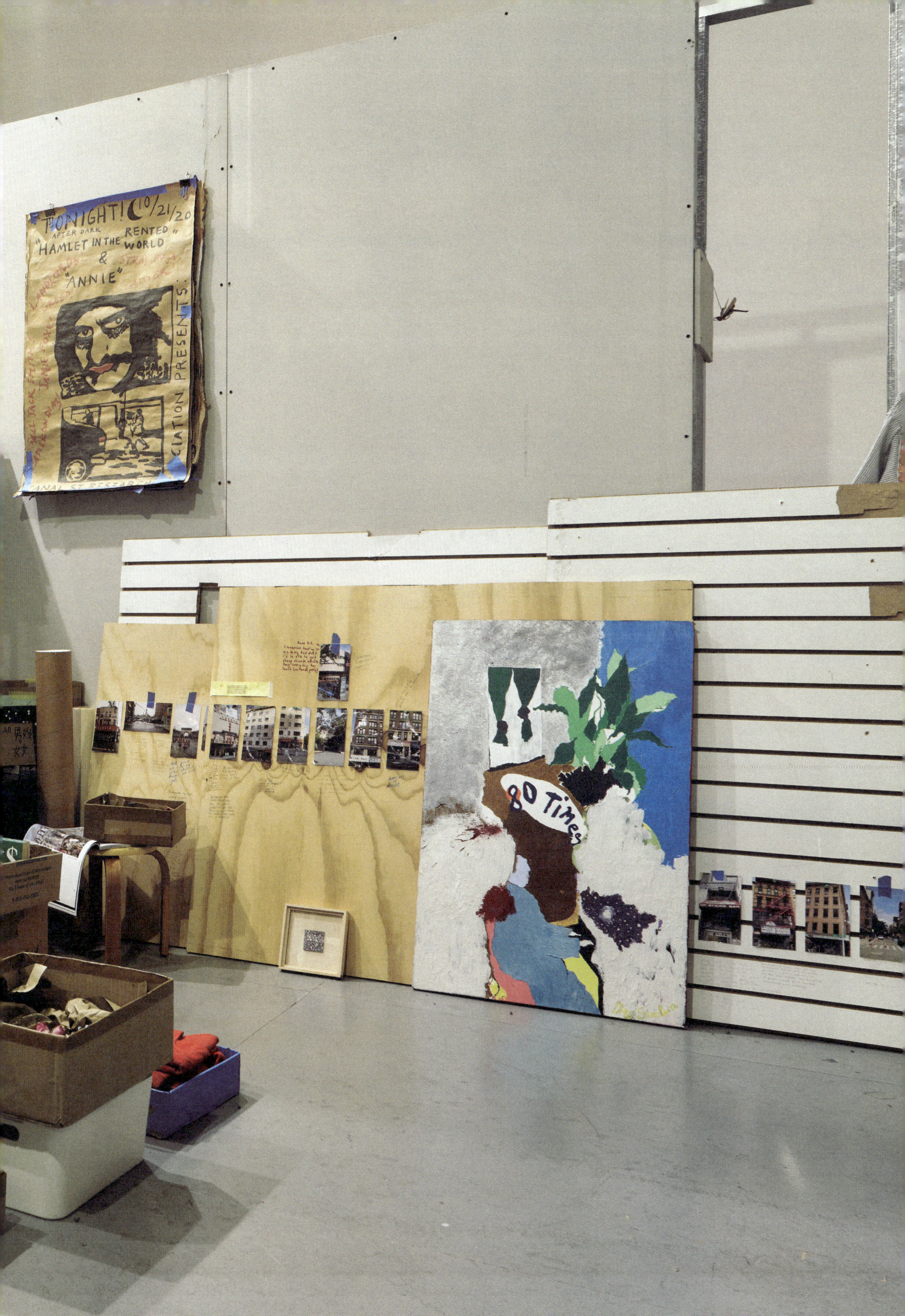
TONIGHT! 10/21/20
AFTER DARK
"HAMLET IN THE RENTED WORLD"
&
"ANNIE"
80 Times

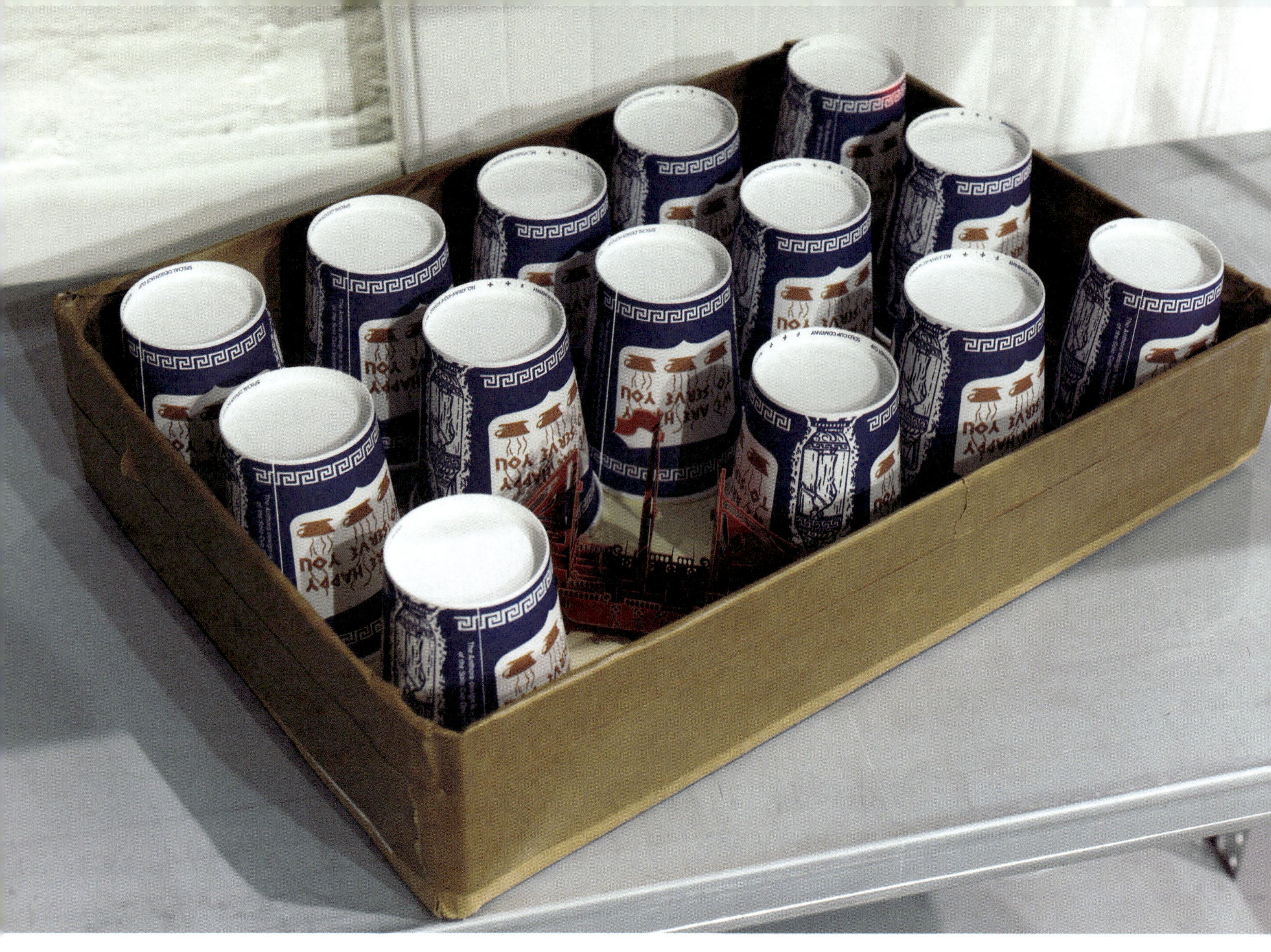

Shanzhai Lyric
Detail, *Canal Street Research Association (storage)*, 2021

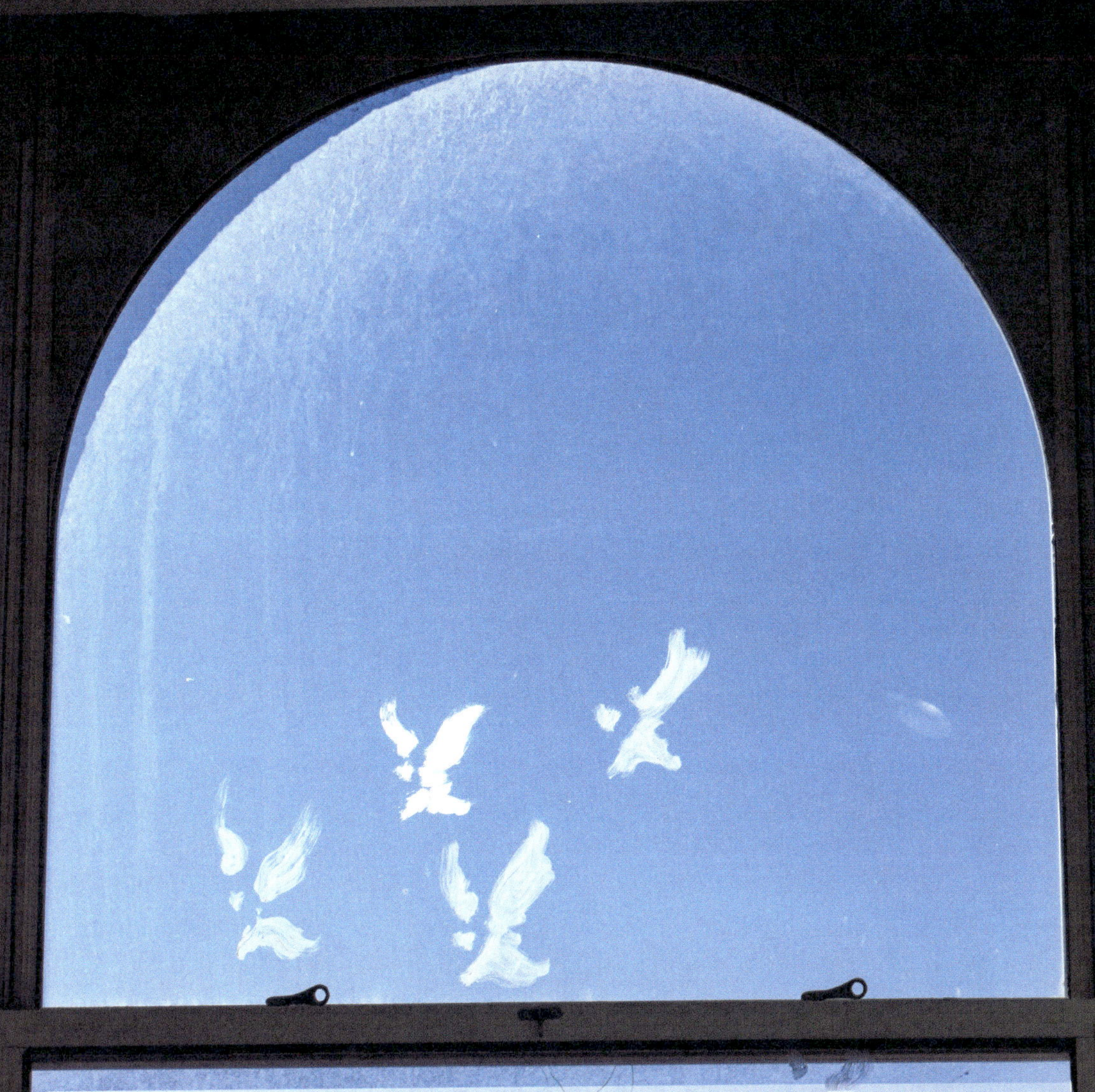

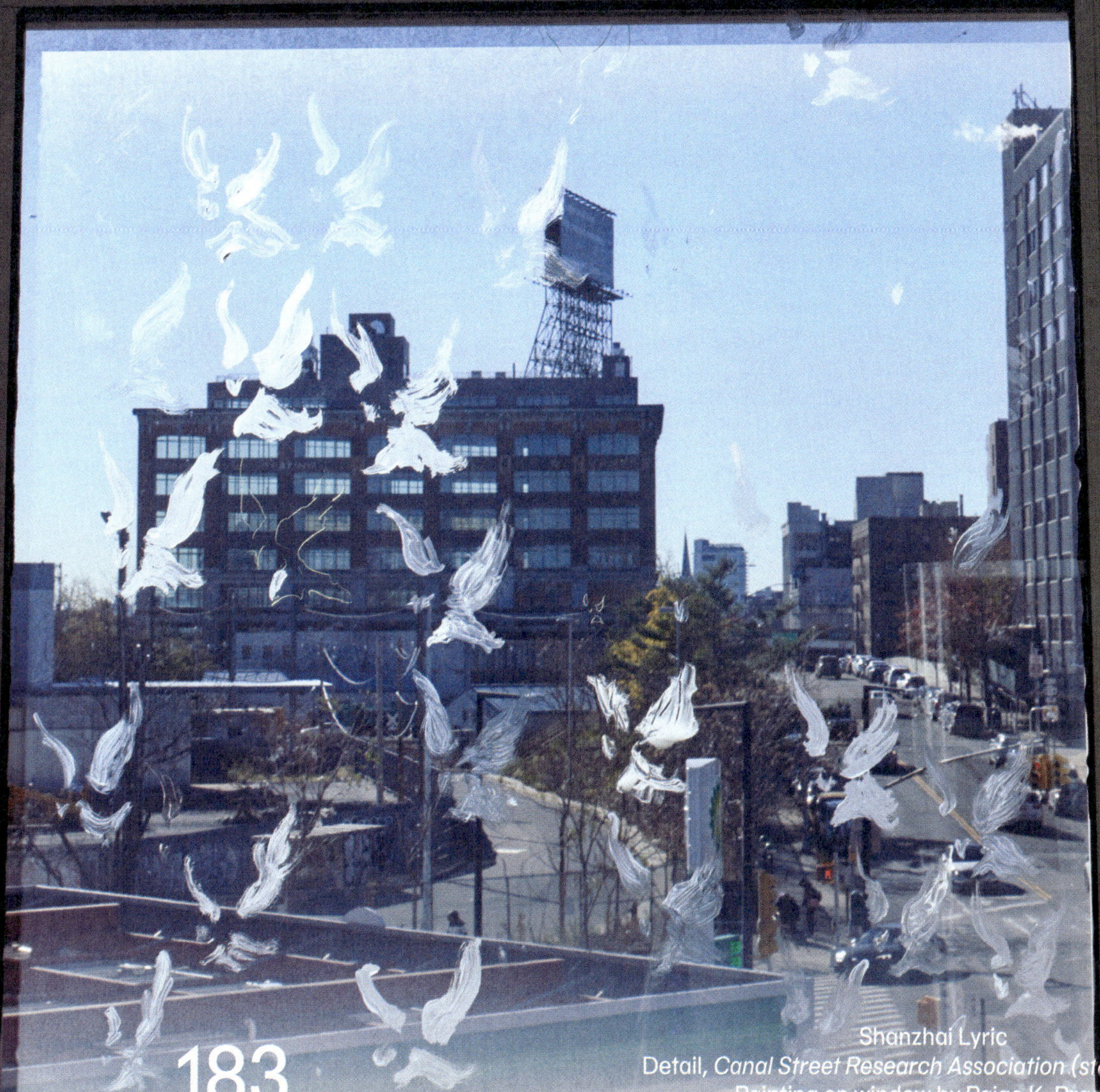

Shanzhai Lyric
Detail, *Canal Street Research Association (storage)*, 2021
Painting on window by Paige K. Bradley

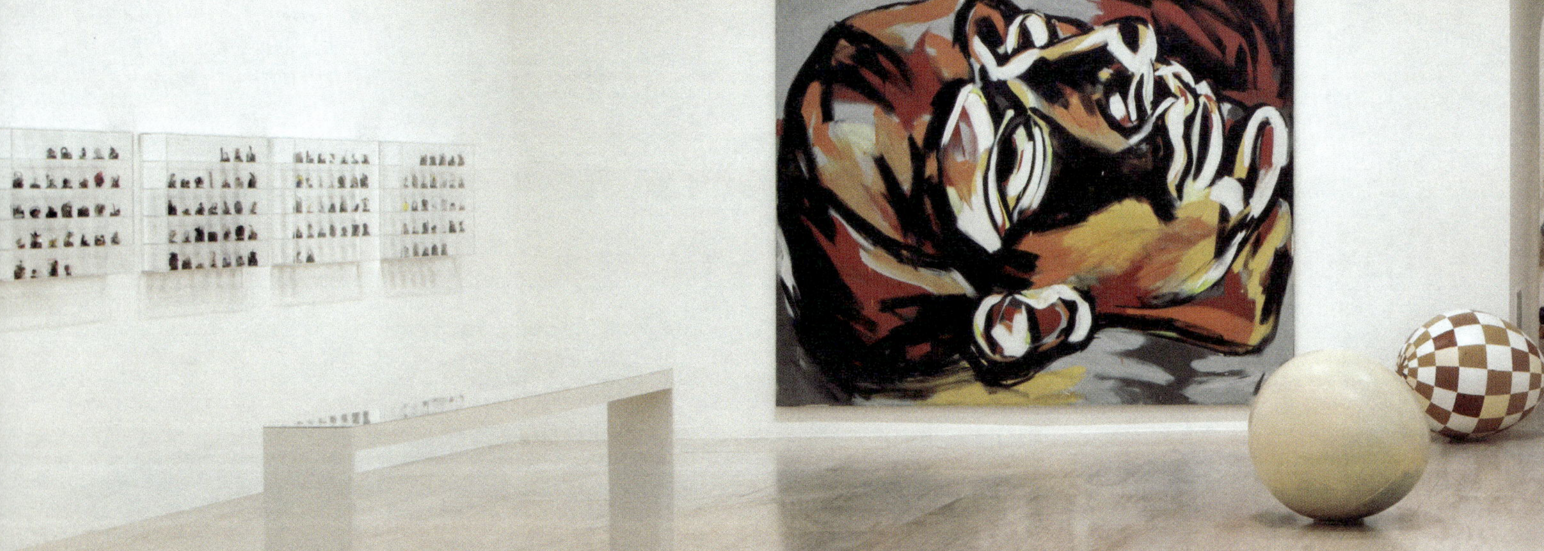

Left to right
Yuji Agematsu, Luis Frangella, Matthew Langan-Peck, Hadi Fallahpisheh, Robin Graubard, Kristi Cavataro, Andy Robert

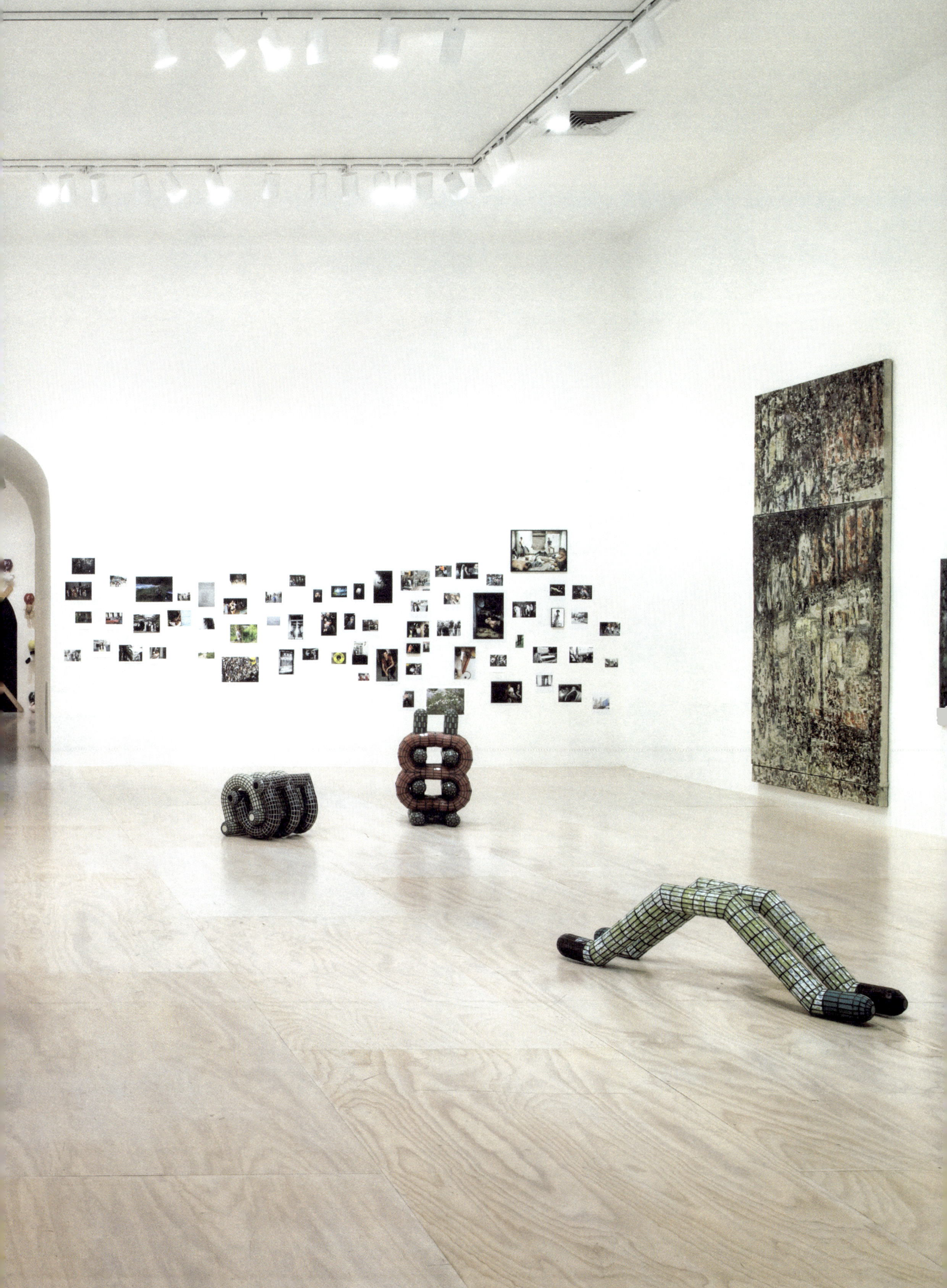

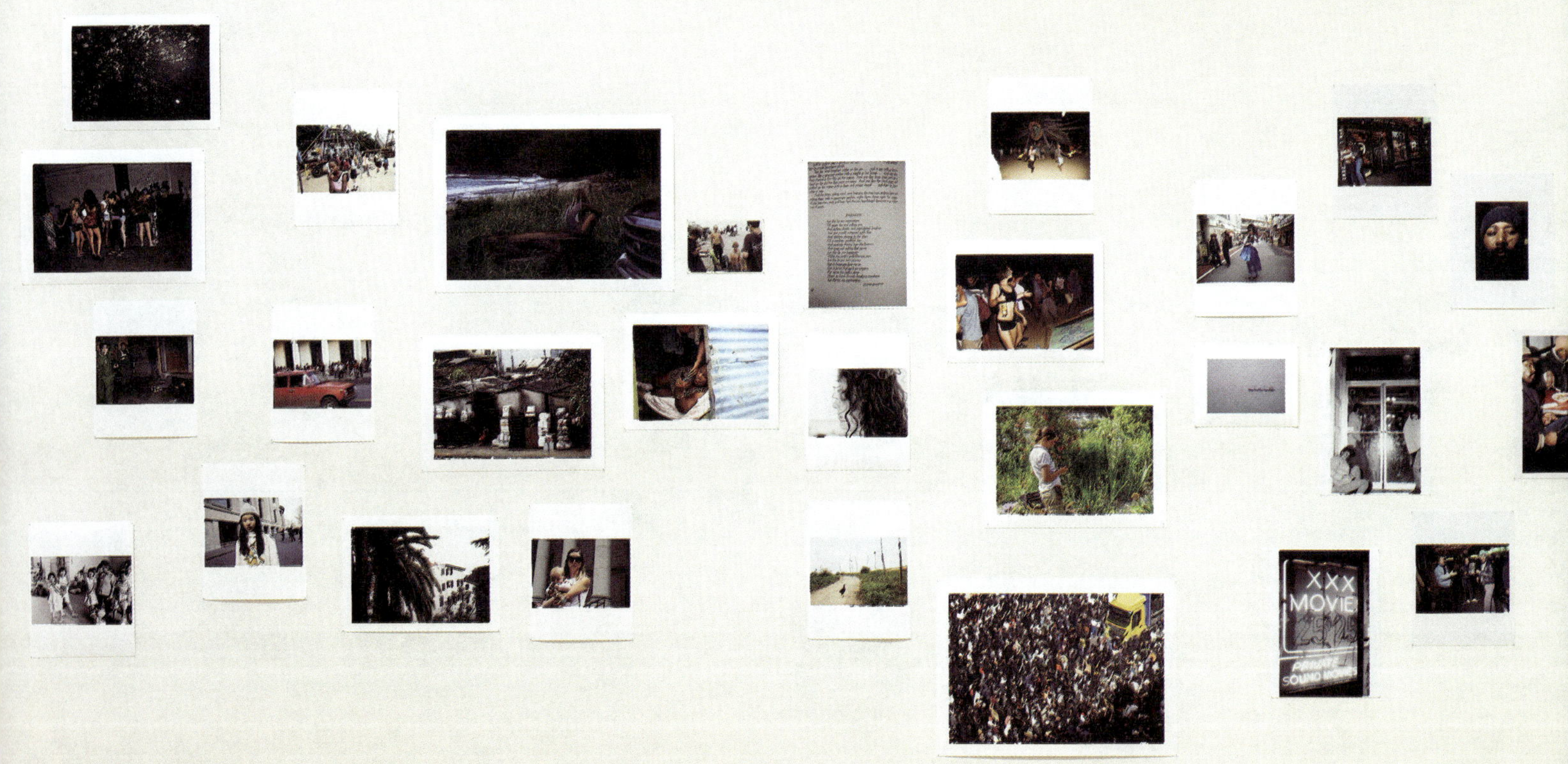
XXX
MOVIE

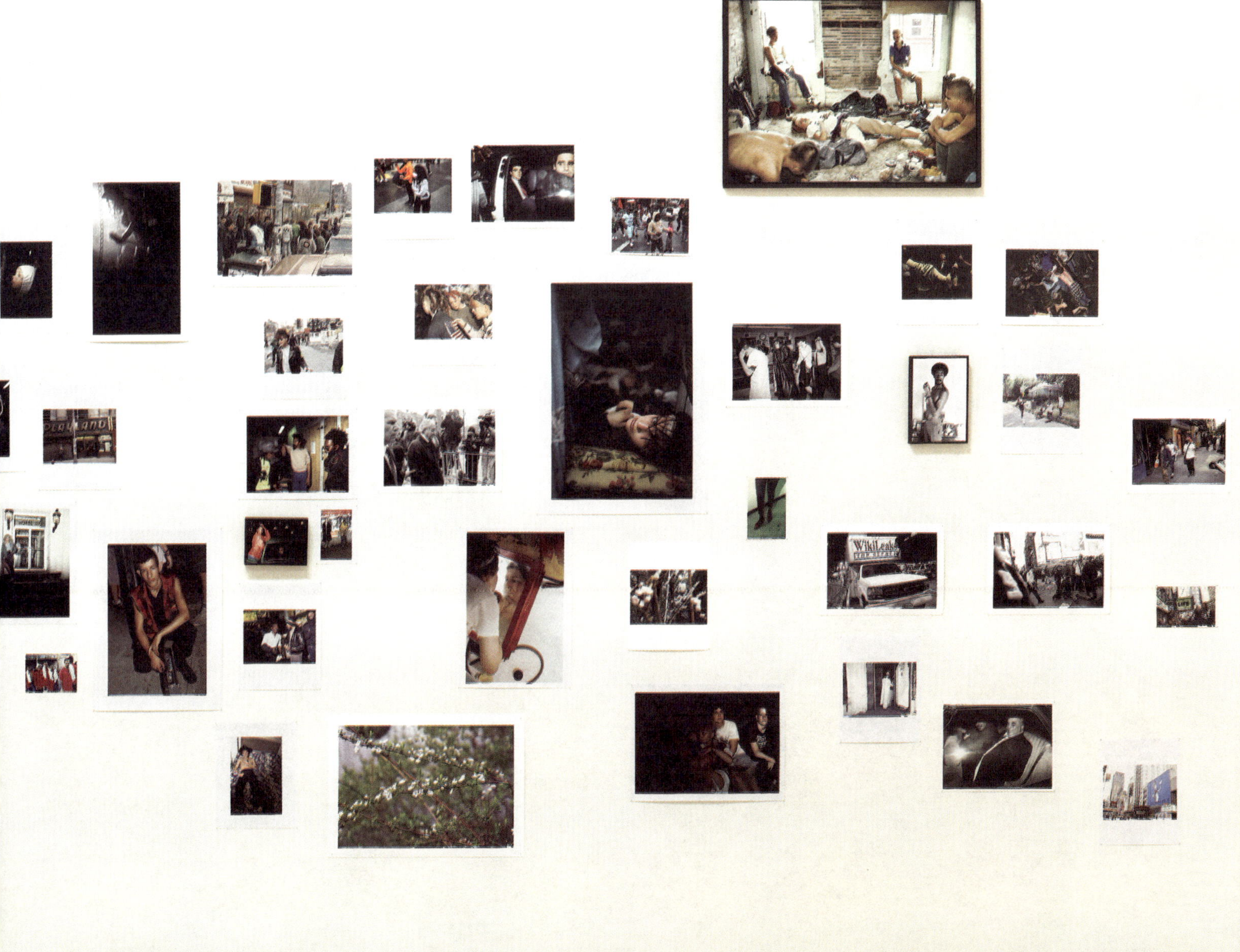
WikiLeaks

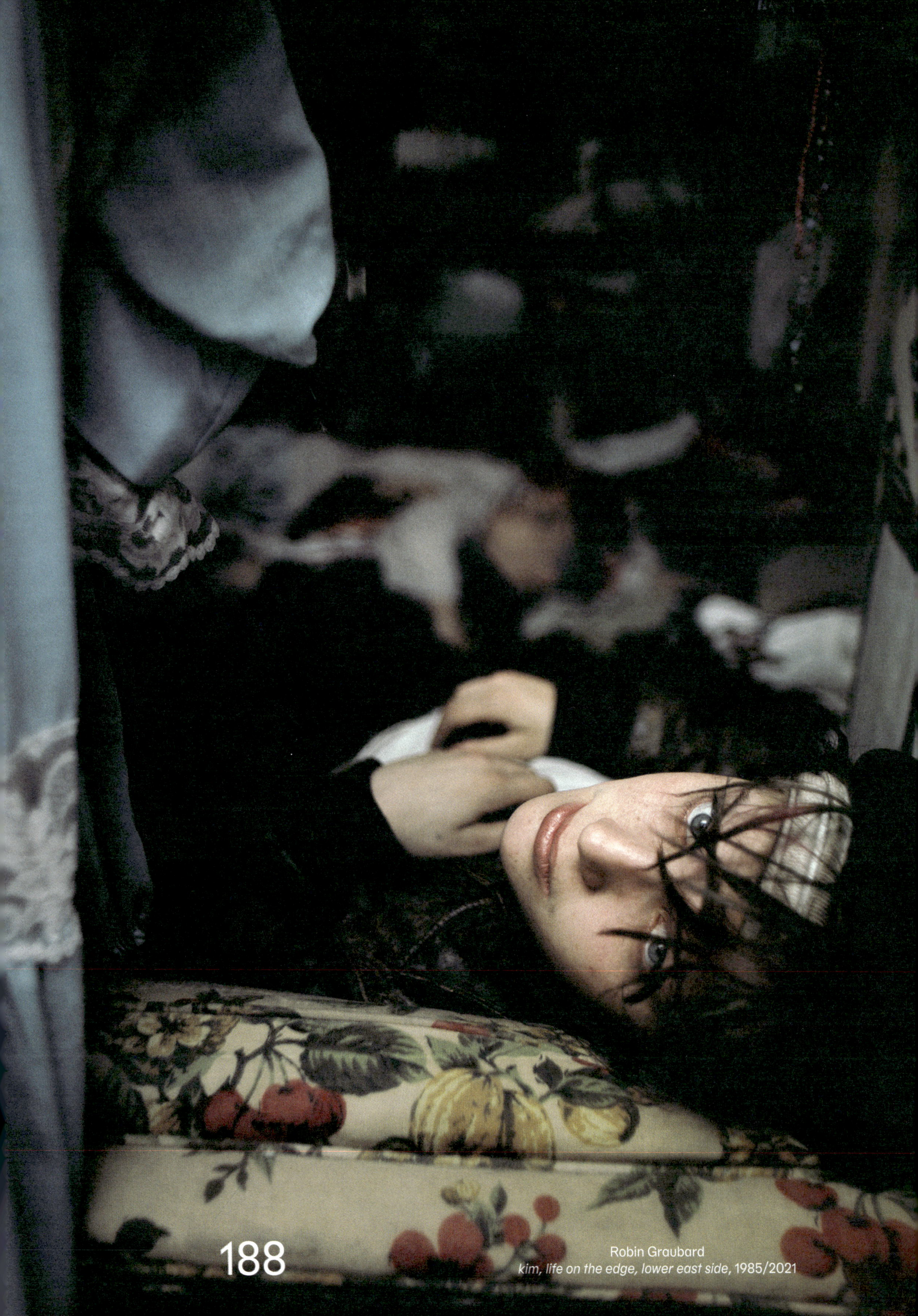

Robin Graubard
kim, life on the edge, lower east side, 1985/2021

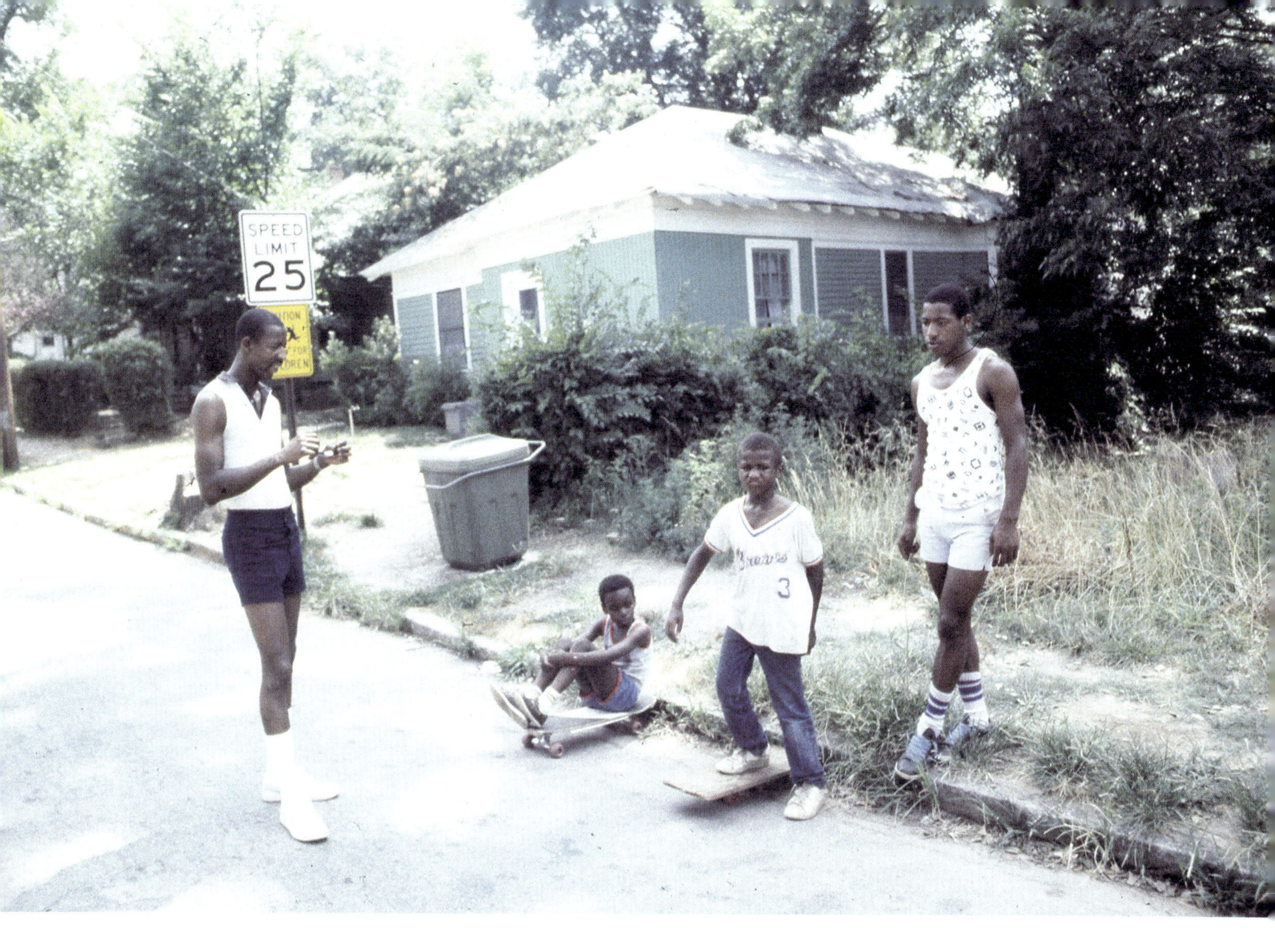

Robin Graubard
atlanta child murders story, 1986/2021

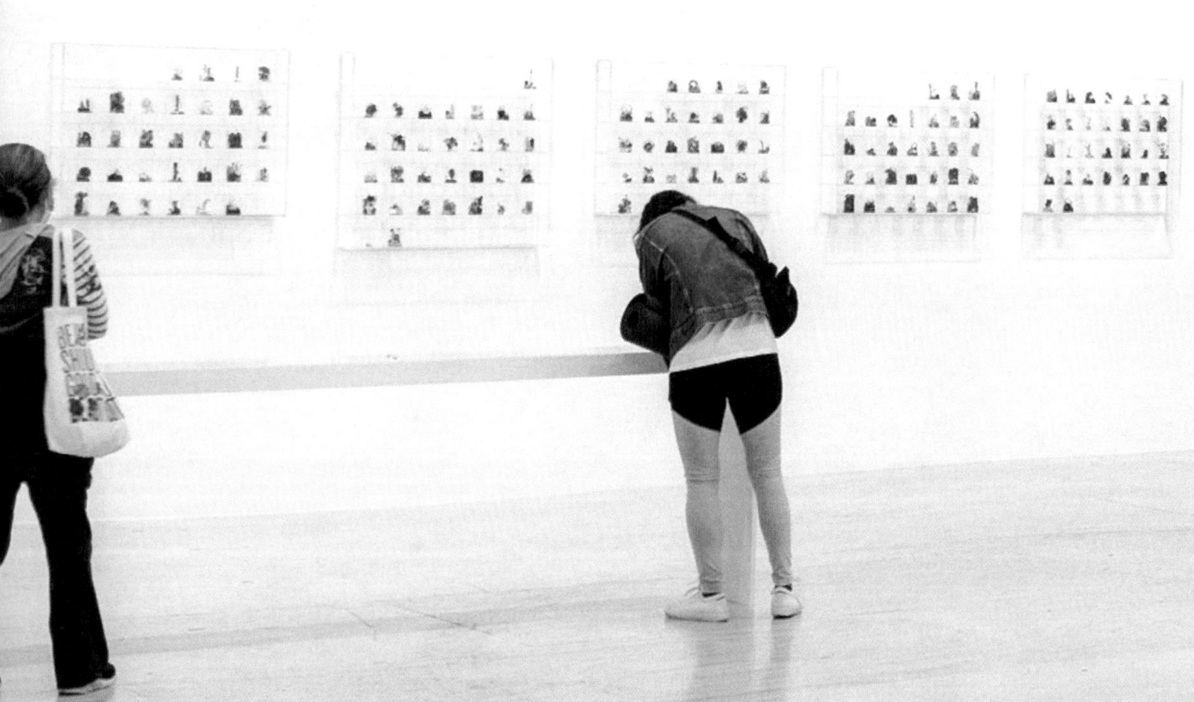

Left to right
Yuji Agematsu, Matthew Langan-Peck,
Luis Frangella, Kristi Cavataro

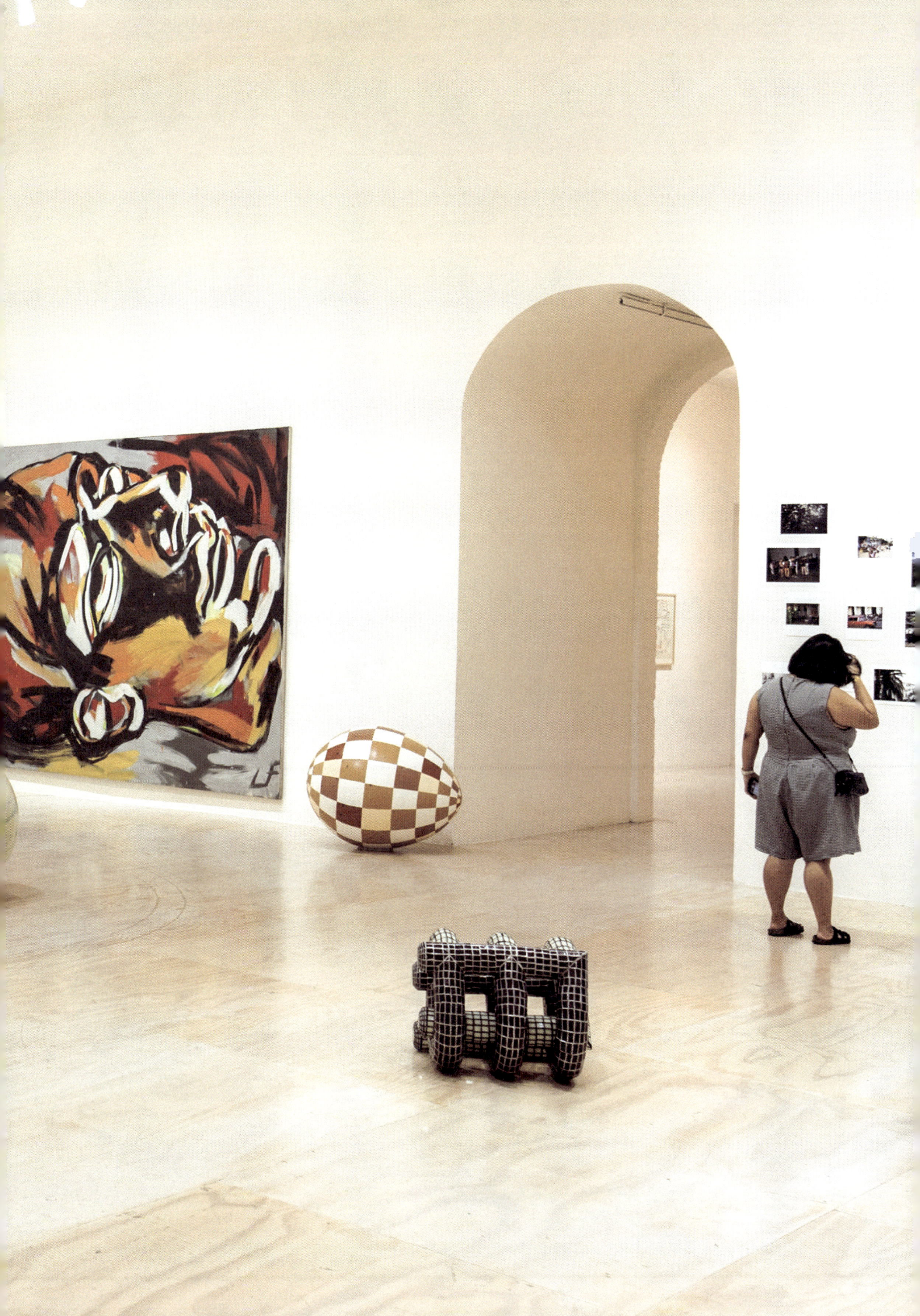

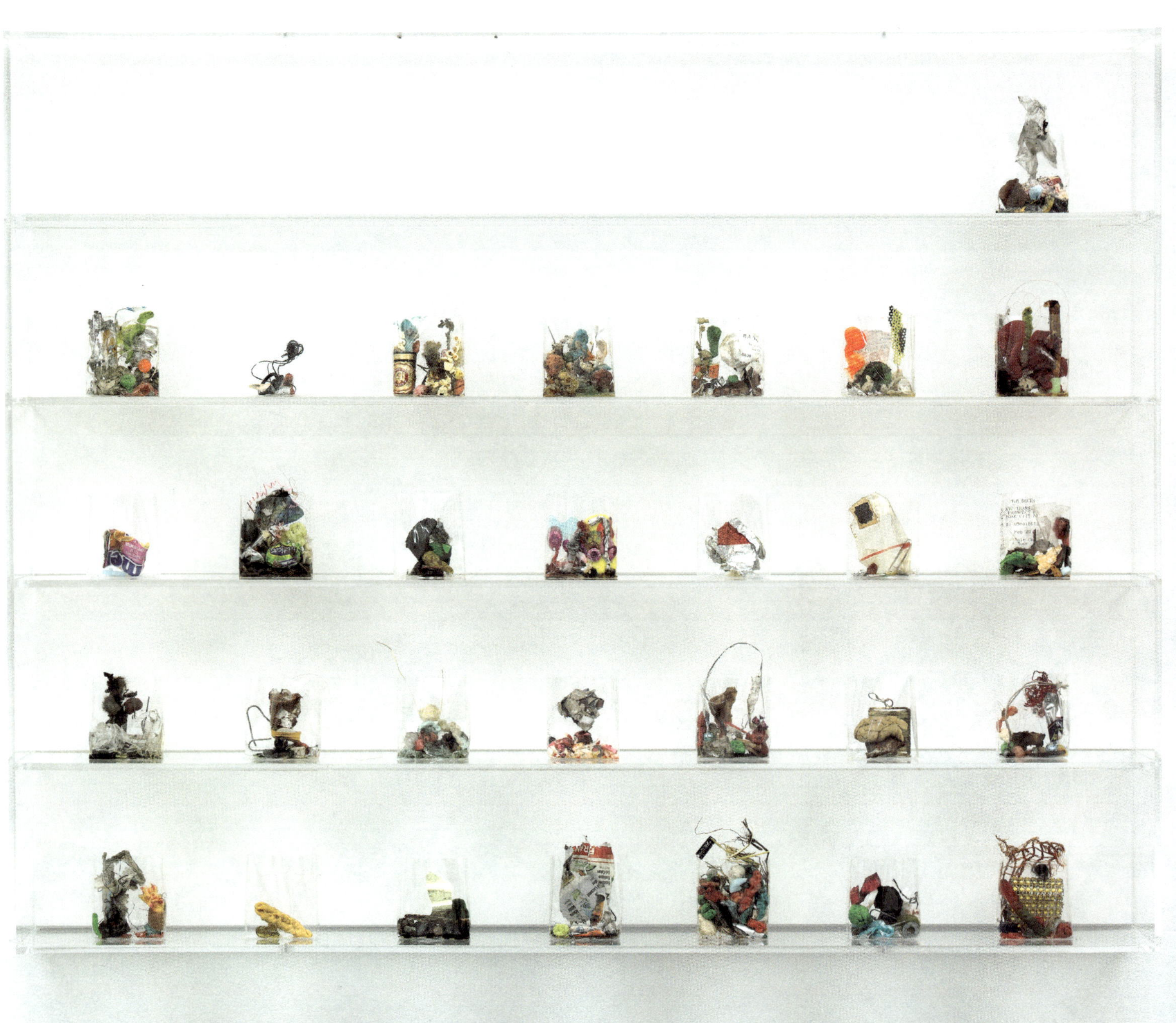

Yuji Agematsu
Details, *zip: 01.01.20 ... 12.31.20*, 2020

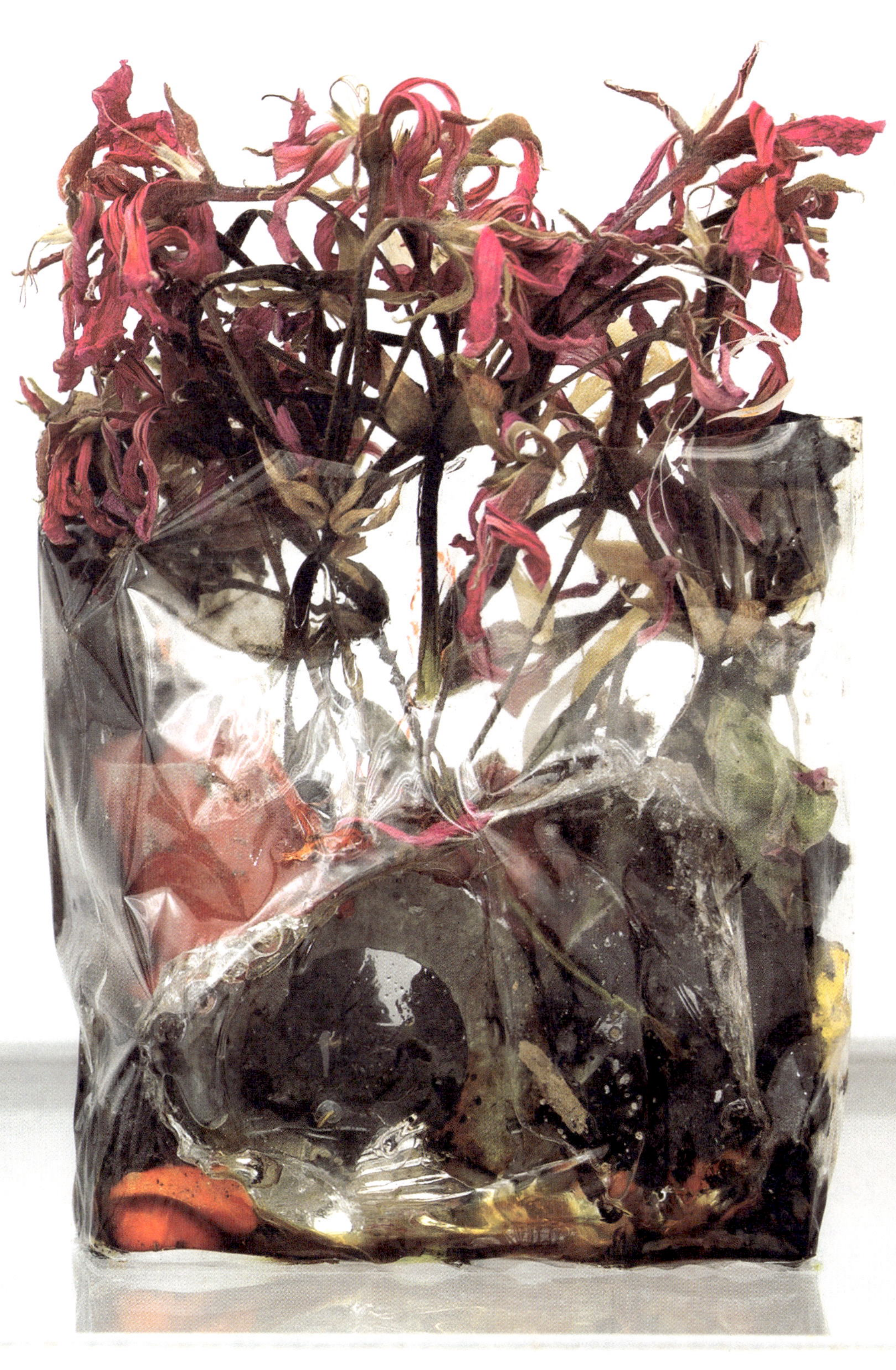

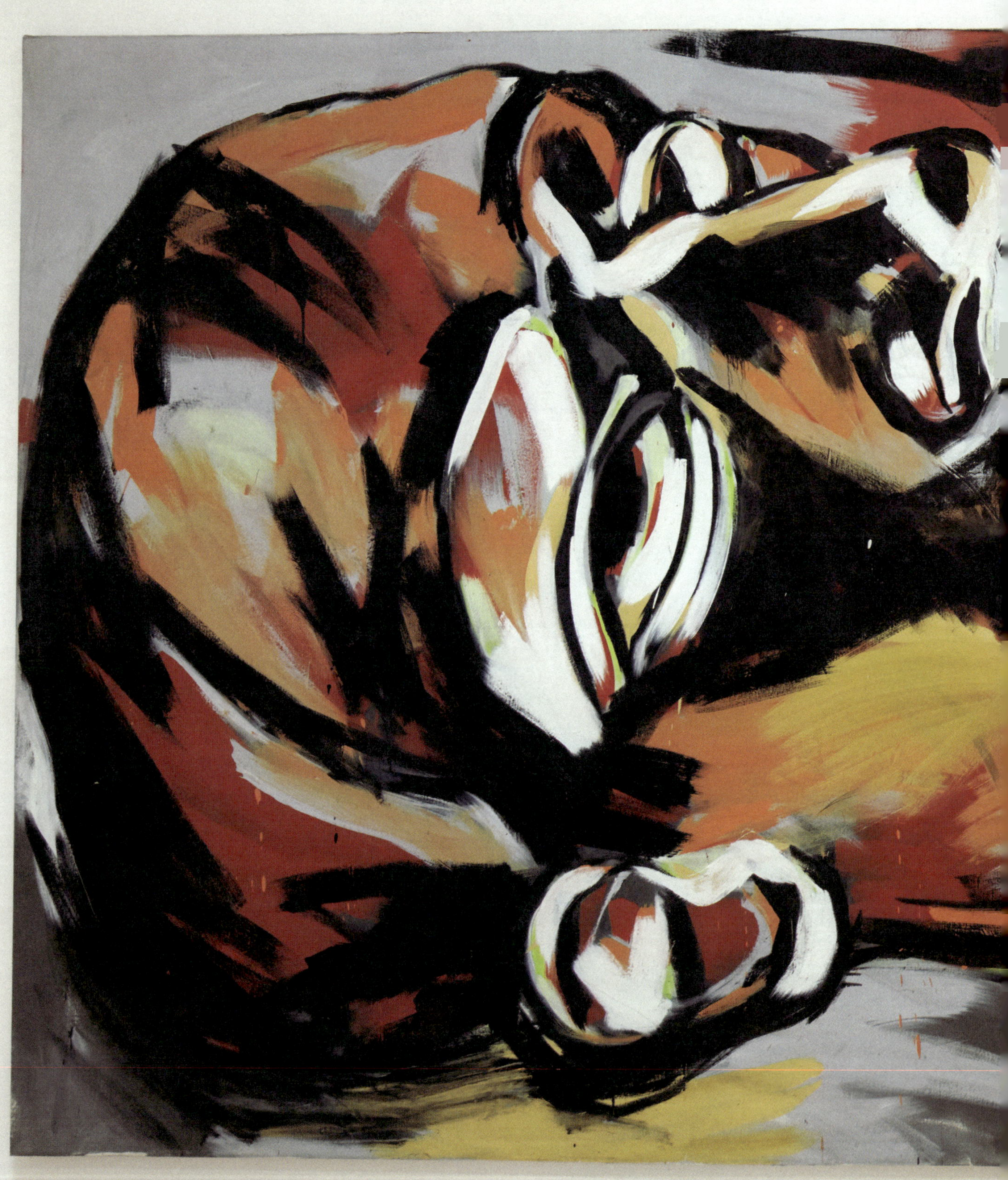

Luis Frangella, *Dreamer*, 1983 (left)
Matthew Langan-Peck, *4 Baskets 4*, 2021 (right)

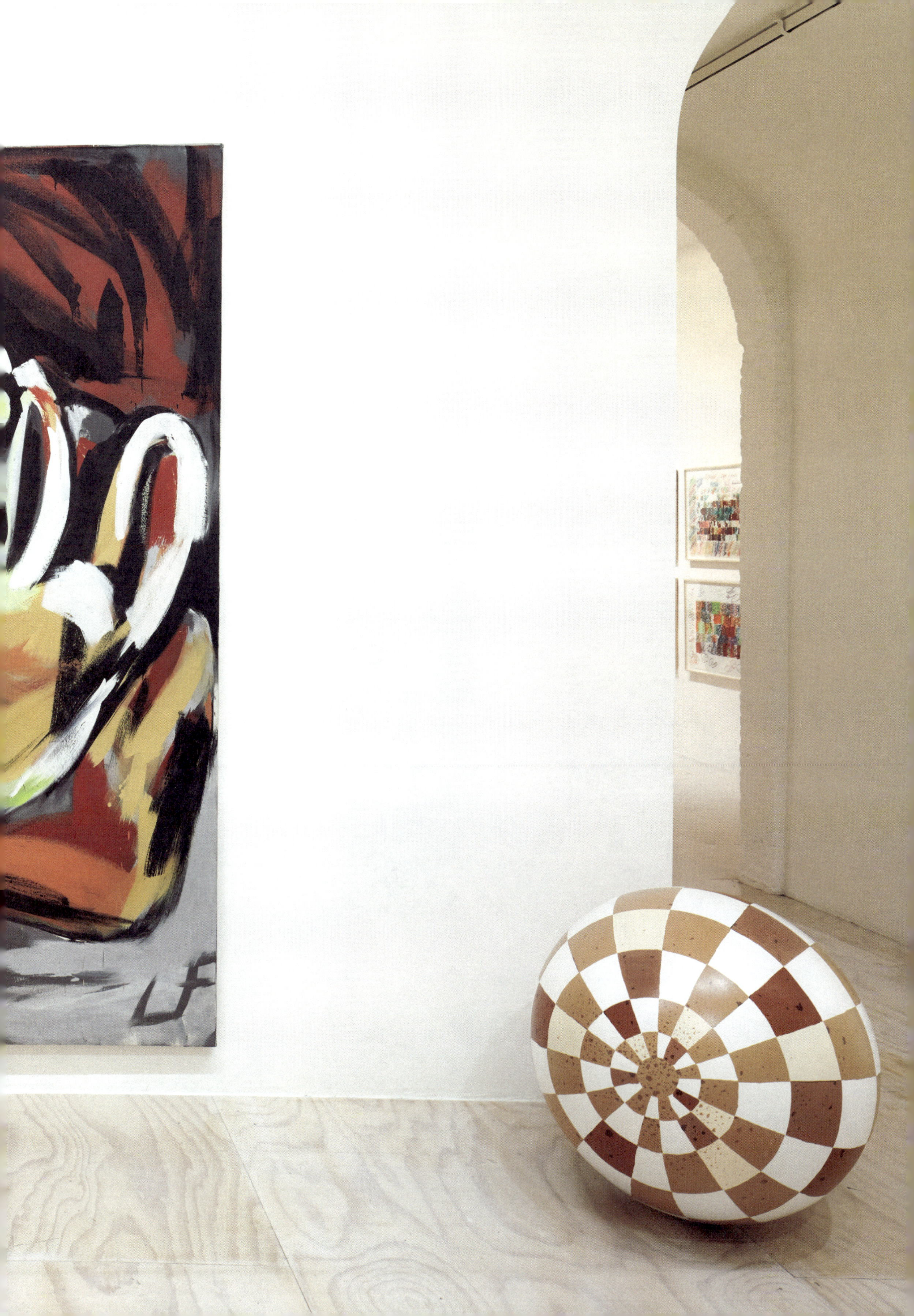

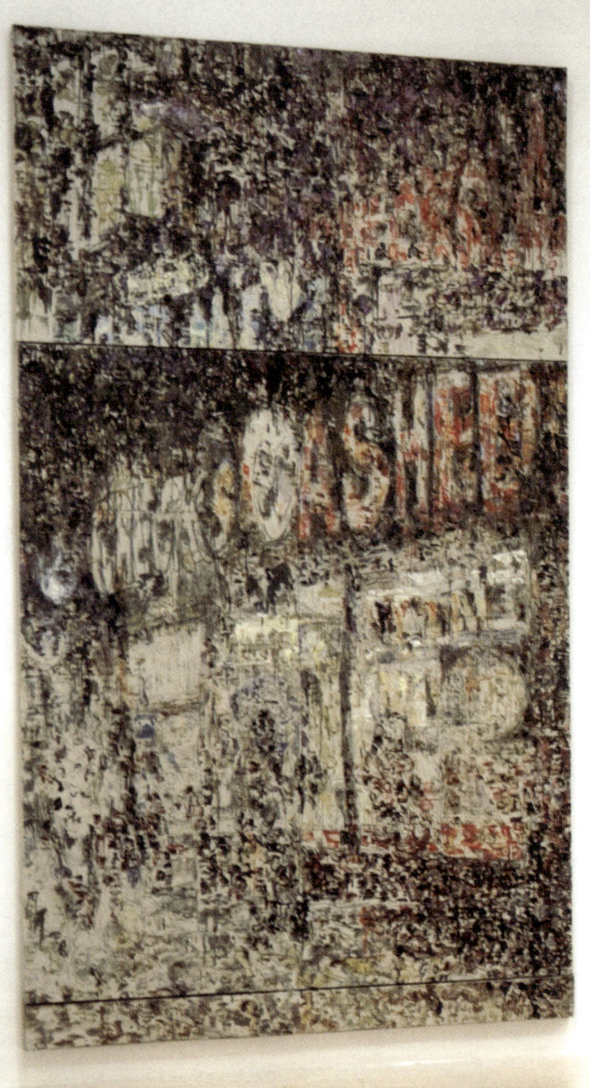
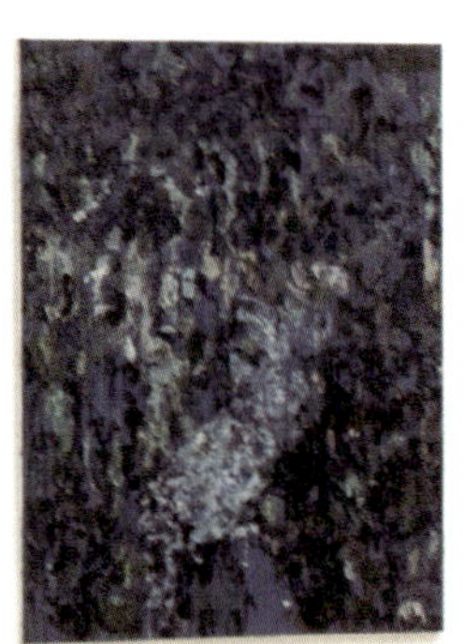

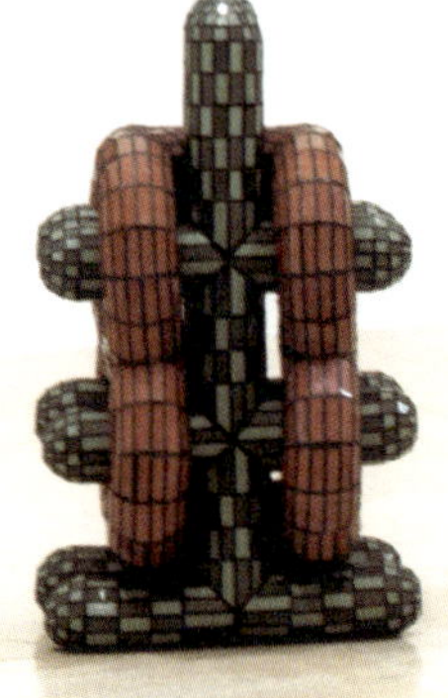
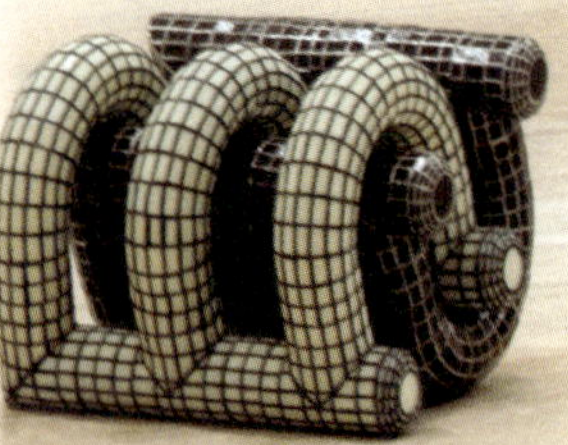

Left to right
Andy Robert, Kristi Cavataro, Matthew Langan-Peck, Shelley Niro

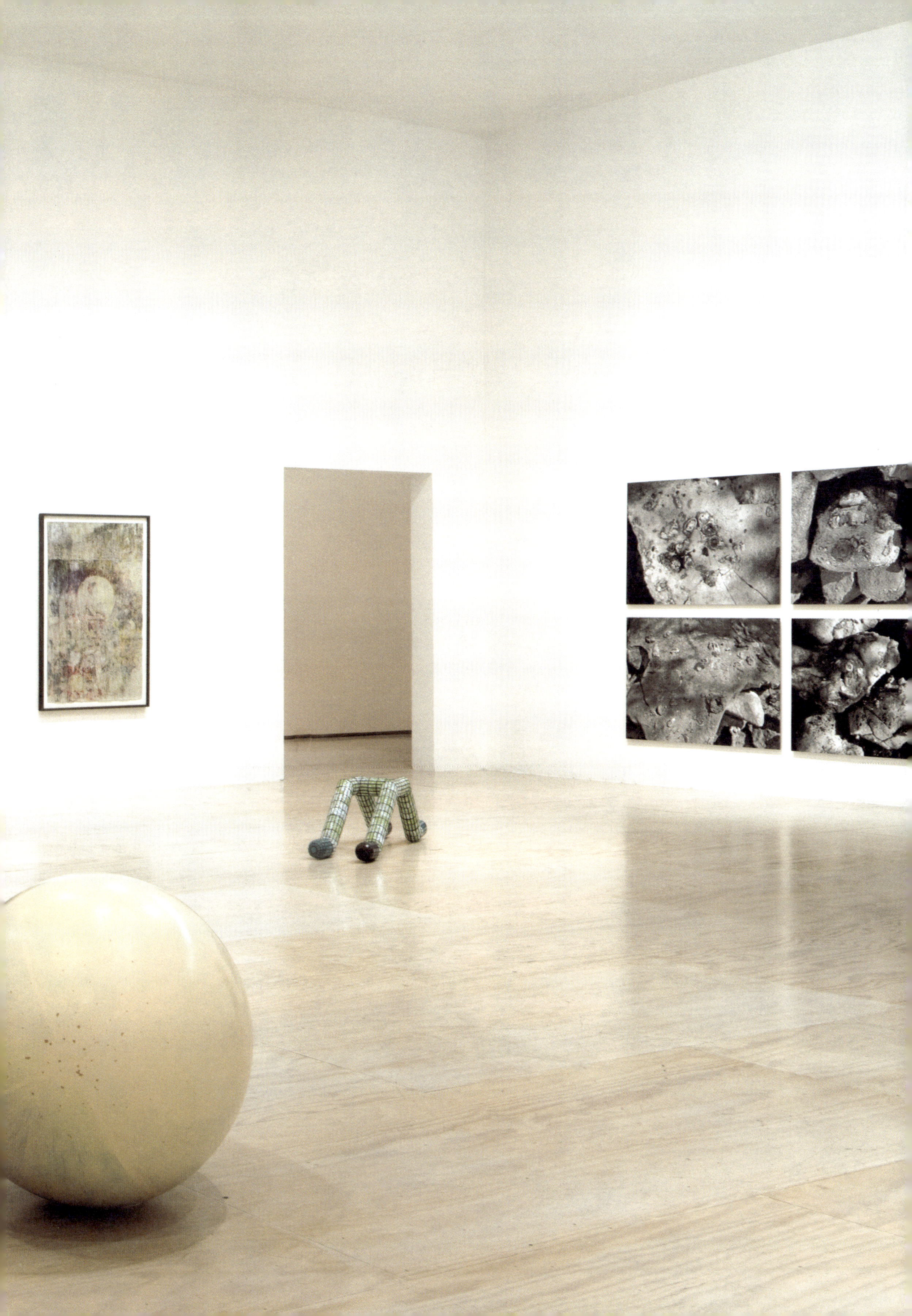

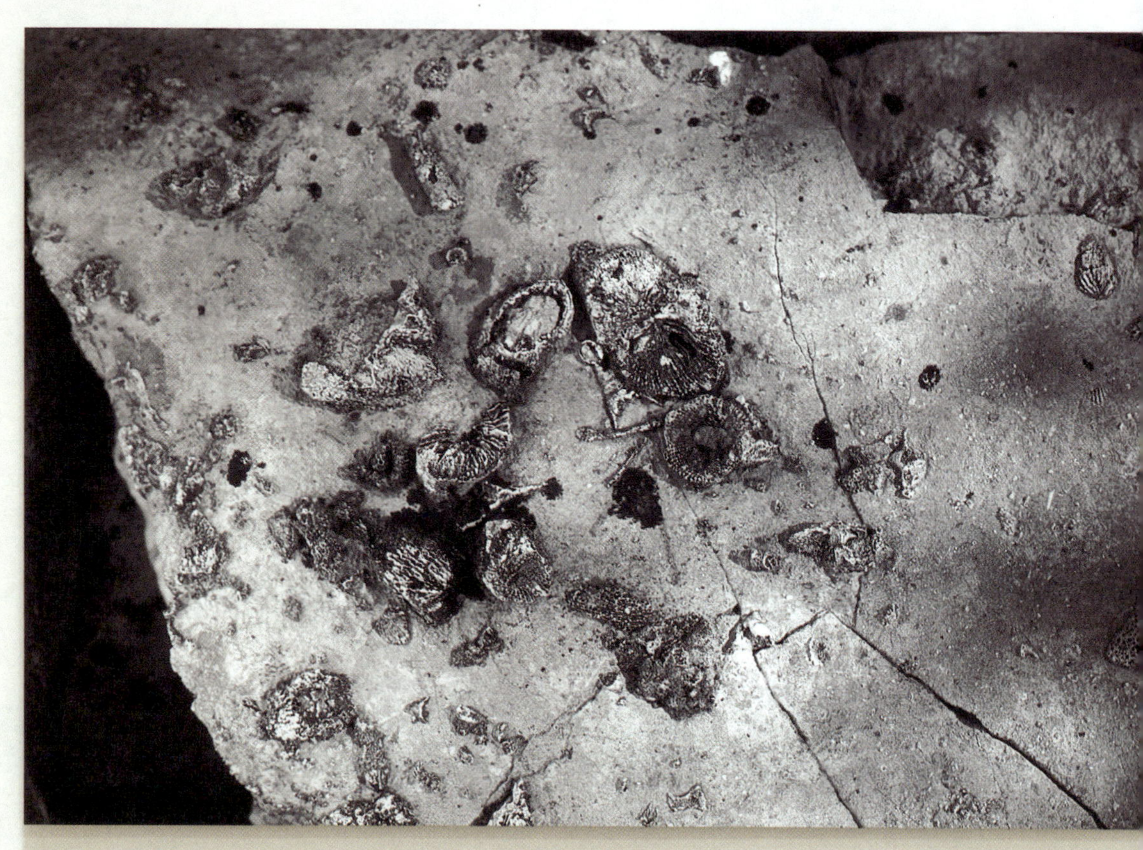

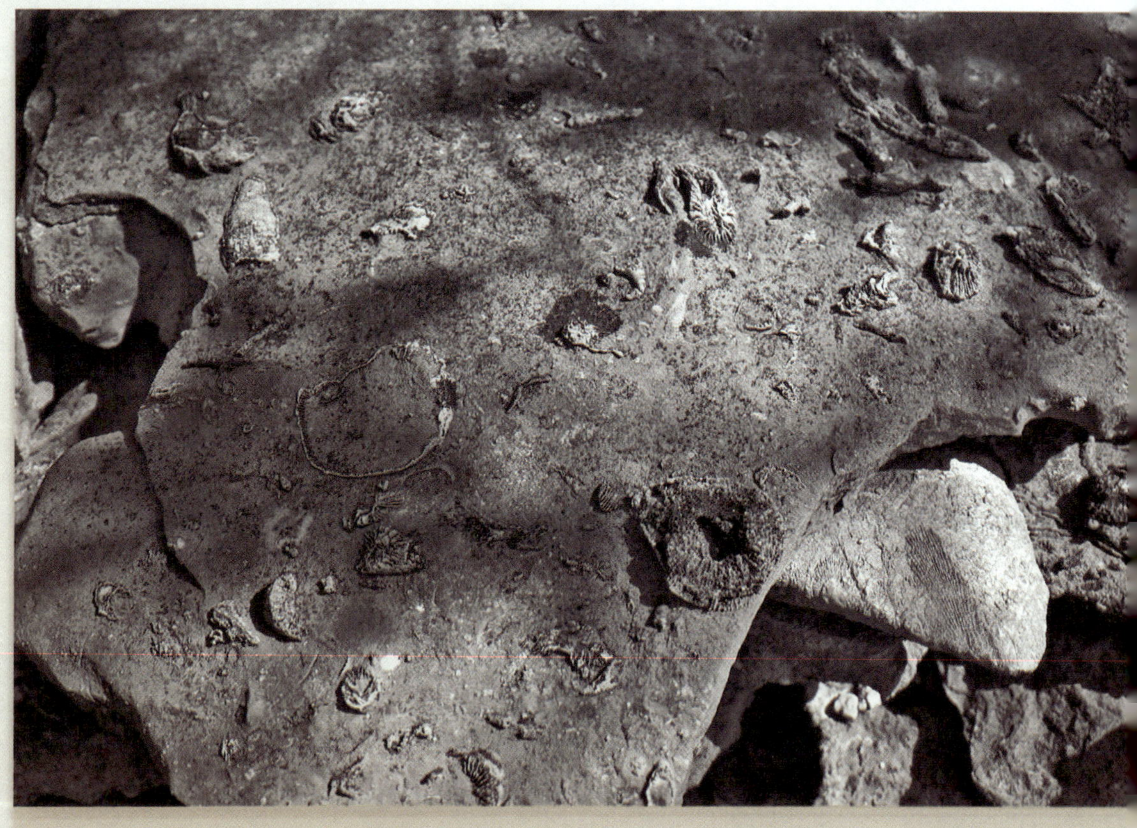

Shelley Niro
Resting Place of Our Ancestors 1–4, 2019

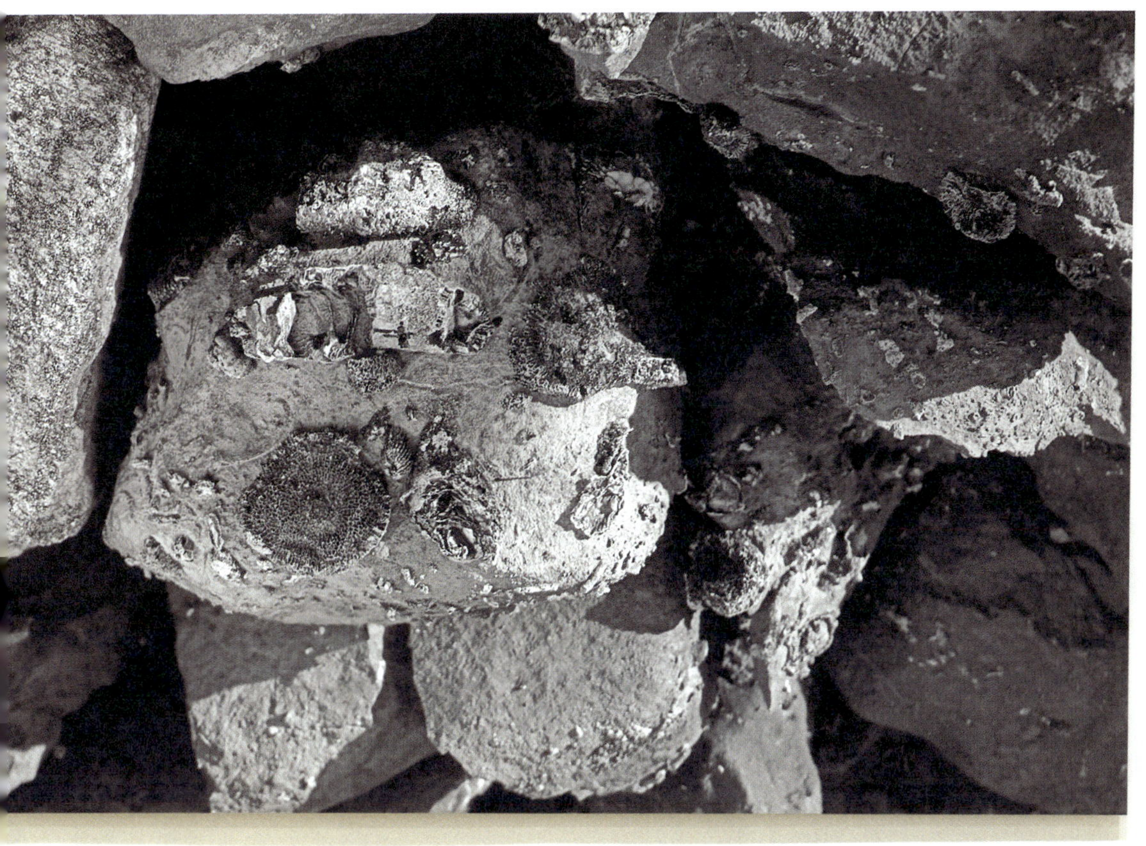

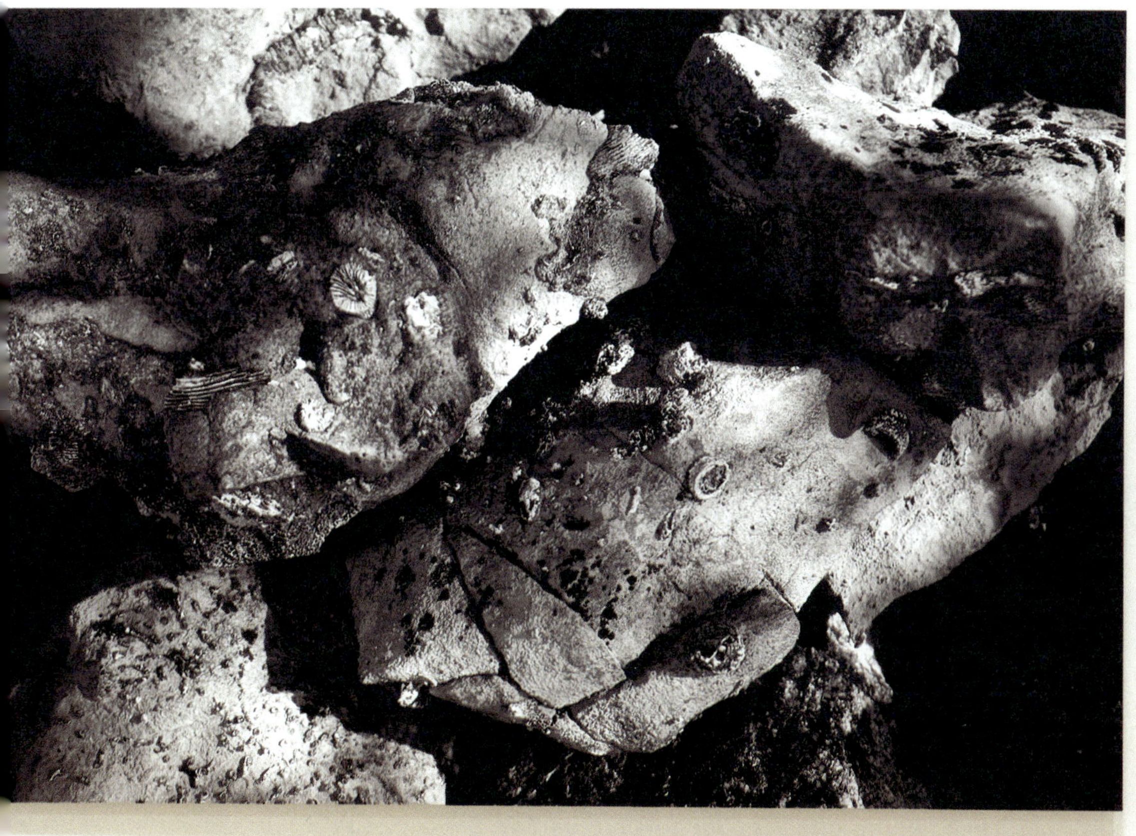

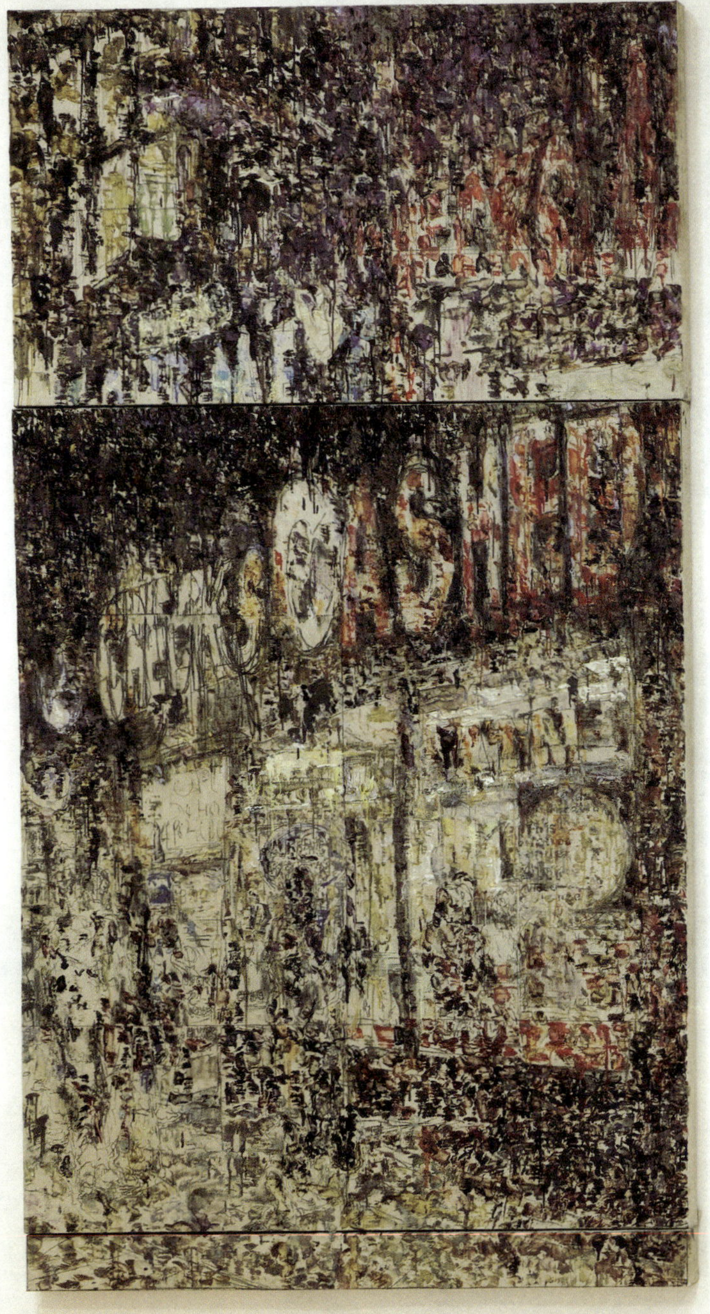

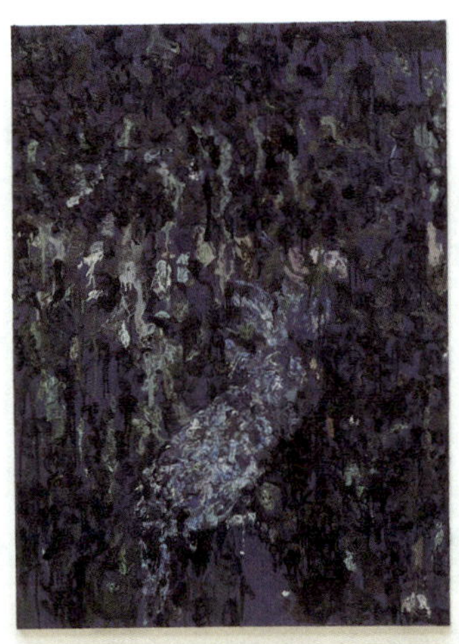

Left to right
Andy Robert
Check II Check, 2017
Harlem Sings the Blues, 2017
Mid Atlantic, 2020
The Original, 2021

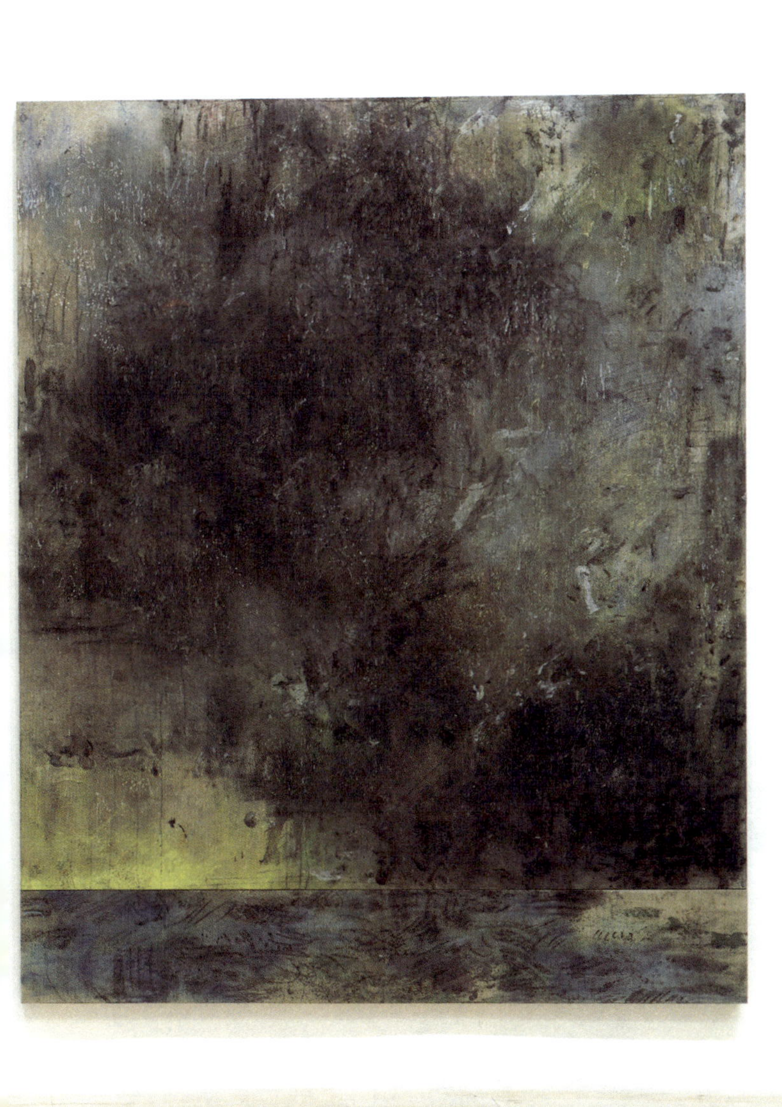

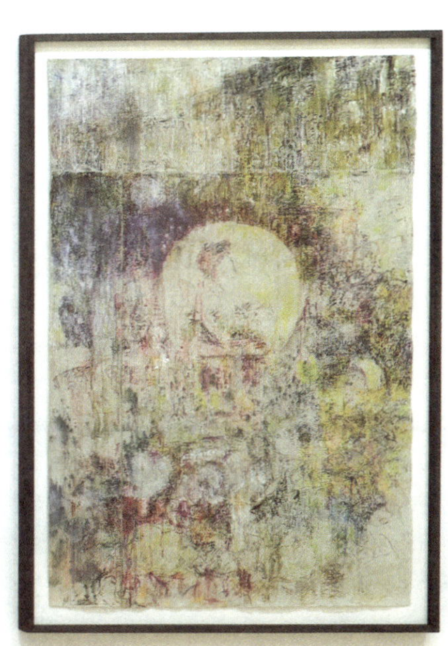

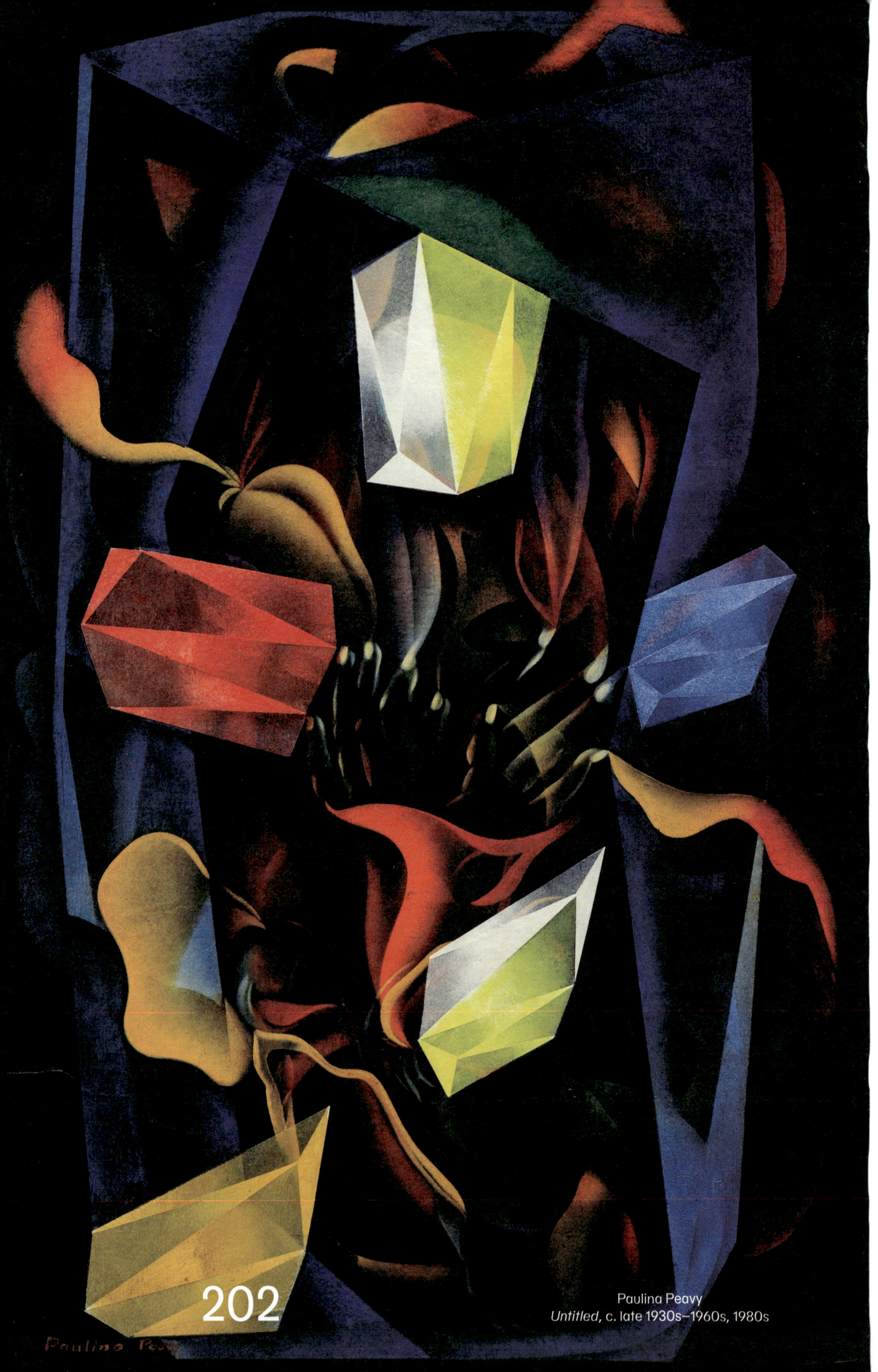

Paulina Peavy
Untitled, c. late 1930s–1960s, 1980s

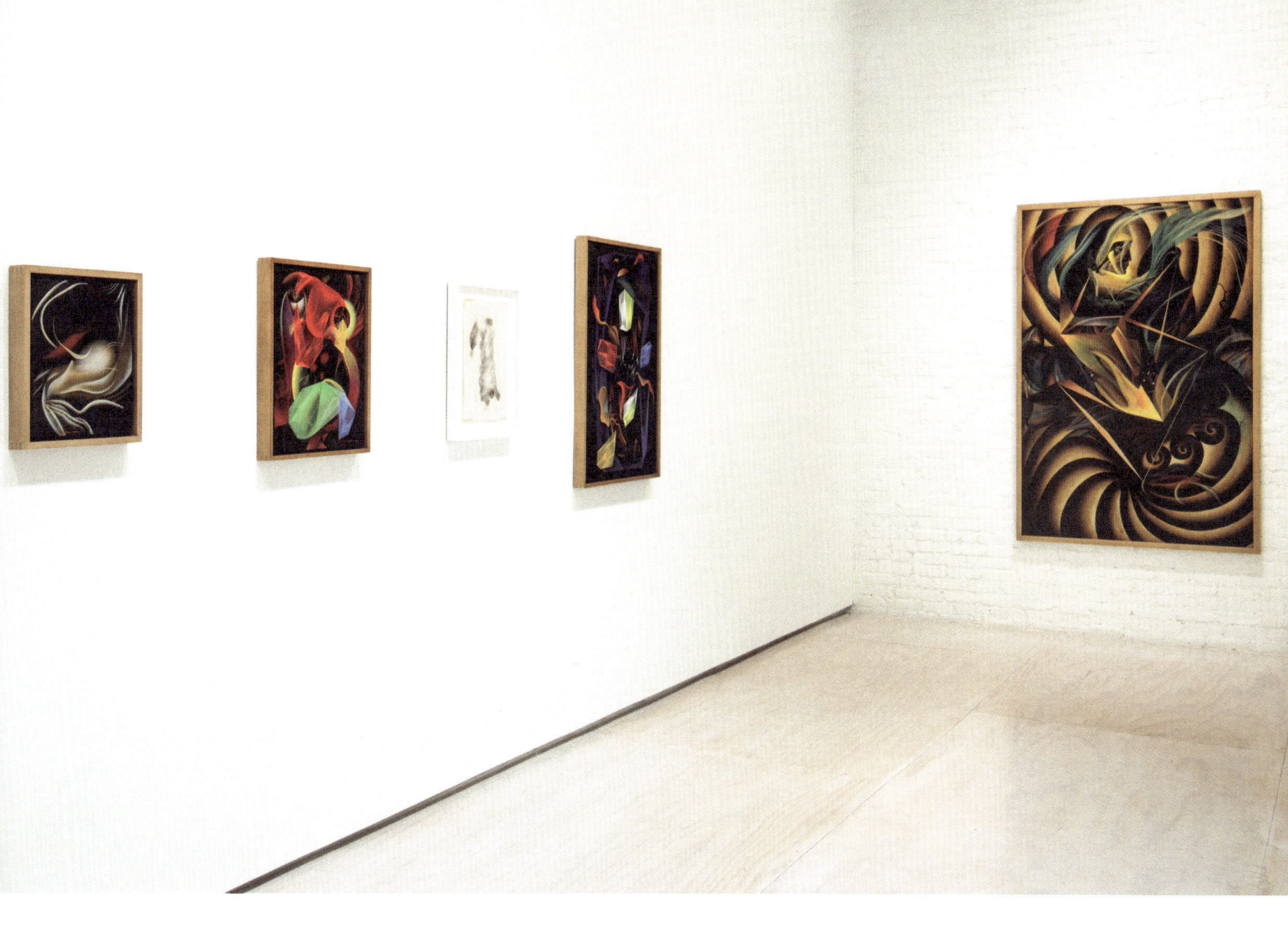

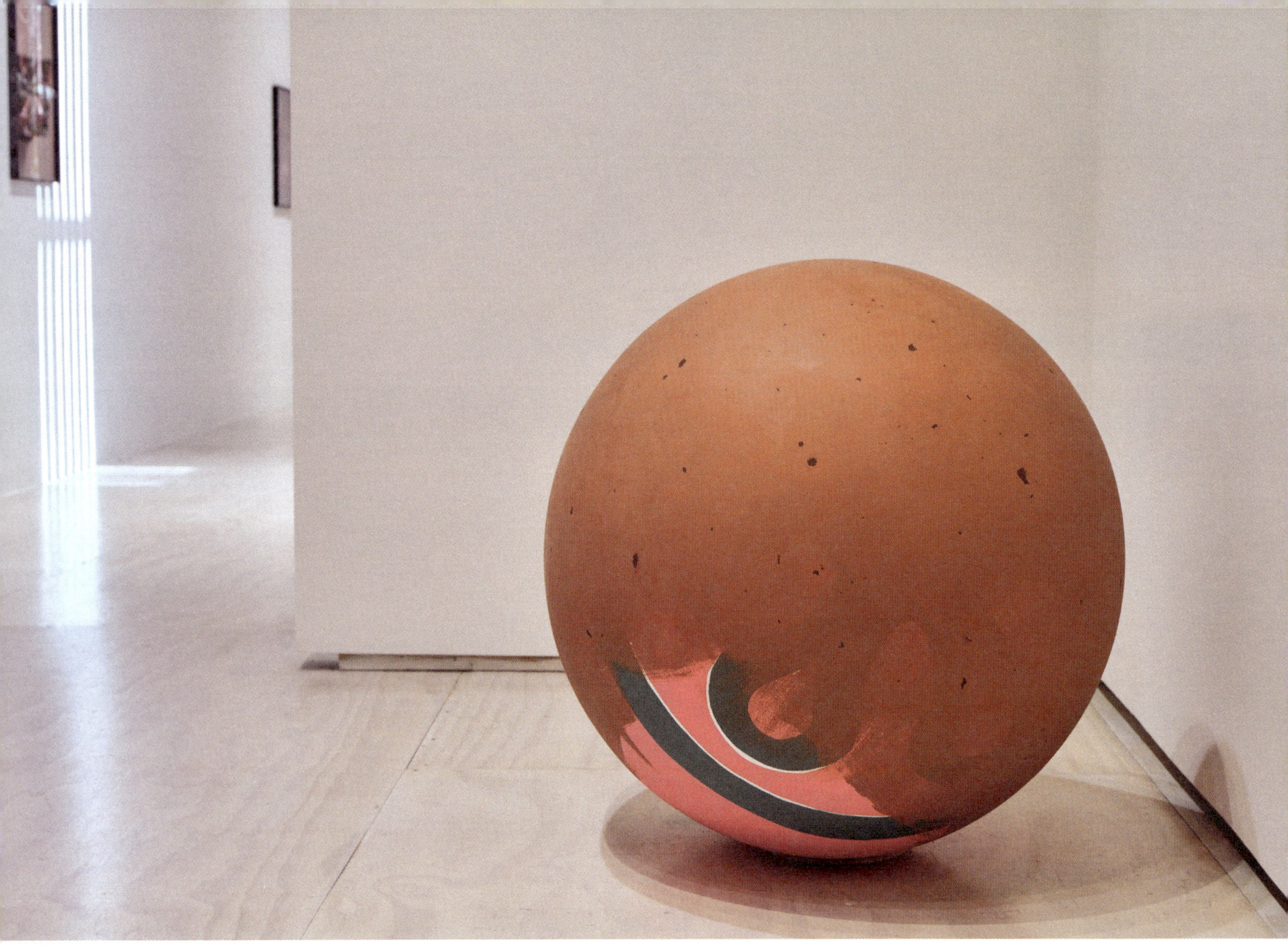

Matthew Langan-Peck
4 Baskets 1, 2021

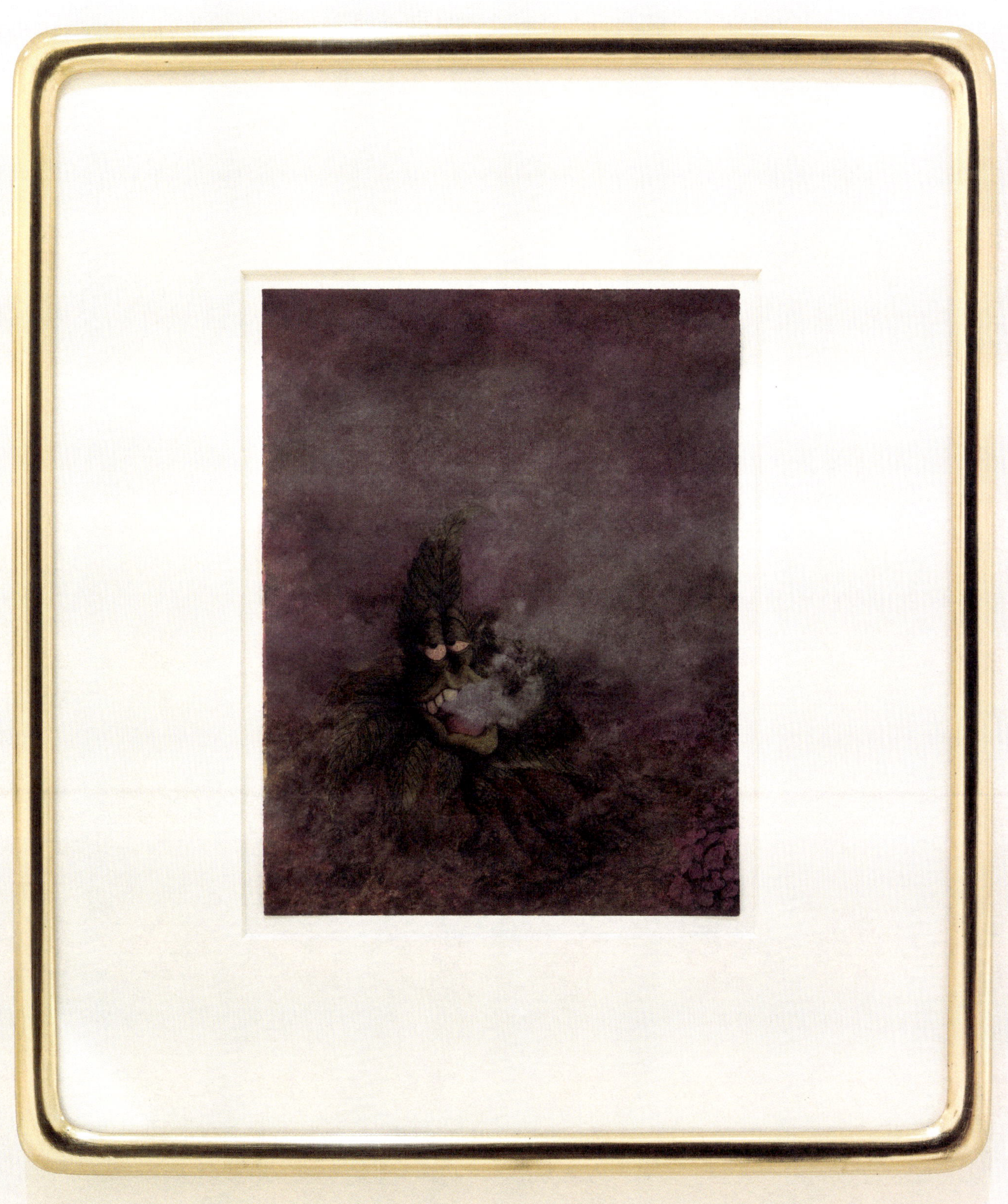

Bill Hayden
WEED, 2021

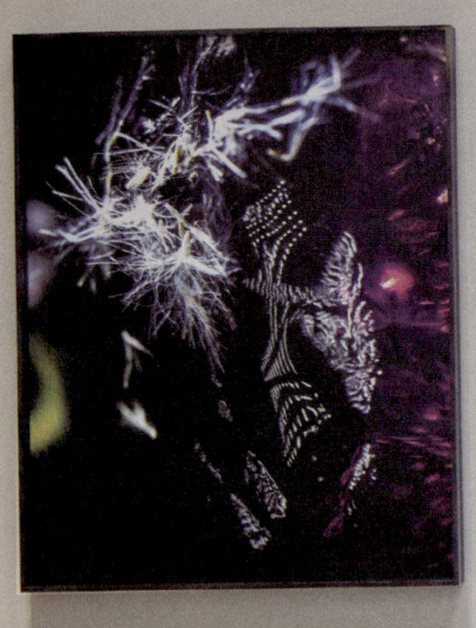

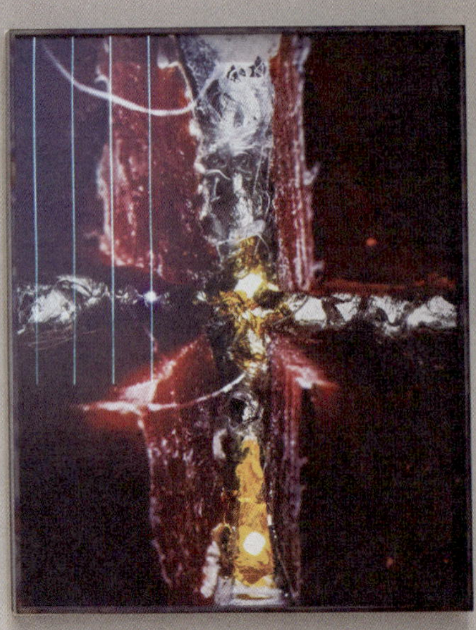

Diane Severin Nguyen
Southern Star, 2021 (left)
Your Reversal, 2021 (right)

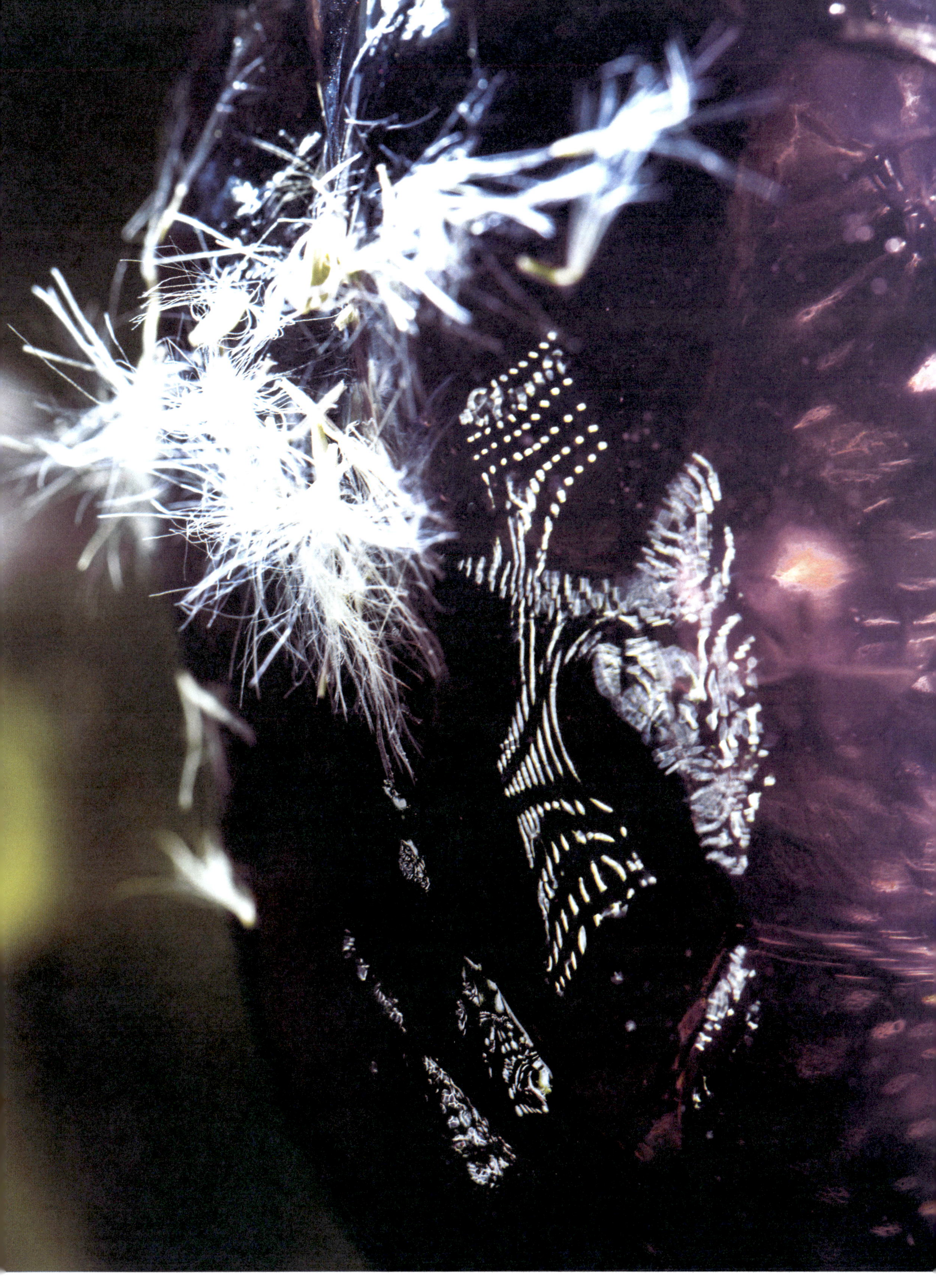

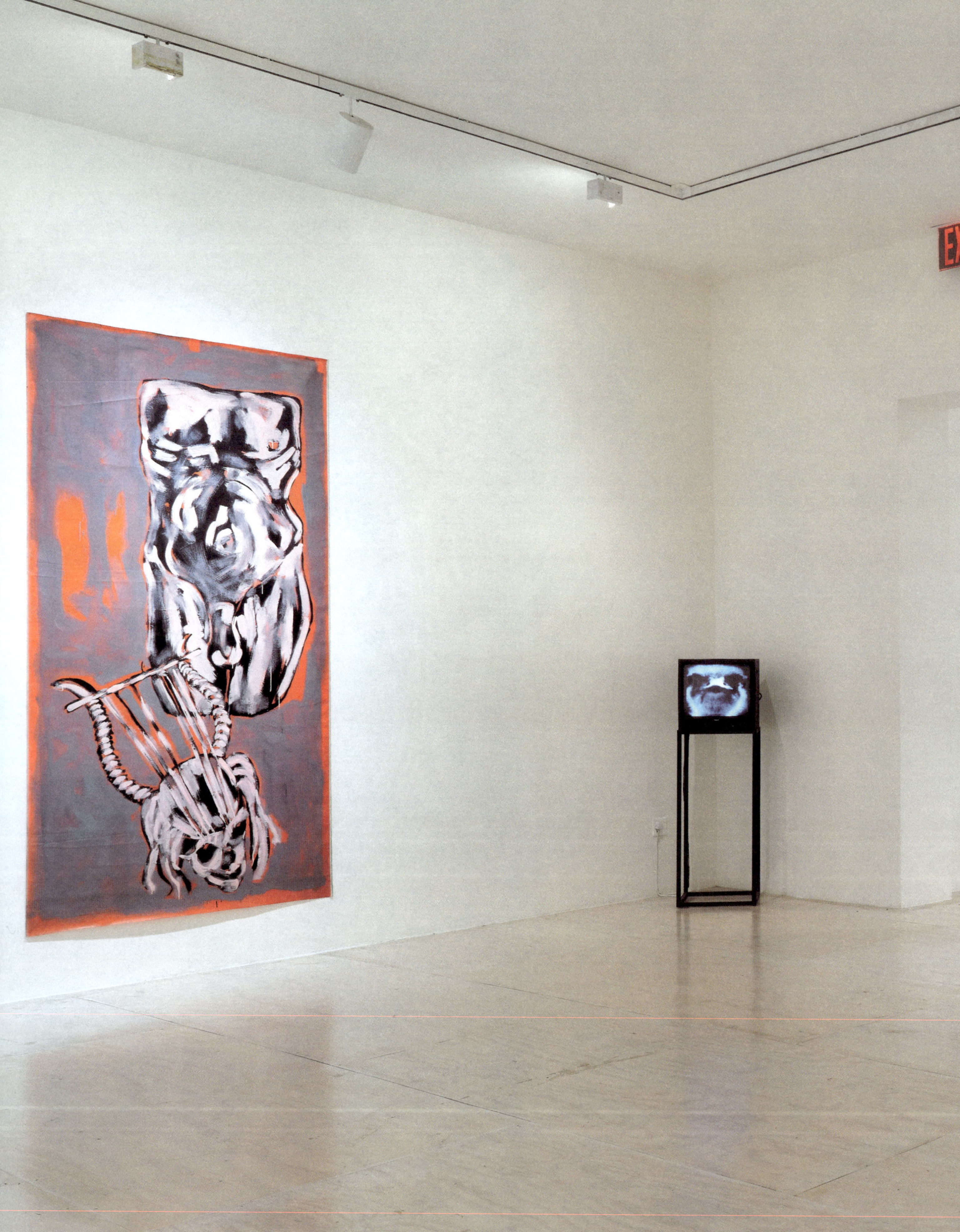

Left to right
Luis Frangella, Regina Vater, Julio Galán, Doreen Garner

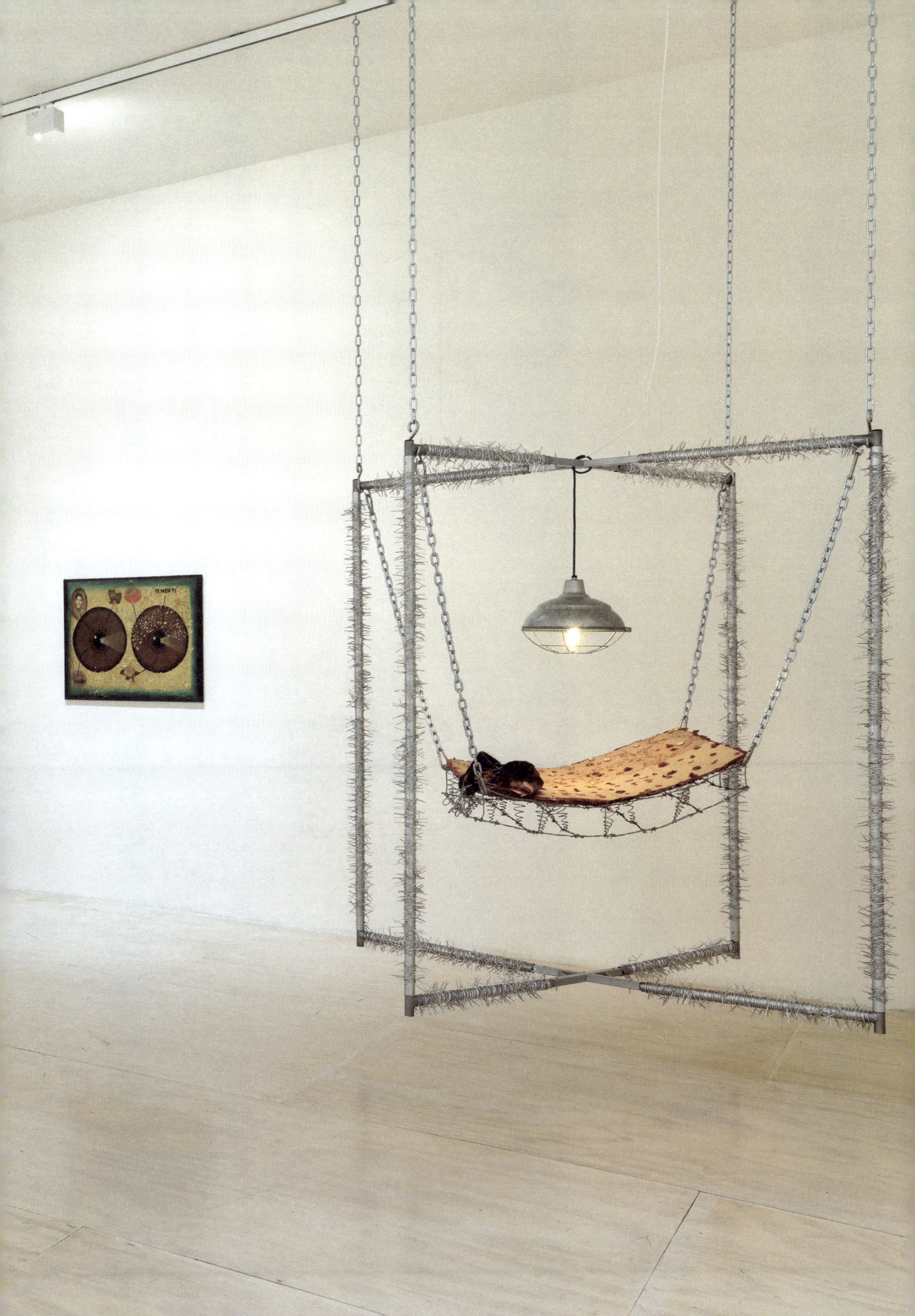
"TE MENTI"

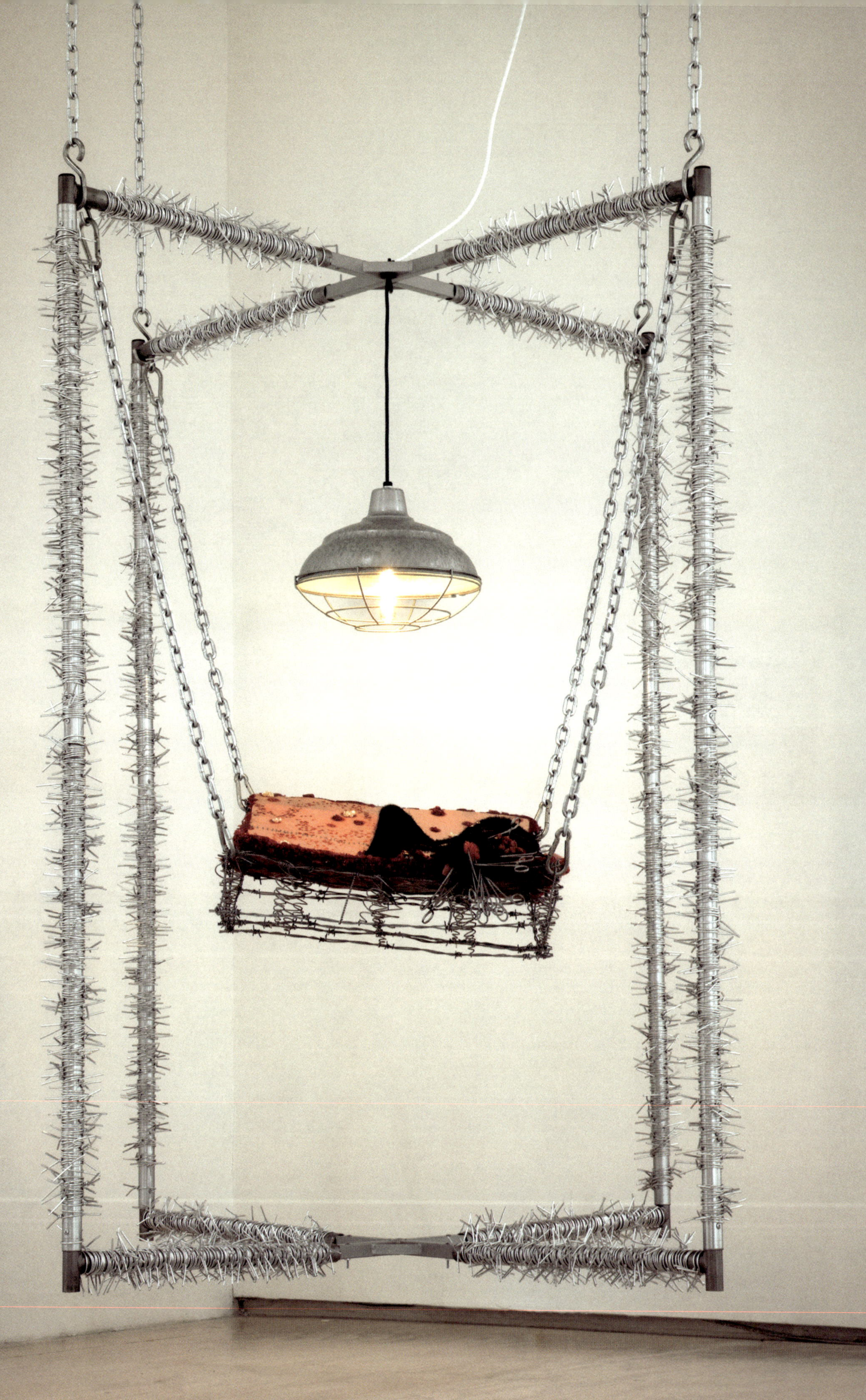

Doreen Garner
Lucy's Agony, 2021

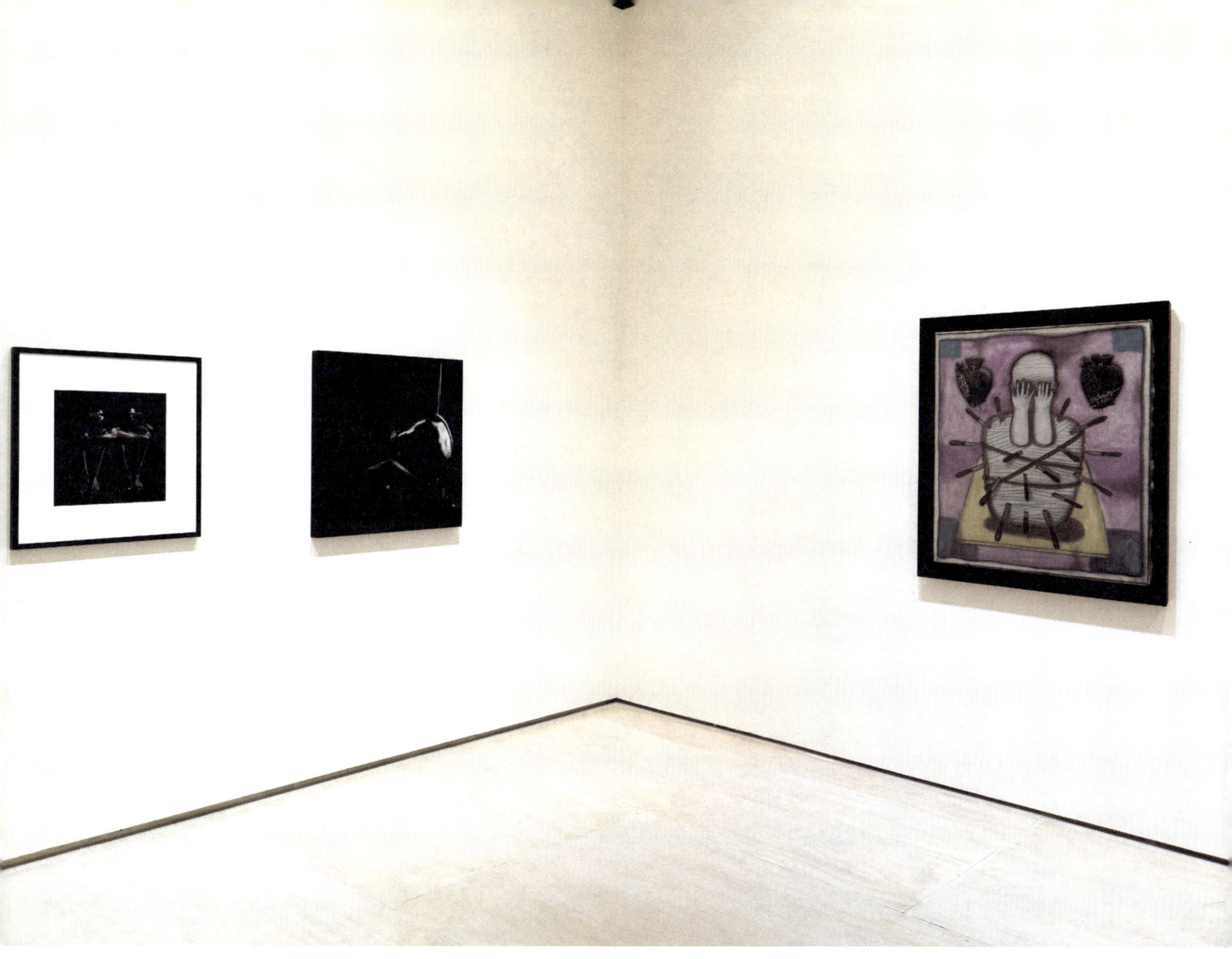

Left to right
Rotimi Fani-Kayode, Julio Galán

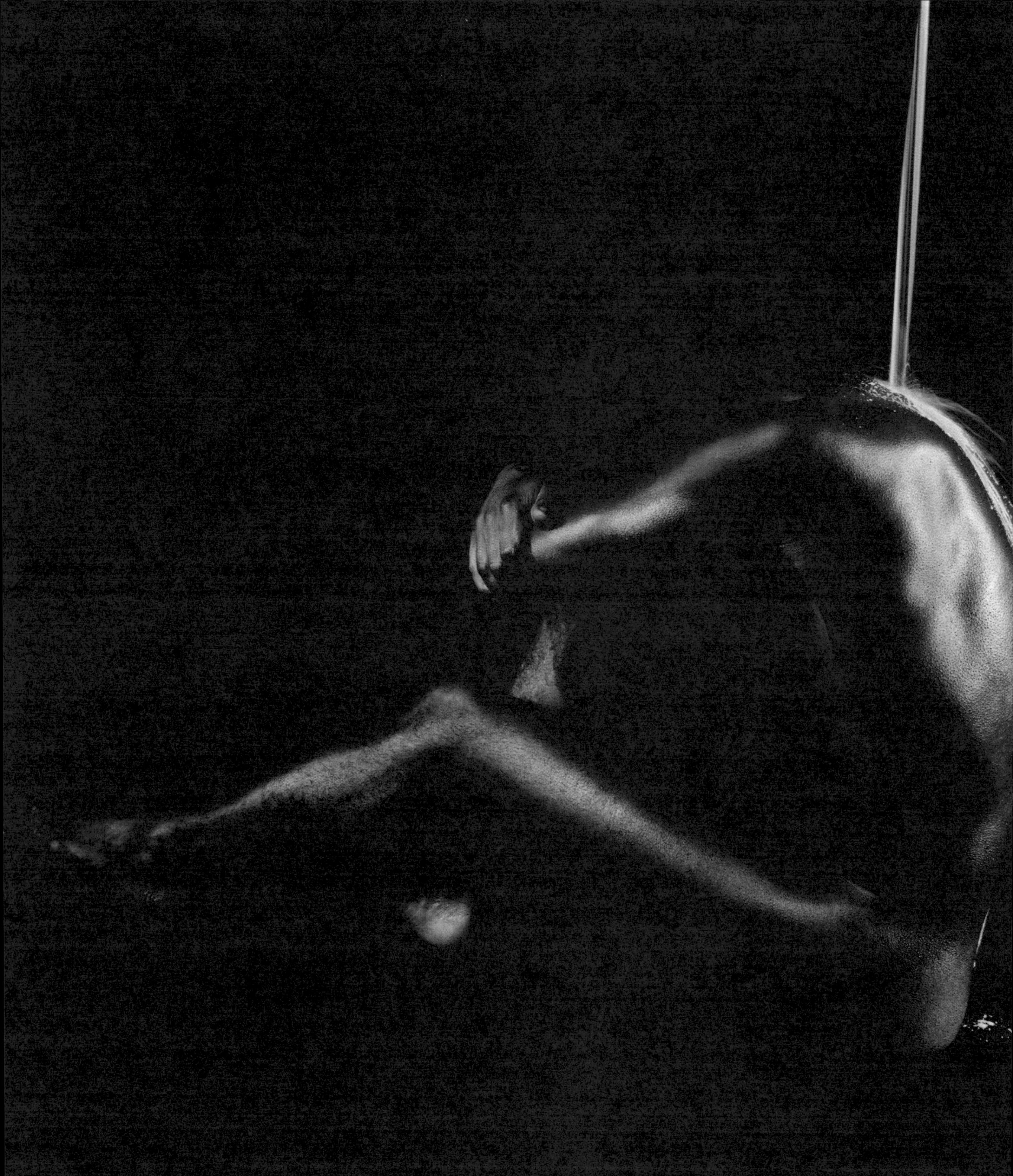

Rotimi Fani-Kayode
Maternal Milk, 1983

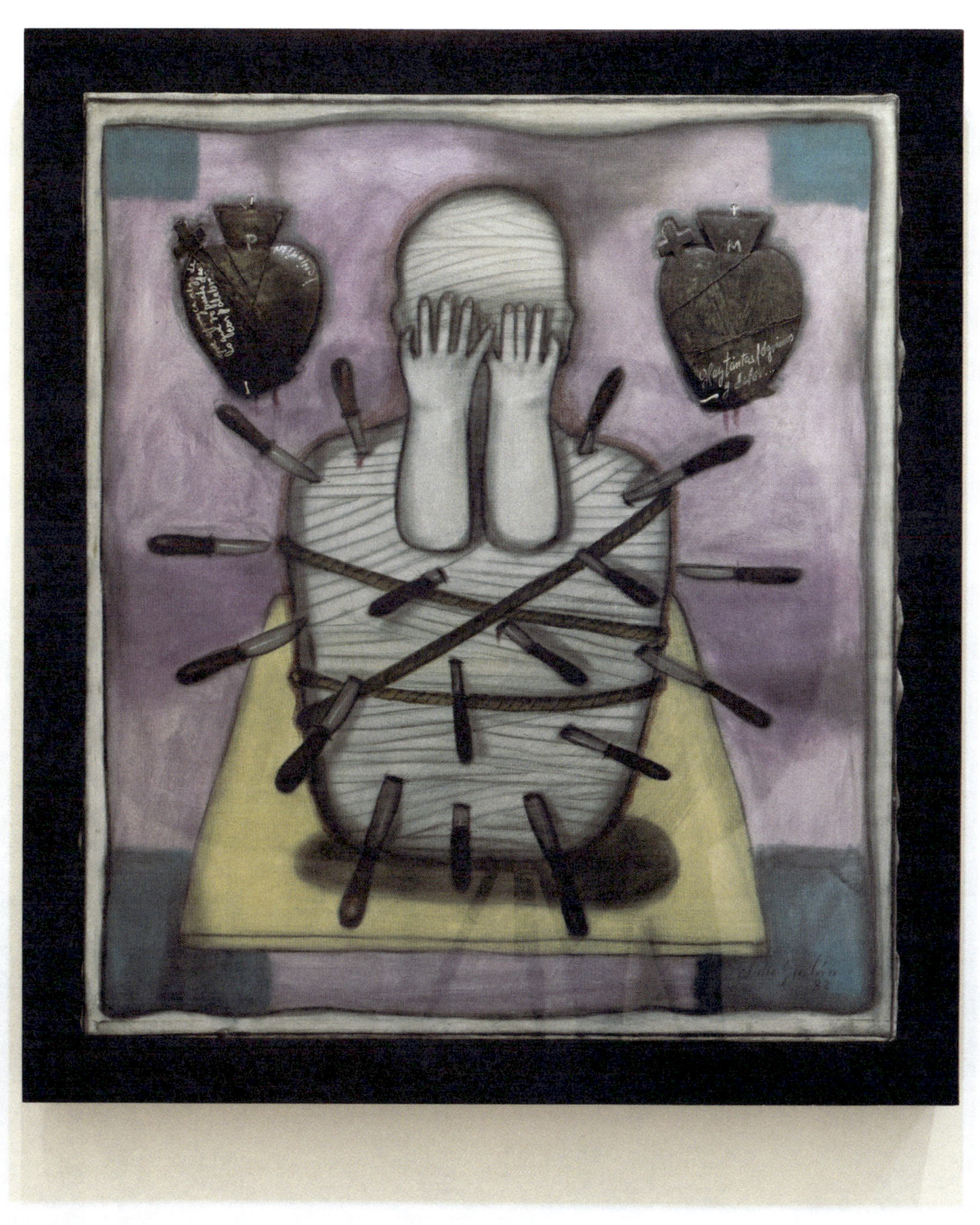

213

Julio Galán
Untitled, 1982

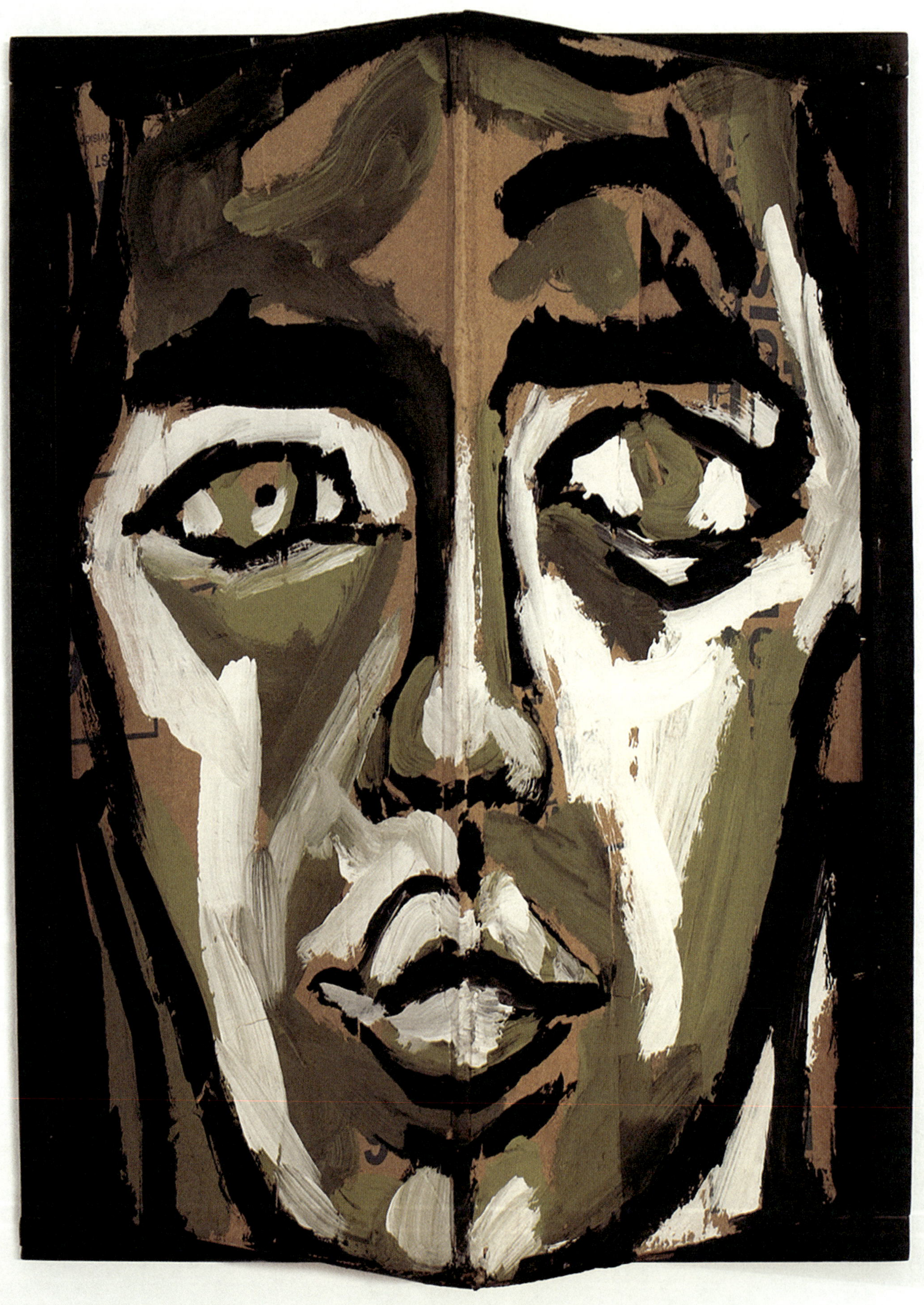

Luis Frangella
David Wojnarowicz, 1984

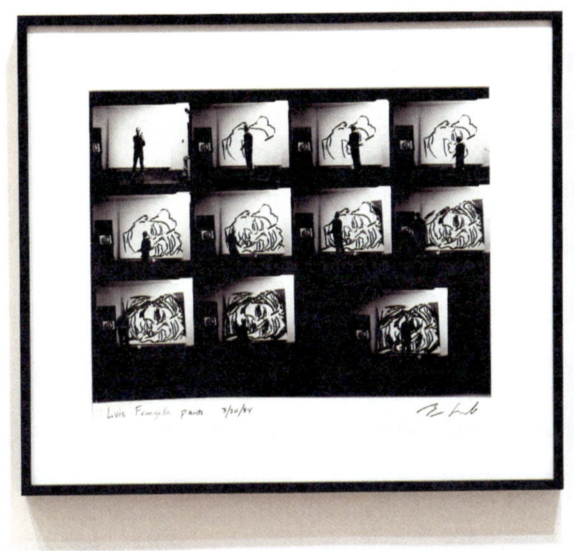

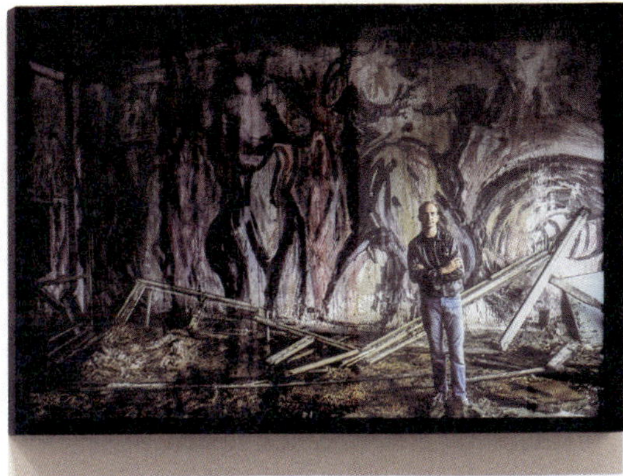

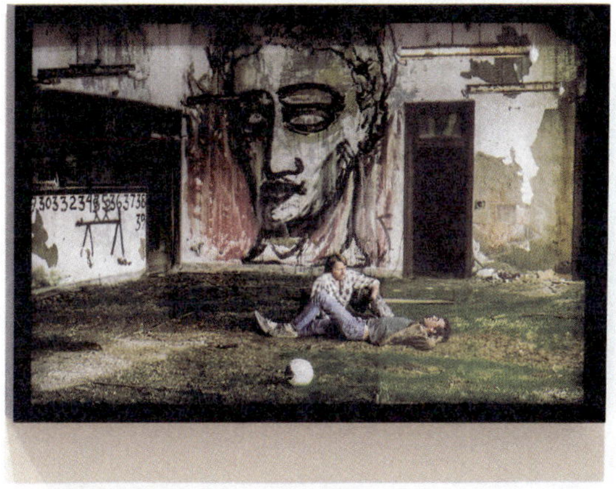

Luis Frangella Paints, 1984 (left)
Photographs by Eric Kroll

Pier 34, Luis Frangella, 1983 (right, top)
David Wojnarowicz and Mike Bidlo at Pier 34 (with painting by Luis Frangella), 1983 (right, bottom)
Photographs by Andreas Sterzing

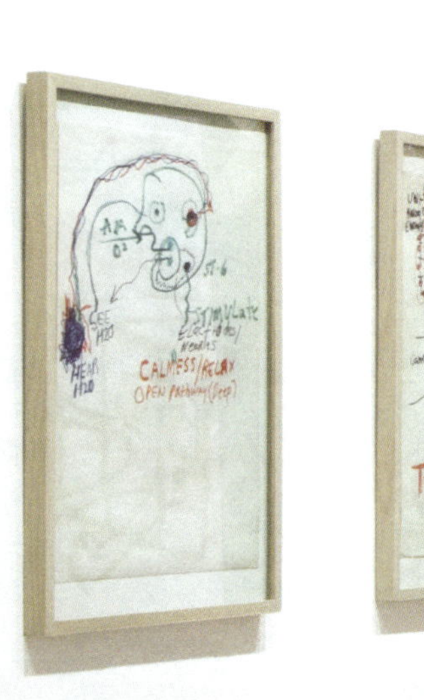

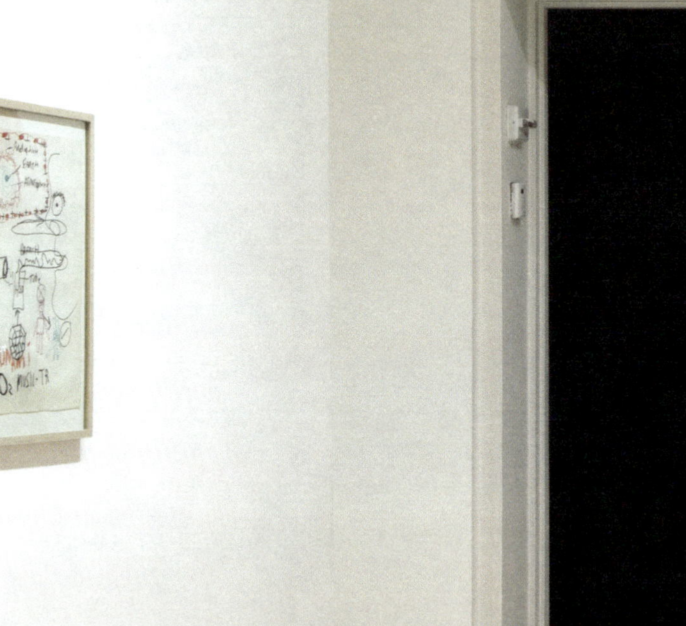

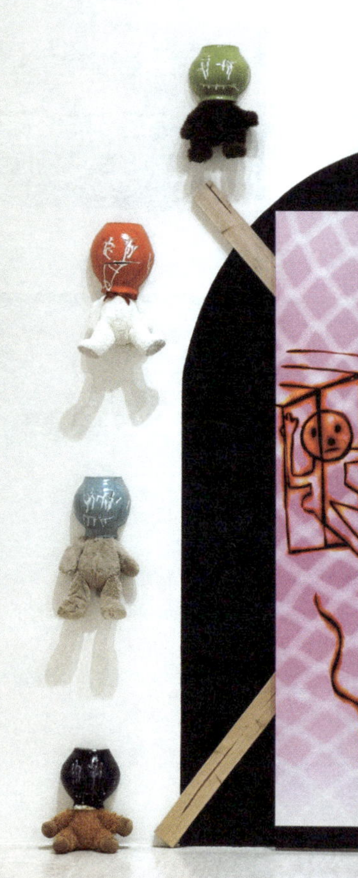

Left to right
Milford Graves, Hadi Fallahpisheh, Rosemary Mayer

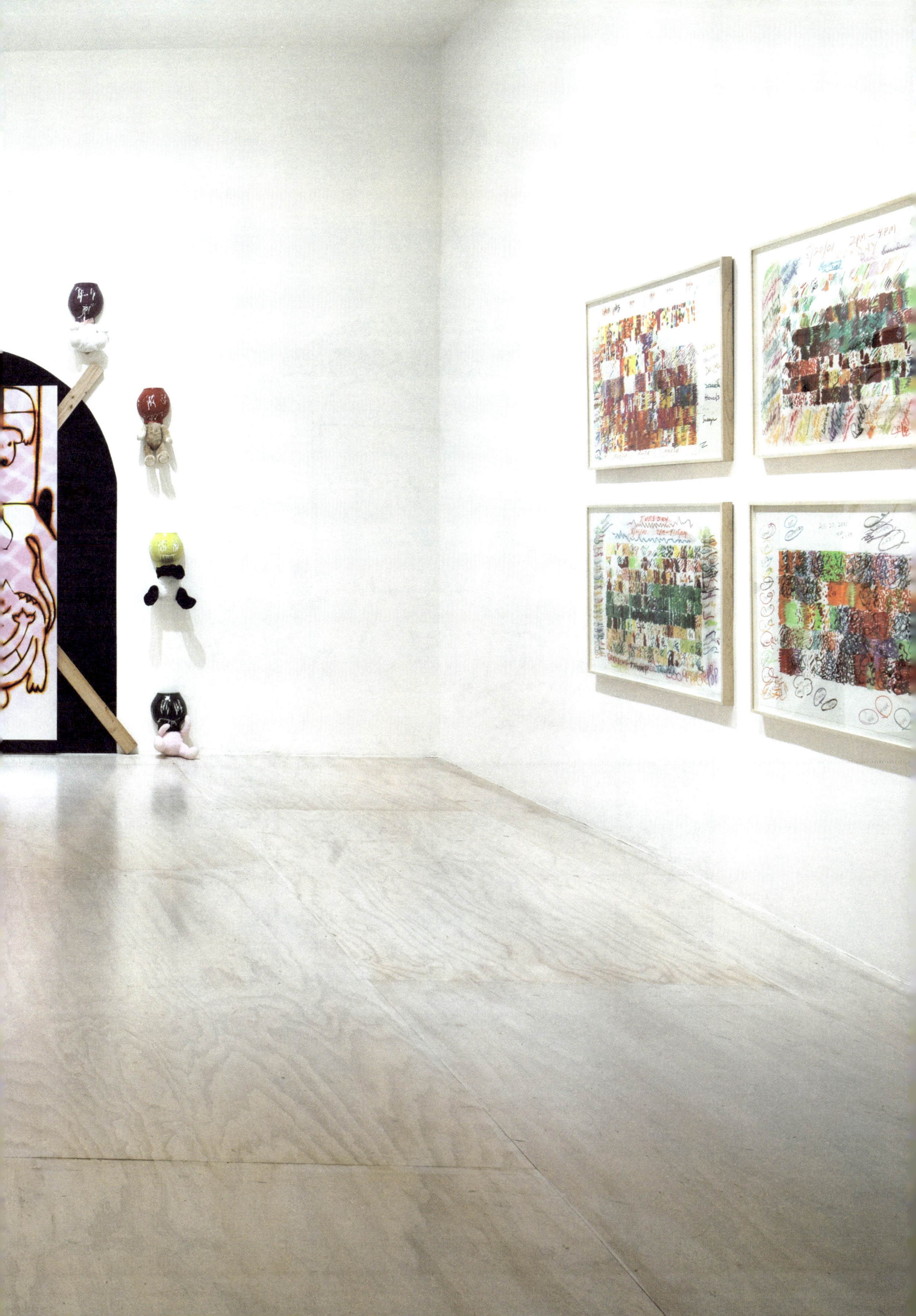

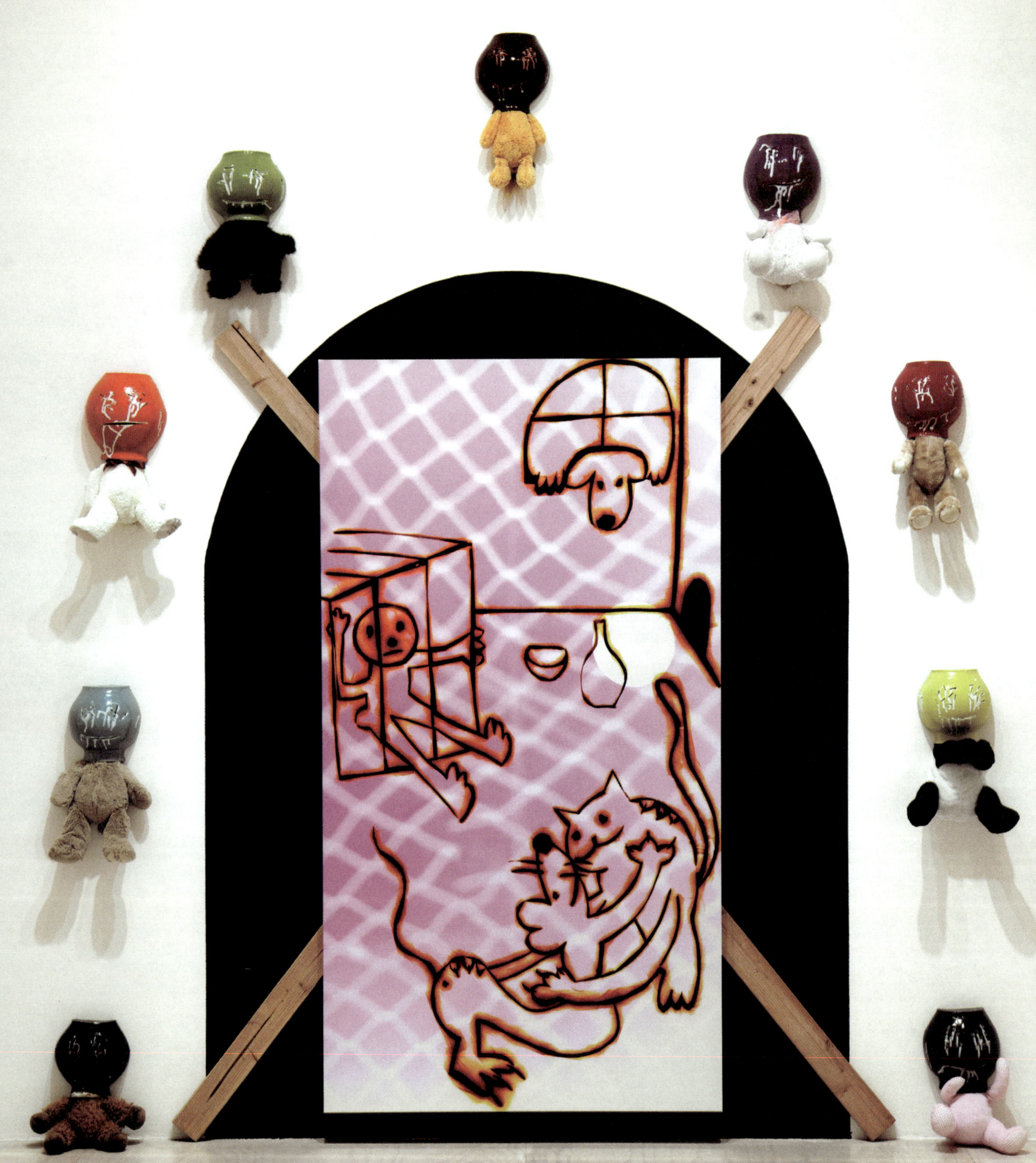

Hadi Fallahpisheh
Young and Clueless, 2021

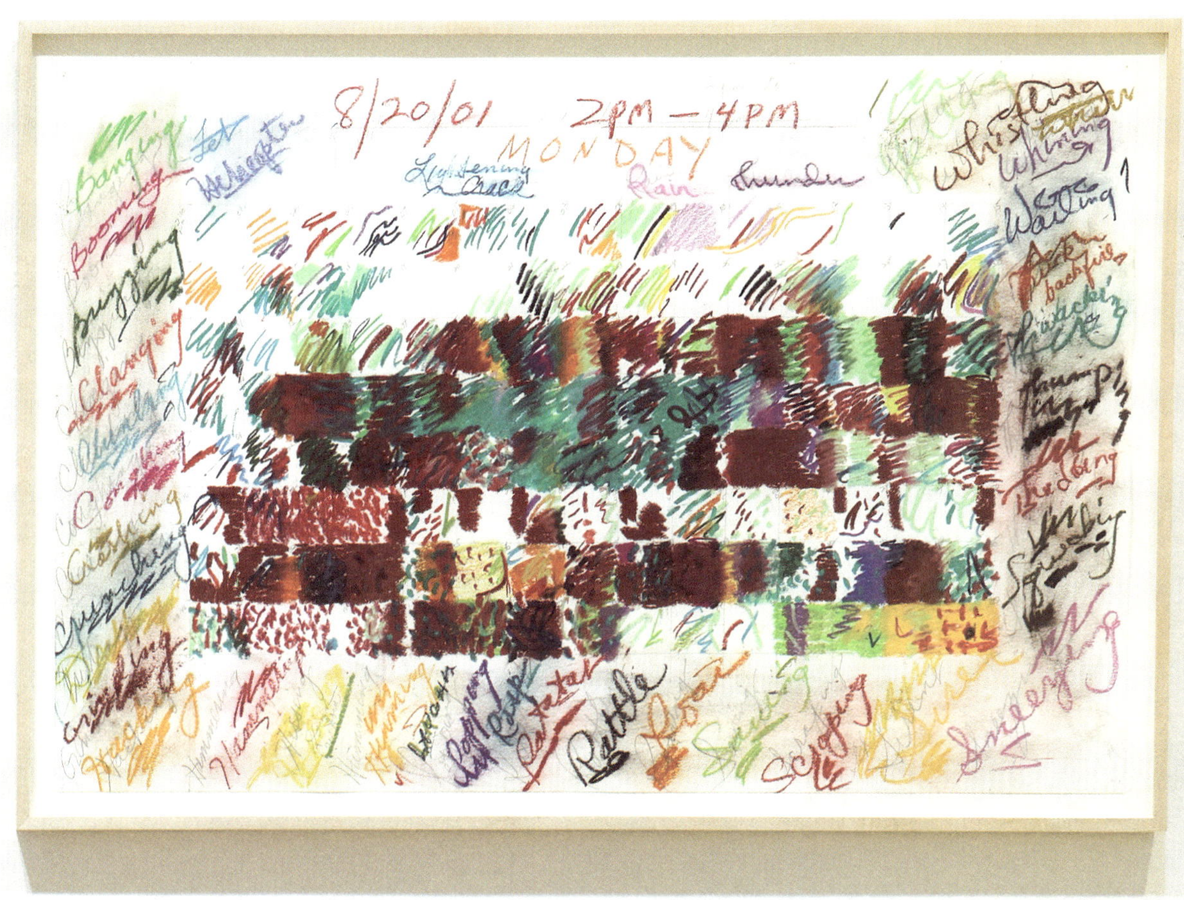

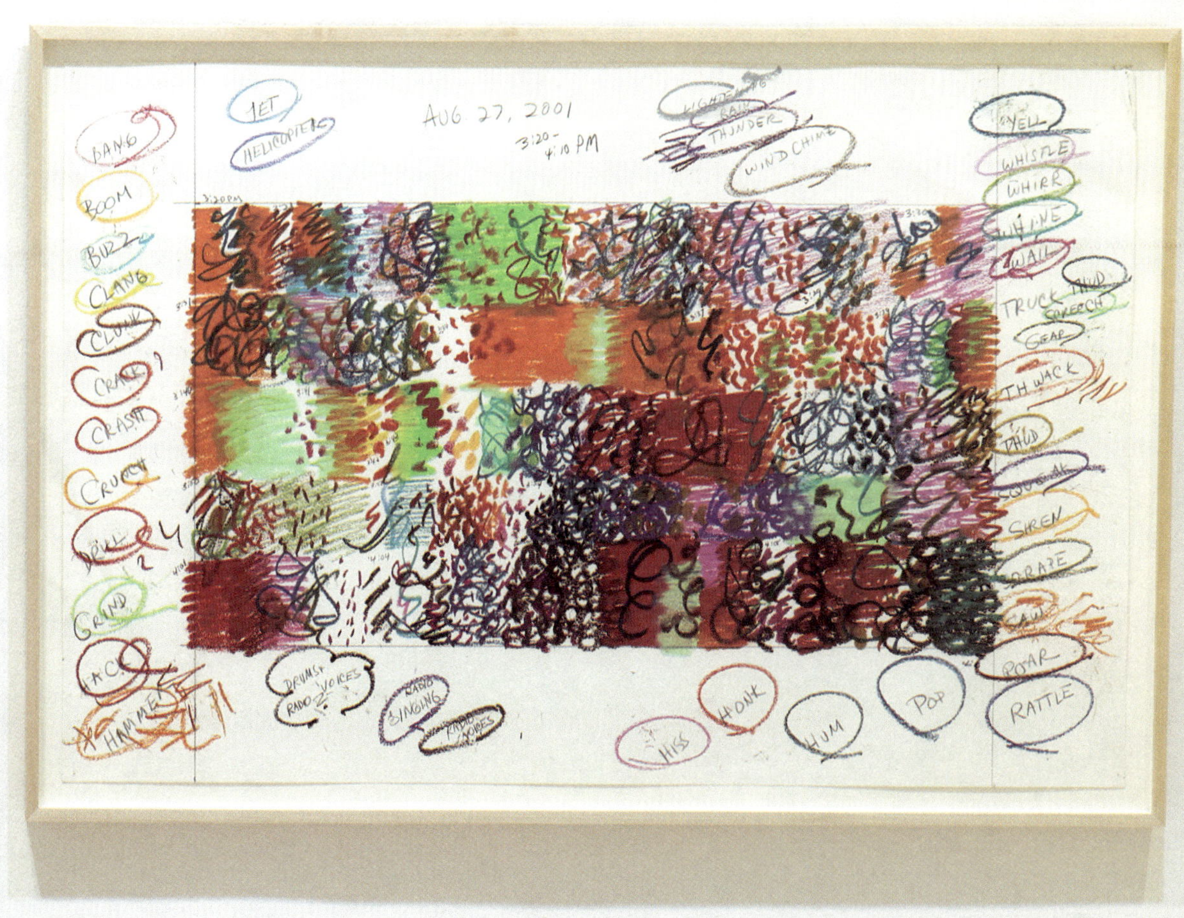

Rosemary Mayer
Untitled (8/20/01, 2PM–4PM), 2001 (top)
Untitled (8/27/01, 3:20PM–4:10PM), 2001 (bottom)

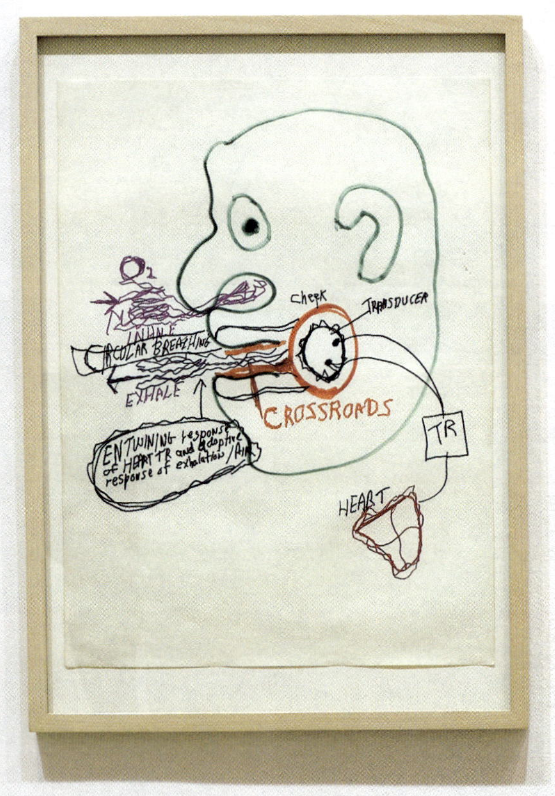

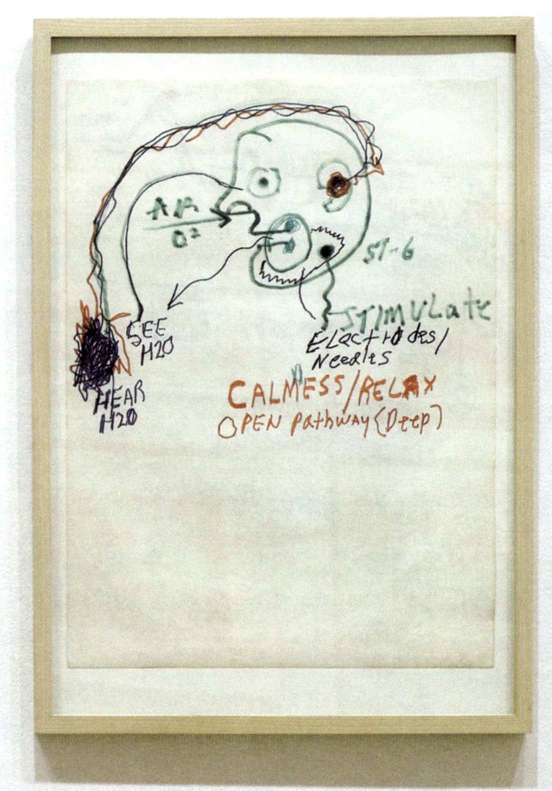

Milford Graves
Crossroads, 2020 (left)
Calmness/Relax, 2020 (right)

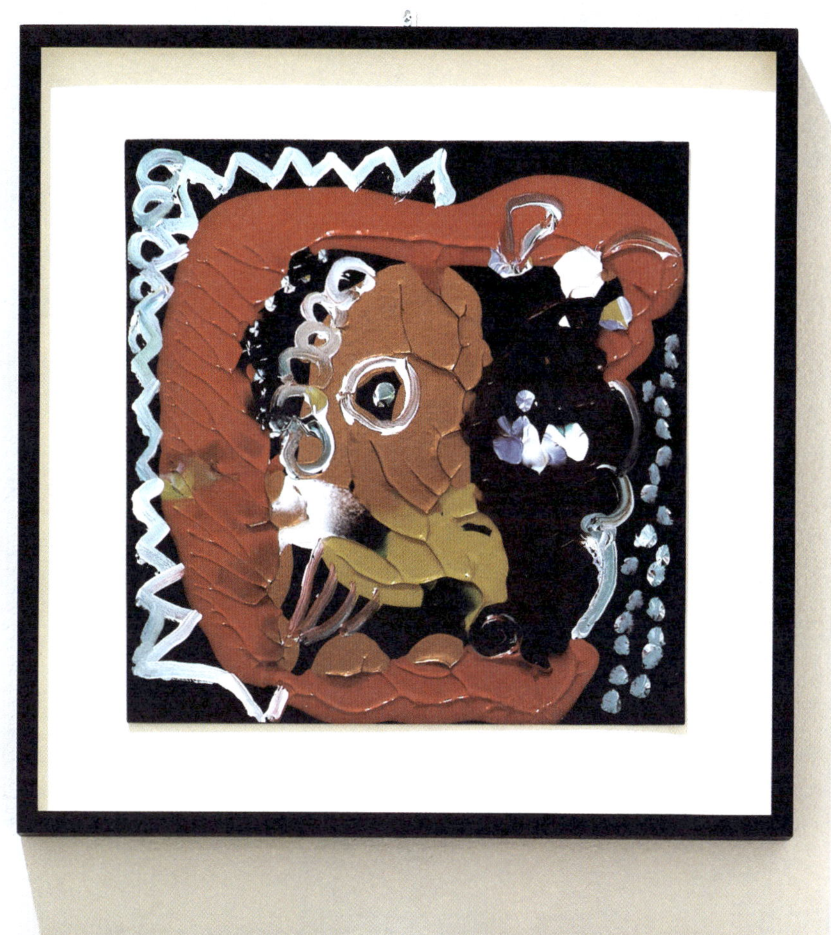

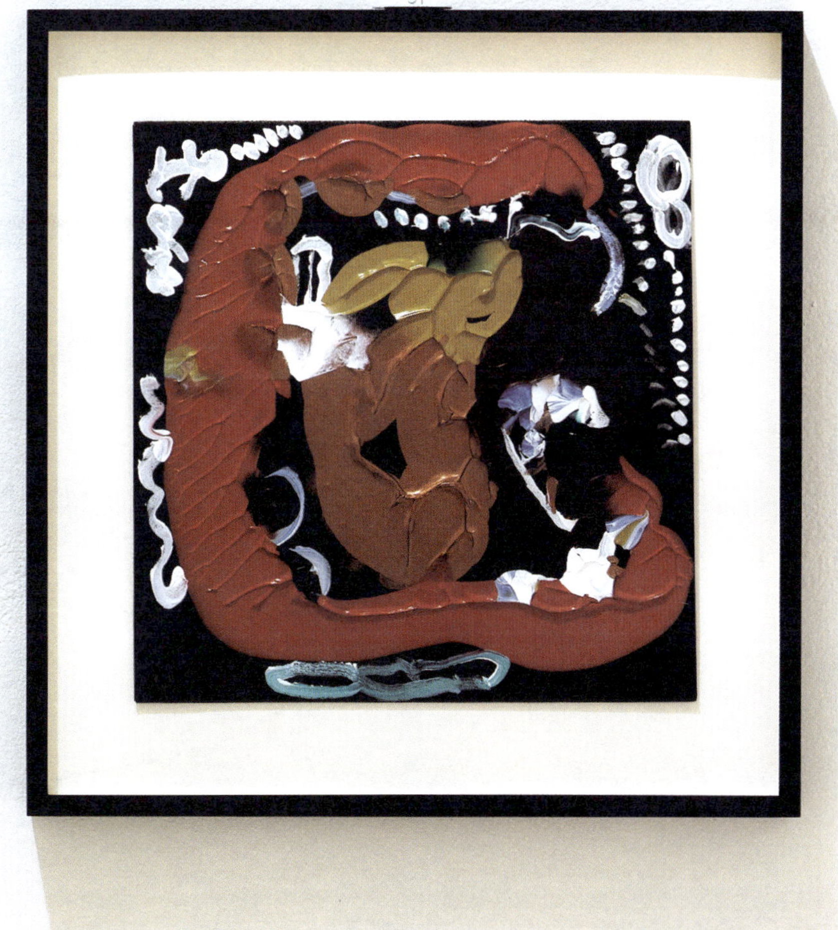

Milford Graves
Untitled 6, 2020 (top)
Untitled 9, 2020 (bottom)

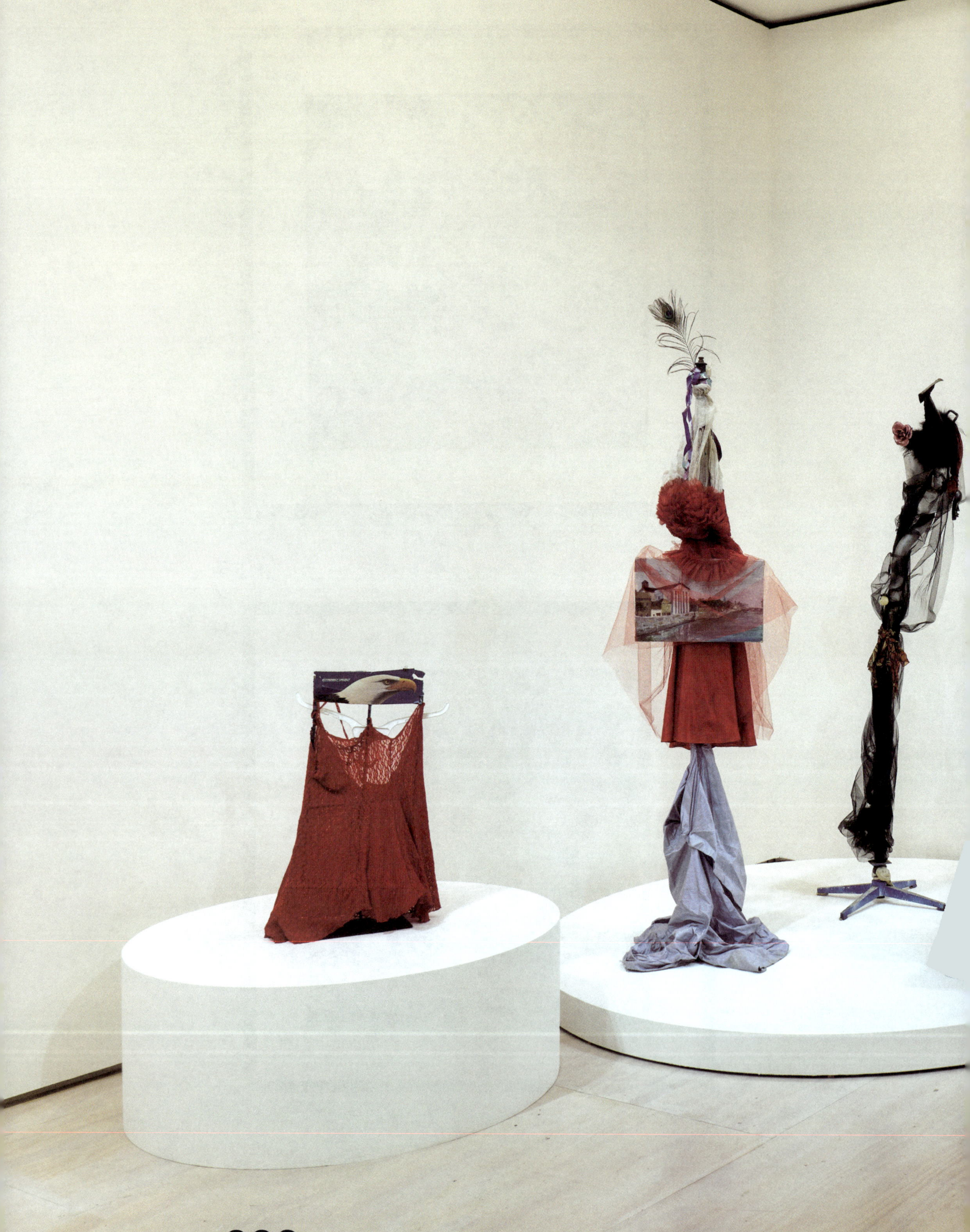

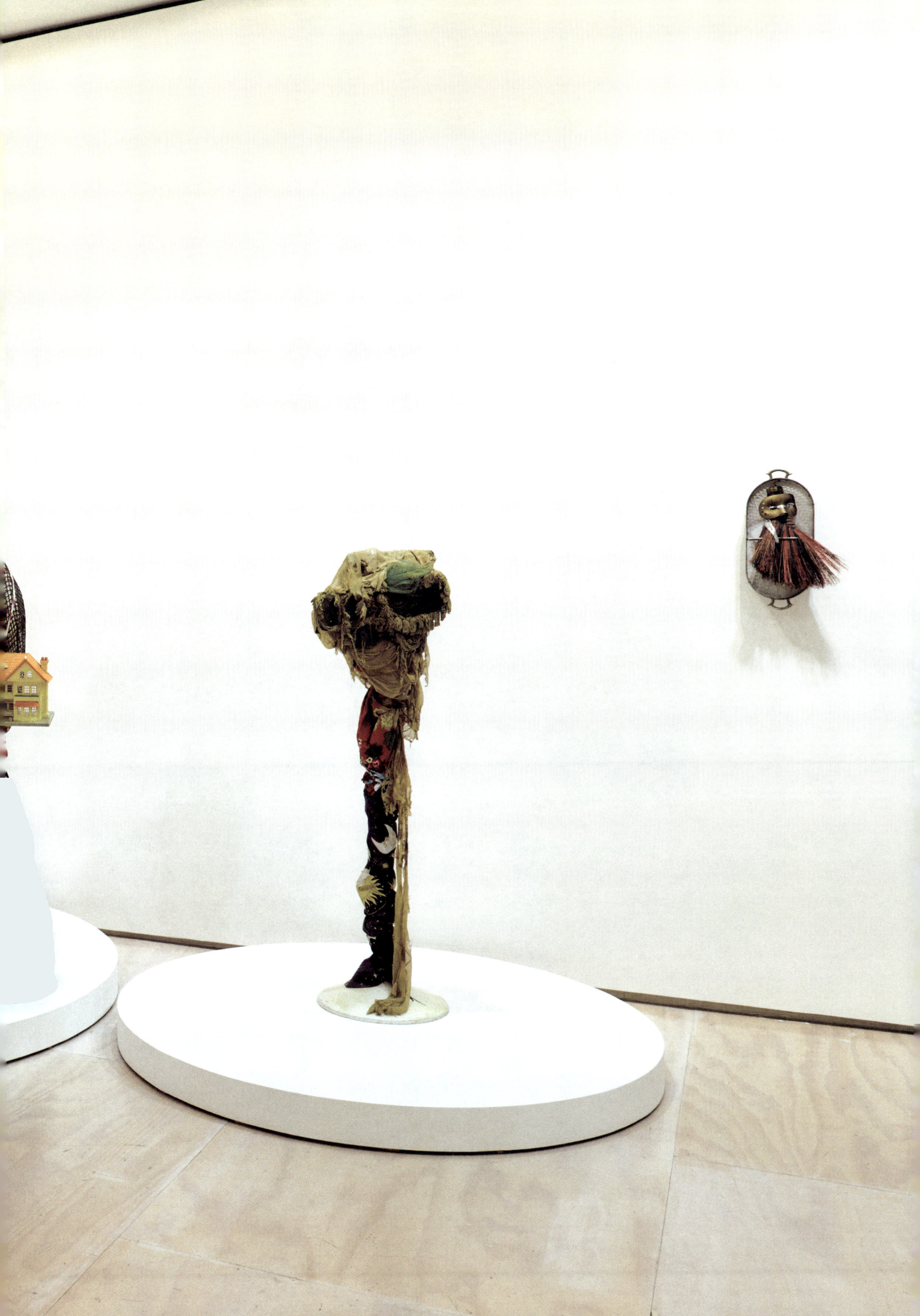

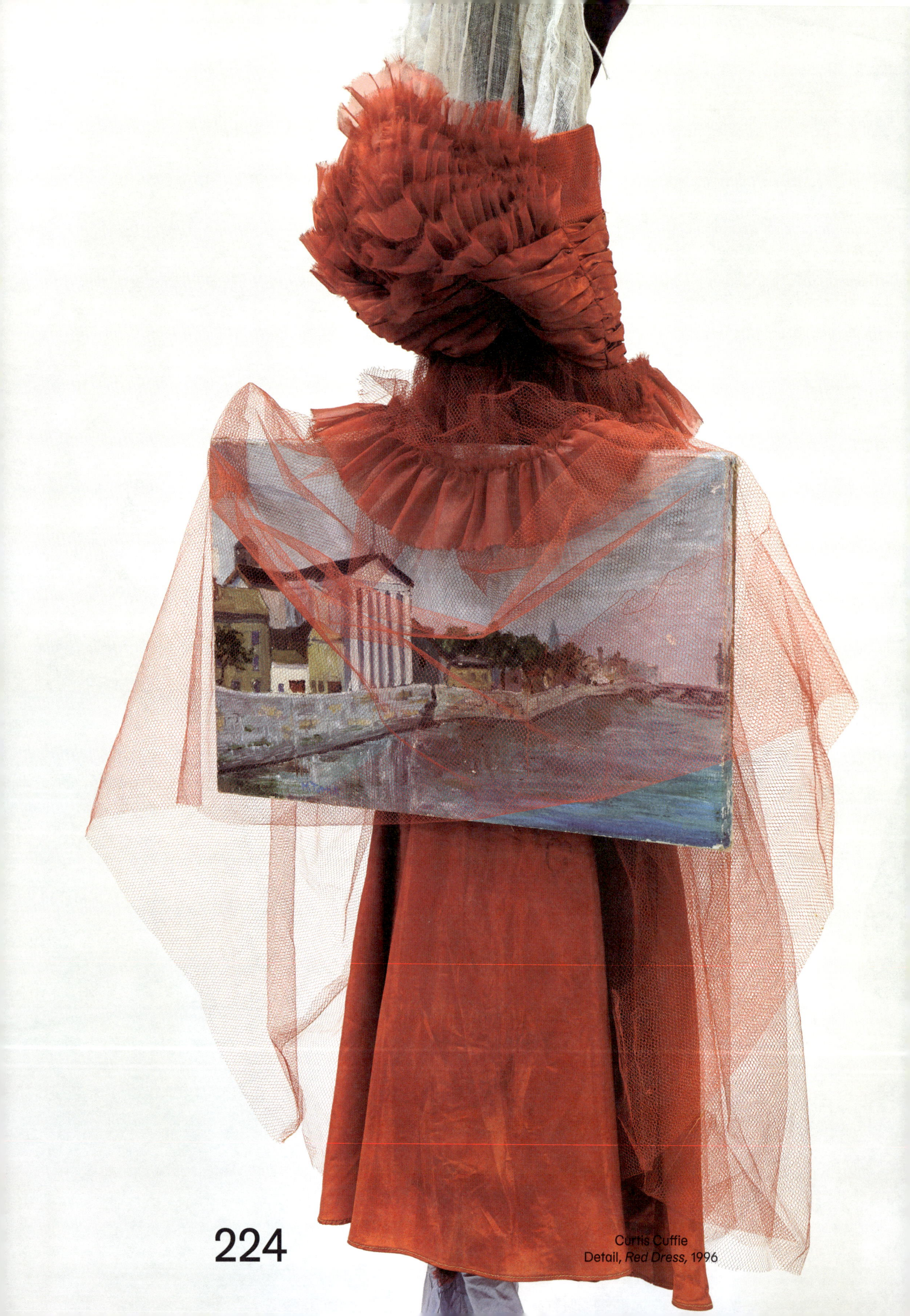

Curtis Cuffie
Detail, *Red Dress*, 1996

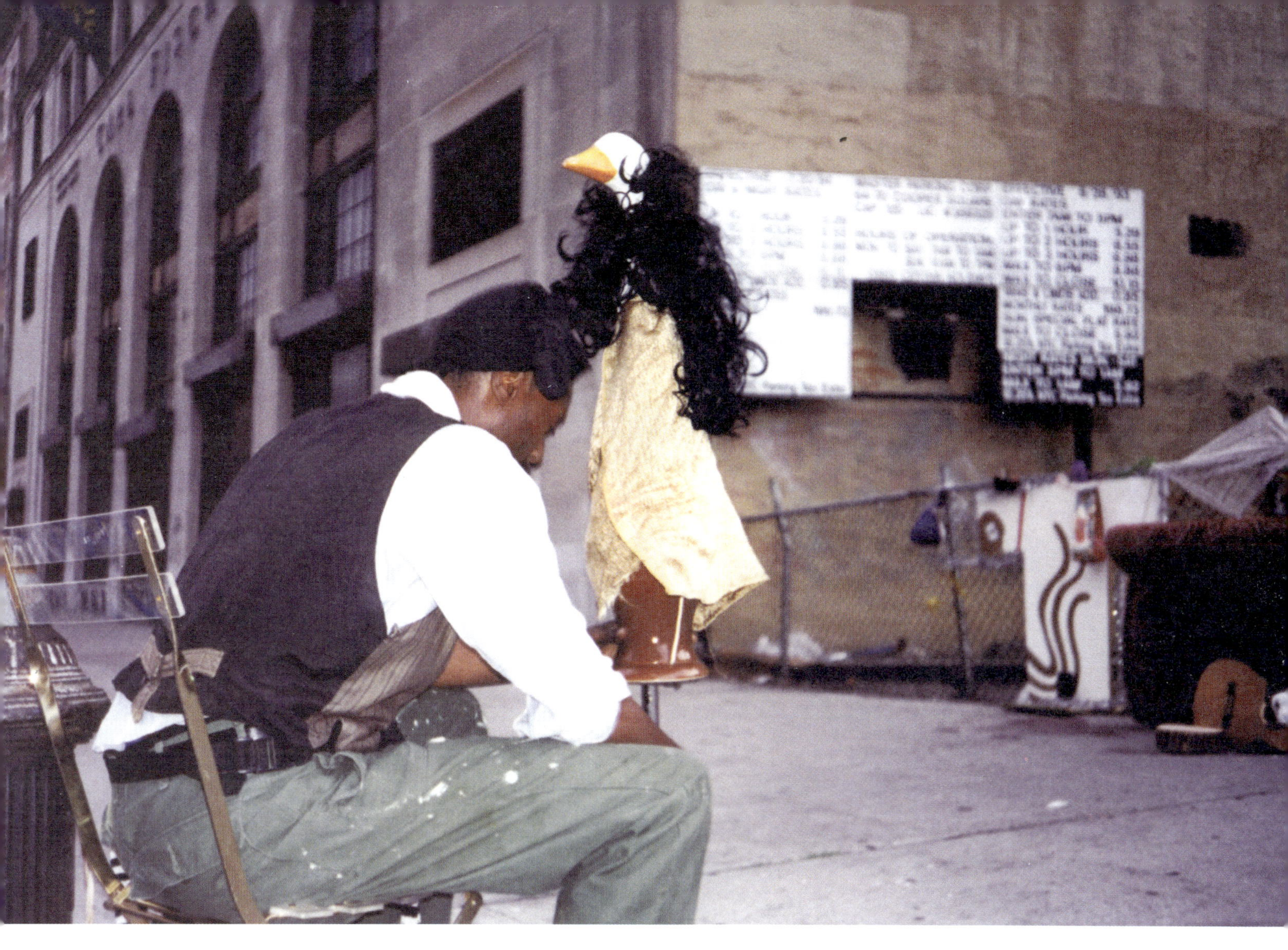

Sculptures by Curtis Cuffie on the streets of New York City, near Astor Place, c. 1990s
Photograph by Katy Abel

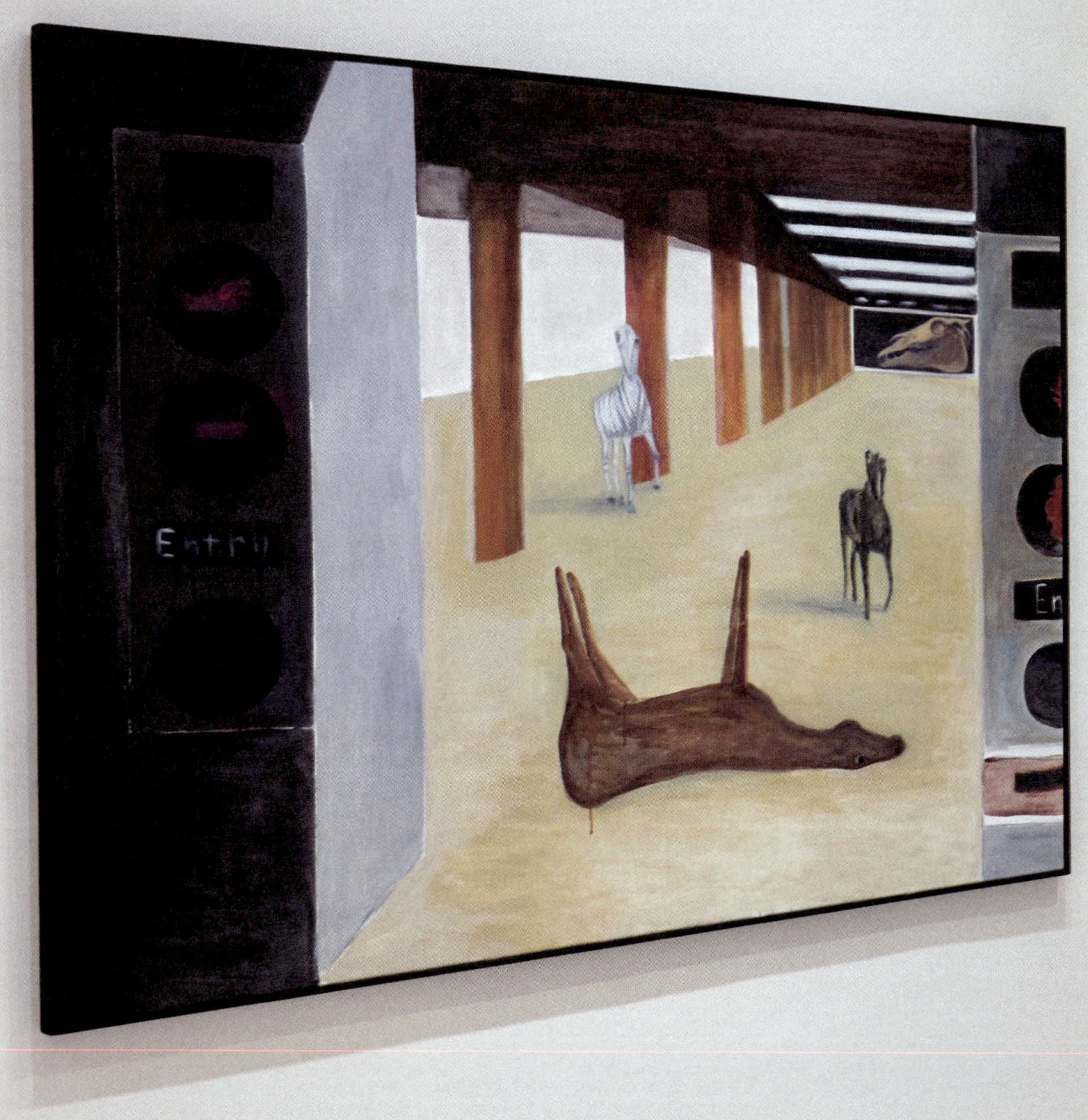

Ahmed Morsi
Subway Station III, 2015 (left)
Green Horse I, 2001 (right)

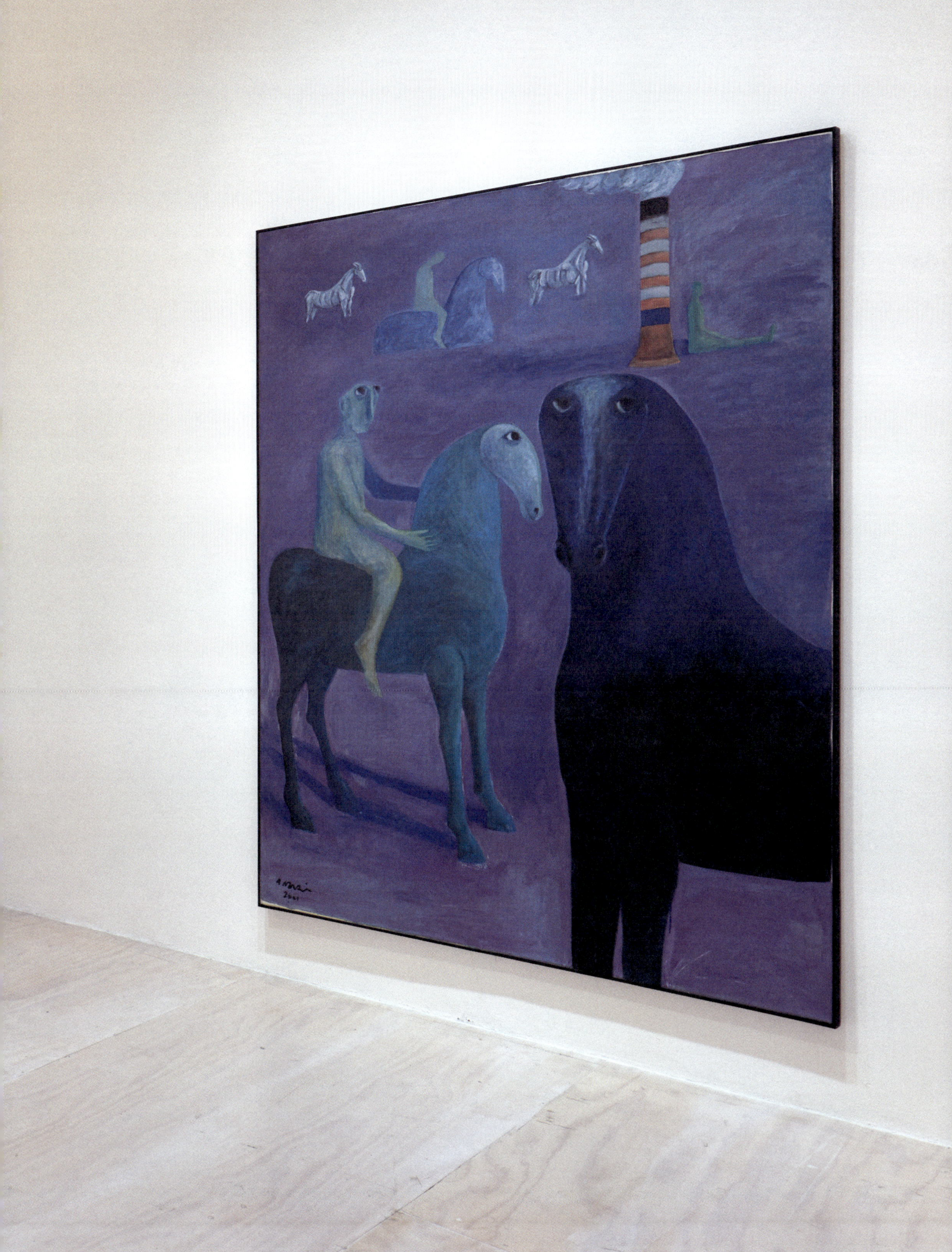

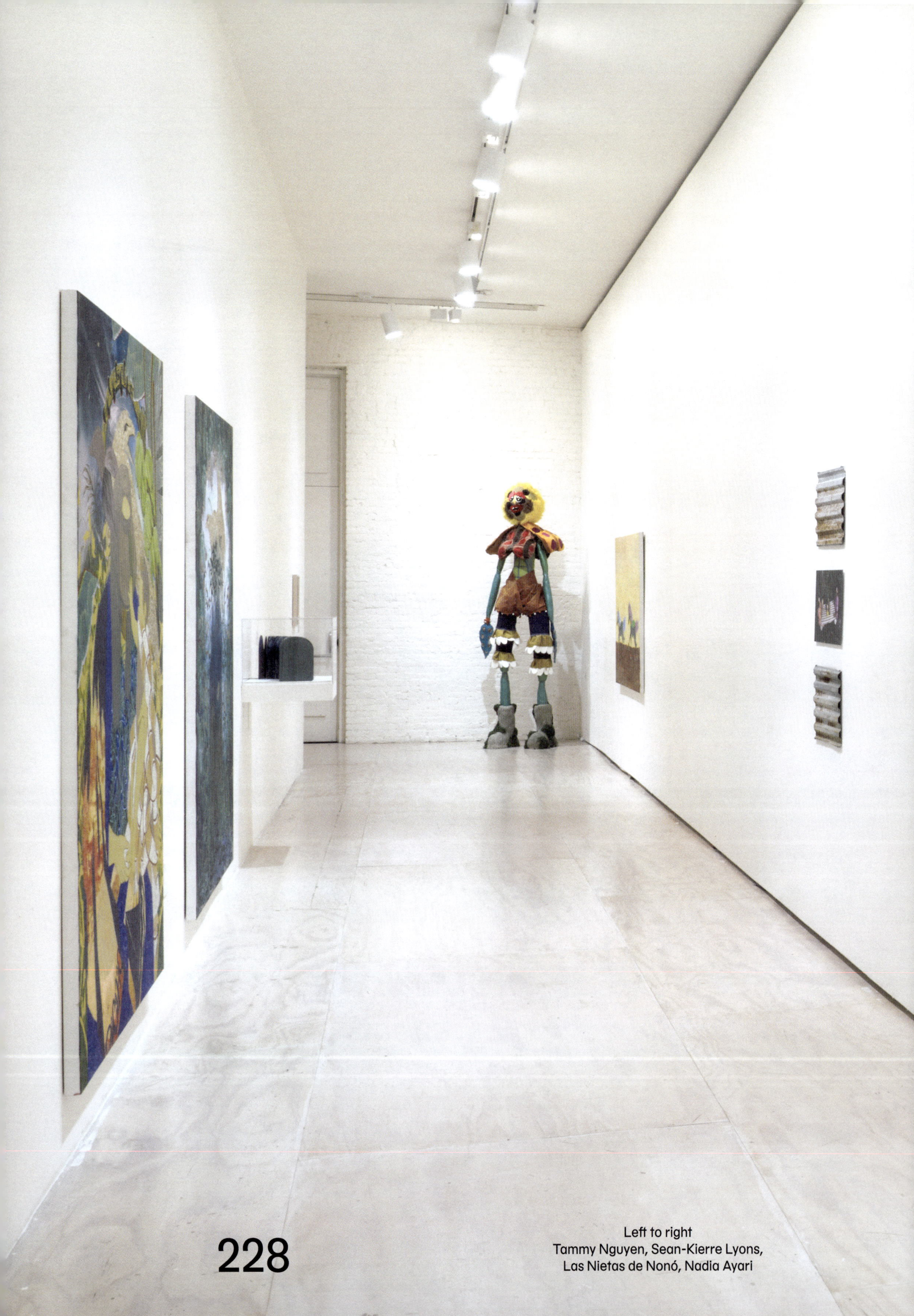

Left to right
Tammy Nguyen, Sean-Kierre Lyons,
Las Nietas de Nonó, Nadia Ayari

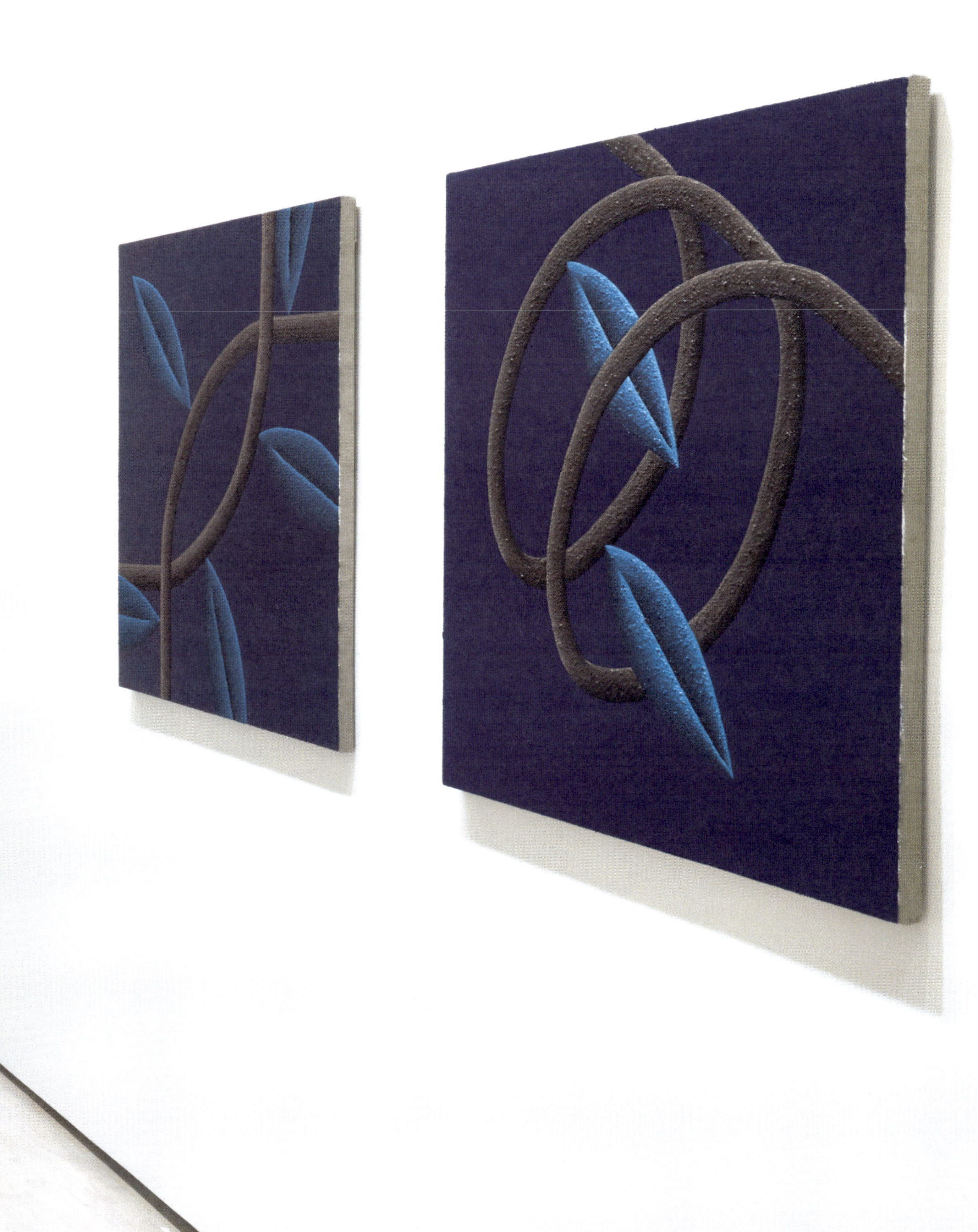

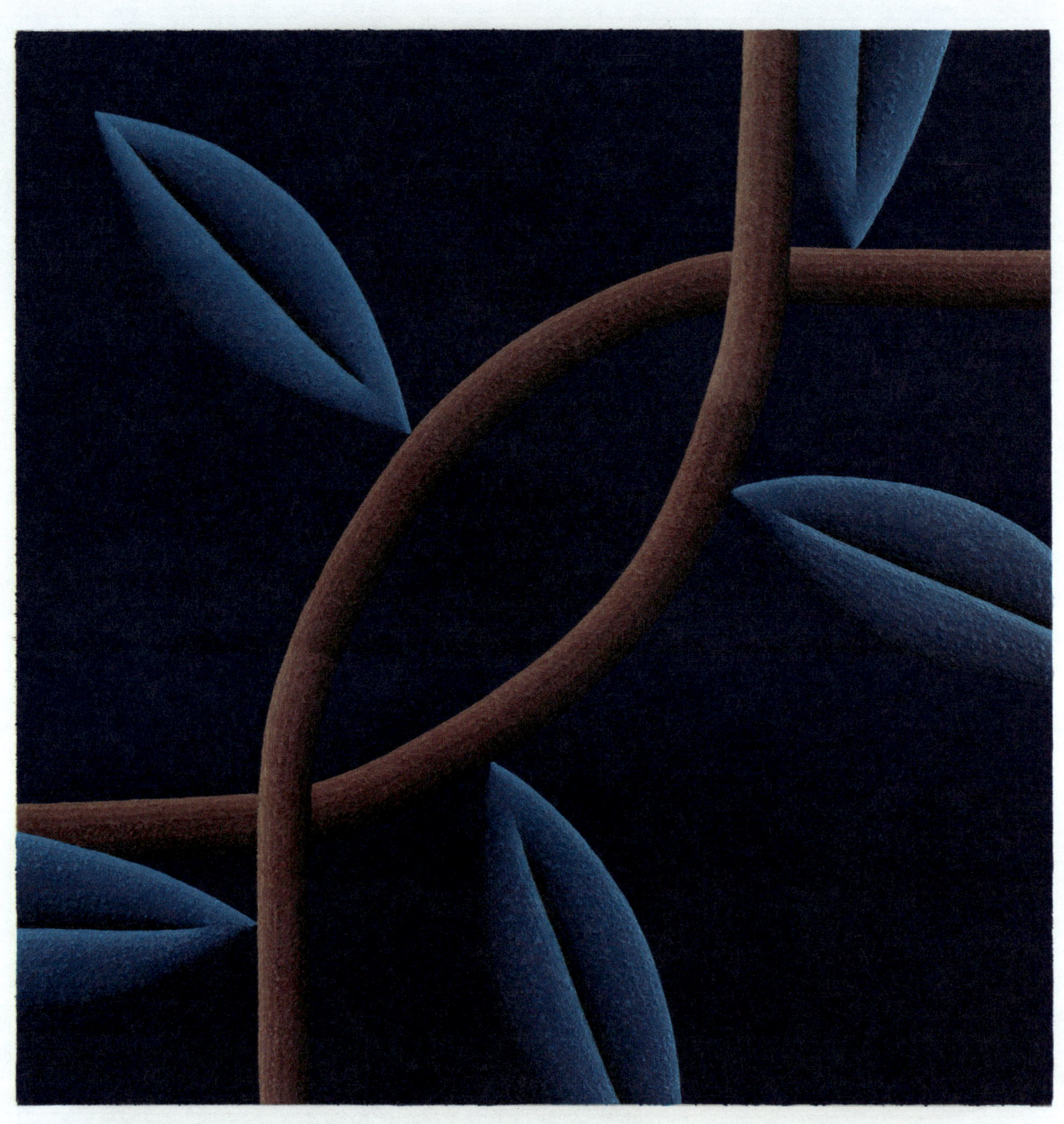

Nadia Ayari
Loop II, 2019

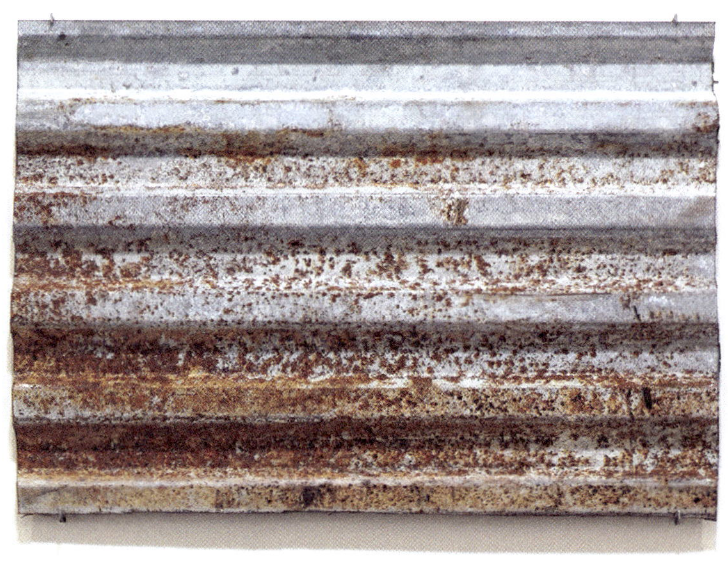

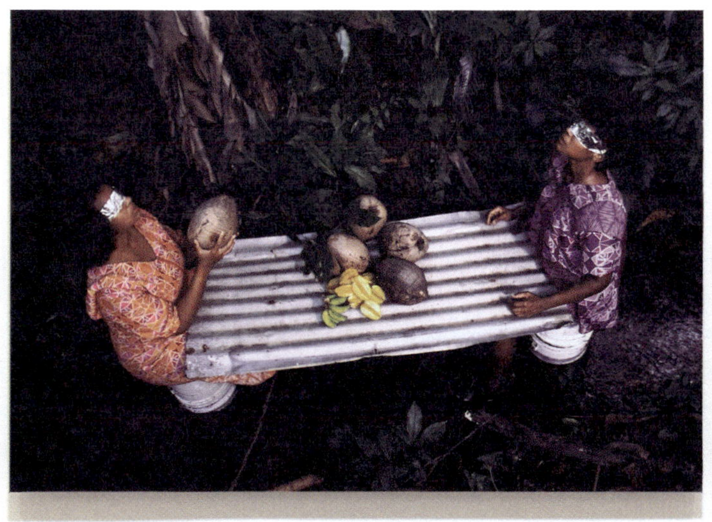

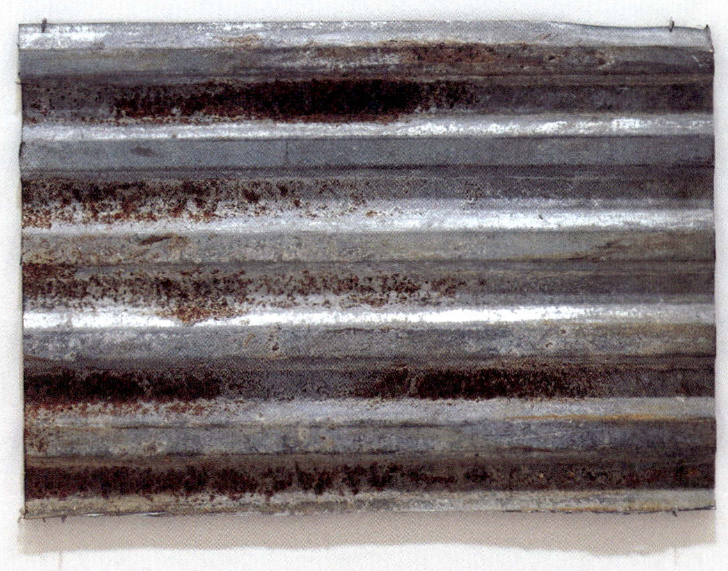

Las Nietas de Nonó
FOODTOPIA: después de todo territorio, 2020

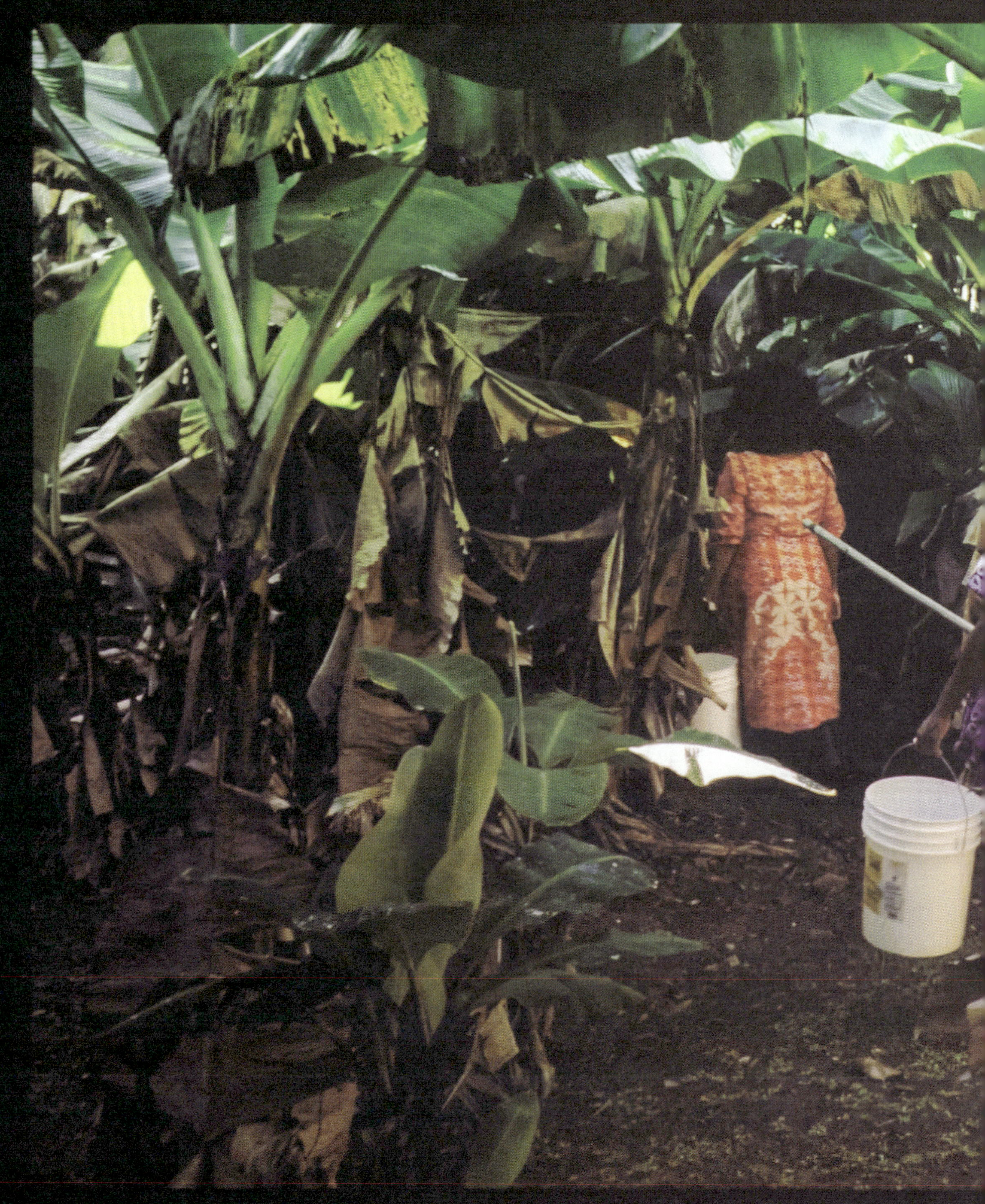

Las Nietas de Nonó
FOODTOPIA: después de todo territorio, 2020–2021

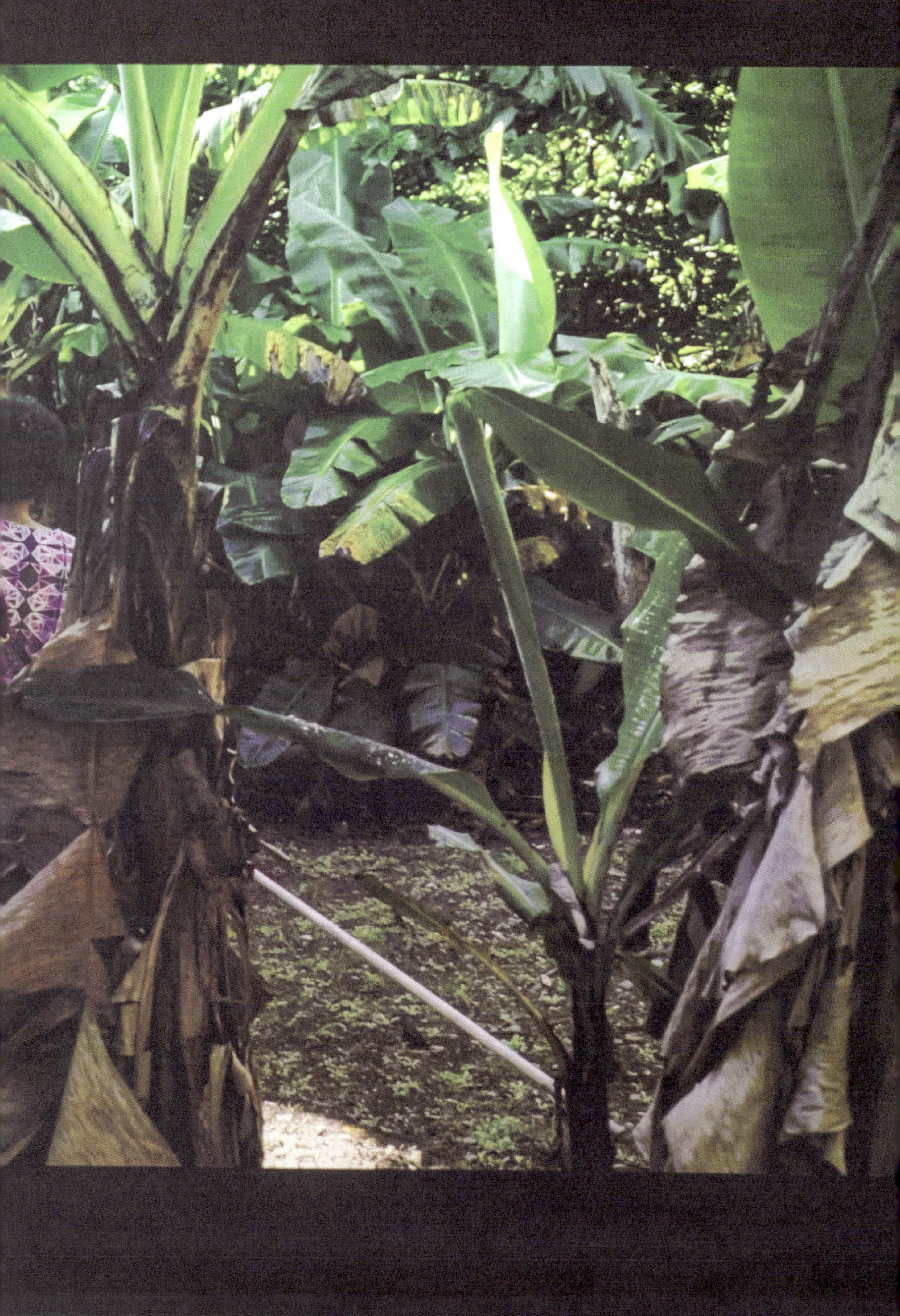

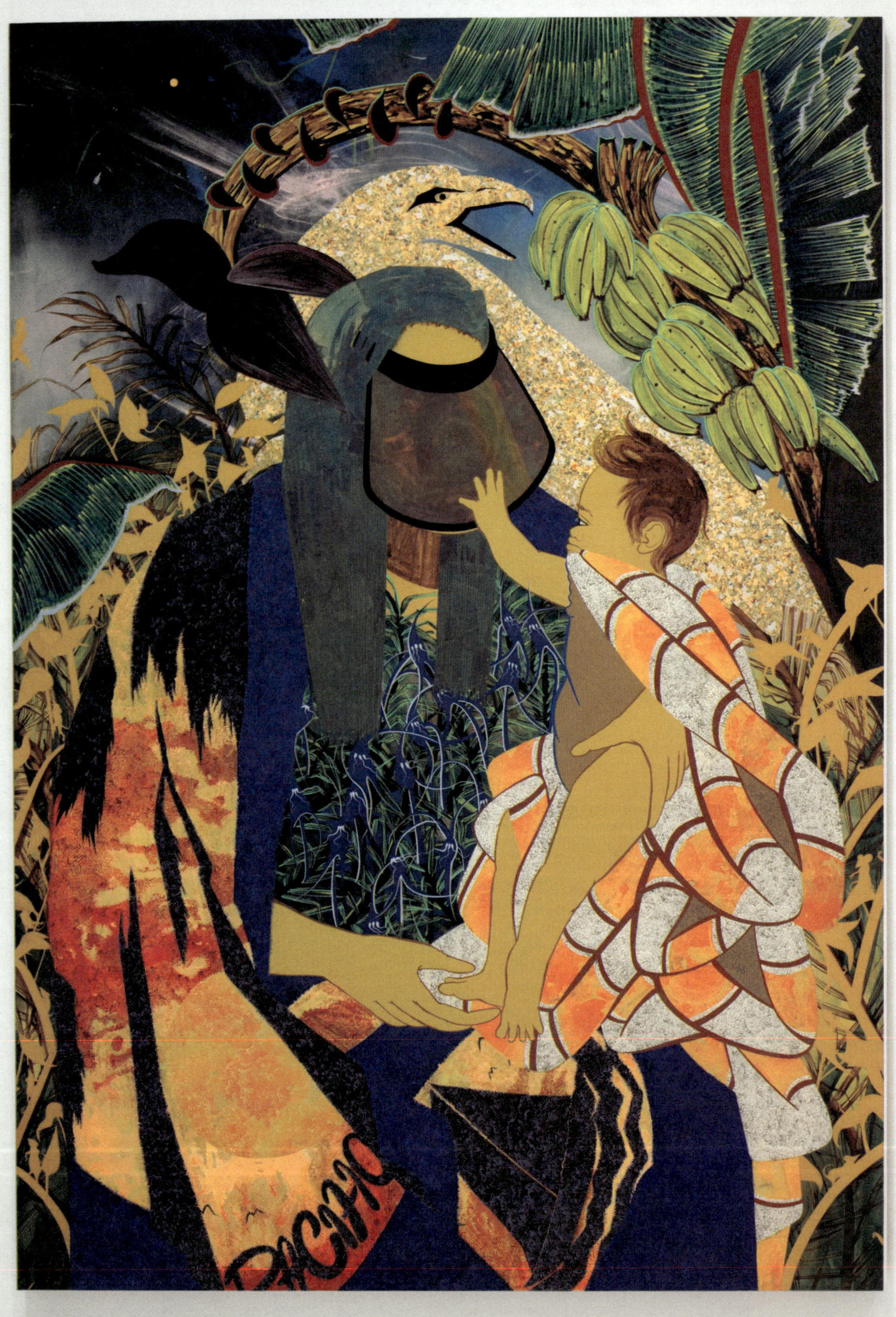

Tammy Nguyen
In the Heart of Rimland, 2021 (left)
Citizens' Cauldron, 2021 (right)

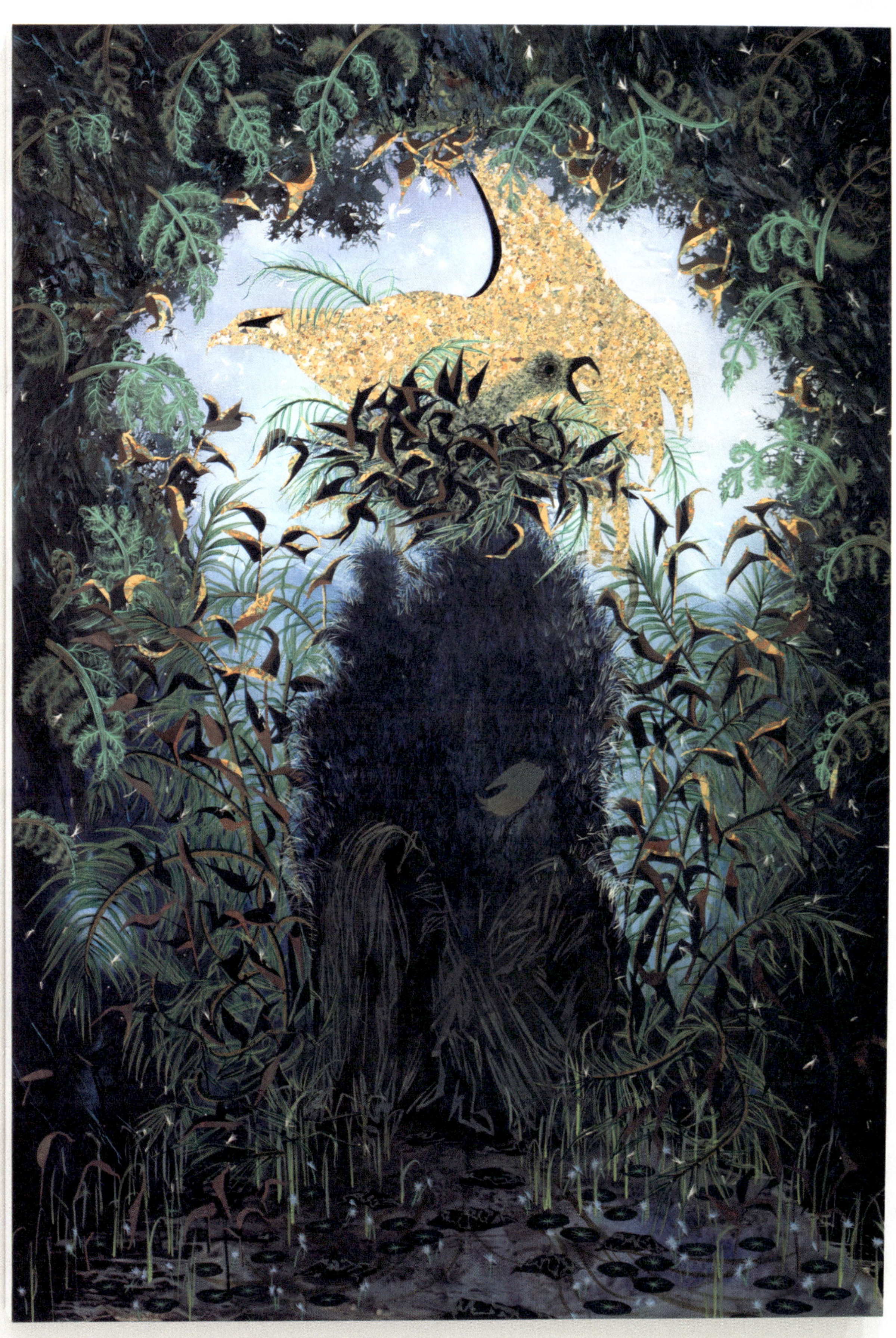

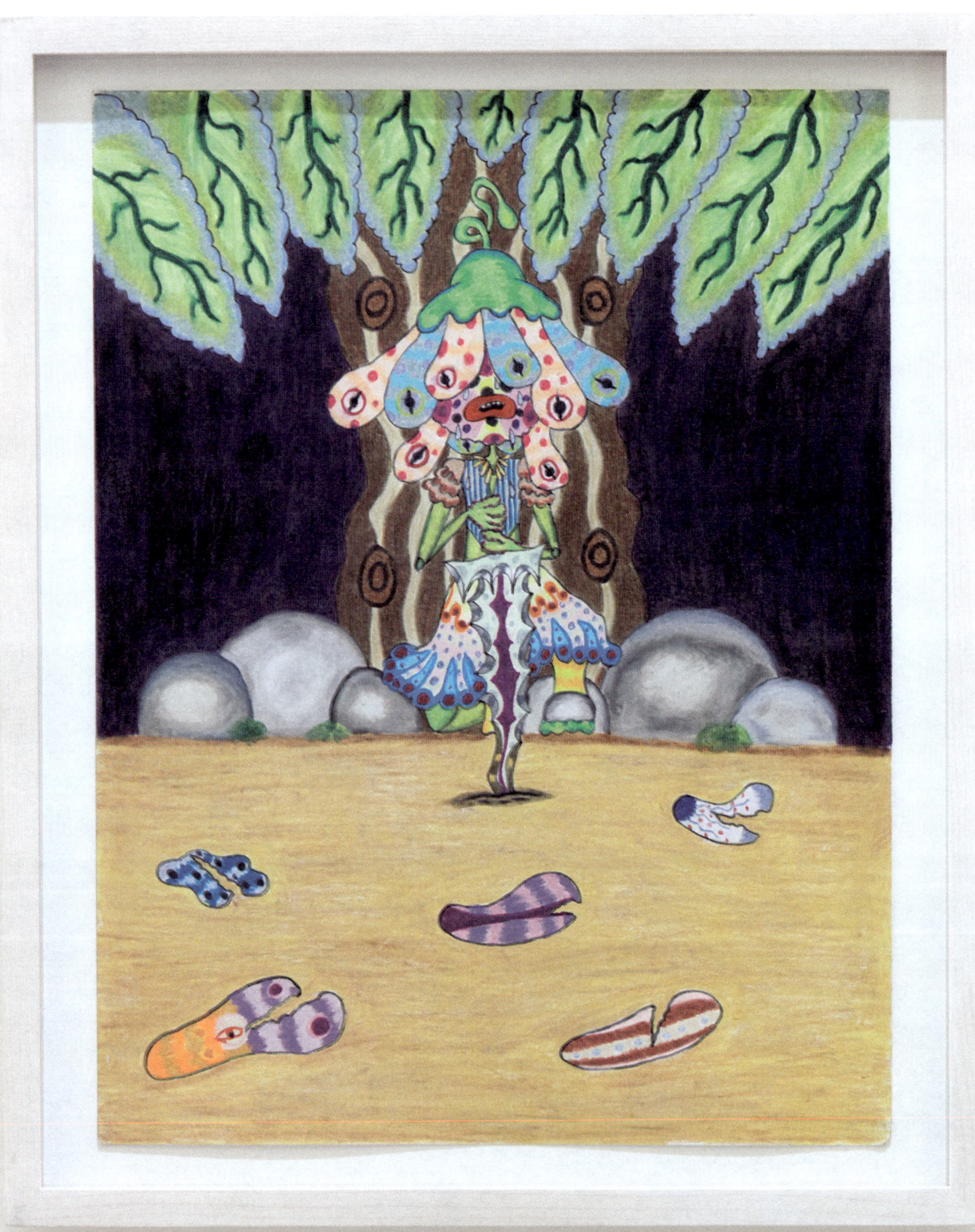

Sean-Kierre Lyons
All My Friends Are Dead, 2021

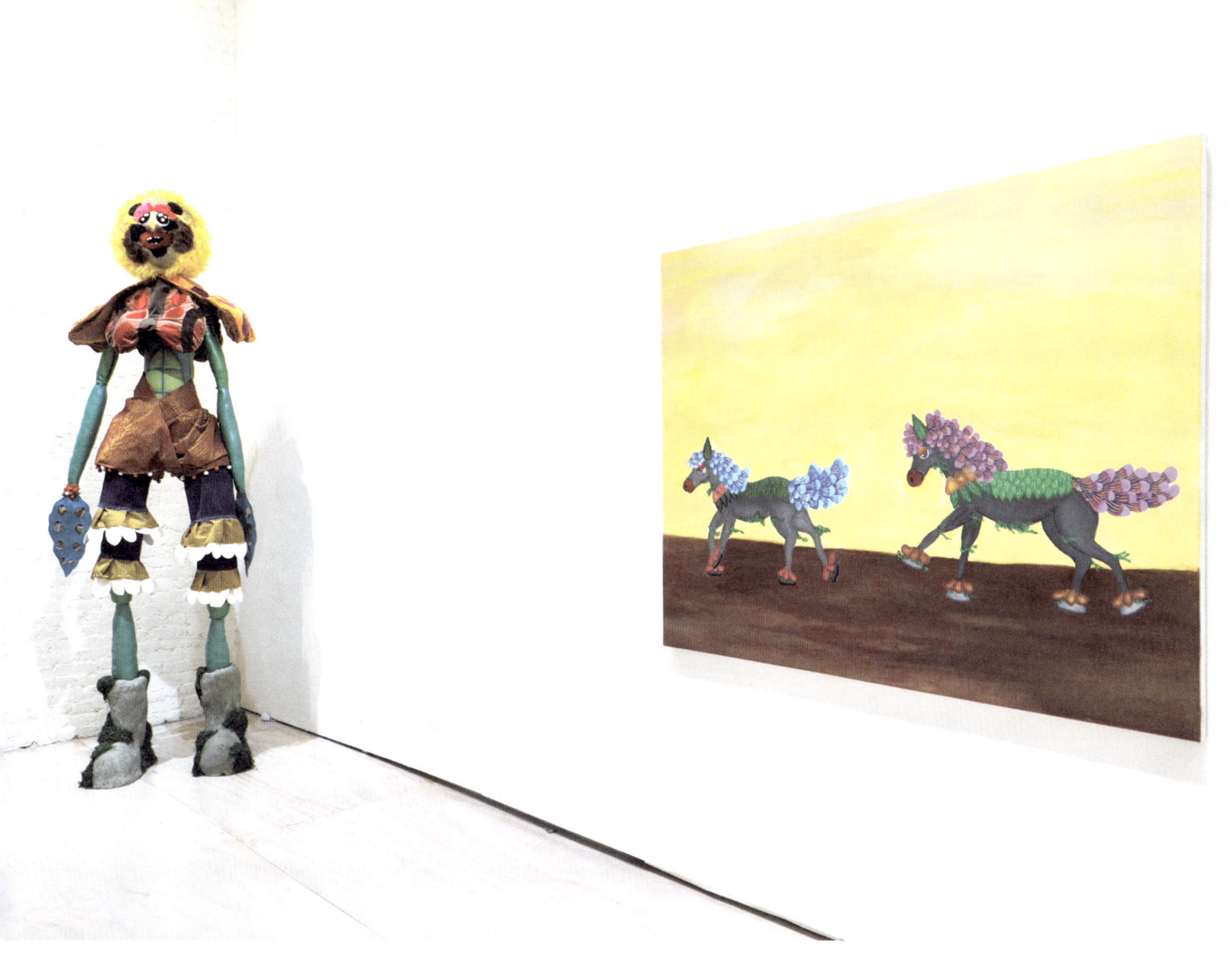

Sean-Kierre Lyons
Prometheus, redacted, 2021 (left)
Symphonic Sounds of Freedom, 2021 (right)

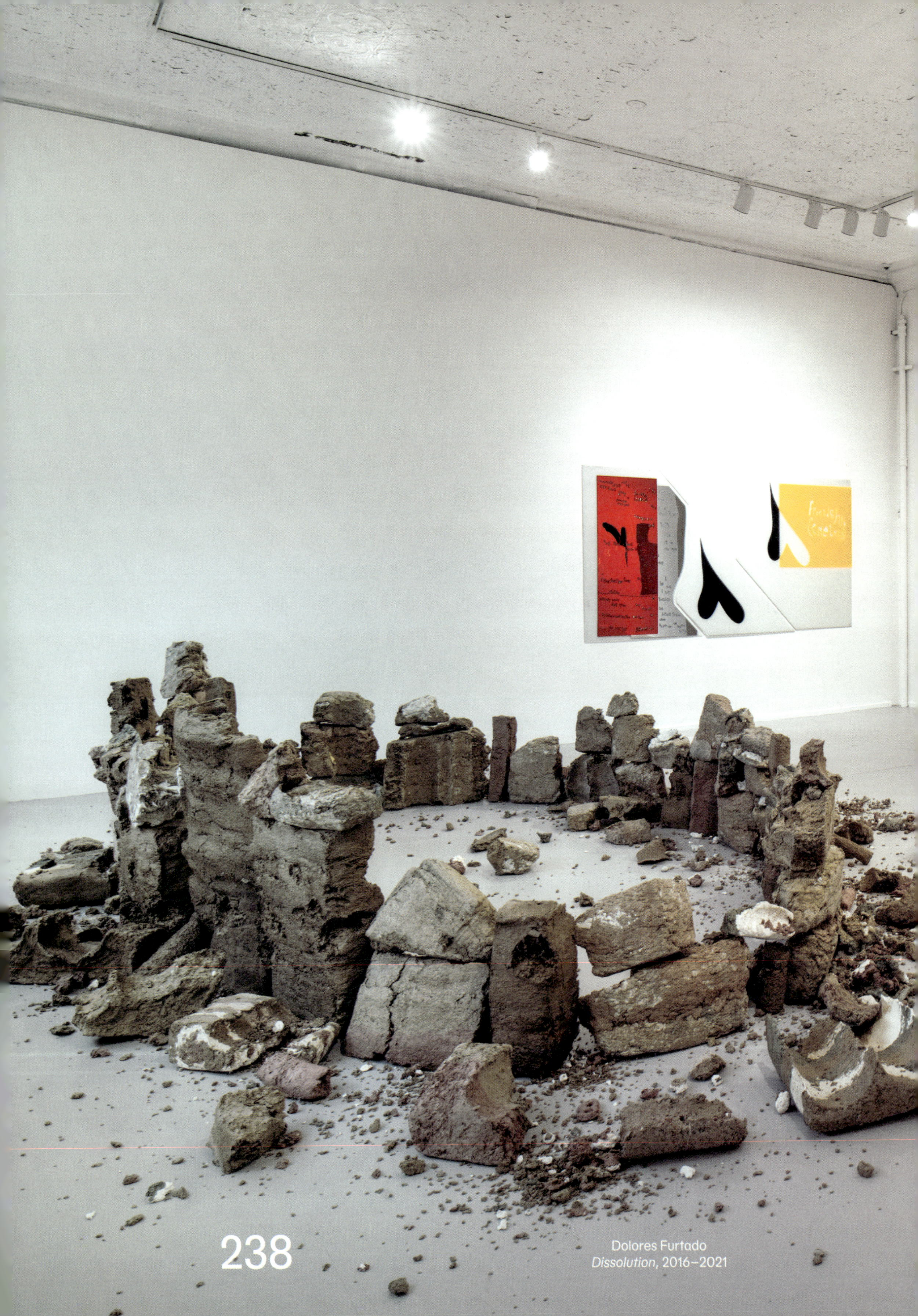

Dolores Furtado
Dissolution, 2016–2021

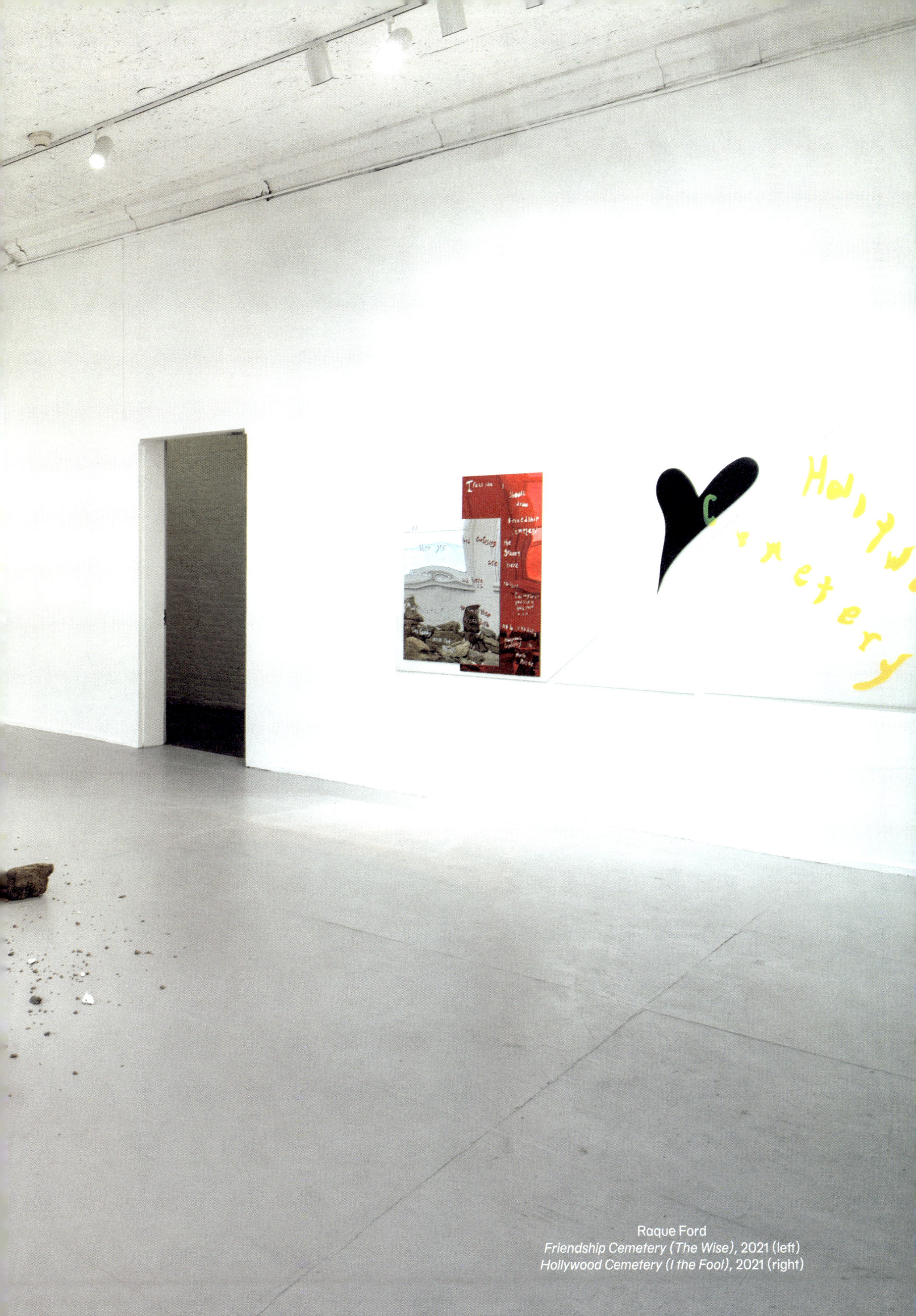

Raque Ford
Friendship Cemetery (The Wise), 2021 (left)
Hollywood Cemetery (I the Fool), 2021 (right)

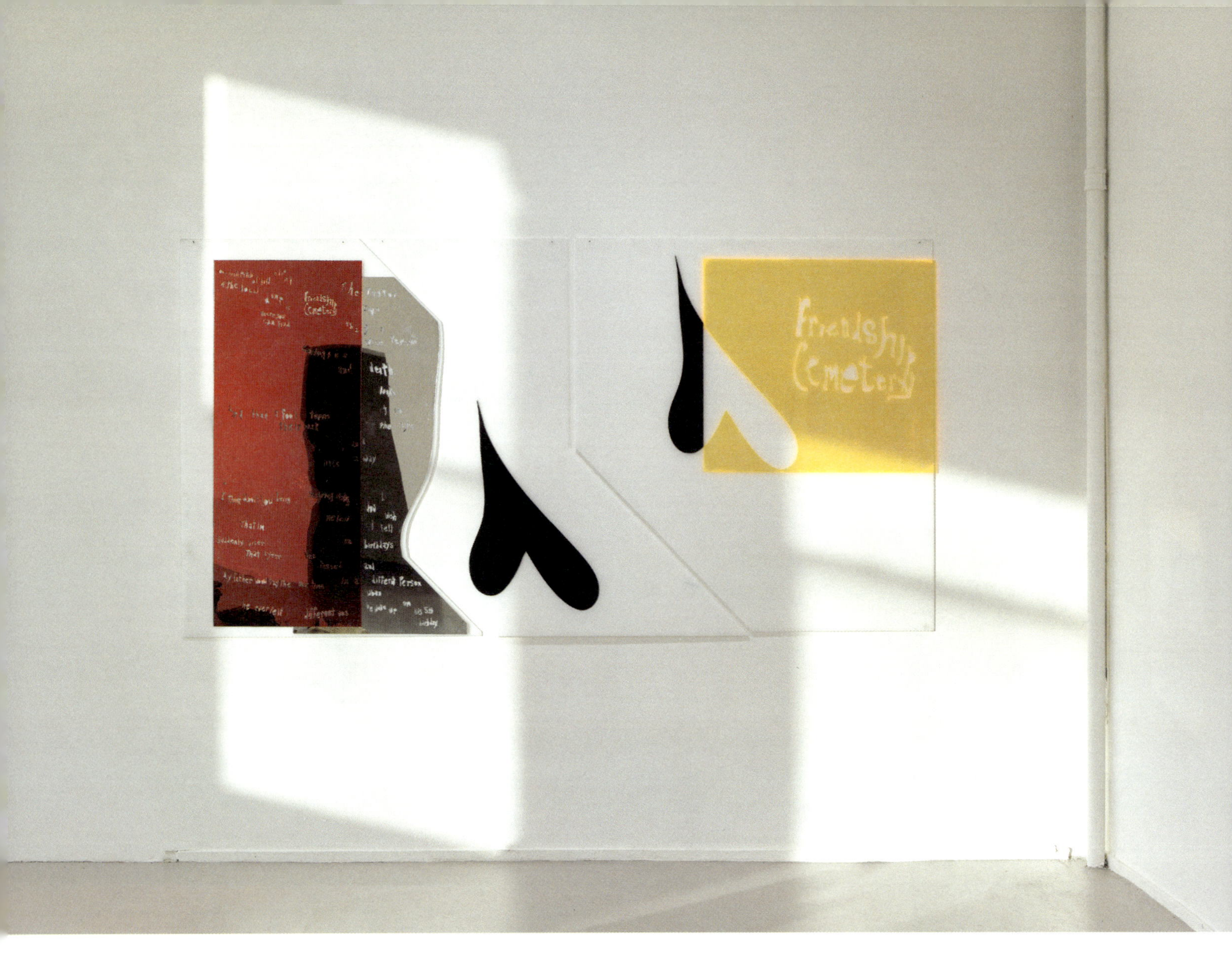

Raque Ford
Friendship Cemetery (The Wise), 2021

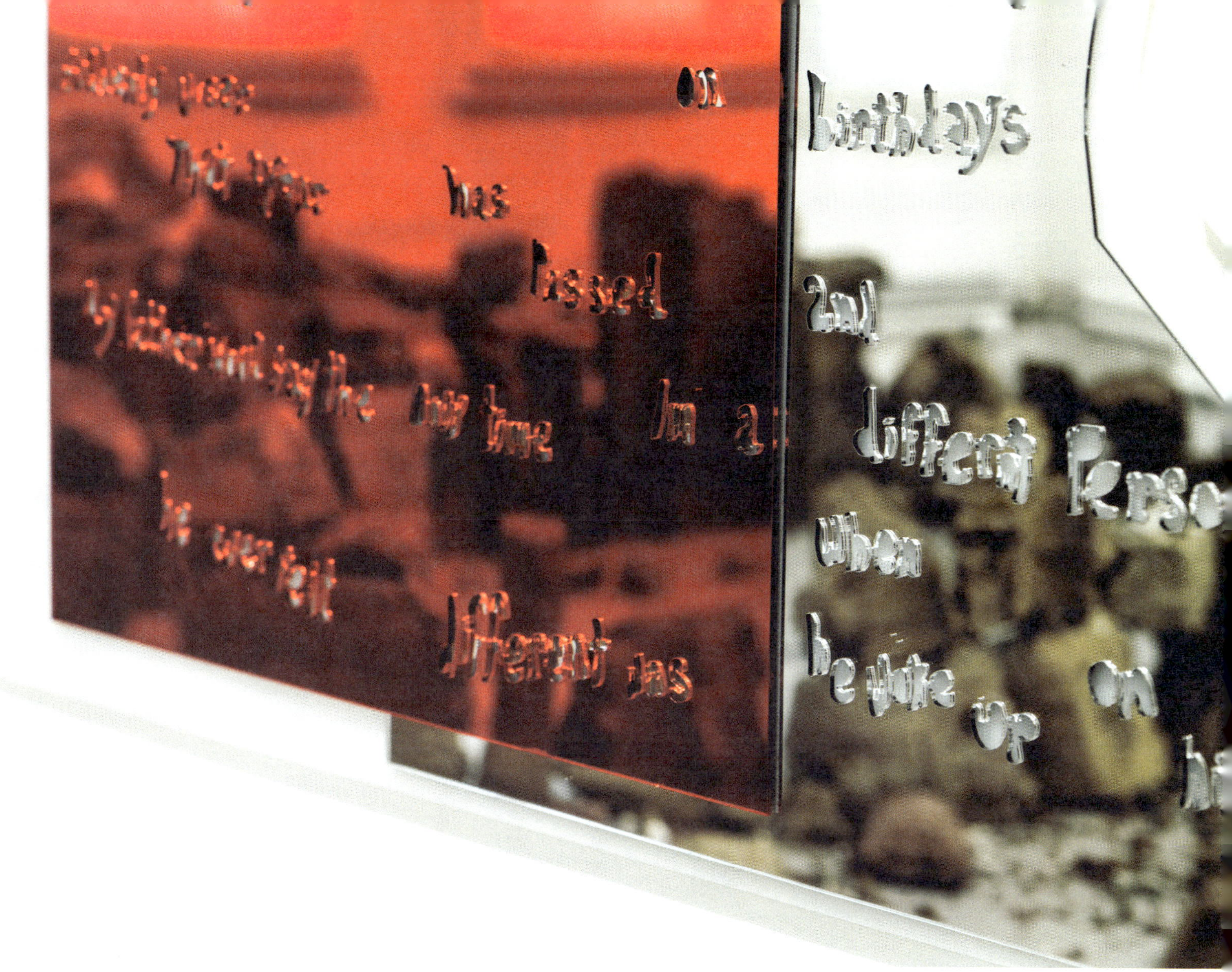

on
has
passed
felt
different days
birthdays
and
different
when
on

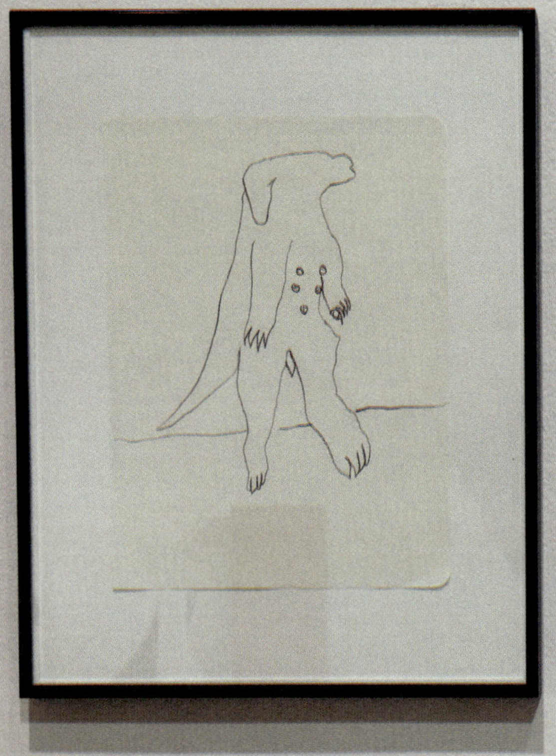

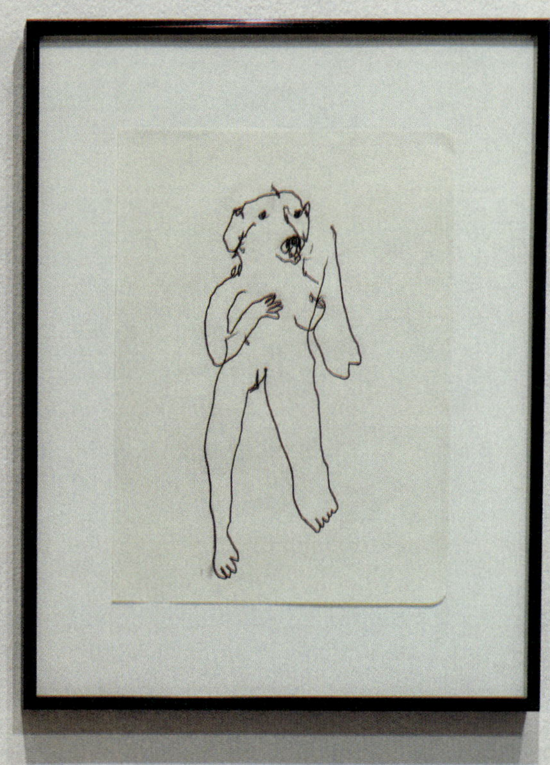

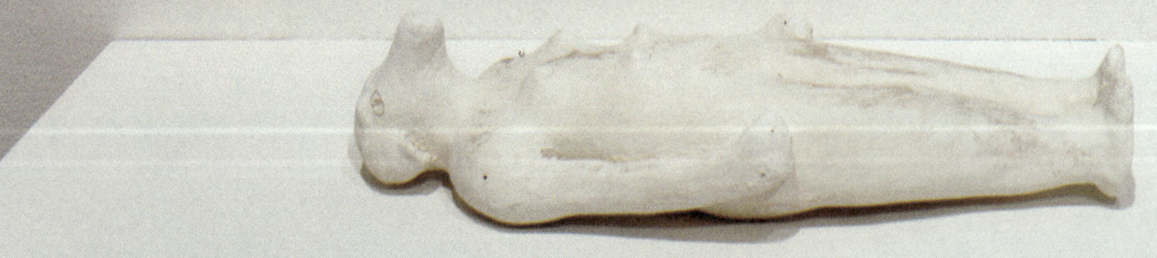

Emilie Louise Gossiaux
London stands up on her hind legs, 2020 (left)
London, in my dreams, 2020 (right)
Dog Girl, they called me, 2021 (bottom)

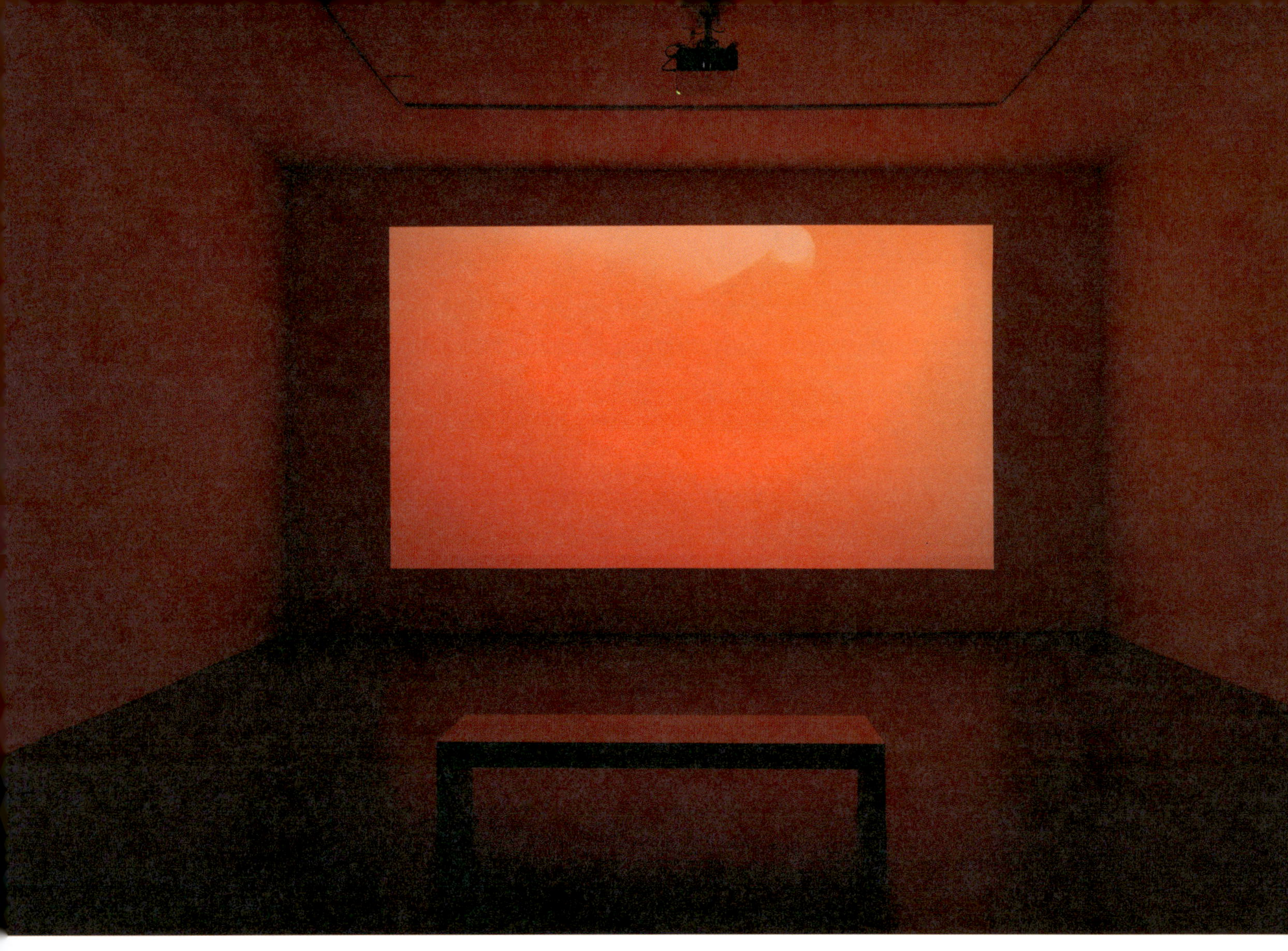

Carolyn Lazard
Red, 2021

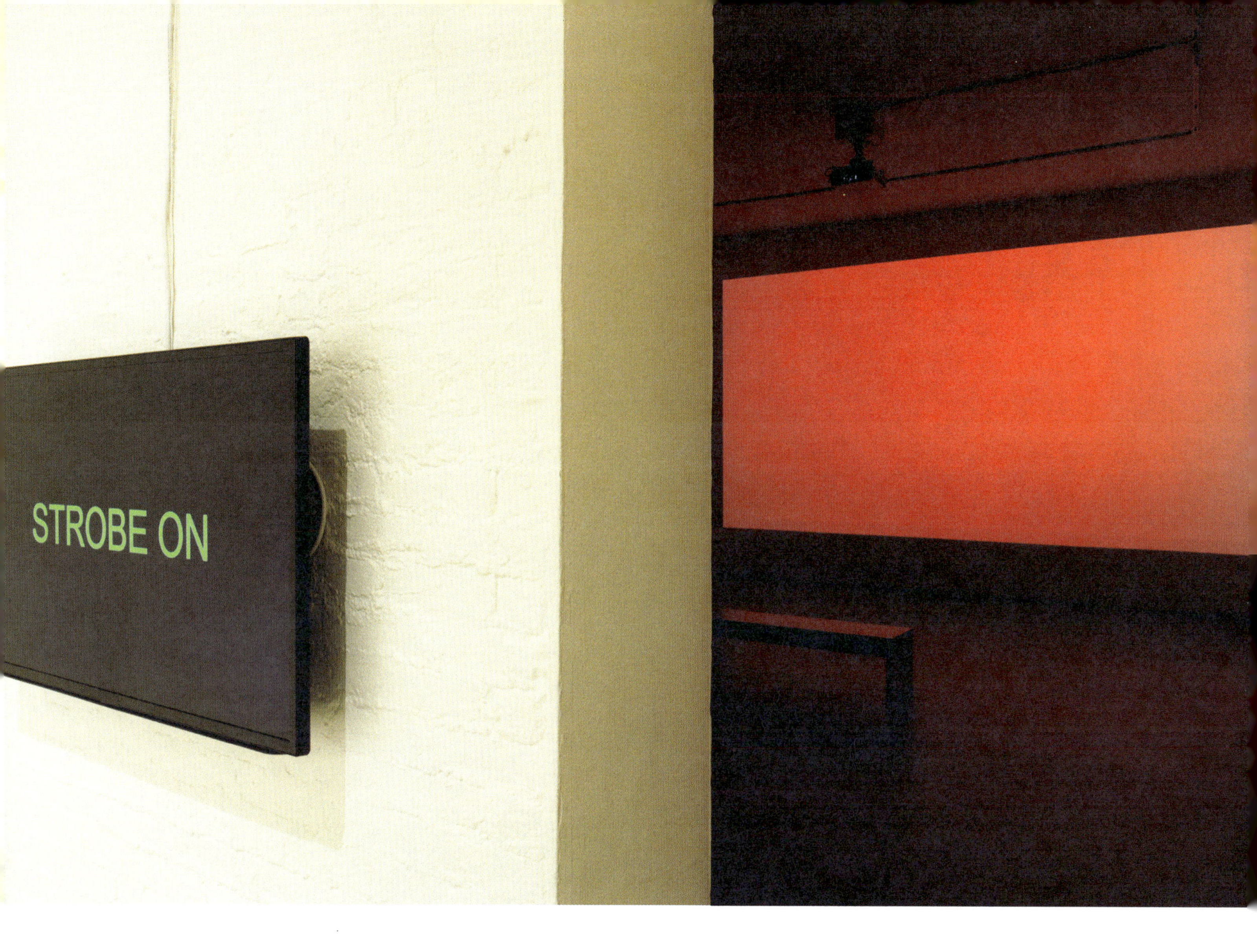
STROBE ON

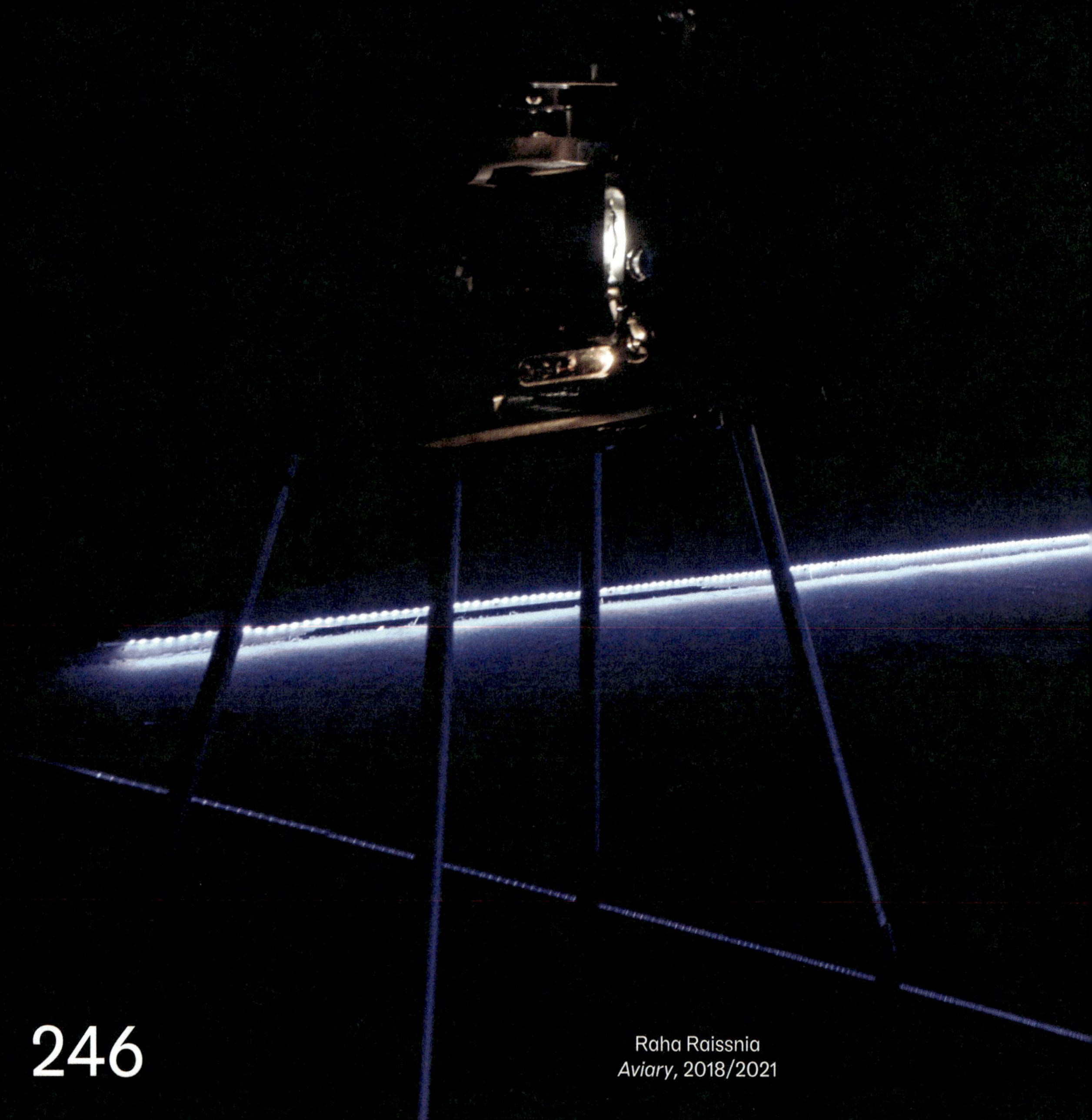

Raha Raissnia
Aviary, 2018/2021

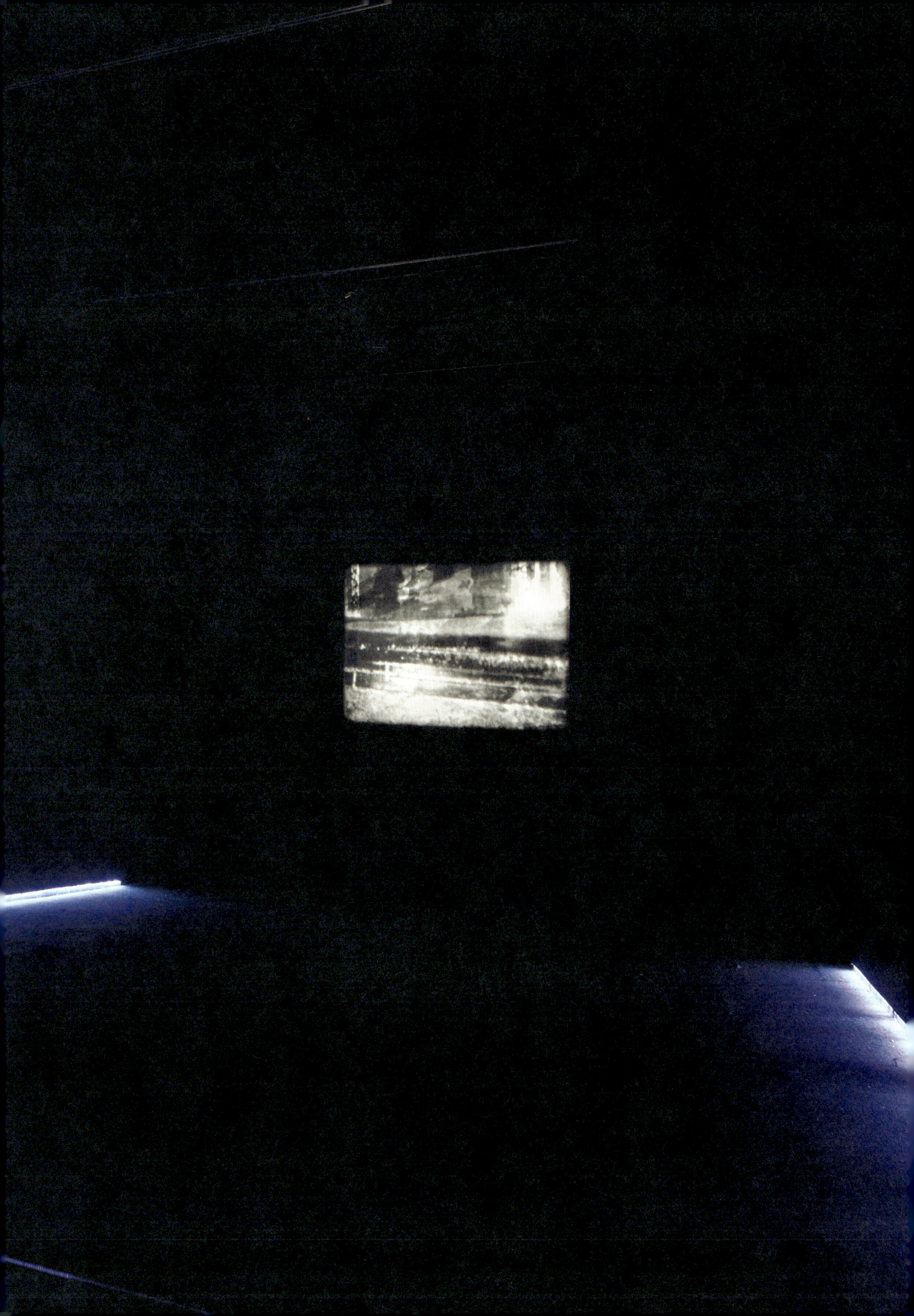

Yuji Agematsu
American, b. 1956, Japan

Yuji Agematsu has cultivated a daily practice of walking and collecting scraps of debris—chewed gum, foil, bottle caps, feathers, thread—from city streets since 1980, when he moved to New York City from Japan. In the mid-1980s, he began assembling his daily foraged treasures within the cellophane wrappers of cigarette packs: each cellophane pouch holds the residue of a particular path through space on a particular day. Influenced by his early involvement in music, including ten years studying with percussionist Milford Graves (whose work is also included in *Greater New York*), Agematsu offers a picture and pulse of the city through his practice. "I see each object as a notation in terms of music," he has stated. "Each has its own sound and rhythm." *zip: 01.01.20 ... 12.31.20* (2020) records the 366 daily walks that Agematsu took between January 1 and December 31, 2020. Arranged by month, they stand as an archive, map, and portrait of the streets of New York throughout the COVID-19 pandemic.

Nadia Ayari
Tunisian and American, b. 1981

Nadia Ayari uses representations of abstracted plant life, divorced from clear context, to hint at memories and depictions of specific locales. Her paintings often use seriality to develop nonhuman characters or "protagonists," isolating and repeating motifs across multiple works, the surfaces of which she builds up with layers of minute brushstrokes. In the series on view in *Greater New York*, Ayari channels the nocturnal life of night-blooming jasmine through tense and illogical compositions of branches, flowers, and leaves, the curvatures of which serve as both supports and enclosures.

BlackMass Publishing
Est. 2018

BlackMass Publishing is a New York–based collective that publishes zines and books of new and archival content by black artists and cultural producers. Printing "on anything as long as it'll feed through the printer," the collective produces new conversations on black cultural production across the diaspora, intermixing known and lesser-known, historical and contemporary, art, music, poetry, and critical writing in an improvisational manner. Their methods of sourcing, collecting, and distributing materials are essential to their work: they often pull from archives and special collections and then reinsert their books into those very institutions, helping to change the ways in which black histories are constructed and preserved. Their publications are included in the Schomburg Center for Research in Black Culture, the Langston Hughes Library, the Thomas J. Watson Library at the Metropolitan Museum of Art, Harvard's Houghton Library, and the library of the Whitney Museum of American Art. For *Greater New York*, BlackMass Publishing has created a multimedia study hall in which visitors can engage with their process. As part of their BlackMass Mail Program, which launched in 2020, viewers are invited to take an envelope in which to send the collective materials to be added to the BlackMass Publishing archive.

Diane Burns
Chemehuevi and Anishinabe, 1957–2006

Born in Lawrence, Kansas, to a Chemehuevi father and an Anishinabe mother, Diane Burns moved to New York in the 1970s to attend Barnard College. After dropping out her senior year, she became active in the poetry scene of the Lower East Side, where she lived. She was a founding poet of the Nuyorican Poets Cafe, a frequent performer at the Bowery Poetry Club and the Poetry Project at St. Mark's Church, and published a book of poems entitled *Riding the One-Eyed Ford* (1981), illustrated with her pen and ink drawings. Burns's poems take on the anachronistic stereotypes she faced as a Native American woman living in downtown New York. "Most people think American Indians are just skulking in the desert or wandering around the woods or something like that," she once noted. "People don't realize how much of New York is Indian country." In *Poetry Spots: Diane Burns reads "Alphabet City Serenade"* (1989) Burns recites a poem while strolling through the streets and empty lots of the Lower East Side. Filmed for the series *Poetry Spots*—produced by poet Bob Holman and shown as interstitial videos in between segments on WNYC-TV—the video alludes to the entwined histories of Native American dispossession, diaspora, and urban poverty: "But here I am on Avenue D," she recites, "a sacrifice of manifest destiny."

A number of archival photos depict Burns while on a trip to Nicaragua in 1986 with peers including Allen Ginsberg, Joy Harjo, and Pedro Pietri (one of the founders of the Nuyorican Poets Cafe). The group was invited to the Ruben Dario Poetry Festival by the Sandinista government. This trip took place during the Contra War and the same year as *Nicaragua v. United States*, the case against the US military's illegal intervention into the country.

Kristi Cavataro
American, b. 1992

Kristi Cavataro's handmade, modular sculptures destabilize and disorient spatial coordinates. She cuts and solders stained glass before wrapping it onto various geometric forms, so that the resulting sculptures intersect, interlock, and conjoin in unexpected and improbable ways. Their tiled surfaces and curvatures at times suggest the city's built environment, harkening to Art Deco forms common to urban public infrastructure. In fact, the works are non-referential, each its own original form with infinite possible permutations. Cavataro has written, "I am skeptical of linear thinking, and linear notions of progress. Moving linearly is a dangerous myth." Through the labyrinthine abstraction of her sculptures, she expands familiar spatial systems.

Curtis Cuffie
American, 1955–2002

Born in Hartsville, South Carolina, Curtis Cuffie moved to Brooklyn at age fifteen. He became known in the 1990s for the impromptu performative sculptures that he installed on sidewalks, walls, and fences around Astor Place and throughout the East Village. Poetically titled and elaborately constructed from salvaged objects and trash, his works used the street as a generative site for materials as well as audiences, often interacting with passersby. At times, his installations were removed by the city or otherwise destroyed, but new works would crop up around the city soon after. While the artist was mostly unhoused while he was living in New York City, he was a recognizable figure: he was featured on local news programs, he and his work were documented by other artists and friends, and he periodically showed his work in local galleries. His proximity to Cooper Union—an art school located on Astor Place, at the edge of the East Village—solidified his relationships with many students and faculty, extending his influence from the street into the art world. However, Cuffie was committed to his mode of working through improvisation and saw the sidewalk as his primary venue.

Hadi Fallahpisheh
Iranian, b. 1987

Hadi Fallahpisheh's photographic works result from private performances in the darkroom, where the artist uses a flashlight to "draw" on the surface of photosensitive paper. The resulting cartoonlike drawings illustrate a cast of entangled domestic characters—usually a person, a cat, a dog, and a mouse. Their slapstick escapades and power struggles allegorize the travails of contemporary immigrants and the effects of cultural displacement, which Fallahpisheh, who was born and raised in Iran, has experienced firsthand. In *Young and Clueless* (2021), as in similar installations, he places his images in relation to sculptural objects, extending the scene of the image into the space of the gallery. Narrating literal cat-and-mouse stories of dislocation and ensnarement, Fallahpisheh plays with the line between what is visible and what is concealed, who must hide and who is forced to be cunning.

Rotimi Fani-Kayode
British and Nigerian, 1955–1989

Raised in England after fleeing civil war in Nigeria, Rotimi Fani-Kayode moved to New York in 1980 to study at Pratt Institute. His photographs include conceptual and staged portraiture as well as travel and street photography. They explore interlocking themes of Black queer desire, erotic transcendence, and spiritual ecstasy—oftentimes drawing from the Ifá divination system of the Yoruba people. His own sense of dislocation and exile informs this inquiry into belonging. As Fani-Kayode noted, "On three counts I am an outsider: in matters of sexuality; in terms of geographical and cultural dislocation; and in the sense of not having become the sort of respectably married professional my parents might have hoped for. Such a position gives me the feeling of having very little to lose." Made in 1983 and 1989, the two photographs featured in *Greater New York* bookend his brief career, which was cut short by his death from complications from AIDS in 1989. A reckoning with mortality and alienation informs much of his work, mirroring the escalating HIV/AIDS epidemic.

Raque Ford
American, b. 1986

Raque Ford etches and inscribes new and salvaged plexiglass with text to create sculptural reliefs that merge industrial materials with intimate content. Ford is interested in the tension that arises from transforming the "personal touch of handwriting . . . into these clunky acrylic sheets." Creating a second skin on the gallery walls, Ford spatializes narratives compiled from her own remembrances and imagination, as well as found text including lyrics and fan letters. Her works broadcast diaristic content at an architectural scale historically deemed inappropriate for celebrations of feminine desire, grief, fabulation, and rumination. In *Hollywood Cemetery (I The Fool)* and *Friendship Cemetery (The Wise)* (both 2021), Ford reflects on two graveyards near her mother's hometown in Arkansas: Friendship Cemetery (where many of her family members are buried), and Hollywood Cemetery. Located across the street from one another, the odd proximity and juxtaposition of their names becomes a means of thinking through the intersection of grief, escapism, and humor.

Luis Frangella
Argentine, 1944–1990

Born in Buenos Aires, Argentina, Luis Frangella studied architecture before moving to the US in the mid-1970s to work as a research fellow at MIT. There, he developed a scientific investigation into vision that led him to begin his career as a painter. Frangella's initial approach to art was conceptual: through painting he examined questions of light, perspective, and color. In New York City, where he lived from 1976 until his death from AIDS-related illness in 1990, he became embedded in the East Village art scene and developed a more expansive and expressive painting style. Many of his works explore sensuality and death, attending to queer desire and revisiting the historical symbols of vanitas paintings. His paintings are often figurative, featuring statuesque heads and torsos. Frangella also painted murals throughout the city, including on construction site barriers, in abandoned piers, and in nightclubs such as the Pyramid Club, Mudd Club, and the Limbo Lounge. The large-scale painting *Dreamer* (1983) was featured in Frangella's 1983 exhibition at Hal Bromm Gallery, where it was installed atop a mural of headless torsos that covered the gallery's walls. These wall paintings echoed a series of murals Frangella began that same year inside Pier 34—a former shipping terminal on Manhattan's west side, near Canal Street—alongside artists David Wojnarowicz and Mike Bidlo. Inviting artists to make work inside the pier, they transformed its walls and floors into an ad hoc and shifting exhibition. In the wake of New York's deindustrialization, many artists and queer communities used abandoned industrial sites such as piers as unregulated spaces in which to congregate, create, and cruise. For his contribution, Frangella painted a procession of totemic heads and torsos, exemplifying his tendency to conflate classical motifs with nontraditional supports such as cardboard boxes, buildings, or abandoned, squatted sites.

Frangella was a close friend and mentor to Wojnarowicz, a central figure of the East Village scene, with whom Frangella shared his painting technique and whom he depicted in a 1984 painting on view in *Greater New York*. Frangella and Wojnarowicz traveled together to Buenos Aires carrying the work of some of their peers for the exhibition *From New York: 37 East Village Painters* at the Centro de Arte y Comunicación in 1984. The exhibition included their own work alongside that of Bidlo, Andreas Sterzing, Keiko Bonk, Judy Glantzman, Russell Sharon, Kiki Smith, and others.

Dolores Furtado
Argentine, b. 1977

Based in New York since 2013, Dolores Furtado investigates relations between the body, form, and history through a physical and spiritual process of direct engagement with matter. Her resin, ceramic, and paper pulp sculptures tend to deliberately expose traces of the artist's hand as marks of the intensity of the production process. *Dissolution* (2016–2021) is one of the most expansive installations Furtado has created. Made of paper pulp that has solidified like rock, the work references adobe structures and vernacular construction techniques. As with many sculptures by Furtado, *Dissolution* presents an entropic architectural form that conjures the residues of an uncertain, catastrophic event.

Julio Galán
Mexican, 1958–2006

In the 1980s and early 1990s, Julio Galán was among the most internationally recognized representatives of neo-Mexicanism, a movement of artists interested in reclaiming traditional features of Mexican culture, including Catholic imagery, a preoccupation with death and suffering, a strong surrealist tradition, and images typical of popular markets. Galán, who was born in Northern Mexico in 1958, was also obsessed with the representation of sexuality and pain, which manifested in his practice through a sustained exploration of self-portraiture. In his works, images of a queer Galán at various ages, performing different characteristic Mexican archetypes in hyper-dramatic and allegorical situations, are often accompanied by confessional texts depicting the artist as suffering, oppressed by homophobia and by the racial and class biases he experienced. Successful from a very early age, the young and eccentric Galán moved to New York in 1984. Here, he caught the attention of Andy Warhol, who reproduced some of his works in the pages of *Interview* magazine. Galán stayed intermittently in the city until his death in 2006.

Doreen Garner
American, b. 1986

Doreen Garner's visceral sculptures unearth historical traumas that echo into the present, focusing on the long history of medical racism in the United States. From the time of the transatlantic slave trade, Black people have been systematically denied medical care and forcibly subjected to dangerous procedures without anesthesia. Garner states, "The era that I reference in my work is a period where Black people were not only enslaved, but were also used as test subjects. There is racist theory that medical practitioners still use to this day that Black people can uniquely endure excruciating amounts of pain, which is completely false." In *Lucy's Agony* (2021) Garner reflects on the brutal gynecological operations undertaken by J. Marion Sims on unconsenting Black women in the mid-nineteenth century. Sims, known as the father of modern gynecology, kept a shack on his property with sixteen cots for the enslaved women on whom he performed procedures without anesthesia, as he recounts in his medical journals. Reminiscent of surgical stirrups, a bed, and a sex sling, Garner's sculpture references the cots upon which Sims cut apart women and stitched them back together, recalling the agency stripped from them as they were subjected to his medical torture and sexual fantasies.

Emilie Louise Gossiaux
American, b. 1989

Emilie Louise Gossiaux's work explores dreams, recollections, and multisensory experience. Since the loss of her vision in 2010, Gossiaux's practice has evolved to rely on her other senses; she often renders her subjects from memory or observes them through touch. Her guide dog, a yellow Labrador Retriever named London, appears frequently in her work. In both drawings and tactile sculptures of shaped clay, Gossiaux renders her dog's physical presence and interiority through hypersensitivity to texture, form, and affect. In the works on view in *Greater New York*, portraits of herself and London, Gossiaux merges human and canine bodily traits, such as giving herself a tail. The lines between the human and non-human are blurred, emphasizing an interconnectedness between these companion species.

Robin Graubard
American, b. 1951

Robin Graubard's artistic career spans forty years, encompassing multiple epochs and social worlds. Though deeply embedded in New York City, Graubard also documents her wanderings and travels, photographing the many people and places she has crossed paths with over the years. The artist first moved to New York in the early 1970s, after dropping out of school at age sixteen and hitchhiking around the country. Much of her work documents the lives of young punks on the Lower East Side, to whom she herself was connected for a time, and the street life of Times Square prior to its gentrification and into the present. In the 1980s, Graubard began tracking and documenting the mafia in New York City, and has worked off and on as a journalist for major newspapers and magazines in the US and abroad. Her photographs intermix the autobiographical, editorial, and documentary, distilling experience while complicating understandings of chronology and geography.

Milford Graves
American, 1941–2021

Born in Jamaica, Queens, Milford Graves was a pioneer of free jazz and a key figure of the Black Arts Movement. In addition to being a musician, Graves was an inventor, herbalist, and visual artist. He developed his own form of martial arts called Yara, which was partially inspired by studying the movements of mantis insects. His disparate practices often fed into one another, forming an integrated and holistic approach to sound and the body—a complete lifestyle dedicated to healing as a form of connection and protection. Graves developed extensive research on human heartbeats and music's medicinal potential, for which he received a Guggenheim Fellowship in 2000. As he once stated, "The objective of music is to train you to understand motion, oscillations. . . . The cosmos, everything we know, plants . . . everything is moving in all these different kinds of directions. . . . We've got so much cosmic energy going through us! And the drumming is supposed to be very related to the intake of this cosmic energy." His drawings explore correlations between breath, rhythm, vibration, the body, and the natural world. In 2018, Graves was diagnosed with amyloid cardiomyopathy and told he had only six months to live. He passed away in Queens in 2021, in the same home where he had lived and worked for nearly his entire life.

Bettina Grossman
American, 1927–2021

A lifelong New Yorker, Bettina Grossman lived and worked at the legendary Chelsea Hotel for the four decades prior to her passing in November 2021. Working in sculpture, photography, drawing, printmaking, and film, Grossman explored techniques of seriality and simplification, translating and iterating forms across media to hone perception. Her works are often abstract, yet they attend to the daily activities and rhythms of city life, upending documentary techniques by introducing or intensifying moments of distortion and surreality. After losing twenty years of artwork to a devastating fire in 1968, Grossman redoubled her artistic explorations. In *Phenomenology Project* (1979–1980), Grossman imaged the city via its warped reflection in storefront windows and glass-paneled skyscrapers; these photographs serve as both unreliable portals and distillations of lived experience.

Avijit Halder
American, b. 1988, India

Avijit Halder's photographs explore the fluidity and shifting legibility of identity; they also register a search for home in the wake of loss and displacement. The photographs in *Greater New York* evoke a symbiotic exchange between the artist and his friends as they wrap themselves in his late mother's saris, which Halder carried with him when he moved to the United States from Kolkata, India. The sari has become a leitmotif in the artist's recent photographs: tied to the memory of the violent death of his mother in a Kolkata brothel, the saris bear the weight of absence and erasure. Yet their literal veiling also forms a womb-like shelter, allowing for play with gender. By enveloping and permeating his body—as well as those of others—with these symbols of femininity and residues of motherhood, Halder discovered space for an exploration of his own nonbinary identity. The fabrics are, in the artist's words, "like brushstrokes of color," exuberant even as they record loss.

Bill Hayden
American, b. 1984

Working across drawing, photography, and sculpture, Bill Hayden reflects on the position of contemporary artists in New York as both purveyors of fantasy and precarious subjects within an extractive economy. In his painstakingly rendered drawings, he weaves city scenes into trippy tableaux populated with fairies, monsters, deli sandwiches, buckets, and, in *WEED* (2021) a stoned marijuana leaf exhaling smoke—a nod to the notion of consumption as self-depletion, and even a form of cannibalism. Ideas around artistic currency—energy, "buzz," image, and intoxication—are put into play as well as thrown into question.

G. Peter Jemison
Enrolled member of the Seneca Nation of Indians, Heron Clan, b. 1945

G. Peter Jemison is a Seneca artist, historian, and curator. His work explores autobiographical subjects alongside the history of Native American people and the injustices perpetrated against them by the United States government. Some of his drawings use paper bags as substrates, a material he first turned to while serving as curator of the American Indian Community House Gallery in New York, where he worked from 1978 to 1985. In doing so, he considered the material and cultural significance of Native American bags, and contemplated how bags of all types were a common denominator between himself and his fellow commuters from Brooklyn into Manhattan. Jemison has since continued to use paper bags in his practice, alongside painting, collage, embroidery, and film.

A number of works in *Greater New York* reference the Canandaigua Treaty of 1794, in which the nascent US government acknowledged the sovereignty of the Haudenosaunee—a confederacy of the Mohawk, Oneida, Onondaga, Cayuga, Seneca, and Tuscarora people, whose name means "our people built an extended house"—in what is now known as upstate New York. The treaty remains in place despite violations and subsequent treaties in 1797, 1838, and 1842 that significantly reduced Haudenosaunee territory. As part of the original treaty, the federal government set aside $4500 for the Haudenosaunee people each year, an amount that has never changed. With these funds, the US Army Corps of Engineers buys yardage of cloth to send to the Haudenosaunee, a tradition that continues, as evidenced in the cloth still given annually to Jemison's family and incorporated into works such as *Canandaigua Treaty 1794 Land Guaranteed* (2021). A form of historical preservation, Jemison's works combat the geographic and cultural erasure his people have faced. As he has stated, "What the army and the government could not accomplish, the church and educational institutions tried. The plan was to eradicate our language and cultural traditions." Jemison is currently the site manager at the Ganondagan State Historic Site in Victor, New York.

Steffani Jemison
American, b. 1981

Steffani Jemison's research-based practice draws on vernacular traditions such as miming, acrobatics, and vaudeville to investigate the embodied nature of language and knowledge. In the video *Similitude* (2019), an actor engages in the tradition of modernist mime. Performing in anonymous sites across New York, he mirrors the gestures of various subjects as they carry out their daily activities, imitating their values and demeanor while also producing moments of lag and play. Jemison is interested in the political implications of this slippage: while mimicry designates a leader and a follower, it is inherently imprecise, offering room for dissemblance and resistance within the performance of submission. The title of the work, *Similitude*, refers to the most concise form of parable in the Bible, which narrates a typical or recurring event to transmit belief through familiarity.

Jemison also presents a series of kinetic sculptures made of retrofitted rock tumblers, which transform rough materials such as stones, hardware, coins, and bits of glass into smooth objects, accelerating the entropic effects of time. The agitated movement of the tumblers renders some materials, like coins, unusable; others, like the stones, become polished and more conventionally desirable. The materials, both rough and tumbled, are displayed on a nearby pedestal.

E'wao Kagoshima
Japanese, b. 1945

E'wao Kagoshima moved from Japan to New York City in 1976, where he became part of the budding East Village art scene. Currently living in Queens, Kagoshima has spent the past decades producing works in an idiosyncratic style that combines a range of found and invented pop imagery in surrealist tableaux. Many of Kagoshima's works explore desire and estrangement; he creates a world of characters and geographies that borrow references from his physical environment to mine psychological depths. In the 1980s, Kagoshima became close to fellow artist Nicolas Moufarrege and was featured in a series of essays on art that Moufarrege wrote, titled "The Mutant International" (1983–1984). In one essay, Moufarrege remarks, "E'wao Kagoshima opens his world: spectral and fiendish portraitures with demon eyes. Wild and ghastly vivacity transforms blurred and indefinite colors. All assumes a startling and intense brilliancy. The lurid luster of a strange fire gleams, bearing witness against the everlasting and incorrigible barbarity of man; all is set alight and smoking like a terrible hymn composed in honor of fate and inescapable grief."

Marie Karlberg
Swedish, b. 1985

Marie Karlberg works across performance, installation, and video to elucidate the psychology and power dynamics that govern social conventions. Parodying the self-seriousness of the art world, Karlberg questions how one learns to play their role—and how to rewrite the script. *The Good Terrorist* (2021) is based on a 1985 novel of the same name by Doris Lessing. The book, set in 1980s Thatcher-era London, follows a young woman named Alice as she joins a group of radical leftists living together in a squatted apartment and negotiating how to practice collective politics. An update on Lessing's novel, Karlberg's film satirizes tropes of romantic bohemians and self-styled revolutionaries, exploring the friction between personal ego, ingrained prejudices, a desire for ideological purity, and necessary compromises. Karlberg filmed *The Good Terrorist* in a vacant luxury apartment on New York's Upper East Side while the city was under lockdown for the COVID-19 pandemic, casting fellow artists as her actors.

Matthew Langan-Peck
American, b. 1988

Matthew Langan-Peck creates sculptural versions of familiar objects to question the transmission of beliefs, meanings, and values. In a series of sculptures featured in *Greater New York*, the artist has dramatically enlarged eggs to gargantuan scale, transforming them into spaces for painting. Their interiors hidden, the eggs are simultaneously pure potential and all surface, devoid of fixed meaning and burdened with symbolism. Their painted shells invite a range of associations: birth, gender, cultural reproduction, religious tradition. One might think of something as luxurious as a Fabergé egg or as commonplace as the supermarket staple.

Las Nietas de Nonó
Afro-Carribean, est. 2011

mulowayi and mapenzi, afro-diasporic siblings who live in the barrio of San Antón in Carolina, Puerto Rico, make interdisciplinary works as Las Nietas de Nonó. In their formerly rural, currently industrializing working-class neighborhood, Las Nietas de Nonó draw on their lived experience to explore the reverberations of their ancestral past and examine histories of colonialism within the context of Puerto Rico. The multimedia work *FOODTOPIA: después de todo territorio* (2020) documents a project for which the artists subsisted entirely on wild food foraged from their neighborhood over a one-month period. Framing their own survival and nutrition as a performance, they highlight the threatened ecology in their neighborhood as well as the over-industrialization of food in the Caribbean. This project continues in a film of the same name, debuted as part of *Greater New York*, which takes as its setting the Blasina stream, a natural space threatened by development and water extraction located near their home. Both a film and a record of their durational performance, the work documents Las Nietas de Nonó walking through abandoned buildings and streams filled with debris, harvesting wild fruits, hunting an invasive species of iguana, and cooking a meal with their gathered food. These moments were captured during peak pandemic times, when supermarkets and other public spaces were considered sites of infection and danger. In their search for a "foodtopia," Las Nietas de Nonó reflect on the conditions of both utopia and dystopia inherent in life on an island-colony.

As part of their practice, Las Nietas de Nonó also cofounded Parceleras Afrocaribeñas, an organization run by Black women that advocates for environmental and racial justice in their neighborhood, and La Conde, a community project that seeks to recover the campus of the recently closed Carlos Conde Marín School and turn it into a community space. Based outside of New York, Las Nietas de Nonó intervene in the parameters of *Greater New York*, suggesting an understanding of belonging and place that foregrounds diasporic ties rather than colonial borders, and emphasizing the interconnectedness between artists in New York and Puerto Rico.

Athena LaTocha
American, Standing Rock Lakota, Keweenaw Bay Ojibwe, b. 1969

Athena LaTocha's monumental landscapes are inspired by memories of the wilderness of Alaska, where she was born and raised, as well as long drives to visit North Dakota and Michigan, where her family comes from. She creates representations and site-specific molds of the natural environment, engaging the history of landscape painting through abstraction. Working flat on the ground, LaTocha uses industrial materials like bricks and shredded tires—found discarded on the sides of highways—to manipulate pigments, debris, and elemental materials like lead and earth, and to mark the surface of her landscapes. In contrast to art-historical interventions upon the landscape, such as those of the Earthworks artists of the 1960s and '70s, LaTocha strives for an understanding of nature as inseparable and erupting from within human experience. "I look at how humans are shaping the earth," she has stated. "Human power versus nature's power. Both are incredible forces, but nature's always going to win." In *It Came From The North* (2021) LaTocha intermingles debris from contemporary construction sites in New York City with remnants of preindustrial geographies: lead sheets that bear the imprint of schist (a form of bedrock that sits below Manhattan and is visible in rare locations throughout the city) and dirt from Green-Wood Cemetery, one of the few places where soil predating the city's development can be found.

Carolyn Lazard
French, Haitian, and American, b. 1987

Based between New York and Philadelphia, Carolyn Lazard questions how ideas of sickness and health are determined and accounted for—or not—within contemporary society. Lazard's work examines the body in relation to the institutions, architectures, and media that structure experience and our access to it. Challenging ingrained assumptions of what productivity looks like, Lazard's work privileges slowness, dependency, and the manifold rhythms of the body. In *Red* (2021), Lazard repeatedly taps and brushes their thumb over the lens of an iPhone camera to create an abstract video in the tradition of avant-garde "flicker films." Flicker films use pulsating light and sound to create visceral, nonnarrative films with stroboscopic effects that can provoke hallucinations in the viewer. Flicker films can also cause seizures in people with photosensitivity, such as those with epilepsy. Lazard has turned their video into a two-channel installation, in which a flatscreen alerts viewers to whether the projected strobe is currently in effect. This juxtaposition builds sensitivity to the ways bodies react to stimuli into the very layout of the installation, transforming the access notice from an incidental accompaniment to a structural aspect of the work itself.

Sean-Kierre Lyons
American, b. 1991

Sean-Kierre Lyons's practice reimagines collective memory with sardonic whimsy. Mining the tropes of American history as well as those of the present, Lyons's works open portals to an alternate universe: a fantastic planet called the *Black Flower Forest*. In this ever-evolving universe, a cast of anthropomorphic characters seek to shape consciousness through radical worldbuilding. Lyons depicts these psychedelic figures as intricately embellished natural beings, such as flowers and insects; benevolent keepers of the forest, they form a community rooted in resilience, reciprocity, and joy. As Lyons has stated of their historical precedents, specifically minstrel figures, "These characters were made without our permission." In resurrecting them from the dustbin of history in reimagined form, Lyons finds a way to honor them, "giving these entities a way to exist where they can live their lives out."

Hiram Maristany
Puerto Rican–American, b. 1945

Born in East Harlem (El Barrio), Hiram Maristany is a photographer who served as the official documentarian for the New York chapter of the Young Lords Party. Arising from the Civil Rights and Black Power movements of the 1960s, the Young Lords was founded in 1968 by Puerto Rican youth demanding civil rights and self-determination for their communities and all colonized people. Though ideologically internationalist, they directed the bulk of their efforts toward addressing local concerns: they organized social services such as dental clinics, daycare, and free lunch for their immediate community, filling a void in segregated government services. In one of their most legendary actions, known as the Garbage Offensive of 1969, the Young Lords gathered garbage that wasn't being collected, dumped it at a major intersection, and set it aflame in protest of the sanitation crisis in East Harlem. Maristany's photographs in *Greater New York* document the Garbage Offensive as well as other key episodes in the Party's history, such as their occupation of the First Spanish United Methodist Church in East Harlem—which they renamed "The People's Church" and transformed into a community center and headquarters—and the funeral of Young Lords activist Julio Roldan, who died in custody at the infamous "Tombs" jail complex in Lower Manhattan. Maristany's photographs also capture moments of everyday beauty and solidarity in the life of his neighborhood. Maristany has stated, "Truly, my work is a reflection of a love affair that I've had with my community. One day hopefully I will give some inspiration to some young people or an evolving artist to know their community, to preserve their community, and not allow someone else to do it for them. We have to take responsibility and title to our own history."

Servane Mary
French, b. 1972

Servane Mary is known for conceptual work in which she prints historical images of women on unconventional materials such as glass or silk. *Stay in the middle two lanes* (2020–2021), however, marks the artist's recent return to painting. Although highly abstract, the painting shares with her previous work an interest in reproducibility and technical processes. Reduced to cyan, magenta, and yellow—the primary colors of CMYK printing—on a silver background, the painting highlights Mary's interest in ceding control rather than producing expressive or intentional brushstrokes. To make the work, Mary pours paint from behind large surfaces made of pegboard sheets that have been sprayed with silver paint, allowing for uncertain results. The artist reflects, "I think these new paintings relate to my previous work through the belief that mistakes and suggestive gestures can be a way to re-assert feminism as a critique of power. I like this post-feminist perspective that a painting can be good and bad at the same time."

Rosemary Mayer
American, 1943–2014

Born and raised in Ridgewood, Queens, Rosemary Mayer worked for decades in New York City, making drawings, objects, and ephemeral outdoor sculptures she termed "temporary monuments." A founding member of A.I.R. Gallery—a collectively run art space that has championed the work of women artists since 1972—Mayer combined feminist concerns with a post-minimalist interest in transient materials and the passing of time. The charting of time, from mundane moments to birthdays and memorials, was central to her practice. In a series of drawings from the summer of 2001, she annotates the cacophony of urban noises—from coughing to clanging—she heard throughout her days in Lower Manhattan. The drawings document a city under construction and development—a growth that has created inhospitable conditions for many communities. In 1969, thirty years prior, she created a similar piece: a visual recording of the firecrackers she heard between 9:00 p.m. and 1:30 a.m. on July 4, 1969, which was published in the avant-garde poetry journal *0-9* and records a very different moment in the city's life.

Alan Michelson
Mohawk, b. 1953

In his multimedia artworks, Alan Michelson uncovers the Indigenous pasts and colonial legacies of geographical sites in New York and elsewhere, examining the intersection of urban and natural realms. In a newly commissioned installation, titled *Midden* (2021), Michelson pays homage to Lenapehoking, the ancestral Lenape homelands that include present-day New York City, and to its bounty of oysters, which fed generations of Lenape and New Yorkers until pollution made them unsafe to eat and decimated the oyster population. Four hundred years ago, when the Dutch first arrived here, monumental shell mounds—or middens—dotted the landscape, some dating as far back as 6950 BCE. These middens testified to not only the natural abundance of the waters but the Indigenous presence and stewardship of the land from time immemorial. Michelson shot the video component of *Midden*, which is projected atop oyster shells, along Newtown Creek and the Gowanus Canal—key waterways where middens were once located but have disappeared as a result of shoreline development and extraction. In revealing their absence, Michelson underscores how an ecosystem nurtured for millennia by Indigenous people was ravaged by mere centuries of colonization, urban development, and environmental destruction. The work also incorporates an audio recording of the Gane' whae' (Delaware Skin Dance), a dance entrusted to the artist's Haudenosaunee (Iroquois) ancestors by the Lenape (Delaware) during a period of great colonial upheaval, honoring their historical connection.

Michelson collaborated with the Billion Oyster Project to source the oyster shells included in the installation. The nonprofit organization aims to restore one billion live oysters to New York Harbor by 2035 by collecting empty shells from local restaurants, reseeding them, and strategically releasing them back into the harbor, where they restore ecological diversity, prevent erosion, and mitigate the effects of climate change. Following the exhibition, the shells will be returned to Billion Oyster Project and used to repopulate the harbor. More than a memorial to the cultural and ecological practices destroyed by colonization, *Midden,* in hopeful homage, reaffirms the survivance of the land and its Indigenous people.

Ahmed Morsi
Egyptian, b. 1930

A critic, poet, and artist, Ahmed Morsi's painting and poetry are affiliated with the Alexandria School, a group of artists who came of age in 1940s Alexandria, Egypt, and had ties to Surrealism. Morsi subsequently lived in Baghdad, Iraq, from 1955 to 1957 and became part of its thriving art scene as a critic; returning to Egypt in 1957, Morsi expanded his practice into costume and set design, and cofounded the avant-garde magazine *Galerie '68*. In 1974, Morsi moved with his family to New York City, where he has continued to play an important role in the development of Arabic art criticism, reporting on cultural developments in New York and the United States more broadly for major Egyptian, Lebanese, and Kuwaiti publications such as *Al Watan* and *Al Hayat*. Morsi's paintings, drawings, and prints combine human and animal figures—primarily horses—with masklike faces in a myriad of unlikely settings and situations. Many of his works evoke estrangement and isolation—themes informed by his own experience as an immigrant.

Nicolas Moufarrege
Lebanese, 1947–1985

Nicolas Moufarrege was a critic, curator, and artist born in Alexandria, Egypt and raised in Beirut, Lebanon. In 1981, he moved to New York City from Paris, France, where he had relocated at the onset of the Lebanese Civil War. Moufarrege settled on St. Marks Place and became part of a close-knit group of East Village artists that included Keith Haring, Martin Wong, Peter Hujar, and E'wao Kagoshima. Moufarrege's work as a critic also helped support the emerging Lower East Side scene, bringing early attention to artists Jean-Michel Basquiat, Fab 5 Freddy, and David Wojnarowicz, and galleries Gracie Mansion, Civilian Warfare, FUN Gallery, and Nature Morte. As an artist, Moufarrege developed a distinct technique of embroidering paintings that mixed references to classicism, Pop art, Islamic tilework, Arabic calligraphy, and comic book illustration. From 1982 to 1984, Moufarrege was an artist in residence at PS1 through the International Studio Program. He had been eagerly anticipating his solo exhibition at FUN Gallery in 1985, but was too ill to attend the opening and passed away of AIDS-related complications shortly thereafter.

Marilyn Nance
American, b. 1953

Marilyn Nance's photographs show moments of irony, protest, revelry, and absurdity in New York City in the 1970s and '80s. The photographs featured in *Greater New York* depict scenes ranging from George Edward Tait (a polymath poet, activist, and musician) playing the horn on a Harlem stoop, to Chinese New Year festivities, elephants crossing a Midtown street, and a standoff between police and demonstrators during a Martin Luther King Jr. Day march. Over decades working as a photographer, Nance has documented the beauty and quirkiness of New York City celebrations and the intensity of the city's struggles—many of which remain ongoing. In 1977, Nance travelled to Lagos, Nigeria, to serve as the official photographer of the North American contingent to FESTAC '77, the Second World Black and African Festival of Arts and Culture. Her photographs, letters, artifacts, and memorabilia from the event have been crucial in bringing wider awareness to the historic festival.

Tammy Nguyen
Vietnamese-American, b. 1984

Tammy Nguyen investigates the intersection of geopolitics, ecology, and myth in paintings and artist books. Her works are dense with foliage and characters built up from ornate patterning that is both seductive and sinister. Drawing from a range of sources that are traditional as well as contemporary, Nguyen brings ancestral thinking to bear on present day understandings of ecological destruction. Often looking specifically at the effects of contemporary globalization and capitalist development on Southeast Asia, where her family is from, her works suggest the interconnected fates of humanity and the environment in the age of existential climate disaster.

Shelley Niro
Bay of Quinte Mohawk, Member of the Six
Nations Reserve Turtle Clan, b. 1954

Shelley Niro was born in Niagara Falls, New York, and raised on the Six Nations of the Grand River reserve near Brantford, Ontario, Canada, where she still lives and works. Her practice encompasses photography, painting, beadwork, film, and new media, exploring the history and self-determination of First Nations people and using humor to counter stereotypes of how Native people—and women in particular—should look or act. Niro also brings focus to the centrality of land within human histories. In *Resting Place of Our Ancestors* (2019) she photographs fossils of ancient life forms encrusted in rock faces near Lake Erie, drawing a continuum between human mortality and the deep time of the earth's lifespan. She has stated of these works, "I'm not a paleontologist but I am curious about life that existed before and during the era of the big bang. I've become attached to the narrative of these small creatures as they went about their daily tranquil lives and suddenly they are now the centrefolds for explaining my own existence as I slither along the edges of this century. These imprints of long-gone life unite us all as evidence of where we come from."

Kayode Ojo
American, b. 1990

Kayode Ojo's sculptural assemblages explore the intersection of artifice, identity, desire, and commodity culture. Combining chrome and mirrored surfaces with seemingly high-end brand names, Ojo's works suggest luxury and the high-gloss, flashy aesthetics of the 1980s. In fact, the artist constructs his sculptures from cheap readymade items he buys online, tapping into an economy of knockoffs, fast fashion, and aspirational lifestyle products. Ojo's works raise questions around class anxiety and the fetishization of, or erotic investment in, objects. They draw out a tension between the violent history of ownership and the intoxicating pleasures of consumption.

Paulina Peavy
American, 1901–1999

Paulina Peavy had a life-changing encounter with a spirit who identified as a genderless UFO voyager named Lacamo while attending a séance in Santa Ana, California, in 1932. From that moment forward, Peavy's artistic expression began to focus on promoting Lacamo's teachings, among them a radical theory that humankind would evolve into an androgynous species. From 1923 to 1943, Peavy lived and worked in California, where she played an important role in its emerging abstract art scene of the 1920s, becoming closely affiliated with the first group of California Surrealists in the 1930s. After creating a series of paintings for the *Golden Gate International Exposition*, Peavy relocated to New York City, where she lived and worked until the age of ninety-seven. It was in New York, guided by Lacamo, where Peavy began to add incremental layers to her paintings, which she saw as progressively preparing the viewer to receive extraterrestrial wisdom. While working in her studio, Peavy would wear elaborate mixed-media masks of her own design to channel Lacamo's spirit.

Freya Powell
English-American, b. 1983

Freya Powell's *Only Remains Remain* (performed at MoMA PS1 October 22–23, 2021) uses the structure of a Sophoclean chorus to create an elegy for the hundreds of unidentified migrants buried in mass graves in Sacred Heart Cemetery in Brooks County, Texas. Working with an ensemble of fifteen performers, Powell explores the mournful potential of the voice. Through a collaborative process, the work utilizes pitch, intonation, breath, movement, and silence to embody a contemporary tragedy drawn from the story of Antigone. The chorus of women seeks to recognize the lives of those laid to rest as unknowns by addressing the silence of their burial and our complicity and grief in the process.

Raha Raissnia
Iranian, b. 1968

Raha Raissnia gained early exposure to analog technologies through her father's amateur photography of demonstrations during the Iranian Revolution (1978–1979). In one of her early professional experiences in New York City, she worked at Anthology Film Archives, where she became steeped in the cinematic avant-garde. In *Aviary* (2018/2021), Raissnia projects a 16-milimeter film featuring slides of a fourteenth-century mosque in India onto a double-screen box, which also functions as a painting. She re-photographed, cropped, spliced, and painted over the found footage, which had been discarded by Brooklyn College's visual resource archive, layering and distorting its images to the point of abstraction. The box intercepts the film projection to produce the illusion of depth and added texture, echoing Raissnia's archaeological process of excavating the discarded filmic fragments of architectural history.

Andy Robert
Haitian-American, b. 1984

Drawing from direct observation, source photographs, and memory, Andy Robert balances abstraction with recognizable imagery—and presence with absence—in his large-scale gestural paintings. In *Harlem Sings the Blues* (2017), Robert depicts a street performer in Harlem, rendered amid shimmering layers of blue paint that conjure the quality of nocturnal light just before daybreak. The painting also nods to the jazz and blues of the Harlem Renaissance. *Check II Check* (2017) captures the neighborhood's check-cashing businesses, which are emblematic of the cycles of economic disenfranchisement and networks of international remittances within which many Black communities are enmeshed. As the artist has explained, "I am critically reflecting on a mass inequality of wealth and power, on economic debt as linked invariably to a 'maroonage,' a marginalization, and autonomy—a making due, a brokenness of being." In *Mid Atlantic* (2020), Robert focuses on landscape as a site of historical violence; as with many of his works, this take on the sublime is also charged with trauma.

Diane Severin Nguyen
Vietnamese-American, b. 1990

Diane Severin Nguyen's photographs begin as intricate, ephemeral sculptural arrangements that the artist improvises from found materials, both natural and synthetic. Operating outside of a typical studio setting, Nguyen shoots these small-scale assemblages up close under artificial light sources like LEDs or the flash of an iPhone camera. The resulting images amplify and distort her material experiments, recasting them as decaying organisms and glistening interiors that seem to shift shape and scale, refusing to cohere. For *Greater New York*, the artist has cut a number of slits into the gallery walls opposite her photographs, partially uncovering the windows hidden below and allowing ribbons of natural light to punctuate the space in conversation with her images.

Shanzhai Lyric
Founded 2015

Shanzhai Lyric investigates global trade networks, informal economies, and the poetics of counterfeit goods. 山寨, or *shanzhai*, means "counterfeit" in contemporary Chinese usage but translates literally to "mountain hamlet," a reference to a tale of outlaws absconding with goods from the empire to redistribute among those on the margins. The group takes inspiration from *shanzhai* T-shirts that are produced in China but circulate globally, oftentimes emblazoned with experimental English phrases and designs expressing a radical disregard for the norms of branding. Shanzhai Lyric notes: "There is delightful humour in the unexpected collisions of meaning, but what really resonates with us about these garments is how deeply we can be moved by apparent nonsense, how it actually seems to describe with poetic precision the experience of living in an utterly nonsensical world. With devoted irreverence, shanzhai poems highlight the arbitrary line between real and fake—designed to exploit and criminalize the many for the gain of the few." An installation in the museum's lobby presents a new iteration of *Incomplete Poem* (2015–ongoing), a shifting archive of *shanzhai* T-shirts sourced over the years in cities from Hong Kong to New York. The artists consider these accumulated shirts to be one long poem moving across bodies and landscapes. Purpose-built reading apparatuses, designed with architectural collective common room, reference structures where text and textile trouble the border between public and private space: laundry lines, newspaper racks, billboards, trash heaps. They draw upon the wall as a structure that demarcates property while also serving as a locus of collective inscription, commentary, protest, and critique.

In the fall of 2020, Shanzhai Lyric founded Canal Street Research Association in an empty storefront on Canal Street, New York City's counterfeit epicenter, to delve into the cultural and material ecologies of the street and its long history as a site that probes the limits of ownership and authorship. Canal Street was once an actual canal, which was polluted by industrial dumping and sewage and then filled in to cover the stench; it became a thoroughfare in the nineteenth century. The street has had many lives as a conduit of excess and overflow: supply hub, landing place for waves of immigrants, site of factories-turned-artist-lofts, and, today, a locus of unofficial street markets and dwindling economies in garment production and NYC souvenirs. Through ongoing collaborations with local vendors, artisans, and community members, and various restagings (or "bootlegs") of ephemeral moments on the storied block, Canal Street Research Association celebrates Canal Street as yet another "hamlet" where semilegal gatherings at the edge of town allow for the redistribution of resources and a reimagined relationship to property. Canal Street Research Association left its temporary center of operations on Canal Street in early 2021, a casualty of ongoing cycles of development that use artists in beautification efforts only to displace them with higher paying tenants. For *Greater New York*, the artists stored the office and its contents in a gallery at MoMA PS1. For the duration of the show, objects cycling between the storage unit and Canal Street form the basis of a series of associative meanders—from the springs under Canal Street to the inlets of Long Island City—that surface buried flows of goods and ideas, currents and currencies.

For *Greater New York*, Shanzhai Lyric also collaborated with the cafe Mina's and coffee proprietor Birane Seck of Jeef Jeel to offer Café Touba to visitors to PS1. Café Touba is a spiced coffee drink often shared among West African vendors on Canal Street. Sufi spiritual leader Sheikh Ahmadou Bamba, who led peaceful resistance against French colonization in Senegal, is said to have invented Café Touba and brought it to Senegal upon his return from exile. Thus the drink, which combines coffee beans with *djar*, or Selim pepper, is imbued with both religious and political import—a spiritual and anti-colonial beverage to sip with intention. In Wolof, the word *touba* means "bliss."

Research notes can be found at:
shanzhailyric.info/money-has-no-smell.

Regina Vater
Brazilian, b. 1943

Born in Rio de Janeiro, Brazil, Regina Vater lived intermittently in New York City during the 1970s and '80s. There, she began to make conceptual art, films, and performances exploring the intersection of urban ecologies, nature, ritual traditions, and diasporic experience. In *LuxoLixo* (1973/1974), which means "luxury garbage" in Portuguese, Vater intersperses photographs of trash on New York City streets—in both wealthy and low-income neighborhoods—with images of storefronts and people shopping. First shown in the 1976 Venice Biennale, the film connects themes of waste and excess to a culture of consumerism. The soundtrack, made collaboratively with Brazilian artist Hélio Oiticica (who she met while living in New York) combines recordings of commercials, advertising jingles, and Oiticica reading a poem written by Vater. Vater's films serve as archaeologies of her present, framing urban life and refuse as key to understanding issues of economic and environmental precarity. *Saudades do Brazil* (1984) juxtaposes footage of New York City and Brazil, highlighting their connections and disparities. The footage is accompanied by a recording of Vater on the phone with American artist Suzan Frecon. Through discussion of filmmakers such as Glauber Rocha and Dziga Vertov, Vater weighs the cultural and aesthetic differences between the two locales, noting a Brazilian "aesthetics of precariousness," whereby art and life intermingle in public space under conditions of economic precarity. The conversation also highlights the ways in which cultural references were being circulated between the countries in a newly globalized world.

Stanley Wolukau-Wanambwa
British and Ugandan, b. 1980

Stanley Wolukau-Wanambwa's artistic practice engages the contemporaneity of history, exploring the relationship between visual conventions and constructions of racial and gendered difference. Intermingling his own photographs with archival images, Wolukau-Wanambwa considers histories of violence. For his installation in *Greater New York*, he brings together a mix of photographic and sculptural elements to examine racialized hierarchies of value and meaning. The actress Anna May Wong (the first Asian-American movie star) pivots across two halves of a diptych; an anonymous man recurs across multiple exposures; an ashtray becomes a mask. Doublings and replications abound in antagonistic relation to photographic realism. As the artist states, "Images make matter, matter becomes image, imaged lives matter and disappear."

Lachell Workman
American, b. 1989

Lachell Workman's collaborative, research-based practice is rooted in social justice movements of the last decade as well as histories of African American migration and settlement. Her works reflect an interest in Black urban space—stoops, sidewalks, and natural environments—as it relates to practices of mourning and memorialization. Employing materials such as asphalt and cotton T-shirts, Workman uses abstraction to explore the vernacular forms and spaces that grief can take. Her installations sharply critique the insistent violence visited upon Black people in the United States—by both police and the American public. She writes, "I am particularly interested in the formal and aesthetic language of the street-side memorial and the cultural coding of the 'R.I.P. T-shirt.' This work shows up in my practice as a series of questions: what constitutes a memorial, a public monument, and who, specifically, are the people and events that matter enough to be publicly memorialized?"

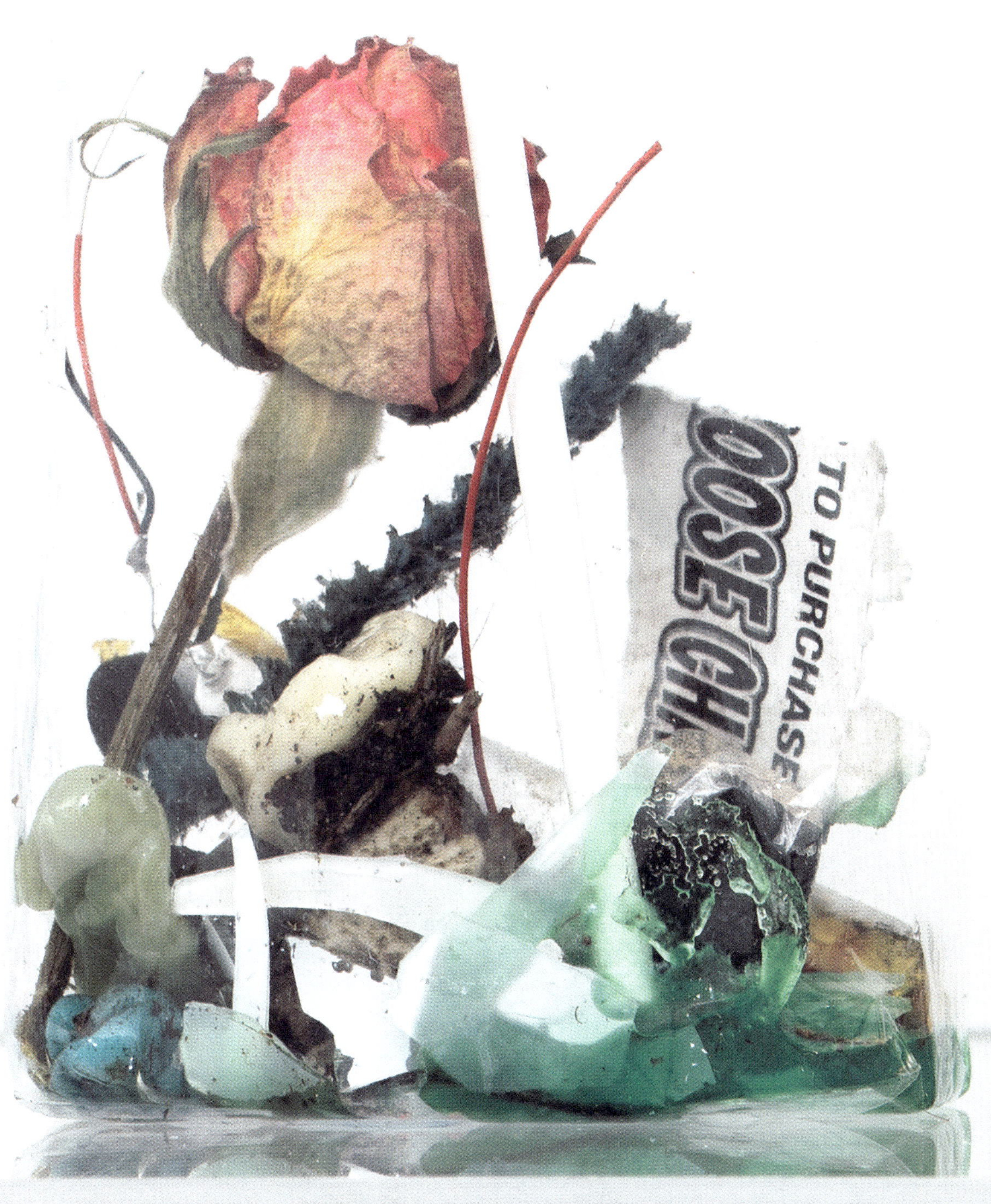
TO PURCHASE

Yuji Agematsu
American, b. 1956, Japan

zip: 01.01.20 ... 12.31.20, 2020
Mixed media in cigarette pack cellophane wrappers (366 units) on wood backed acrylic shelves, latex paint (12 units)
Wrappers, each approx.: 2 ½ x 2 ⅛ x 1" (6.3 x 5.3 x 2.5 cm); 10 shelving units, each: 26 ½ x 34 ¼ x 5 ¼" (67.3 x 87 x 13.3 cm); 2 shelving units, each: 31 ¾ x 34 ¼ x 5 ¼" (80.6 x 87 x 13.3 cm); overall dimensions variable
Collection Lonti Ebers, New York

Notebooks for zip: 01.01.20 . . . 12.31.20, 2020
Twelve notebooks
5 × 3" (12.7 × 7.6 cm) each; overall dimensions variable
Courtesy the artist and Miguel Abreu Gallery, New York

Nadia Ayari
Tunisian and American, b. 1981

Kiss I, 2021
Fresco on cast glass
19 × 8 ½ × 8 ½" (48.3 × 21.6 × 21.6 cm)
Courtesy the artist and Taymour Grahne Projects

Kiss II, 2021
Fresco on cast glass
19 × 8 ½ × 8 ½" (48.3 × 21.6 × 21.6 cm)
Courtesy the artist and Taymour Grahne Projects

Loop I, 2020
Oil on linen
35 × 35" (88.9 × 88.9 cm)
Courtesy the artist and Taymour Grahne Projects

Loop II, 2019
Oil on linen
35 × 35" (88.9 × 88.9 cm)
Courtesy the artist and Taymour Grahne Projects

Jetty I, 2020
Oil on linen
60 × 60" (152.4 × 152.4 cm)
Courtesy Fundación MEDIANOCHE0

Orbs I, 2021
Oil on linen
60 × 60" (152.4 × 152.4 cm)
Courtesy the artist and Taymour Grahne Projects

Orbs II, 2021
Oil on linen
60 × 60" (152.4 × 152.4 cm)
Courtesy the artist and Taymour Grahne Projects

BlackMass Publishing
Est. 2018

Study Hall, 2021
Mixed media installation
Dimensions variable
Courtesy the artists

Diane Burns
Chemehuevi and Anishinabe, 1957–2006

Poetry Spots: Diane Burns reads "Alphabet City Serenade," 1989
Video (color, sound)
1 min., 59 sec.
Courtesy Bob Holman
www.poetryspots.com

Riding the One-Eyed Ford, 1981
Chapbook with poems and illustrations by Diane Burns
Courtesy Bob Holman
www.poetryspots.com

"Sure You Can Ask Me A Personal Question," 1983
Poem
Courtesy Bob Holman
www.poetryspots.com

Diane Burns archival materials:

Diane Burns and Pedro Pietri, 1986
Photograph by Joy Harjo
5 × 7" (12.7 × 17.8 cm)
Courtesy Hale Schulman Archives

Allen Ginsberg and Poets in Nicaragua, 1986
Photograph by Ilka Hartmann
5 × 7" (12.7 × 17.8 cm)
Courtesy Hale Schulman Archives

Bob Holman and Diane Burns, 1986
Photograph by Patrick Warner
5 × 7" (12.7 × 17.8 cm)
Courtesy Hale Schulman Archives

Carlos Reyes, Ernesto Cardenal, Pedro Pietri, Allen Ginsberg, Diane Burns, 1986
Photograph by Patrick Warner
5 × 7" (12.7 × 17.8 cm)
Courtesy Hale Schulman Archives

Diane Burns, Pedro Pietri, Carlos Reyes, 1986
Photograph by Patrick Warner
5 × 7" (12.7 × 17.8 cm)
Courtesy Hale Schulman Archives

Kristi Cavataro
American, b. 1992

Untitled, 2019
Stained glass
21 × 24 × 9" (53.3 × 61 × 22.9 cm)
Courtesy the artist and Ramiken, New York

Untitled, 2019
Stained glass
17 × 57 × 16" (43.2 × 144.8 × 40.6 cm)
Courtesy the artist and Ramiken, New York

Untitled, 2021
Stained glass
35 × 21 ½ × 20" (88.9 × 54.6 × 50.8 cm)
Courtesy the artist and Ramiken, New York

Untitled, 2021
Stained glass
Interlocked: 24 × 23 ½ × 23 ½" (61 × 59.7 × 59.7 cm)
Each: 23 ½ × 16 ½ × 16" (59.7 × 41.9 × 40.6 cm)
Courtesy the artist and Ramiken, New York

Untitled, 2021
Stained glass
40 × 23 × 14 ½" (101.6 × 58.4 × 36.8 cm)
Courtesy the artist and Ramiken, New York

Curtis Cuffie
American, 1955–2002

Red Dress, 1996
Dress, recycled painting on canvas, fabric, tulle, ribbon, and peacock feather assemblage on metal stand
90 × 29 × 15" (228.6 × 73.7 × 38.1 cm)
Courtesy Carol Ann Thompson

Every House Deserves A Happy Home, Every Home Deserves A Happy Family, 1996
Doll house, various fabrics, basketry, and metal frame assemblage
60 × 23 × 23" (152.4 × 58.4 × 58.4 cm)
Courtesy Carol Ann Thompson

Untitled, c. 1995
Metal, muffler, tailpipe, fabric, iron, fake fur, African passport mask, metal stand, beads, and rubber eyeball
80 × 24 × 24" (203.2 × 61 × 61 cm)
Courtesy Aarne and Tina Anton

Drive Safe / Hoot Owl, 1994
Auto dashboard gauges, lamp base, and fabrics
63 × 20 × 19" (160 × 50.8 × 48.3 cm)
Courtesy Aarne and Tina Anton

Extremely Urgent, 1994
Metal display rack, negligee, express mail

envelope, and plastic hanger
31 × 17 × 11″ (78.7 × 43.2 × 27.9 cm)
Courtesy Aarne and Tina Anton

Untitled, 1994
Metal, plastic mask, and broom bottom
19 ½ × 12 × 6 ½″ (49.5 × 30.5 × 16.5 cm)
Courtesy Aarne and Tina Anton

Curtis Cuffie archival materials:

Sculptures by Curtis Cuffie on the streets of New York City, near Astor Place, c. 1990s
Photographs by Katy Abel
Courtesy Aarne and Tina Anton

Curtis Cuffie installing work in the exhibition Assemblage: Reordering Chaos at American Primitive Gallery, 1995
Photograph by Tina Anton
Courtesy Aarne and Tina Anton

Hadi Fallahpisheh
Iranian, b. 1987

Young and Clueless, 2021
Light drawing on photosensitive paper, ceramic, stuffed animals, wood and paint
144 × 84″ (365.8 × 213.4 cm)
Courtesy the artist and Andrew Kreps Gallery, New York

Rotimi Fani-Kayode
British and Nigerian, 1955–1989

Maternal Milk, 1983
Gelatin silver print
30 × 30″ (76.2 × 76.2 cm)
Courtesy The Walther Collection

Half Opened Eyes Twins, 1989
Gelatin silver print
24 × 24″ (61 × 61 cm)
Courtesy The Walther Collection

Raque Ford
American, b. 1986

Friendship Cemetery (The Wise), 2021
Acrylic
53 ¼ × 110 × ⅜″ (135.3 × 279.4 × 1 cm)
Courtesy the artist and Greene Naftali, New York

Hollywood Cemetery (I The Fool), 2021
Acrylic
53 ¼ × 110 × ⅜″ (135.3 × 279.4 × 1 cm)
Courtesy the artist and Greene Naftali, New York

Luis Frangella
Argentine, 1944–1990

David Wojnarowicz, 1984
Acrylic on cardboard and wood
25 3⁄16 × 18 11⁄16 × 9 ⅛″ (64 × 47.5 × 23 cm)
Collection Mr. Michael Ettner; courtesy Cosmocosa, Buenos Aires

Untitled (Torso y Lira), 1985
Acrylic on plastic vinyl canvas
110 3⁄16 × 56 5⁄16″ (279.9 × 143 cm)
Collection Alec Oxenford; courtesy Cosmocosa, Buenos Aires

Dreamer, 1983
Oil on canvas
108 × 136″ (274.3 × 345.4 cm)
Courtesy Hal Bromm Gallery / Tribeca

Luis Frangella archival materials:

Luis Frangella Paints, 1984
Photographic contact sheet
Photographs by Eric Kroll
15 ⅗ × 15 7⁄10″ (39.5 x 40 cm)
Collection Mr. Ferdinand Porak; courtesy Cosmocosa, Buenos Aires

David Wojnarowicz and Mike Bidlo at Pier 34 (with painting by Luis Frangella), 1983
Photograph by Andreas Sterzing
15 ¾ × 23 ⅝″ (40 × 60 cm)
Courtesy the artist and PPOW, New York

Pier 34, Luis Frangella, 1983
Photograph by Andreas Sterzing
15 7⁄10 × 23 ⅗″ (40 × 60 cm)
Courtesy Cosmocosa, Buenos Aires

Canal Street Piers: Man Painting Figure Studies, 1983
Gelatin silver print
Photograph by Peter Hujar
14 × 11″ (35.6 × 28 cm)
Courtesy the Peter Hujar Archive, LLC

Dolores Furtado
Argentine, b. 1977

Dissolution, 2016–2021
Paper pulp
Dimensions variable
Courtesy the artist

Julio Galán
Mexican, 1958–2006

Untitled, 1982
Oil on canvas and ex-voto
39 × 32″ (99.1 × 81.3 cm)
Courtesy the Helios Trust, UK

Te Mentí (Sofía), 1986
Oil and collage on canvas
27 × 36″ (68.6 × 91.4 cm)
Collection Francesco Pellizzi, New York

El Que Se Viene Se Va, 1988
Oil on canvas
68 × 90″ (172.7 × 228.6 cm)
Courtesy the Helios Trust, UK

Doreen Garner
American, b. 1986

Lucy's Agony, 2021
Mattress swing, metal poles with spikes, crossbars and light fixture
Dimensions variable
Courtesy the artist and JTT, New York

Emilie Louise Gossiaux
American, b. 1989

Dog Girl, they called me, 2021
Earthenware ceramic
15 × 6 × 3″ (38.1 × 15.2 × 7.6 cm)
Courtesy the artist

London, in my dreams, 2020
Ballpoint pen on paper
9 13⁄16 × 7 ⅜″ (24.9 × 18.7 cm)
Courtesy the artist

London stands up on her hind legs, 2020
Ballpoint pen on paper
9 13⁄16 × 7 ⅜″ (24.9 × 18.7 cm)
Courtesy the artist

True Love Will Find You in the End, 2021
Ballpoint pen on paper
23 × 17″ (58.4 × 43.2 cm)
Courtesy the artist

Robin Graubard
American, b. 1951

Peripheral Vision, 1979–2021
Selection of photographs
Dimensions variable
Courtesy the artist and Office Baroque, Antwerp

Milford Graves
American, 1941–2021

Calmness / Relax, 2020
Drawing
24 × 18″ (61 × 45.7 cm)
Courtesy the Estate of Milford Graves

Crossroads, 2020
Drawing
24 × 18″ (61 × 45.7 cm)
Courtesy the Estate of Milford Graves

TIR + CIR, BRe Cood, 2020
Drawing
24 × 18″ (61 × 45.7 cm)
Courtesy the Estate of Milford Graves

Tsunami, 2020
Drawing
24 × 18″ (61 × 45.7 cm)
Courtesy the Estate of Milford Graves

Untitled 6, 2020
Acrylic on vinyl sleeve
12 ½ × 13 ½″ (31.8 × 34.3 cm)
Courtesy the Estate of Milford Graves and Fridman Gallery, New York

Untitled 9, 2020
Acrylic on vinyl sleeve
12 ½ × 13 ½″ (31.8 × 34.3 cm)
Courtesy the Estate of Milford Graves and Fridman Gallery, New York

Bettina Grossman
American, 1927–2021

options for an angle, 24 inconstants from one constant, 1971
Marble
4 × 1 ½″ (10.2 × 3.8 cm) each; overall dimensions variable
Courtesy the Estate of Bettina Grossman

Phenomenology Project, 1979–1980
C-prints
14 × 11″ (35.6 × 27.9 cm) each; overall dimensions variable
Courtesy the Estate of Bettina Grossman

Avijit Halder
American, b. 1988, India

Birth, 2018
Pigment print
38 × 57″ (96.5 × 144.8 cm)
Courtesy the artist

Arrival, 2019
Pigment print
21 × 14″ (53.3 × 35.6 cm)
Courtesy the artist

Enviando Cartas, 2019
Pigment print
35 × 21″ (88.9 × 53.3 cm)
Courtesy the artist

Portal, 2019
Pigment print
35 × 23 ¼″ (88.9 × 59.1 cm)
Courtesy the artist

Jewlz, 2018
Pigment print
30 × 45″ (76.2 × 114.3 cm)
Courtesy the artist

Untitled (Kitchen), 2019
Pigment print
21 × 32 ⅜″ (53.3 × 82.3 cm)
Courtesy the artist

Untitled (Fly), 2019
Pigment print
31 ½ × 21″ (80 × 53.3 cm)
Courtesy the artist

Bill Hayden
American, b. 1984

Untitled, 2021
Cell phone charging station
26 ½ × 16 ¼ × 10 ¼″ (67.3 × 41.3 × 26 cm)
Courtesy the artist

WEED, 2021
Ink on paper
12 × 9 ½″ (30.5 × 24.1 cm)
Courtesy the artist

G. Peter Jemison
Enrolled member of the Seneca Nation of Indians, Heron Clan, b. 1945

Free Use and Enjoyment, 2018–2019
Mixed media on board
38 × 43″ (96.5 × 109.2 cm)
Courtesy the artist

Hunger on Reservations While Children In Africa Starve, 1981
Acrylic, oil pastel, collage and ink on paper
17 × 12 × 7″ (43.2 × 30.5 × 17.8 cm)
Courtesy the artist

In Our Language, 2020
Photocollage photographed and printed on canvas
52 × 48″ (132.1 × 121.9 cm)
Courtesy the artist

Indigenous Victims, 1983
Colored pencil, acrylic, and ink on paper bag
17 ½ × 12 ½″ (44.5 × 31.8 cm)
Courtesy the artist

Jim Thorpe 1, 2019
Marker, colored pencil, gold foil on keybag
16 × 9 ¾ × 6 ¼″ (40.6 × 24.8 × 15.9 cm)
Courtesy the artist

Parasol-NRA, 2018
Egg tempera on parasol
26 × 34″ (66 × 86.4 cm)
Courtesy the artist

Real Indian Land Claims, 2000
Acrylic, collage, and colored pencil on bag
19 ½ × 16 × 6″ (49.5 × 40.6 × 15.2 cm)
Washington's State Art Collection, acquired by the Washington State Arts Commission in partnership with the University of Washington

Party Bag, 1982
Mixed media on paper bag
17 × 12 × 7″ (43.2 × 30.5 × 17.8 cm)
Collection of Cross and Couteau, The Leafarrow Theater

Aotearoa / Ganondagan, 1986
Colored pencil and grease crayon on paper bag
16 × 7 × 6″ (40.6 × 17.8 × 15.2 cm)
Courtesy the artist

Grandmother's Treaty, 1996–2005
Colored pencil and iron-on images
56 × 34″ (142.2 × 86.4 cm)
Courtesy the artist

Canandaigua Treaty 1794 Land Guaranteed, 2021
Treaty cloth, heavy weight paper, heat transferred image, calico beads, and colored pencil
81 × 50″ (205.7 × 127 cm)
Courtesy the artist

Indians Have Always Paid The Price, 2005
Paper, crayon, paint and graphite
30 $^3/_{16}$ × 22 ⅝ × ¼″ (76.6 × 57.5 × 0.7 cm)
Collection National Museum of the American Indian, Smithsonian Institution

Steffani Jemison
American, b. 1981

Similitude, 2019
HD Video (color, sound)
35 min., 51 sec.
Courtesy the artist; Greene Naftali, New York; and Annet Gelink Gallery, Amsterdam

Tumbler, 2021
Aluminum, electric gear, motor, belt, 3D-printed nylon, rubber, PET, water, ceramic media, grit, and soap
17 × 17 × 10″ (43.2 × 43.2 × 25.4 cm)
Courtesy the artist; Greene Naftali, New York; and Annet Gelink Gallery, Amsterdam

Tumbler, 2021
Aluminum, electric gear, motor, belt, 3D-printed nylon, rubber, PET, water, ceramic media, grit, and soap
17 × 17 × 10″ (43.2 × 43.2 × 25.4 cm)
Courtesy the artist; Greene Naftali, New York; and Annet Gelink Gallery, Amsterdam

Tumbler, 2021
Aluminum, electric gear, motor, belt, 3D- printed nylon, rubber, PET, water, ceramic media, grit, and soap

17 × 17 × 10″ (43.2 × 43.2 × 25.4 cm)
Courtesy the artist; Greene Naftali, New York; and Annet Gelink Gallery, Amsterdam

Tumblers, 2021–2022
Stones, coins, metal, and glass
Courtesy the artist; Greene Naftali, New York; and Annet Gelink Gallery, Amsterdam

E'wao Kagoshima
Japanese, b. 1945

Stick Together, 2011
Ballpoint pen on paper
8 ½ × 14″ (21.6 × 35.6 cm)
Courtesy the artist and Bodega, New York

Stick Together A-J, 1982
Ballpoint pen on paper (11 sheets)
Each: 8 ½ × 14″ (21.6 × 35.6 cm)
Courtesy the artist and Bodega, New York

No Bombo, 1978
Graphite on paper
11 × 14″ (27.9 × 35.6 cm)
Courtesy the artist and Bodega, New York

In Session, 1978
Graphite and colored pencil on paper
11 × 14″ (27.9 × 35.6 cm)
Courtesy the artist and Bodega, New York

Open House, 2016
Graphite, colored pencil on paper, collage and string on paper
11 × 14″ (27.9 × 35.6 cm)
Courtesy the artist and Bodega, New York

Tautology, 2014
Graphite, colored pencil on paper, collage and string on paper
11 × 14″ (27.9 × 35.6 cm)
Courtesy the artist and Bodega, New York

Eat & Drink, 2016
Graphite, colored pencil on paper, collage and string on paper
14 × 17″ (35.6 × 43.2 cm)
Courtesy the artist and Bodega, New York

African Dream, 2021
Colored pencil on paper
14 × 17″ (35.6 × 43.2 cm)
Courtesy the artist and Bodega, New York

Naked Name, 2013
Graphite, collage and acylic on paper
23 ½ × 18″ (59.7 × 45.7 cm)
Courtesy the artist and Bodega, New York

Loop Hole, 2013
Graphite, collage and acrylic on paper
23 ½ × 18″ (59.7 × 45.7 cm)
Courtesy the artist and Bodega, New York

Untitled, 2021
Paint and pencil on canvas
70 ½ × 54″ (179.1 × 137.2 cm)
Courtesy the artist and Bodega, New York

Marie Karlberg
Swedish, b. 1985

The Good Terrorist, 2021
Video (color, sound)
1 hr., 2 min., 40 sec.
Courtesy the artist

Matthew Langan-Peck
American, b. 1988

4 Baskets 1, 2021
Acrylic, vinyl, and MSA varnish on fiberglass
32 × 40 × 32″ (81.3 × 101.6 × 81.3 cm)
Courtesy the artist

4 Baskets 2, 2021
Acrylic, vinyl, and MSA varnish on fiberglass
32 × 40 × 32″ (81.3 × 101.6 × 81.3 cm)
Courtesy the artist

4 Baskets 3, 2021
Acrylic, vinyl, and MSA varnish on fiberglass
32 × 40 × 32″ (81.3 × 101.6 × 81.3 cm)
Courtesy the artist

4 Baskets 4, 2021
Acrylic, vinyl, and MSA varnish on fiberglass
32 × 40 × 32″ (81.3 × 101.6 × 81.3 cm)
Courtesy the artist

Red Light Problem, 2021
Two-channel audio track
10 min.
Courtesy the artist

Las Nietas De Nonó
Afro-Carribean, est. 2011

FOODTOPIA: después de todo territorio, 2020–2021
Video (color, sound)
27 min., 54 sec.
Courtesy the artists

FOODTOPIA: después de todo territorio, 2020
Multimedia project (digital C-print and zinc metal sheets)
Each: 12 3⁄16 × 18 5⁄16″ (31 × 46.5 cm)
Courtesy the artists

Athena LaTocha
American, Standing Rock Lakota, Keweenaw Bay Ojibwe, b. 1969

It Came From The North, 2021
Shellac ink, earth from Green-Wood cemetery, New York City demolition debris on paper and lead
108 × 222″ (274.3 × 563.9 cm)
Courtesy the artist

Carolyn Lazard
French, Haitian, and American, b. 1987

Red, 2021
Two-channel video installation (color, sound)
10 min., 15 sec.
Courtesy the artist and Maxwell Graham / Essex Street, New York

Sean-Kierre Lyons
American, b. 1991

All My Friends Are Dead, 2021
Color pencil on Bristol paper
11 × 14″ (27.9 × 35.6 cm)
Courtesy the artist and Larrie

Symphonic Sounds of Freedom, 2021
Acrylic on canvas
48 × 60″ (121.9 × 152.4 cm)
Courtesy the artist and Larrie

Prometheus, redacted, 2021
PVC piping, Poly-Fil, cement, rubber boots, dry moss, faux leather, velvet, faux fur and felt
99 5⁄8 × 24 × 24″ (253 × 61 × 61 cm)
Courtesy the artist and Larrie

Hiram Maristany
Puerto Rican–American, b. 1945

Night View, 1961
Gelatin silver print
18 x 14 3⁄8″ (45.7 x 36.5 cm)
Courtesy the artist

The Gathering, 1964
Gelatin silver print
15 x 15″ (38.1 x 38.1 cm)
Courtesy the artist

Lechón / Roasting Pig in Alley, 1971
Gelatin silver print
14 3⁄8 x 18″ (36.5 x 45.7 cm)
Courtesy the artist

Clothing Drive, 1971
Gelatin silver print
14 1⁄16 x 18″ (35.7 x 45.7 cm)
Courtesy the artist

Juan Gonzalez at the Original Headquarters of the Young Lords Party in East Harlem, 1969
Gelatin silver print

12 11/16 x 18″ (32.3 x 45.7 cm)
Courtesy the artist

Take-over of the TB-testing truck, 1970
Gelatin silver print
12 ½ x 18″ (31.8 x 45.7 cm)
Courtesy the artist

Young Lords Member with Pa'lante Newspaper, 1970
Gelatin silver print
15 x 14 3/16″ (38.1 x 36.1 cm)
Courtesy the artist

First Takeover of The People's Church, 1970
Gelatin silver print
12 7/16 x 18″ (31.6 x 45.7 cm)
Courtesy the artist

Children in the Funeral March of Julio Roldán, 1970
Gelatin silver print
15 ¼ x 15″ (38.8 x 38.1 cm)
Courtesy the artist

Garbage Offensive, 1969
Gelatin silver print
10 ⅛ x 18″ (25.8 x 45.7 cm)
Courtesy the artist

Buttons, 1969
Gelatin silver print
11 13/16 x 18″ (30 x 45.7 cm)
Courtesy the artist

Abuelita, March to Free the Panther 21, 1969
Gelatin silver print
12 3/16 x 18″ (31 x 45.7 cm)
Courtesy the artist

Kite Flying on Rooftop, 1964
Gelatin silver print
13 ¼ x 18″ (33.7 x 45.7 cm)
Courtesy the artist

The Bronx March, 1969
Gelatin silver print
11 ¾ x 18″ (29.8 x 45.7 cm)
Courtesy the artist

Servane Mary
French, b. 1972

Stay in the middle two lanes, 2020–2021
Spray paint, acrylic, and silkscreen ink on laminated pegboard panel
96 × 96″ (243.8 × 243.8 cm)
Private collection, New York

Rosemary Mayer
American, 1943–2014

Untitled (7/19/01–8/16/01), 2001
Pencil and pastel on paper
26 × 40″ (66 × 101.6 cm)
Courtesy the Estate of Rosemary Mayer and Gordon Robichaux, New York

Untitled (8/20/01, 2PM–4PM), 2001
Pencil and pastel on paper
26 × 40″ (66 × 101.6 cm)
Courtesy the Estate of Rosemary Mayer and Gordon Robichaux, New York

Untitled (8/21/01, 2PM–4:15PM), 2001
Pencil and pastel on paper
26 × 40″ (66 × 101.6 cm)
Courtesy the Estate of Rosemary Mayer and Gordon Robichaux, New York

Untitled (8/27/01, 3:20PM–4:10PM), 2001
Pencil and pastel on paper
26 × 40″ (66 × 101.6 cm)
Courtesy the Estate of Rosemary Mayer and Gordon Robichaux, New York

Alan Michelson
Mohawk, b. 1953

Midden, 2021
HD video (color, sound) and oyster shells
346 ¾ × 86 ½ × 20″ (880.7 × 219.7 × 50.8 cm)
12 min., 17 sec.
Delaware Skin Dance (Stick Dance) singers: Shatekaronhioton Fox, Tioniatarishon Jacobs, Tehonienhtaronweh Thompson, Enhakahnhoton Norton and Ronekonhnatste Norton
Native North American Traveling College, Akwesasne Territory, 2017
Courtesy the artist

Ahmed Morsi
Egyptian, b. 1930

Green Horse I, 2001
Acrylic on canvas
89 ¾ × 70 1/16″ (228 × 178 cm)
Courtesy the artist and Salon 94, New York

Clocks, 1996
Acrylic on canvas
90 3/16 × 140 9/16″ (229 × 357 cm)
Courtesy the artist and Salon 94, New York

Untitled, 1998
Acrylic on canvas
61 × 48 1/16″ (155 × 122 cm)
Courtesy the artist and Salon 94, New York

Subway Station III, 2015
Acrylic on canvas
60 ¼ × 74″ (153 × 188 cm)
Courtesy the artist and Salon 94, New York

Ahmed Morsi archival materials:

Edwar El Kharrat, The Artist Ahmed Morsi (A Study), 1990
Courtesy Ahmed Morsi

Ibdaa magazine, July 1989
Courtesy Ahmed Morsi

Manuscript for *Pictures from the New York Album*, a collection of poetry by Ahmed Morsi, 1998
Courtesy Ahmed Morsi

Nicolas Moufarrege
Lebanese, 1947–1985

Laocoon Quest #2, 1980
Thread and oil on needlepoint canvas
40 × 32″ (101.6 × 81.3 cm)
Collection Joshua P. Smith

Worry War Rid, 1983
Mixed media on needlepoint canvas
18 × 54″ (45.7 × 137.2 cm)
Collection Joshua P. Smith

Marilyn Nance
American, b. 1953

George Edward Tait on Horn, 1978
Inkjet print
11 × 17″ (27.9 × 43.2 cm)
Courtesy the artist and The Marilyn Nance Archive / Artists Rights Society (ARS), New York

Day of Outrage. Subway. Zizwe Ngafua, 1987
Inkjet print
11 × 17″ (27.9 × 43.2 cm)
Courtesy the artist and The Marilyn Nance Archive / Artists Rights Society (ARS), New York

Chinese New Year, 1988
Inkjet print
11 × 17″ (27.9 × 43.2 cm)
Courtesy the artist and The Marilyn Nance Archive / Artists Rights Society (ARS), New York

Revelers On Eastern Parkway. Labor Day Carnival, 1986
Inkjet print
11 × 17″ (27.9 × 43.2 cm)
Courtesy the artist and The Marilyn Nance Archive / Artists Rights Society (ARS), New York

Revelers On Eastern Parkway. Labor Day Carnival (ii), 1986
Inkjet print
11 × 17″ (27.9 × 43.2 cm)

Courtesy the artist and The Marilyn Nance Archive / Artists Rights Society (ARS), New York

Boy With Gun, 1975
Inkjet print
11 × 17″ (27.9 × 43.2 cm)
Courtesy the artist and The Marilyn Nance Archive / Artists Rights Society (ARS), New York

Jumping Subway Turnstiles. James Scruggs. John Mitchell, December, 1975
Inkjet print
11 × 17″ (27.9 × 43.2 cm)
Courtesy the artist and The Marilyn Nance Archive / Artists Rights Society (ARS), New York

Police and Demonstrators. MLK Day March. Little Black Book. Carol Taylor, 1/18/1998
Inkjet print
11 × 17″ (27.9 × 43.2 cm)
Courtesy the artist and The Marilyn Nance Archive / Artists Rights Society (ARS), New York

Girls Listening to Rap Music, 1986
Inkjet print
11 × 17″ (27.9 × 43.2 cm)
Courtesy the artist and The Marilyn Nance Archive / Artists Rights Society (ARS), New York

Banco Theatre, 1975
Inkjet print
11 × 17″ (27.9 × 43.2 cm)
Courtesy the artist and The Marilyn Nance Archive / Artists Rights Society (ARS), New York

Elephants In The Street, 1985
Inkjet print
11 × 17″ (27.9 × 43.2 cm)
Courtesy the artist and The Marilyn Nance Archive / Artists Rights Society (ARS), New York

The Circus Is In Town, 1980
Inkjet print
11 × 17″ (27.9 × 43.2 cm)
Courtesy the artist and The Marilyn Nance Archive / Artists Rights Society (ARS), New York

Tammy Nguyen
Vietnamese-American, b. 1984

In The Heart of Rimland, 2021
Watercolor, vinyl paint, acrylic paint, pastel, and metal leaf on paper stretched over panel
84 × 60″ (213.4 × 152.4 cm)
Courtesy the artist

Citizens' Cauldron, 2021
Watercolor, vinyl paint, pastel, and metal leaf on paper stretched over panel
84 × 60″ (213.4 × 152.4 cm)
Courtesy the artist

Four Ways Through A Cave 1, 2021
Leather, bookboard, letterpress, digital print, and collage on paper
9 ¾ × 6 ½ × 1″ (24.8 × 16.5 × 2.5 cm)
Courtesy the artist

Shelley Niro
Bay of Quinte Mohawk, Member of the Six Nations Reserve Turtle Clan, b. 1954

Resting Place of Our Ancestors 1, 2019
Inkjet print
40 × 60″ (101.6 × 152.4 cm)
Courtesy the artist

Resting Place of Our Ancestors 2, 2019
Inkjet print
40 × 60″ (101.6 × 152.4 cm)
Courtesy the artist

Resting Place of Our Ancestors 3, 2019
Inkjet print
40 × 60″ (101.6 × 152.4 cm)
Courtesy the artist

Resting Place of Our Ancestors 4, 2019
Inkjet print
40 × 60″ (101.6 × 152.4 cm)
Courtesy the artist

Kayode Ojo
American, b. 1990

You need to prove to me that I can count on you to be loyal, 2021
ASOS Moss London – Gray Velvet Suit Jacket, ASOS Moss London – Gray Velvet Suit Pants, Liberty Imports Heavy Duty Diecast Metal Stainless Steel Handcuffs with Keys Bulk Party Favors for Police Kids Role Play, Vorage Set of 20 Keyrings with Stainless Steel Key Rings, Carabiner Hooks with Key Fob 25mm (Silver), Ikea Tobias Chairs, Clear Amac Boxes, Mirrors
45 ¼ × 72 ⅛ × 23 ⅝″ (114.9 × 183.2 × 60 cm)
Courtesy the artist; Sweetwater, Berlin; and Balice Hertling, Paris

You are incredibly sexy but you are way too much work, 2021
Searchlight Waterfall 3 Light Gold Chandelier Ceiling Light Ceiling Light 3 Lights, Christoph Palme Leuchten Crystal Birnel L. 63mm 7pcs Crystal Lace Pendulum Rainbow Crystal Window Decoration Feng Shui 30% Lead Crystal Sun Catcher, You've Got Chainmail Cowl Dress
92 ½ × 16 ½ × 16 ½″ (235 × 41.9 × 41.9 cm)
Courtesy the artist; Sweetwater, Berlin; and Balice Hertling, Paris

Afterparty for Mirror Cells, Whitney Museum of American Art, The Jane Hotel, New York (Elaine), 2016
Inkjet print
27 × 40 ½″ (68.6 × 102.9 cm)
Courtesy the artist; Sweetwater, Berlin; and Balice Hertling, Paris

Gift Message (TOM FORD METALLIC COTTON BOXER BRIEFS), Sweetwater, Berlin, 2021
Inkjet print
27 × 40 ½″ (68.6 × 102.9 cm)
Courtesy the artist; Sweetwater, Berlin; and Balice Hertling, Paris

Paulina Peavy
American, 1901–1999

Untitled, 1938–1947
Oil on masonite board
72 × 48″ (182.9 × 121.9 cm)
Courtesy Andrew Edlin Gallery and the Estate of Paulina Peavy

Untitled, c. late 1930s–1960s, 1980s
Oil and paper on masonite board
36 × 24″ (91.4 × 61 cm)
Courtesy Andrew Edlin Gallery and the Estate of Paulina Peavy

Untitled, c. 1930s–1960s, 1980s
Oil and paper on masonite board
20 × 16″ (50.8 × 40.6 cm)
Courtesy Andrew Edlin Gallery and the Estate of Paulina Peavy

Untitled, c. 1940s
Oil on masonite board
14 × 11 ½″ (35.6 × 29.2 cm)
Courtesy Andrew Edlin Gallery and the Estate of Paulina Peavy

Untitled (Smokies Series), 1978
Smoke on paper
16 × 11″ (40.6 × 27.9 cm)
Courtesy Andrew Edlin Gallery and the Estate of Paulina Peavy

Freya Powell
English-American, b. 1983

Only Remains Remain
Performance at MoMA PS1, October 22–23, 2021

Raha Raissnia
Iranian, b. 1968

Aviary, 2018/2021
Projector, 16mm film, wood, scrim and acrylic on canvas
(b/w, no sound)
3 min.
Courtesy the artist and Miguel Abreu Gallery, New York

Domain of Silenus, 2021
Oil, ink and acrylic medium on canvas
60 × 90 × 1 ½″ (152.4 × 228.6 × 3.8 cm)
Courtesy the artist and Miguel Abreu Gallery, New York

Andy Robert
Haitian-American, b. 1984

Harlem Sings the Blues, 2017
Oil on canvas
48 × 36″ (121.9 × 91.4 cm)
Courtesy The Studio Museum in Harlem; Museum purchase with funds provided by the Acquisition Committee

Check II Check, 2017
Oil and pencil on linen
Overall dimensions: 138 × 75″ (350.5 × 190.5 cm)
Top panel dimensions:
44 × 74″ (111.8 × 188 cm)
Bottom panel dimensions:
94 × 74″ (238.8 × 188 cm)
Kravis Collection

Mid Atlantic, 2020
Oil, acrylic, charcoal, pastel, pencil, gesso and mixed media on canvas
96 × 80 × 2″ (243.8 × 203.2 × 5.1 cm)
Private collection, New York

The Original, 2021
Mixed media drawing on paper
56 × 38″ (142.2 × 96.5 cm)
Courtesy the artist and Hannah Hoffman Gallery, Los Angeles

Diane Severin Nguyen
Vietnamese-American, b. 1990

Confession of a mask, 2021
LightJet C-print and steel frame
25 × 20″ (63.5 × 50.8 cm)
Courtesy the artist and Bureau, New York

Your Reversal, 2021
LightJet C-print and steel frame
25 × 20″ (63.5 × 50.8 cm)
Courtesy the artist and Bureau, New York

Southern Star, 2021
LightJet C-print and steel frame
25 × 20″ (63.5 × 50.8 cm)
Courtesy the artist and Bureau, New York

Artist intervention in wall, 2021
Dimensions variable
Courtesy the artist

Shanzhai Lyric
founded 2015

Incomplete Poem, 2015–ongoing
Mixed media
Dimensions variable
Courtesy the artists

Canal Street Research Association (storage), 2021
Mixed media
Dimensions variable
Courtesy the artists

Canal Street Research Association (Money Has No Smell), 2021
Café Touba and coffee cups
Courtesy the artists

Regina Vater
Brazilian, b. 1943

LuxoLixo, 1973/1974
Video (color, sound)
16 min., 30 sec.
Courtesy the artist and Galeria Jaqueline Martins, São Paulo and Brussels

Saudades do Brasil, 1984
Video (color, sound)
25 min., 27 sec.
Courtesy the artist and Galeria Jaqueline Martins, São Paulo and Brussels

Stanley Wolukau-Wanambwa
British and Ugandan, b. 1980

AMWMA, 2021
Inkjet prints
Each: 71 ¼ × 57″ (181 × 144.8 cm)
Courtesy the artist

Mask(s), 2021
Inkjet print
35 × 28″ (88.9 × 71.1 cm)
Courtesy the artist

Separation(s), 2021
Triptych of inkjet prints and images on plexiglass
Each: 5 × 7″ (12.7 × 17.8 cm)
Courtesy the artist

Skins, 2021
Inkjet print
45 × 36″ (114.3 × 91.4 cm)
Courtesy the artist

Fractions, 2021
Found object and plaster
Dimensions variable
Courtesy the artist

Gun Hill, 2018–2021
Brick and wood
12 × 12 × 5 ½″ (30.5 × 30.5 × 14)
Courtesy the artist

Lachell Workman
American, b. 1989

A Sartorial Monument, 2021
T-shirts, 35mm slide projector and slides
Dimensions variable
Courtesy the artist

The Cenotaph Won't Hold, 2021
Asphalt and T-shirt
Dimensions variable
Courtesy the artist

Ruba Katrib

Ruba Katrib is Curator at MoMA PS1. At MoMA PS1 she has curated exhibitions such as *Niki de Saint Phalle: Structures for Life* (2021), *Theater of Operations: The Gulf Wars 1991–2011* (2019) (co-curated with Peter Eleey), the retrospective of Simone Fattal in 2019, and the solo shows of Edgar Heap of Birds (2019), Karrabing Collective (2019), Fernando Palma Rodríguez (2018), and Julia Phillips (2018). From 2012 to 2018 she was Curator at SculptureCenter in New York where she curated over twenty solo and group exhibitions, including solo shows by Carissa Rodriguez (2018), Kelly Akashi, Sam Anderson, Teresa Burga, Nicola L., Charlotte Prodger (all 2017), Rochelle Goldberg, Aki Sasamoto, Cosima von Bonin (all 2016), Anthea Hamilton, Araya Rasdjarmrearnsook, Magali Reus, Gabriel Sierra, Michael E. Smith, Erika Verzutti (all 2015), David Douard, and Jumana Manna (both 2014). Previously, Katrib was the Associate Curator at the Museum of Contemporary Art North Miami from 2007 to 2012. Katrib was also cofounder of the residency and exhibition space Threewalls in Chicago, and has also held positions at the Renaissance Society and the Center for Curatorial Studies at Bard College, where she currently serves on the Graduate Committee. She was a research advisor for the 2018 Carnegie International and a member of the Advisory Board for Recess, a nonprofit artist residency and exhibition space in New York. Katrib co-curated SITE Santa Fe's 2018 biennial, *Casa Tomada*, along with José Luis Blondet and Candice Hopkins.

Inés Katzenstein

Inés Katzenstein is Curator of Latin American Art and Director of the Patricia Phelps de Cisneros Institute for the Study of the Art of Latin America at MoMA. She received a masters degree from the Center for Curatorial Studies, Bard College, New York (2001). She has written extensively about contemporary art and curated exhibitions like *Sur Moderno: Journeys of Abstraction* (MoMA, 2019), *Liliana Porter: Fotografía y ficción* (Centro Cultural Recoleta, Buenos Aires, 2003), *David Lamelas, Extranjero, Foreigner, Ètranger, Aüslander* (Museo Rufino Tamayo, Mexico, 2005) *Marcelo Pombo, un artista del pueblo* (Collection Fortabat, Buenos Aires, 2015). She co-curated *Televisión, El Di Tella y un episodio en la vida de la TV* (Espacio Telefónica, Buenos Aires, 2010) and *Aquella mañana...* (Parque de la memoria, Buenos Aires, 2014). She was curator of the Argentine pavilion at the 52nd Venice Biennale, where she presented the project *Guillermo Kuitca, si yo fuera el invierno mismo* and was co-curator of *Zona Franca*, Mercosur Biennial, 2007.

Among other books, she edited *Listen, Here, Now! Argentine Art of the Sixties: Writings of the Avant-Garde* (The Museum of Modern Art, New York, 2004). From 2004 to 2008 she served as curator at Malba-Fundación Costantini in Buenos Aires, where among other programming projects she initiated the collection of contemporary Argentine art. Also in Buenos Aires, in 2008 she founded the Department of Art at the University Torcuato Di Tella, where she served as director of educational programs and exhibitions for ten years.

Serubiri Moses

Serubiri Moses is a writer and curator who currently lives in New York. He is currently Adjunct Assistant Professor in the Department of Art and Art History at Hunter College, where he teaches contemporary African and Afro-diaspora art history. Previously, Moses was part of the curatorial team for the tenth Berlin Biennale of Contemporary Art entitled *We Don't Need Another Hero* (2017–2018). From 2013 to 2017 Moses travelled extensively to participate in curatorial residencies, conferences, and juries across Africa, Asia, Latin America, and Europe.
In 2015, Moses held the position of Stadtschreiber, an academic fellowship, at the Bayreuth Academy of Advanced African Studies and in 2014 he co-curated the second public art biennial in Kampala, KLA ART, entitled *Unmapped*, and organized a four-volume public program at the Goethe Zentrum Kampala. From 2011 to 2012 he was a critic at the Ugandan daily newspaper *New Vision Daily*. With his interests ranging from historical narration and exhibition history to African feminist theory and iconography, Moses is currently an associate researcher in "African Art History and the Formation of a Modern Aesthetic," a long-term project founded by the Bayreuth Academy of Advanced African Studies in Germany. Moses completed the MA in Curatorial Studies from the Center for Curatorial Studies, Bard College, where his thesis focused on exhibition histories of small projects in Africa.

Kate Fowle

Kate Fowle is the Director of MoMA PS1. From 2013 to 2019 she was the inaugural chief curator at Garage Museum of Contemporary Art in Moscow and director-at-large of Independent Curators International (ICI) in New York, where she was the executive director from 2009 to 2013. Prior to this she was the inaugural international curator at the Ullens Center for Contemporary Art in Beijing (2007–2008). In 2002 she cofounded the Master's Program in Curatorial Practice for California College of the Arts in San Francisco, for which she was the Chair until 2007. Before moving to the United States, Fowle was codirector of Smith + Fowle in London from 1996 to 2002. From 1994 to 1996 she was curator at the Towner Art Gallery and Museum in Eastbourne, East Sussex.

Fowle's recent projects include solo exhibitions with David Adjaye, Rasheed Araeen, John Baldessari, Sammy Baloji, Louise Bourgeois, Marcel Broodthaers, Urs Fischer, Rashid Johnson, Irina Korina, Robert Longo, Anri Sala, Taryn Simon, Juergen Teller, and Rirkrit Tirivanija, as well as extended essays on Ilya Kabakov, Sterling Ruby, and Qiu Zhijie, and numerous extended articles on curating and exhibition histories. Fowle has written three books: *Exhibit Russia: The New International Decade 1986–1996* (2016); *Rashid Johnson: Within Our Gates* (2016); and *Proof: Francisco Goya, Sergei Eisenstein, Robert Longo* (2017).

STAFF LIST

Herbert Armstrong
Maintenance Technician

Arnold Ayala
Maintainer

Philip Brand
Development Associate, Foundation & Corporate Relations

Bhagwandat Budhu
Maintenance Technician

Taja Cheek
Associate Curator at Large

Samuel N. Denitz
Assistant Director, Operations

Joya Erickson
Registrar

Kate Fowle
Director

Jody Graf
Assistant Curator

Anna Grofik
Exhibition Assistant

Odean Groves
Maintainer

Angela Hallinan
Project Manager, Exhibitions

Emily A. Harr
Visitor Engagement Associate

Hannah Howe
Director of Individual Giving

Ruba Katrib
Curator

Elena Ketelsen González
Assistant Curator

Molly Kurzius
Director of External Affairs

Yasmel Lorenzo Rodriguez
Accountant

Christopher Masullo
Project Manager, Performance and Events

Kai Mora
Press Assistant

Jose A. Ortiz
Deputy Director

Citlali Ortiz
VW Fellow, Public Programs & Community Engagement

Jose Paz
Maintenance Technician

Zechariah Philippe
Visitor Engagement Associate

Jack Radley
Special Projects Coordinator & Executive Assistant, Director's Office

Nora Rodriguez
Digital Strategy and Content Manager

Andrea Sánchez
Administrative Assistant, Curatorial

Carlos Santana
Visitor Engagement Associate

Carley E. Santori
VW Fellow, Production and Events

Amber Sasse
Assistant Director of Institutional Giving

Molly Taylor
Assistant Manager of Visitor Engagement

Jinelle S. Thompson
Manager of Strategic Partnerships

Vance Wellenstein
Head of Design

Richard Wilson
Exhibition and Production Designer

Noel P. Woodford
VW Fellow, Digital Marketing & Media

Laura Zapp
Manager of Visitor Engagement

MoMA PS1 TRUSTEES

GREATER NEW YORKERS

FOUNDING MEMBERS

John Alex

Sarah Arison

Julia Arnhold & Lane Gerson

Paul Arnhold & Wes Gordon

Eboné Bishop

The Here and There Collective – Lisa Young, Steven Abraham, Dan Nguyen

Jukay Hsu

Michi Jigargian

Kent Kelley

Will Leung

Liza Mauer

Melissa Passman and Ryan Stevens

Anna Raginskaya

Lisa Roumell

Emma Scully

Antonio and Anna Valverde

Debi Wisch

Anonymous

ARTWORK IMAGES

All artwork images copyright and courtesy of the artist unless otherwise indicated

pp. 6–7: Hiram Maristany, *Kite Flying on Rooftop*, 1964. Courtesy the artist

pp. 22–23: Marie Karlberg, still from *The Good Terrorist*, 2021. Courtesy the artist

p. 40: Yuji Agematsu, detail, *zip: 01.01.20 . . . 12.31.20*, 2020. Courtesy the artist and Miguel Abreu Gallery, New York. Photo: Stephen Faught

p. 42: *Sculptures by Curtis Cuffie on the streets of New York City, near Astor Place*, c. 1990s. Photograph by Katy Abel. Courtesy Aarne and Tina Anton

p. 44: Julio Galán, *El Que Se Viene Se Va*, 1988. Courtesy the Helios Trust, UK

p. 46: Robin Graubard, *kim crashpad 1985 nyc*, 1985/2021, selection from *Peripheral Vision*, 1979–2021. Courtesy the artist and Office Baroque, Antwerp

p. 48: Bettina Grossman, detail, *Phenomenology Project*, 1979–1980. Courtesy the estate of Bettina Grossman

p. 50: E'wao Kagoshima, *Full Moon Cat*, 1978, 2018. Courtesy the artist and Bodega, New York. Photo: Eric Veit

p. 52: Ahmed Morsi, *Green Horse I*, 2001. Courtesy the artist and Salon 94, New York. Photo: Dan Bradica

p. 55: Diane Burns, illustration from *Riding the One-Eyed Ford*, 1981

pp. 82–87: Courtesy the Estate of Rosemary Mayer

p. 139: Courtesy the artist and Ramiken, New York. Photo: Dario Lasagni

pp. 142–143: Courtesy the artist and Salon 94, New York. Photo: Dan Bradica

p. 163: Courtesy the National Museum of the American Indian, Smithsonian Institution (26/9746). Photo: NMAI Photo Services

p. 164: © 2022 Marilyn Nance / Artists Rights Society (ARS), New York

p. 168: Courtesy the artist and Sweetwater, Berlin

p. 170. Courtesy the artist and Bodega, New York. Photo: Eric Veit

p. 171: Photo: Lily Engelmaier

p. 192–193: Courtesy the artist and Miguel Abreu Gallery, New York. Photo: Stephen Faught

p. 202: Courtesy Andrew Edlin Gallery and the Estate of Paulina Peavy. Photo: Nicholas Knight

p. 212: © Rotimi Fani-Kayode/Autograph ABP. Courtesy Autograph, London

p. 214: Courtesy the Estate of Luis Frangella and Galería Cosmocosa. Photo: Ignacio Iasparra

p. 225: Courtesy Aarne and Tina Anton

p. 230: Courtesy the artist and Taymour Grahne Projects. Photo: Susan Alzner

p. 257: Yuji Agematsu, detail, *zip: 01.01.20 . . . 12.31.20*, 2020. Courtesy the artist and Miguel Abreu Gallery, New York. Photo: Stephen Faught

p. 271: Shanzhai Lyric, detail, *Incomplete Poem*, 2015–ongoing. Photo: Steven Paneccasio

p. 272: Matthew Langan-Peck, detail, *4 Baskets 3*, 2021. Photo: Steven Paneccasio

INSTALLATION IMAGES

Marissa Alper: p. 190

Jason Mandella: p. 176

Steven Paneccasio: pp. 122–125, 131, 133–138, 144, 160–162, 172, 174, 180–182, 186, 198–201, 205, 208, 211, 213, 215, 219–224, 226–229, 231, 237, 240, 242–245

Martin Seck: pp. 128–130, 133, 146, 150–155, 157, 166, 178, 184, 196, 203, 210, 216–218, 234, 238, 241, 246

Matthew Septimus: pp. 81, 126, 140, 158, 164, 183, 194, 204, 206, 236

Julia Schäfer: p. 120, 147–149, 173

Noel Woodford: pp. 118, 232